Mesoamerica – southeastern Mexico and western Central America – has become one of the world's most important areas for research into the emergence of complex human societies. In the last two decades, a number of ambitious research efforts have contributed a voluminous body of new data on culture change, data that make it possible to evaluate cultural evolutionary theories with a much greater degree of sophistication than before. In this substantially revised second edition of a book first published in 1981, the authors synthesize the major contributions of this recent research and place these discoveries in an original framework for explaining change.

The book treats Mesoamerica's first inhabitants more than 10,000 years ago, but focuses on the time period from the earliest agricultural villages to the Spanish conquest. Included in this span were changes that are among the most significant in the evolution of human societies, such as the emergence of agriculture and of sedentary villages, the growth of centralized governments (chiefdoms and states), and the rise of market systems, cities, and highly stratified social systems. The authors add to our understanding of cultural evolution in a general sense by assessing similarities and differences in the evolutionary sequences of three of prehispanic Mesoamerica's most important nuclear zones, the valleys of Oaxaca and Mexico and the eastern Mesoamerican Maya lowlands. In addition to drawing on their own extensive fieldwork experiences in various parts of Mesoamerica, the authors utilize the abundant literature on Mesoamerica and other areas of early civilizations, including the recently reported results of new research.

No prior knowledge of Mesoamerican archaeology or cultural evolution is assumed in this volume. The findings should be of value to all who are interested in prehispanic Mesoamerica and in the rise of complex human societies.

Ancient Mesoamerica

NEW STUDIES IN ARCHAEOLOGY

Series editors

Colin Renfrew, *University of Cambridge*
Jeremy Sabloff, *University of Pittsburgh*

Ancient Mesoamerica

A comparison of change in three regions

SECOND EDITION

RICHARD E. BLANTON
STEPHEN A. KOWALEWSKI
GARY M. FEINMAN
LAURA M. FINSTEN

CAMBRIDGE
UNIVERSITY PRESS

Published by the Press Syndicate of the University of Cambridge
The Pitt Building, Trumpington Street, Cambridge CB2 1RP
40 West 20th Street, New York, NY 10011-4211, USA
10 Stamford Road, Oakleigh, Victoria 3166, Australia

First published 1981
Second edition 1993

Printed in Canada

Library of Congress Cataloging-in-Publication Data

Ancient Mesoamerica : a comparison of change in three regions /
Richard E. Blanton . . . [et al.]. – 2nd ed.
p. cm. – (New studies in archaeology)
Includes bibliographical references and indexes.
ISBN 0-521-22858-1. – ISBN 0-521-29682-X (pbk.)
1. Indians of Mexico – Antiquities. 2. Indians of Mexico – History.
3. Indians of Central America – Antiquities. 4. Indians of Central
America – History. 5. Mexico – Antiquities. 6. Central America –
Antiquities. I. Blanton, Richard E. II. Series.
F1219.A595   1993
972.01 – dc20   92-32389
                                                     CIP

A catalog record for this book is available from the British Library.

ISBN 0-521-22858-1 hardback
ISBN 0-521-29682-X paperback

CONTENTS

ILLUSTRATIONS AND TABLES

The historian Will Durant argued that the best way to understand the nature of our species is to observe human behavior as it has manifested itself over the sixty centuries of history. Only with a long historical perspective is it possible to identify those aspects of culture and society that undergo significant evolutionary change, and to distinguish the dynamic and changeable features from the more perdurable. In this book our goal is similar to Durant's. We want to contribute to a better understanding of human behavior and cultural evolution by interpreting some aspects of change and continuity in the prehispanic societies of Mesoamerica over roughly ten thousand years. To offer a full scholarly study and interpretation of Mesoamerica's rich record of sociocultural evolution – from its nomadic bands to the settled communities of chiefdoms, states, and empires – would be an undertaking of greater scope than we attempt here, but we hope we have made some real advances toward that objective. Our first effort to realize this goal was the first edition of this book, published in 1981. Since the pace of research on the prehispanic societies of Mesoamerica has been so rapid over the past ten years, we felt that the book required an updating. This revised edition takes into consideration developments in our field since 1981, including important new findings relevant to understanding Teotihuacan and the nature of its connections to the rest of Mesoamerica, research on Aztec society and culture and the Aztec empire, the completion of the regional survey of the Valley of Oaxaca, and new research that helps us better comprehend the enigmatic Maya region. This edition also adds to the scope of the first by including a chapter on those archaeological periods predating the rise of agricultural villages, from the first human occupation of Mesoamerica through those periods during which Mesoamericans first domesticated the suite of plants that later became the energetic basis for the rise of complex society. Laura Finsten, who has worked with us for many years in the Valley of Oaxaca, brings her expertise to this edition.

If our arguments do turn out to represent an important contribution to the theoretical understanding of human behavior and sociocultural evolution, most of the credit is due to those individuals who stimulated our thinking and those institutions who provided resources for field research. We acknowledge especially the help provided by the National Science Foundation of the United States, which financially supported not only the bulk of our own research and analyses, but also that of many of the other researchers whose work we discuss. We are also thankful for funding provided by the Social Sciences and Humanities Research Council of Canada. We are appreciative of the permits and aid of various sorts given by Mexico's Instituto

Nacional de Antropología e Historia, both from its offices in Mexico City and from its regional center in Oaxaca. We thank especially those individuals who directed the Oaxaca regional center during the years we worked there, Manuel Esparza, Maria de la Luz Topete V., and Ernesto Gonzalez Licon. Several universities have provided support, including Rice University, Hunter College of the City University of New York, Purdue University, the University of Georgia, the University of Wisconsin, McMaster University, and Arizona State University.

The last few decades have seen many new developments in the study of sociocultural dynamics. Many people working in diverse regions and disciplines have made valuable contributions. We would like to acknowledge especially the intellectual stimulation and help provided to us by Kent Flannery, whose efforts were instrumental in getting us started on the archaeological survey of the Valley of Oaxaca. A list of other scholars whose writings have been of exceptional value to us would include Gregory Johnson, Joyce Marcus, Roy Rappaport, G. William Skinner, Carol Smith, Immanuel Wallerstein, Eric Wolf, and Henry Wright.

We thank Linda Nicholas and Jackie Saindon, for their help in many capacities, Ruth Ann Brooks, Mark Borland, Gail Newton, and Gisela Weis.

1

The growth of Mesoamerican archaeology and ethnohistory

Our commission in this volume is a dual one: to investigate both cultural evolution itself and the civilization that was ancient Mesoamerica. Our method will be to use Mesoamerica's past to learn more about cultural evolution in general, and to deploy as much as is known about cultural evolution in an effort to understand Mesoamerica better. In this first chapter we describe the field and array the main concepts in preparation for the ensuing attack. First we briefly review how Mesoamerica has been studied, then we inspect several strategies that have been devised for explaining the development of civilization. In the rest of the chapter we present the plan that we think will be most effective, and define its theoretical capabilities and date requirements.

Pioneering research

The advancement of archaeological and ethnohistorical methods for learning about Mesoamerica's past has always been a reflection of the state of knowledge in those fields in general, but Mesoamerican specialists have contributed at least their share to progress in general method and theory. Early Mesoamerican archaeology had its decades of exploration, by brave men of character – and some real characters – whose wonderful and often wonky reports of ruins in the rain forests drew the attention of the public and inspired others to begin serious, scholarly investigation. Toward the end of the nineteenth century, anthropology was being established as a recognized discipline by persons such as Frederic Ward Putnam and John Wesley Powell in the United States, and by Manuel Gamio (in the second decade of this century) in Mexico. Formal, scientific expeditions were sent to Middle America by foreign institutions, including the Peabody Museum of Harvard University, the American Museum of Natural History, and the Carnegie Institution of Washington. These enterprises usually produced lengthy, descriptive monographs, many of which are still very useful (see Fig. 1.1). Sylvanus G. Morley, for example, recorded and published five volumes of Maya inscriptions. The objectives of these early studies were frankly observational and descriptive. The work of Manuel Gamio, however, had a broad theoretical conception more in line with the multidisciplinary, regional projects of modern anthropology. Gamio believed that any improvements in the social conditions of Mexico could come only with a thorough understanding of the historical trajectories and peculiarities of the country's distinctive geographical and ethnic regions, each of which was to be studied on its own. His major work traced the prehistorical and historical antecedents as well as the contemporary

1

condition of the population of the Teotihuacan Valley, drawing on the resources of archaeology, ethnohistoric documents, ethnography, census data, physical anthropology, and the environmental sciences.

A significant result of the investigations in Mesoamerica prior to the 1950s was the discovery of "culture areas." These are broad areas with a readily identifiable flavor and a distinct sequence of historical development, like the Maya lowlands, the Valley of Oaxaca, the Mixteca, the Huasteca, and the Basin of Mexico. The archaeologists of the first half of the twentieth century established chronologies for the major culture areas of Mesoamerica using the methods of stratigraphic excavation, seriation of pottery types, and cross-dating. But more than anything else, these investigators contributed a realization of the temporal and spatial dimensions, and the nearly overwhelming vastness and complexity, of Mesoamerica's pre-Columbian archaeological record. Mesoamerica was thus coming to be recognized by archaeologists as a nucleus for the development of civilizations of considerable time depth. Though all across the area the general similarities set Mesoamerica apart from other centers of high culture, it was not all of one piece. Mesoamerica consisted of dissimilar regional components.

Ethnohistory

At the same time, historians were trying to make sense out of the traditions and ethnohistoric documents describing the predecessors – mythical or factual – of the sixteenth-century Mesoamericans. Gradually, ethnohistorians learned that the existing documents could shed considerable light on the last two or three centuries before the Spanish conquest. For example, Tollan, the capital of the Toltecs of legend, was identified by the historian Wigberto Jiménez Moreno as a real place: Tula, in the state of Hidalgo. The huge site of Teotihuacan, on the other hand, was recognized as representing an earlier, "classic" stage of Mesoamerican civilization. The decipherment of the Maya calendar, which in one respect allowed archaeologists to date to the year the cities of the Maya lowlands "old Empire," also helped fix the Mesoamerica-wide Classic time span at A.D. 300–900. This enabled the relative chronologies from different regions to be tied together and to an absolute time scale even before radiocarbon came into use in the 1950s.

The discovery of early culture horizons

Stratigraphic excavations by George C. Vaillant at Ticoman and Zacatenco in the 1920s uncovered remains of an "Archaic" stage prior to the Classic in the Valley of Mexico. A few years before 1862, while clearing a milpa (the traditional maize field) on the slopes of the Cerro de San Martín, near San Andres Tuxtla, Veracruz, a peasant uncovered the first known colossal stone head. Many more of these twenty-ton basalt monuments were found later. By the 1950s, these were recognized to be part of the "Olmec" art style contemporary with part of Vaillant's Archaic, and dated by radiocarbon to around 1000 B.C. This was Mesoamerica's earliest "Great Tradition." Simpler societies that existed prior to settled villages became better known in the 1950s and 1960s, especially through the work of Richard S.

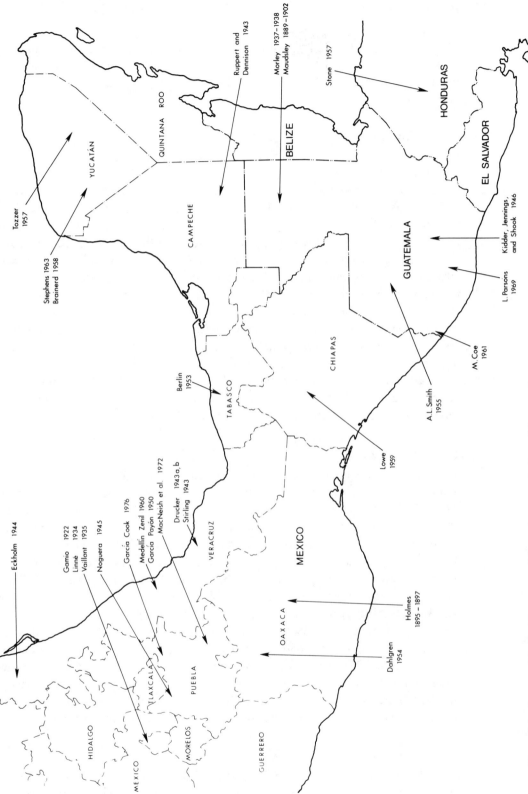

Figure 1.1. A geographical guide to some of the major monographs on Mesoamerica.

3

MacNeish, whose band of botanists, zoologists, geomorphologists, and archaeologists recorded the origins and development of agriculture from its nomadic hunting-and-collecting beginnings in the dry but archaeologically favorable caves of the Tehuacán Valley.

Settlement patterns

In Mesoamerica, as in other ancient civilizations, the grandest and the most spectacular ruined cities, the most aesthetically pleasing art objects, and, at times, the romantic, the bizarre, and the sensational have lured the attention of the public and archaeologists alike. Since the 1950s, however, some professionals, recognizing the importance of a broader sociological base, have initiated "settlement pattern" studies designed to discover the full layout of large cities (that is, the residential areas as well as the downtown, "ceremonial" precincts) and the distribution of the towns, villages, farmsteads, and special places that were the various centers of activity of the whole society, not just the ancient elite. In Mesoamerica, where natural and archaeological conditions permit, walking surveys could map the sizes and dispositions of nearly all human settlements for each prehistoric time period over large areas. The goal of these large-scale projects was to integrate the data from excavations and surveys of whole regions in order to describe and account for change from the beginning of human occupation to the present. Because the anthropological objective was to explain the evolution of societies, studying only a few communities was not sufficient – societies were much larger.

The Valley of Mexico

These aims are easier stated than accomplished. In the 1950s, for example, Pedro Armillas, Angel Palerm, and Eric Wolf published papers on irrigation agriculture in the Valley of Mexico and its possible relation to social evolution. Excavations, mainly at Teotihuacan, had been carried out by Jorge Acosta, Roman Piña Chan, and others. At a 1960 conference of Valley of Mexico specialists, the major step of deciding on priorities and coordinating research efforts was taken. Mapping the urban center of Teotihuacan was to be the responsibility of René Millon; William T. Sanders was to direct the survey of the valley, beginning in its northeastern corner. Almost twenty years of persistent, difficult, and costly study have been invested since the plan to map the Valley of Mexico was initiated – an indication that the serious investigation of Mesoamerican civilization is indeed not a casual undertaking. Was the effort worth it? Might not some short cuts have been taken to save valuable time and expense? Probably not, for as we are finding at every turn, what is needed is more, not less. The Valley of Mexico scholars were right in the first place: There is no substitute for the mapping of every site over very broad areas.

The Valley of Oaxaca

In this book we draw on data from the Valley of Oaxaca and the lowlands of eastern Mesoamerica in addition to information from the Valley of Mexico (Fig. 1.2). The

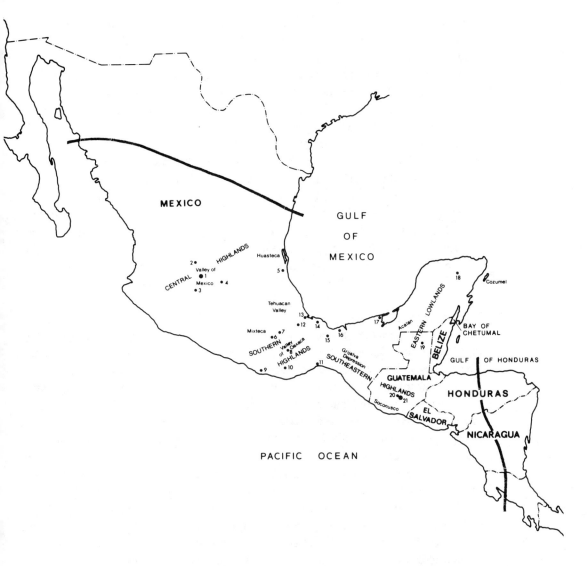

Figure 1.2. Map of Mesoamerica showing modern political boundaries and places mentioned in the text. Mexico City (1), Tula (2), Xochicalco (3), Cholula (4), El Tajín (5), Coixtlahuaca (6), Cuicatlán (7), Oaxaca (8), Tututepec (9), Miahuatlán (10), Tehuantepec (11), Tuxtepec (12), Cerro de las Mesas (13), Matacapan (14), San Lorenzo (15), La Venta (16), Xicalango (17), Chichén Itzá (18), Tikal (19), Kaminaljuyú (20), Guatemala City (21).

Valley of Oaxaca, like the Valley of Mexico, has been the scene of coordinated, regionally oriented research efforts; the eastern lowlands have not. The differences in research results are instructive. The Valley of Oaxaca had its share of archaeological explorers and pioneers, like Leopoldo Batres and Adolphe Francis Alphonse Bandelier, who described the famous hilltop city of Monte Albán and the excellently preserved palaces of Mitla. But it was the nearly fifty-year career of Alfonso Caso that established Oaxaca's ancient Zapotecs as one of Mesoamerica's key societies. By the 1950s Caso had cleared and reconstructed Monte Albán's Main Plaza, established the master ceramic chronology, excavated over 100 tombs, including one of Mesoamerica's richest, published the first systematic study of ancient Zapotec writing and calendrics, and founded the *indigenista* movement for the protection of native peoples in Mexico. Caso trained Ignacio Bernal, who, with his student John Paddock, carried out stratigraphic excavations at important valley sites away from Monte Albán. In 1966, Kent Flannery, himself a scion of this Oaxacan anthropological lineage, founded the Human Ecology Project, a long-term multidisciplinary group patterned after MacNeish's Tehuacán Project and Robert Braidwood's study of the origins of plant and animal domestication in the Near East. Flannery's associates have concentrated on paleoenvironmental research and the excavation of the early living floors critical for documenting the transitions from nomadic hunting and gathering to sedentary agriculture and the rise of ranked society. In cooperation with the Human Ecology Project, Richard E. Blanton took charge of the surface survey and the mapping of all sites in the valley. The regional survey is now complete, and the results are described in Chapter 3.

The eastern lowlands

The regionally oriented research designs that have been so rewarding in the valleys of Mexico and Oaxaca have not been implemented in the lowlands of eastern Mesoamerica. Partly because of the dense vegetation, the standard practice among Maya archaeologists has been to map only the "ceremonial" precincts of centers; but Mayapán, central Tikal, and Dzibilchaltún have been mapped so that every visible structure is now located and drawn. In the 1950s William Bullard, by following mule trails through the rain forest of the Department of Petén, in Guatemala, found many sites of varying internal complexity and size away from the main centers. He suggested a functional hierarchy (major center, secondary center, zone, and hamlet) that is still useful in spite of the hit-or-miss search method that he had to employ.

The basic problem with these eastern lowlands settlement pattern studies, and with research in the eastern lowlands as a whole, has been that for the most part studies are "site centered." Archaeologists mapped sites already known to them or to their local informants, or they did unsystematic reconnaissance, mapping "sites" as they chanced to run (literally, at times) into them. The drawback with this method is that it results in a sample of settlements that is neither complete nor representative. So far the best resolution of this problem has been provided by Dennis E. Puleston, who began systematically covering whole blocks of *area*. This technique allows one to learn about all of the settlements in a defined study area (the areas with sites as well as the demonstrably vacant areas), from the smallest to the major centers: their relative spacing, density, and relationship to the land. Unfortunately this kind of survey is slow and difficult, and so far very little area in the eastern lowlands has been systematically surveyed. Of course complete wide-area settlement pattern studies would not be a panacea, here or anywhere else. What is clearly needed, on the other hand, is a coordinated effort to define research goals on at least a regional scale. Some method of studying settlement patterns would be essential, but just as important would be more detailed work at sites selected with some foreknowledge of their role in regional behavioral networks.

Progress in Mesoamerican research

Overall, from our present perspective, major progress has been made on the quality and quantity of knowledge about Mesoamerica. Four main factors have been behind the improvement over the years in the gathering of the basic data on Mesoamerica's past. First, better theories have allowed archaeologists to go for the right *kinds* of information. For example, the theoretical concern with population and human ecology led to the systematic settlement pattern surveys, which have located thousands of sites. We discuss this point about the relationship between theoretical questions and data more specifically toward the end of this chapter.

A second way data collection has improved is that in many cases dedicated researchers have labored in the same areas of study for a decade or more. E. Willys Andrews IV, for one, worked for thirty-seven years in the northern Yucatan; Ronald Spore's continuing archaeological, ethnohistorical, and ethnographic research on the Mixteca Alta began over twenty-five years ago. This kind of sustained effort is apparently almost necessary for a person to make sense of a civilization's potentially overwhelming amount of information. To understand what we mean by "potentially overwhelming," consider the following example: Lambityeco, an Early Postclassic site of only moderate size in the Valley of Oaxaca, has over *60 million* potsherds on the surface of the ground alone. Think of the difficulty in trying to find out the important facts; imagine the possibilities of being enticed away from the main goal and becoming mired forever in a myriad of minutiae.

This brings us to the third facet of the explanation for the advancement of knowledge about Mesoamerica. With a few exceptions, Mesoamericanists have generally avoided entangling themselves in sterile, purely methodological exercises. Indeed, Mesoamerican archaeologists and ethnohistorians have been instrumental in introducing new techniques and methods to their disciplines. But they have usually done so without making it seem as though the way in which knowledge was gained were more important to them than the knowledge itself. Mesoamericanists have directed their energies instead to learning as much as possible about past human behavior. Their subject is people, not archaeology or its practitioners.

Finally, since about 1960 more money has been made available for archaeology in Mesoamerica, a worldly fact that incontrovertibly makes a difference. Jorge Acosta, in three field seasons of excavation and reconstruction of major public buildings at Tula in the mid-1950s, had a total budget of less than $7,500 – an impossibly small sum even in those days. Nowadays even a surface survey in which a shovel never breaks the ground may cost fifteen times as much. The increase in funds has supported more projects and provided for the enlistment of many more trained specialists for field and laboratory tasks. Gone are the projects in which one archaeologist tried to supervise fifty or a hundred workmen. The result is an improvement in the amount and quality of information. Pride in new theories is permitted, but it always helps to have the material support.

Our discussion in succeeding chapters constitutes only an attempt to struggle with the archaeological information. The data are so rich that a whole variety of analyses can be done. We are sure that many more satisfying hypotheses can be formed and tested than we are able to offer. Nevertheless, consonant with the vastly improved quality of the archaeological data that have come to light in recent years, we try here to develop better ways of thinking about how to interpret the information. A better understanding of the factors at work in the growth of civilization should be the result. But before developing our approach to the problem, it will be valuable to have a retrospective view of how other investigators thought about the growth of civilization.

Thinking about Mesoamerican civilization

Anthropology's goal is to understand similarities, differences, and changes in human societies, wherever and whenever people lived. As anthropologists our contribution to the world will be measured by the extent to which we can bring meaning to both the greatly variable and the broadly universal ways of human life. No matter what else an anthropologist does well – digging holes in the ground, questioning an informant, editing a native document – explaining cultural variability is the real and perhaps only worthwhile goal.

In the history of the social sciences several fundamentally conflicting approaches have been advocated by one or another of the scholars who have studied Mesoamerica. Some of the ideas proved quite useful for a time, but today they are unsatisfactory. In our opinion the search for a good theory about the dynamics of civilization will sometime meet with success, meaning that in the future people will probably be satisfied that they know the essential workings of human systems well enough to predict the outcomes they consider consequential. Because civilization is readily enough understood in many of its pieces, we reason that it can eventually be understood scientifically as a whole. However, that kind of predictive comprehension of civilization is not available in any past or current approach, and although we offer some specific directions for concrete research in this book, we make no claim that we have a fully explanatory theory. Other social scientists have made such claims, but that is probably why their approaches are so easily shown to be too simple, too general, or just wrong. The next few pages review three broad classes of previous ideas about the dynamics of civilization.

Diffusion

The idea that Mesoamerican civilization did not develop on its own, but was transplanted from somewhere else, has been a persistent but always a minority view. Several Spaniards of the seventeenth century, for example, believed on the most tenuous of evidence that the builders of the large Yucatecan sites of Uxmal and Chichén Itzá were Phoenicians, Carthaginians, or Asians. More recently it has been suggested that the Olmec art style of around 1000–800 B.C. was developed under the auspices of Shang Chinese influence. Once enough knowledge is acquired about the local prehistory, however, gaps that previously could be explained only by foreign contact can usually be filled in with indigenous developments. Experience thus shows that diffusionist theories thrive for areas that are poorly understood, but with adequate archaeology each area is usually shown to have had its own in situ evolution.

How should we comprehend "contact" between societies, the basic diffusionist question? The people of a region use or are used by outside contacts according to their own and more global needs. For instance, in a sense Spanish culture diffused to Mesoamerica with the conquest in the sixteenth century. But this is rather abstract. It would be of far greater relevance to ask how the Indian use of the Spanish fit the needs of the Indian systems, and how the Spanish use of the Indians fit into a system that had evolved the capacity to exploit on a transoceanic scale. Such questions, or better, questions that have been framed even more precisely, seem to go more directly toward the essential aspects of human systems, whereas diffusionism appears to be satisfied with studying more secondary phenomena, such as the spread of traits. Diffusionism has the additional drawback of not addressing the absolutely essential questions of survival and making a living. Diffusionism, in short, has not proven itself a very satisfactory approach.

Culture history
Much of what is known today about ancient Mesoamerica has been contributed by scholars who subscribed to a culture historical paradigm. This is the study of the traditions, beliefs, and customs believed to be distinctive to and held in common by a group of people, and of how these "cultures" fare over time when they come in and out of contact with other cultures. Just as one might trace genealogical roots into the past, this approach digs for the genealogies of particular cultures. The actions of people, according to culture history, are governed by the values of their culture. For the culture history approach, the question, Who were those people – were they Toltecs, Putun Maya, Pipil, Zapotecs, Olmecs? is of great concern, for the answer is believed to be an important fact in itself, and it is held to have explanatory power. In archaeology, the culture historian pays a great deal of attention to defining material culture complexes assumed to be the reflections of commonly held recipes for doing things.

Being able to identify a past culture and to trace it through time is thus the main endeavor of culture history. At one time it was a viewpoint that had a certain attractiveness, because it held out the promise that we would be studying real people and their ways of life. Anthropologists wanted to study the particular histories of traditional lifeways instead of formulating general laws applicable anywhere and anytime. This was a promise never fulfilled. Instead of focusing on people and what they actually did, culture history created a whole new jargon of abstractions. In addition to the troublesome notion of "a culture," one is faced with the idea of cultures influencing one another, being in contact, imploding, efflorescing, blending. Culture's material products, especially ceramics, are said to do the same kinds of things – that is, influence and contact each other, evolve one from another, and become related to one another. As the culture history approach developed, its theory and practice became more arcane and scholastic instead of more precise. Its concepts rarely had real-world referents and were seldom defined so that they could mean only one thing and no other. In reply to a short article about the culture history of a Guatemalan archaeological site, a reviewer noted that the word "influence" appeared at least twenty times in the article, in each case with a variety of potential meanings. A fatal flaw of culture history is that it does not ask, If people behave according to their values, why do they have those values in the first place? To reply that values come from parents through socialization only begs the question.

In anthropology's past, cultural or ethnic affiliation and the question Who were those people? may have been important as a way of carving up and labeling the world's population, suddenly and so recently known to the West. Perhaps too often anthropologists uncritically assumed that cultures recognized in the nineteenth and twentieth centuries had a perdurable reality in the precolonial world. Today, however, this concept of culture may be anachronistic. In most recent studies of societal dynamics, Who were those people? and What culture was that? are unasked, irrelevant questions, because the answers tell us very little about why people and their social systems behave the way they do.

Cultural evolution

Many contemporary anthropologists agree that some kind of evolutionary approach offers the best available prospect for a general theory for understanding sociocultural variability and change. Our discipline is still far from having a completely satisfactory evolutionary theory, but the main directions taken by evolutionary theorists, emphasizing such basic processes as human–environmental interactions, production, energy and material flows, and political organization, are good foundations upon which to build explanations.

Evolution implies change through time. For cultural systems, unfortunately, just what kinds of units – populations, individuals, societies, institutions – should be considered as changing or staying the same or combining in different ways over time are not yet clear. Studying an object whose parts have the important adaptive habits of moving, breaking down, recombining, becoming something else, and still surviving is both challenging and disconcerting (but see the next part of this chapter).

By saying that an evolutionary approach seems like the best direction for anthropology, we mean something other than the construction of general sequences of progressive stages. It should be possible to do more than conduct the speculative enterprise of defining evolutionary stages and the processual sequences between them from existing social types. The aim, after all, it to understand variability and change, not to declare at the outset that all systems are alike. It seems very unlikely that the aim of comprehending variability could be satisfied without actual cases, preferably quite a lot of them. This implies use of not only the ethnographic record but also the techniques of archaeology and history. Static, cross-cultural comparison is not adequate.

By evolution we do not mean to imply progressive development or teleological movement toward an end goal or in a necessary direction. Instead, cultural evolution, like biological evolution, probably moves opportunistically, solving only today's problems, proceeding rather blindly, without a predetermined course, into the future.

In addition, we know that neither biological evolution nor cultural evolution proceeds *necessarily* from the simple to the complex. That view does not fit the facts, either in social organization or in material culture. Industrial societies and many mobile hunter-gatherer societies (like the Inuit) have similar, rather simple kin organizations, whereas often the "middle-range," sedentary village societies (the Hopi, the Trobriand Islanders) have highly segmented and complexly integrated kinship systems. Likewise, in another realm, the Spanish conquest of Mesoamerica actually simplified what had been a rather complicated native market and tribute economy; at the same time the Mesoamerican economy became a specialized part of the developing global system of capitalism. In technology and art, anyone who has had the experience of reconstructing a Mesoamerican ceramic sequence knows that pottery did not start out crudely and become increasingly more sophisticated and beautiful. Some Classic Period assemblages are quite coarse in their entirety, whereas a thousand years earlier very elaborate pots were quite common.

Cultural evolution does not have inevitability as one of its properties, at least in any theoretically meaningful sense. For example, some treatises maintain that civilizations inexorably pass through the stages of birth, development, florescence, senescence, and death. Typically these theories were born of armchair speculation and nourished with a highly biased selection of facts. Many discussions about the course of human history make it sound as though civilization, with all the variability and complication the term implies, was simply the inevitable outcome of the Neolithic revolution, the transition from food collecting to food production. Again, this scenario does injustice to the facts. There are many societies dependent on food production – in North America, New Guinea, lowland South America, and elsewhere – that did not have state-level government, monumental public works, writing systems, or other features found in civilizations. For these societies as well as for those areas where evolutionary processes did produce large-scale, complex developments, we want to be able to account for the varying rates, trajectories, and forms, not sweep them under the rug.

A solid, materialist theoretical foundation for cultural evolutionism in anthropology was established by Leslie A. White. He contended that increase in the ability to harness new energy or to use existing energy sources more efficiently leads to growth in cultural complexity. But this does not explain why people work to capture more energy in the first place. It is often appropriate to continue to ask Why? when confronted with such unicausal explanations.

Given the current state of knowledge, it is most unlikely that cultural systems change primarily because of any one dominating, specific cause. Single-cause explanations have a certain appeal because of their simplicity, but they can easily become almost mythlike, and hence potentially dangerous if as anthropologists we teach these theories to future policymakers. For example, to an extent the green revolution was based on the conviction, taught for years as the conventional wisdom, that technological improvement was at the root of all significant cultural change. It followed that introducing new agricultural technology would promote economic development and hence better people's lives. We need not go into the particular consequences here, but the results were often as bad as the original situation in terms of health, demography, social stratification, prices, and environmental effects. Had the development model reflected some of the complexity of the total human system, at least some of the major consequences might have been predicted. The point is applicable not only to technological solutions, but to other applications of unicausal theories as well. If one believes that population pressure ultimately provides the stress that moves human systems, then perhaps fertility limitation would be a logical public policy. But if one fails to ask why a population is growing, and treats population growth as a purely independent variable, then the fertility policy may be very difficult for people to adopt, or it may well become counterproductive. Because archaeologists are part of a larger intellectual community, their explanations even about past events can have an effect on current opinion. Proposing simple solutions to complex problems is not exemplary practice at this time.

In this connection several archaeologists have invoked Occam's razor, which states that in cases where there are several competing explanations for the same phenomenon, and each is satisfactory on other grounds, the simplest explanation is preferable. We must remember that William of Occam's principle is referred to as a razor, not a data hammer. Unfortunately the study of human history has not yet achieved the sophisticated understanding necessary to allow us the luxury of deciding with the criterion of elegance, for we are still attempting to formulate theory that will be satisfactory on substantive grounds.

Many instructive examples of unicausal theories have been offered to explain prehistoric events in Mesoamerica. In 1970 a group of specialists in eastern Mesoamerica held a symposium to try to account for the dramatic collapse of the eastern lowlands system around A.D. 900. In many respects this was a productive conference, but the tone of the event was set by the competing "prime-mover" arguments that had previously constituted the debate. One scholar argued for outside invasion as the main cause of the downfall, another for peasant uprising, another for a breakdown of long-distance trade, someone else for soil exhaustion, and so forth; the debate also worked its way through cultural exhaustion, yellow fever, drought, and earthquakes. The proponents of all these arguments, of course, did not find it difficult to come up with a few facts in support of their hypotheses.

One solution to this is the "laundry list," wherein one says blithely that all of the factors were no doubt involved. This, for example, is the current status of the debate on subsistence in eastern Mesoamerica. In the case of subsistence, it used to be held by some that the people of eastern Mesoamerica relied on slash-and-burn maize farming. However, many students began to point out that many other techniques were or could have been used. Better than such a list of techniques, of course, would be some information about what proportions of different crops and land-use techniques were used under what circumstances in each area over time. Unfortunately, however, little data exist about the actual variability in ancient subsistence practices.

A somewhat different strategy is to arrange the factors (as in the case of the collapse) in boxes on a piece of paper, and to draw lines between the boxes to show that the factors are related, as are components in a system. This flow-chart method can have the excellent result of clarifying one's thinking, but unfortunately most of our Mesoamerican systems models are of the armchair variety – they would be much more interesting if they were accompanied by the appropriate kinds of facts about past systems.

In this book we use a type of systems approach designed to schematize flows of goods or information or people among actual groups that existed in space, such as households or administrative districts. This approach is introduced in the next section. It is different from the systems models that extract categories of action such as warfare, long-distance trade, political centralization, population growth, and so forth, and then suggest dependent-independent variable relationships among them. Each conceptualization has its own advantages and limitations; neither is worth much without the appropriate facts.

Yet another solution to competition between "pet movers" is to decide by convention. In effect, this is what happened at the Rise of Maya Civilization conference that was held following the success of the collapse seminar. There, virtually all the participants agreed that the development of complexity in the eastern lowlands was due to population increase, which results in agricultural intensification and warfare. What is remarkable and most unjustified about this consensus is that it was reached in the almost total absence of the kinds of data necessary to speak in an informed way about any of these variables.

In summary, of the approaches taken to understanding Mesoamerican civilization, an evolutionary approach seems to offer the best possibilities. Diffusion is clearly unsatisfactory as an explanation on factual as well as theoretical grounds. Culture history, although it has produced much of what is known today about Mesoamerica's past, seems disconnected from the problems faced by people in everyday life. In addition, its concepts are not well suited to the explanation of variation and change. Evolutionism has the advantage of offering hypotheses to explain change and variation, within and between human groups, and it tends to emphasize such fundamental matters as production and energy flows. While we would not want to argue that a purely materialist theory will answer all of our questions, these kinds of factors are important points of departure for evolutionary inquiry. Next we outline some new directions for cultural evolutionary research.

An approach to cultural evolution

As we have pointed out, a problem shared by anthropologists interested in cultural evolution has been that of determining the object of focus. What are the appropriate units? What does cultural evolution involve at base? Historically, technology has been considered to be the essential feature – witness the well-worn evolutionary sequence of Stone, Bronze, and Iron ages. More recently, the focus has turned more to political evolution, specifically the rise of the state, although some researchers have favored urbanism or agricultural intensification. We believe that viewing change from any one of these perspectives may be misleading. The feature in question may prove to be largely epiphenomenal, or reflective of only particular circumstances, not general process. Technology, for one example, is a notably errant indicator of evolutionary development. The aboriginal New World civilizations, as a case in point, were organizationally as complex as their Bronze Age counterparts in the Old World, but the American Indian civilizations had an essentially Stone Age technological base.

In explaining change in human societies one ought to be able to deal with the "core" features. These are characteristics that are not epiphenomenal, but basic to all societies, permitting valid comparison over space and time. Throughout this book we will be concerned with four factors we think are these essential or core features, namely *scale, integration, complexity,* and *boundedness.* Cultural evolution can be defined as change in scale, integration, complexity, and boundedness. When viewed over the very long run, there have been increases in these four variables. Modern nation-states, although varying among themselves, are larger in scale, more integrated, more complex, and have more boundedness than the hunting-gathering bands of the Pleistocene. But when one is looking at the behavior of a particular society over time, those general trends are not often duplicated. This is because culture change is not always linear, unvarying, or unidirectional. Instead, in specific cases it typically involves periods of rapid change followed by plateaus of relative stability, or even collapse and reorganization in new formats, perhaps followed by further periods of substantial change, and so on. This cycling pattern seems very common, as will become clearer in the course of this book. But cycles of change do not necessarily imply repetitive cycles, because the starting point of each new cycle is never the same as the starting point of any prior cycle. Each cycle alters conditions so that a return to the status quo ante is never really possible. This cycling with alteration will result in directional change, but not in a simple unilinear manner. The question of the relationships among our core features of scale, integration, complexity, and boundedness is of prime importance. We begin a more detailed consideration of this further on. First we need to define these core features.

Scale
When one speaks of scale differences among societies, one basically means size differences. The size of a society refers to the number of people incorporated into the society and/or the size of the area involved. In the general course of cultural evolution, the size of human societies has increased in both of these respects. Interesting exceptions occur, however. Large areas that at one time supported a single, spatially large nomadic society were divided at a later time among a number of sedentary societies. Each area was then smaller in size, but the total population was equal to or larger than the population in earlier times. Territorial shrinkage may in

fact be a concomitant of the development of ranked societies from egalitarian societies, in certain situations. Consolidation and expansion of territory may then occur with somewhat more complex ranked organization. Population density increases are also sometimes a concomitant of evolution, although again not in a dependable way.

Social systems exhibit what are referred to as "emergent properties," that is, characteristics of the whole that could not be foreseen by knowing only the nature of the component parts, characteristics that are products of the *relationship* among the parts. Because of differences in their emergent properties, "big" and "little" social systems are not simply different-scale replicas of each other. Their organization and response to new conditions are usually different, due in large part to their differences in scale. Societies or organizations of different scales may differ in some respects because of their size differences alone. Exactly all of what is involved in this aspect of scale is an exciting but poorly developed area of social science research, especially in anthropology. It is not our goal here to discuss all the possibilities, but a couple of examples will suffice to illustrate the point.

A major limitation to growing system size is the limited capacity of the human brain for processing information. A rule of thumb for grade-school size, if it is expected that the principal will know most of the students by their first names, is that the school can hold no more than several hundred students. In larger schools the principal must have assistants, each of whom is responsible for keeping track of some portion of the total student body. As Elizabeth Colson noted in her observations of the Gwembe Tonga of Zambia:

> Local men of influence still depend on an immediate following, which limits their appeal to only a small portion of the local community. If they are to extend their influence to encompass the great majority of those present within their local sphere, as did their predecessors, they will have to develop a system of intermediaries who can serve as channels of communication and buffers between them and the mass of their followers. . . . A differentiation in terms of a set of ranked offices will then have taken place. The net result should be an increased capacity of those who are in close proximity to minimize actual contacts and live in different social spaces. The way will be clear for them to treat the majority of their fellows as objects rather than as demanding personalities. (Colson 1978:161)

In both this example of the Gwembe Tonga and the case of the grade school, large systems had to be organized differently than small systems if certain tasks deemed necessary were to be accomplished. The scale differences called for differences in the character of the system.

Another facet of scale has to do with the working capacity of organizations of differing scales. We have all heard from economists of the advantages of scale factors in production, meaning that large production units are more efficient than small ones, due to the greater possibilities for a division of labor, routinization of tasks, and so on, in the larger units. Beyond a certain size, however, scale advantages turn into the so-called eventually diminishing returns to scale. As Kenneth Boulding put it:

> As institutions grow they have to maintain larger and larger specialized administrative structures in order to overcome the increasing difficulties of communication between the "edges" or outside surfaces of the organization (the classroom, the parish, the retail outlet) and the central executive. Eventually the cost of these administrative structures begins to outweigh any of the other possible benefits of large scale, such as increasing specialization of the more directly productive parts of the organization, and these structural limits bring the growth of the organization to an end. One can visualize, for instance, a university of a hundred thousand students in which the entire organization is made up of administrators, leaving no room at all for faculty. (Boulding 1956:72)

Social systems may increase in scale up to a point, but not indefinitely.

Another aspect of scale considered in this book has to do with the assembly of large organizations such as empires. An expansionist state will have much more difficulty dealing militarily with small, independent polities, even if each of these alone is weak and poorly organized for fighting, than with large, unified entities, because in the latter case military energies can be focused on single nodal points that are the focuses of the larger units. In the former, each of the small units must be separately incorporated, a costly task if a substantially large number of people or a substantially large territory is to be assembled. As Herbert Simon argued:

> Philip assembled his Macedonian empire and gave it to his son, to be later combined with the Persian subassembly and others into Alexander's greater system. On Alexander's death, his empire did not crumble to dust but fragmented into some of the major subsystems that had composed it. . . . [This] implies that if one would be Alexander, one should be born into a world where large stable political systems already exist. Where this condition was not fulfilled, as on the Scythian and Indian frontiers, Alexander found empire building a slippery business. So too, T. E. Lawrence's organizing of the Arab revolt against the Turks was limited by the character of his largest stable building blocks, the separate, suspicious desert tribes. (Simon 1969:98)

Assembling a large-scale system apparently requires considerable preexisting organization, in another way confirming that large systems, if indeed they are to be systems, are structurally different from small ones.

Integration

Integration refers to the interdependence of units. In a society with little overall integration, the units constituting it (for example, households, villages, districts, and so forth) are highly self-sufficient. Higher levels of integration imply more connections among units. Depending on the kind of component units, the connections are established as flows of material, energy, information, or people. The greater the flow through interconnecting channels, the greater the interdependence. This implies that integration can be of several kinds. Of special importance to us throughout this volume are economic integration (referring to the extent to which households or other units are interdependent in terms of the exchange of goods and services) and political integration (referring to the extent to which units are autonomous in power and decision making – more autonomy means less societal integration). In general, cultural evolution has involved increased levels of integration of larger and larger systems. These changes are not necessarily linear or simple, however. Political integration, for example, may decline through time as economic integration increases, or vice versa. Our task is not to proclaim certain general trends as "laws," but to formulate and test hypotheses about how different kinds and amounts of integration and different system sizes affect one another.

Complexity

Complexity refers to the extent to which there is functional differentiation among societal units. An increase in complexity has occurred, for instance, if there is a transition from a high degree of redundancy in the production of household craft items to more diverse and specialized production. Complexity is obviously related to integration, because functionally specialized parts are highly interdependent. Complexity, though, refers to the number of functionally distinct parts, not their degree of integration per se. Households producing the same crops could be highly integrated (but evidence little specialization), for instance, if they were heavily dependent on one another for food exchanges to balance surpluses and deficits.

Complexity has several aspects. *Horizontal differentiation* refers to functional specialization among parts of equivalent rank in a system. This would apply, for example, to an administrative institution that has different offices or bureaus at the same administrative rank. Differentiation can also be vertical in form, wherein rank differences can be seen among functionally diverse parts. A society is vertically differentiated if a chiefship exists that centralizes the making and carrying out of decisions for the society as a whole. In other words, a political hierarchy is present. The more vertical levels that can be distinguished in the hierarchy, the more vertical complexity is present. The state as a type of governmental institution, for example, is conveniently defined by specifying that it has a political hierarchy of at least three levels – something like local officials, district managers, and the ruler, for example. Chiefdoms have one or two levels. Economic institutions can also be described in terms of their degrees of vertical complexity. A region containing a wide range of production specialties in a market system might exhibit a hierarchy of marketing places consisting of local markets that offer relatively little, and high-order markets that offer a wider range of goods to a wider audience over a greater area. Societies lacking much in the way of vertical differentiation politically or economically (for example, a foraging-band society) are said to have a "flat" hierarchy. The degree of vertical complexity will be strongly related to the degree of stratification in the society – that is, the number of different kinds of ranks that are present, and the extent to which these ranks imply unequal privileges.

Boundedness

Boundedness relates to how the population of a social system interacts with other populations outside its boundaries, in exchanges of energy, materials, people, genes, and information. Of particular importance is the degree of permeability of the boundary. Is it more or less open or closed to unimpeded flows? Another way to look at this variable is to ask: How well defined, as a regional entity, is the social system in question? Does it have sharply drawn, regulated boundaries, or "fuzzy" edges? What are the available choices for people who move across boundaries, for example migrants, or merchants engaged in long-distance trade? More centralized states may regulate, impede, or monopolize movements across their territorial boundaries, reducing boundary permeability, and thereby increasing the degree of boundedness. In a case like this, there is likely to be a considerable degree of overlap between what we would regard as the local social system and the area controlled by the state. But economic and political systems do not always coincide, so it is sometimes difficult to say exactly what is the social system in question. If a region is integrated by the flows of people, materials, energy, and information, but is at the same time governed by a series of autonomous states (a "multistate system"), then integration should be understood to apply at the level of the interacting region, and is economic in form, not political. And it is very likely that the complexity of the economic system is greater than the complexity of the individual local polities. As we shall see, Mesoamerica was organized very much like this for part of its history.

In studying the evolution of complex societies, we have found it fruitful to ask questions about the varying ways in which political and economic institutions interrelate, and about the consequences of these interrelationships. In this book we consider, for instance, the problem of whether strong market systems can evolve in the context of powerful governments, and vice versa. We discuss the factors that seem to favor the "imbeddedness" of economic institutions in governmental ones. We ask how scale factors affect the connections between political and economic integrations. In Mesoamerica these relationships were surprisingly variable – and thus very interesting for the investigation of cultural evolution.

Societal taxonomies

In the last few pages we have said that cultural evolution consists of changes in certain core features of a social system – specifically, what we have defined as scale, integration, complexity, and boundedness – particularly in political and economic institutions. However crucial a variable such as technology or environmental relationships might be in a particular situation, cultural evolution means change in these dimensions of the human social system. To us, the object is to explain variation in these core features.

As these dimensions may vary independently to some extent, especially when one considers separately institutions organized for different purposes, we have found it difficult to use the taxonomies often employed in cultural evolutionary studies. These taxonomies attempt to define the level of cultural "complexity" of societies in terms of specific kinds of institutional arrangements. In the most frequently used taxonomy (bands, tribes, chiefdoms, states), for instance, chiefdoms are described as "redistributional" societies (in which surpluses go to the political head, and are then redistributed). As we have noted, in reality societies of roughly that scale and degree of vertical political complexity have a wide range of economic practices, not all of which by any means involve redistribution. This is to be expected, because political and economic institutions are not always the same and do not always evolve together in tightly covarying ways. Taxonomies can thus blind the researcher to the highly variable and sometimes counterintuitive aspects of cultural evolution. Our study of Mesoamerica suggests to us that it is very informative to search out and exploit this variability to better understand how systems evolve in general. Thus, in the remainder of this book, when we use the terms "chiefdom" and "state," we are referring to particular political forms within society, not to types of societies. These political forms are discussed in the earlier section on complexity.

Explaining social change

One approach to understanding societies is to pay attention to the rules that guide behavior and thus govern the cultural system – essentially, this is the strategy of culture history. We favor an approach more compatible with studies of change, one that emphasizes people's diverse strategies for achieving goals or solving problems. Rather than focusing on rules, one is concerned more with why particular rules exist in the first place, with how rules are broken, and with how new forms of behavior develop while old ones are abandoned. Such deviations from the norm are especially likely when new or extreme conditions are encountered, and changed behavior becomes necessary to maintain a traditional way of life (or at least its most desired aspects). Coal, for instance, was only reluctantly adopted as a source of fuel in England in the sixteenth century, when deforestation resulted in an energy crisis. Change may also occur in the absence of any immediate severe stress, as the result of experimentation with the idea of resolving long-standing problems or of simply making life better (for example, by decreasing work loads or minimizing risk).

Actors in social systems thus have certain goals, among which are survival and security, and also, in some cases, prestige. The goals even for a single actor may conflict and cannot all be achieved perfectly at the same time. Actors use strategies and resources in different mixes in order to come close to their goals. The resources, the strategies, and even the goals themselves may be altered to cope with new problems and circumstances. The kinds of problems people face and the kinds of strategies they will employ to cope with extreme situations or to improve conditions will vary depending on the context within which they are making decisions. A king has a very different role and a different perspective than a household head. At the household level, we might generally expect coping behavior or innovation to occur primarily in such areas as work intensity, types of production, fertility and migration decisions, marriage, the devolution of wealth between generations, and consumer behavior. We can thus identify a household as a sphere of organization within which certain kinds of problems are faced, and within which certain kinds of strategies are likely to be used. Although the households in two different societies do not always have to cope with identical problems, and do not respond to problems in an identical fashion, in general there is considerable cross-cultural similarity. Human households often have common features of structure and function. For example, it is very common in agrarian societies for population growth to be the result of increased pressures by government on households for surplus production. Larger families increase the working capacity of the household, thus maintaining acceptable levels of nonwork time in the light of the altered circumstances. In such societies there are commonly found patterns in male – female and adult – child division of labor.

The actors in other organizational spheres face other kinds of problems and employ other kinds of strategies. Cross-culturally, for example, governmental institutions are often involved in problem solving with respect to boundary maintenance for the society as a whole. The strategies employed by heads of state when they are concerned with boundary maintenance are "geopolitical." City managers are typically involved with problems of deviance, fire, disease, the regulation of food supplies, and so on. The actors fulfilling higher-level roles such as head of state or city manager may have somewhat different interests as private individuals. How they shift their loyalties around can be an important factor in fluid situations of social change.

We are interested in how behavioral change occurs in varied organizational contexts. But even more we are concerned with how change in one organizational sphere may reverberate through society, creating new sets of conditions for actors in other spheres, new situations for neighboring societies, or even major alteration in ecological patterns. As people adjust to the new circumstances, their responses in turn create a situation even further from the norm, ramifying through the system to feed back on the original source of change, and requiring even greater efforts to effect an adjustment. We might pursue here our example of increased family size as a strategy to cope with increased production demands. The population growth resulting from larger families could feed back to create additional problems for the governing institution that initiated the change in the first place. Disputes over desirable land or water for irrigation might increase in intensity, threatening the functioning of the whole system. Stepped-up production demands on households may thus in the long run prove to entail more costs than benefits – to the government itself, to agrarian families, or to the society as a whole. Adjustments in one organizational sphere are thus likely to affect other parts of the system, and, to make a further point, they do so in ways often unanticipated by the actors.

Problem solving by actors in one organizational sphere typically ramifies out in complex and unpredictable ways. Humans are rarely able to fully predict the consequences of their actions. In large part this is due to the fact that the causality involved in change is circular and complex, whereas humans tend to think in more simple, linear terms (for example: If we do X, that will solve problem Y). As Roy Rappaport reminds us:

> The circularity . . . blurs the distinction between cause and effect, or rather
> suggests to us that simple linear notions of causality, which lead us to think

of actors, objects upon which they act and the transformation of such objects, are inadequate, for purposeful behavior seldom affects only a single object . . . but usually many other objects as well, often in complex and ramifying ways. Among those being affected in unforeseen and possibly unpleasant ways may be the actor himself. (Rappaport 1978:68)

Let us amplify and summarize our approach to cultural evolution as it has been developed thus far. What evolve are human social systems, impermanent organizations formed by the more or less regular or repeated behavior of social actors. The actors pursue goals according to certain strategies, and both goals and strategies may be changed by the actors to meet new conditions. The systems created and self-defined in this way have emergent properties not completely understood by their participants, including considerable intricacy and unpredictability. Such organizations have different purposes – for example, the allocation of resources or the making and carrying out of decisions – but their key dimensions that we want to study are their scale, complexity, integration, and boundedness. Notice that this approach to the study of cultural variability calls for the simultaneous examination of large-, medium-, and small-scale events and processes. We want to be able to connect the grand and sweeping long-term processes to the nature of local communities, and to how individuals lived and why people behaved in the ways that they did.

To illustrate these points we can look, in preview, at our reconstruction of some of the events of the period from 500 B.C. to about 200 B.C. in the Valley of Oaxaca (Monte Albán phase I in the local terminology). Chapter 3 contains a discussion of the evidence for the patterns and interpretations, but our purpose in the following brief sketch is to indicate the interplay among causes and effects in different organizational spheres of a single system during one time period. Monte Albán phase I was a time of fundamental change in the valley that involved a number of developments, but especially a dramatic growth in governmental institutions, the beginnings of a market system (see Special topic 1), and a general move to increased levels of agricultural production involving, prominently, the construction of piedmont canal irrigation systems. The "kick" initiating this set of changes was the formation of a pan-valley military league or alliance, centered at a newly founded regional capital, Monte Albán. In several respects this new form of regional integration created conditions that resulted in the transformation of society, very likely in ways that the actors could not have anticipated. No doubt the new military league provided benefits to the population of the region, especially in reducing military uncertainties, but its establishment also entailed costs, which increased through time as the new institution became much larger and more powerful. These costs were borne mainly by the numerous households of agricultural producers, who were required to step up their production of goods. A consequence was increased fertility, resulting in a sustained population growth unmatched during any previous period. Growth took the form, under those economic conditions, of the reproduction of many more new household units. (In-migrating families, we think, further augmented growth.) Another response was an intensification of irrigation agriculture – in that region, the key means of assuring a second crop per year. But this required that more time be spent in farming, and by necessity that meant less time spent in nonagricultural pursuits.

In short, the Valley of Oaxaca farmers were being converted into a rural peasantry. Increasing demands for their production made people farm more than they had previously. Farming got in the way of other things that they needed or wanted to do. In other, ethnographically described cases, households in this situation commonly obtain needed manufactures, such as pottery, from outside suppliers instead of trying to maintain self-sufficiency. This is probably what happened in the Valley of Oaxaca in phase I. Items such as pottery were in theory not difficult to produce at home, but they required considerable time and energy expenditure. Specialists, in contrast, produced goods much more efficiently because they became more practiced and because they could take advantage of the benefits of larger-scale production. Purchasing craft items, in other words, became a time-saving strategy, alleviating scheduling difficulties and leaving more free time for the kinds of time-consuming but important activities that people really wanted or needed to do, such as visiting, participating in community ceremonials, or tending irrigation facilities.

A consequence of this set of changes was the development of a set of places in the region where economic exchange and possibly other transactions could take place – a market system. The development of this form of regional economic integration was no doubt also encouraged by the formation of the new capital in the valley's center, and by the new political integration, which facilitated freer and more secure movement. Prior to Monte Albán's establishment, the valley's center zone had been only sparsely occupied, probably indicating that it had been a contested "shatter zone" between competing political entities. After Monte Albán's establishment in the middle of this "no-man's-land," the population of the zone increased substantially. The free movement required for a market system was thus instituted.

The upward-spiraling aspects of the phase I transformation are well illustrated by the fact that in all of these areas we have mentioned – population growth, irrigation agriculture, and the development of a marketing system – increased governmental work loads are implied. Bringing all the parts of the valley together in a single league was the initial kick; that started a whole series of profound changes throughout the system; and those changes increased the administrative work load, causing the government to grow even larger. The result was one of those watersheds in human history after which very little was as before. The changes affected everything right down to the household level. Population growth (especially in the congested area around the new capital, where growth was most pronounced) no doubt led to increased need for adjudication in such areas as land disputes. Comparable irrigation systems in the valley today are so simple that they need little in the way of government on a year-to-year basis. Still, on those rare occasions when the demand for water is greater than the supply, insolvable disputes threaten to bring even these systems to a trickling halt. Only a high-order governmental institution has the power to adjudicate such disputes and assure long-term smooth operation of the agricultural system. Similarly, in an early market system of the sort we think was in operation in phase I, governments have a regulatory role to play – for example, in adjudicating disputes among market participants. The catch in all of this was, of course, that as government work loads increased more administrative personnel were needed. A more elaborate bureaucracy had to be devised. All of this called for increased demands on rural families to produce more to support the growing structure. These demands further intensify the same trends: further population growth, deeper commitment to intensive agriculture, and more market participation, completing the circular chain of causality.

The actual picture was more complex, as we will see in Chapter 3, but this sketch suffices to outline the major trends. A change in one organizational sphere (regional-level politics) ramified through other spheres, transforming the region in the direction of increased scale (as it is very likely that for the first time the entire valley became a unified political and economic unit, at least in some regards, and as there was substantial population growth), integration (more interdependency of local political units and less household self-sufficiency), and complexity (involving more specialization in craft production, and more regional administrative complexity).

These trends continued through phase I, until limits of some sort were reached, at which time a reorganization took place. The result was the smaller, less complex, and less integrated valley system of phase II that we describe in Chapter 3. We lack the data to precisely identify the limiting factors, but we might not be too far off in suggesting that a growing administrative institution experienced "eventually diminishing returns to scale." At the same time the congested area around the new capital began to show signs of environmental degradation due to overly zealous agricultural development. At any rate, the system by no means returned to pre-Monte Albán conditions – it had gone too far for that.

Comments on data and methods

As rough and incomplete as the preceding explanatory sketch is, it is still based on a substantial amount of data. Now we shall discuss the kinds of information necessary to carry out studies of the changing relationships among scale, integration, complexity, and boundedness in political and economic institutions. What we have in mind is what it is like to collect data in Mesoamerica, especially in the highlands, but changing what needs to be changed, the same general data requirements would apply to other areas and to historical, nonarchaeological studies. In our case, a well-understood and well-dated ceramic sequence first had to be in place, because everyone on our survey crews makes decisions about dating sites in the field. Systematic settlement pattern surveys over a broad area provided us with the evidence needed to reconstruct changing political organization. For example, a total survey was necessary to know that prior to Monte Albán's foundation the valley was divided into several largely autonomous local systems, separated by open, probably contested, space. The surface survey data also indicated the magnitude of the population transition and, when combined with some excavated data and land-use studies, evidence for changing agricultural strategies. During these surveys evidence was found for the beginning of specialized ceramic production during Monte Albán phase I, although to a certain extent, according to ceramic specialists, changes in the pottery forms alone independently suggested a move in that direction. The relative "costliness" of the dozens of Monte Albán phase I ceramic categories had to be estimated (Special topic 3), and maps of the distribution of the types made to see how the different types were becoming distributed over the valley. The maps were based on some 3,000 surface collections.

Maps showing the distributions of ceramic categories can also be useful in other regards. For example, if pottery types are relatively uniformly distributed over the region, we infer the presence of a highly integrated economic system through which goods moved long distances. Lesser distribution uniformity would imply, for instance, the presence of a series of local economic systems, with little movement of goods across their boundaries. Each of these local systems may have been highly integrated, but the region as a whole would be considered to have been poorly integrated. The ceramic collections can also be used to assess the relative "affluence" of different sites. For instance, more affluent sites are those with more of the costly ceramic types, or with a wider range of types present. We use the ceramic evidence in still another way. In market systems, purchasers have considerable freedom of choice. Thus, if a potter makes shoddy goods and charges too much, he will go out of business. In those periods in which marketing choices were present, therefore, we could expect more competition among independent potters, and therefore generally higher-quality pots. In periods during which freedom of choice was, for whatever reason, more curtailed (as when the government supplies pottery, or limits competition between independent producers), quality should have declined. Unfortunately these sorts of ceramic analyses cannot be done at the present time except with the Oaxaca data. As we mentioned, the broad regional surveys are relatively unproductive in the eastern lowlands. The appropriate surveys and surface collections have been done in the Valley of Mexico, but the ceramic counts have never been published, and estimates never made of the costliness of types.

Our major tool for analyzing change in administrative institutions is information on the size and distribution of sites showing evidence of administrative functions. Such places are called administrative "central places." Central places could also be loci of economic transactions, or they may have been the sites for some combination of both administrative and economic functions, plus other functions – for example, ritual and other social integrative activities. Administrative activities are indicated archaeologically in Mesoamerica by mounded architecture. This can be somewhat tricky in application, because, for example, an isolated temple-mound could be indicative of religious ceremonial and little else. Too, it is not impossible that a wealthy merchant, for example, could employ the labor force required to build a mounded structure. By and large, however, judging from what one can tell from descriptions of the aboriginal societies made by Spaniards shortly after the conquest, and from descriptions of homotaxial societies, substantial mounded architecture is very likely indicative of governmental functions. Religious institutions in such societies were typically closely bound up with government and the governing elite. Certainly this was by and large true of Mesoamerica at the time of the conquest, and no doubt before that. Recall from our discussion of scale factors that an elite governing a large population must be "buffered" from that population. The information-processing limitations of the human mind preclude direct, open interaction between a leader and a large group of followers. Contact is with inter-mediaries, through which only selected information is channeled. In Mesoamerica this buffering was accomplished architecturally. The governors were isolated behind high walls, and protected by outer offices staffed by intermediaries. They lived in rooms elevated on high platforms, often facing closed patios built to facilitate the control of traffic. The elaborate architecture left behind by a governing elite shows up today as various kinds of pyramid mounds.

The scale of the architecture at an administrative locality was presumably pro-portionate to the importance of that place in the region's hierarchy of administrative places. This follows because the higher-ranking elite has more access to the resources necessary to the construction of the larger buildings. The grandeur of the buildings is also a symbol of power. The sometimes truly monumental buildings in a Meso-american capital such as Monte Albán or Teotihuacan provided information to citizens as well as to members of other societies about the power of the state as a whole. In the Valley of Oaxaca, we have found that low-order administrative central places (centers ranking third, fourth, or fifth in the hierarchy) usually have mounded buildings measuring in the vicinity of 100 or 1,000 cubic meters. Second-level cen-ters are often in the area of 10,000 cubic meters, and Monte Albán at its height as regional capital (around A.D. 600) had mounded buildings totaling over 900,000 cubic meters.

We have another indicator of the relative importance of an administrative place – its population size. High-order administrative places have more functions than low-order places. Low-order places usually have decision-making responsibilities vis-à-vis local agriculture of adjudication and tax collection, for instance. Middle-range places (sometimes called "district capitals") may have similar responsibilities, but may add the coordination of the lower centers and ties with the capital to their list of activities, and they are usually "busier." The regional capital has the additional tasks of boundary maintenance for the society as a whole, diplomacy, regulation of international trade, and so on. More work being done in the more important cen-ters implies more people doing the work, so population size of centers should be roughly proportional to position in the regional administrative hierarchy. If a center also has commercial functions, its population will be even greater, and higher-order commercial central places will have larger populations than low-order ones, for similar reasons. (More functions mean more people.) None of these indicators of the relative importance of central places is perfect. Indeed, some sites had large populations but were probably not administrative places; other sites had mounds but were not included in the administrative hierarchy. These are recognizable exceptions, however, to the general indexes. Such measures are essential to recon-structing the first outlines of regional central-place systems.

These data on site functions can be used in several ways. We can assess the verti-cal complexity of a region's administrative hierarchy by noting how many separate groupings of like administrative sites can be identified. Sites with similar values of population size and mound volume, we infer, would have been similar in numbers and kinds of functions. They are grouped as a "level" in the hierarchy. For instance, returning to our Monte Albán I example, we identified at the outset of this phase (Early I) three administrative levels, corresponding to something like local centers, district centers, and the regional capital (Monte Albán). The following phase (Late I) evidenced four or five such levels, and we interpreted this to mean that a substantial increase in the vertical complexity of the region's administrative hierarchy had occurred.

We can also assess the degree of political integration using these sorts of data along with what we know about the locations of administrative places vis-à-vis the capital and each other. One of the questions we will ask is, To what extent does the region's capital exert control? In cases of extreme regional political integration, most decision making takes place in the one capital, and lower-order places have little power or autonomy. This will result in the capital being far larger (and architecturally far more elaborate) than other centers, a form of regional organization referred to as "primate." (The capital in such cases is referred to as a primate center.) Regional dominance by one center can be magnified if commercial as well as political functions tend to be centralized in the one place. Suppose, though, that the regional capital decreases in population, while secondary centers increase in size and in architectural complexity. This would imply decreased political control by the capital, and a less politically integrated system in which lower-order centers have more functions. This interpretation would be strengthened if it were the case that there had been an increase in stylistic variation in the forms or layouts of public buildings in the region, indicating that local architects were freer to design buildings according to local conventions rather than according to centrally promulgated designs.

In reconstructing the degree of political control by a regional capital, one also looks at where secondary centers are located. In the case of a highly autonomous local center, the major links through which information flows are between the center and its dependent communities. Thus the local center's optimal location (which is referred to as the "demographic center of gravity") is near the center of its territory, minimizing its average distance costs to its dependencies. If that local center is strongly dominated by a regional capital, on the other hand, its major information flows are no longer with its local dependents, but with the capital. Therefore its optimal location is no longer at the demographic center of gravity of its own district, but somewhere closer to the major center. Thus during periods of a high degree of regional integration focused on a single primate center, secondary centers should be "pulled in" toward the capital.

In sum, in the Valley of Oaxaca the basic data we depend on include the sizes of sites, from which population estimates can be made, their locations relative to each other and to environmental features, the nature of mounded architecture, and the ceramic counts by site. For Mesoamerica's eastern lowlands, virtually none of this information is available except at selected sites, although we are aided by the detailed epigraphic and iconographic materials. The systematic settlement pattern surveys carried out in the valleys of Oaxaca and Mexico provide abundant information, but even in those valleys many problems remain and much more work needs to be done. For instance, although it is true that over the years a highly effective set of methods for estimating population based on site size and sherd density has been worked out, it is also true that our ceramic periods are often 200 years or more in length, meaning that we cannot always be sure that all the sites we identified to a period were in fact contemporaneously occupied. Our population totals for the periods, then, may be slightly high. Around Mexico City, but in some cases elsewhere as well, so much contemporary growth has occurred that entire major sites have been wiped out, affecting our abilities not only to estimate populations, but also to reconstruct political and economic systems. Another problem that crops up is in dating the construction and use of mounded buildings in multicomponent sites. Fortunately for our purposes especially in the Valley of Mexico, and during the later periods of Oaxaca, so many major reorganizations of regional settlement systems occurred that in many cases buildings were built, then abandoned and not reused in succeeding periods.

Another major problem we face is that, even though these research projects have been going on for years, in some respects the quality of our data is still meager as compared with the complexity that was once the Mesoamerican world. This can be demonstrated quite tangibly with just one class of archaeological remains, the ceramics. We made some 3,000 surface collections in the Valley of Oaxaca (and more than that have been made in the Valley of Mexico), but by necessity these were all of the "grab-bag" sort, meaning that each collection consists of 50 to 100 or so easily found diagnostic sherds. These collections cannot possibly be considered adequate random samples of the total population of sherds. Recall Lambityeco, where it is estimated that there are some 60 million sherds on the surface. And this is only one of 2,500 archaeological sites in the Valley of Oaxaca. Given our resources it would be impossible to even begin to obtain systematically a much larger and truly representative sample, much less tabulate and then analyze all of the resultant information. The ceramic data we have are very useful for identifying certain broad patterns, but their statistical utility is severely limited. Similarly, in many cases the testing of hypotheses about changing features of household economics (for example) would require excavated data. But the problems involved in excavating a representative sample of communities are immense, and therefore make excavation much more costly than the systematic surface collection of ceramics.

Given these limitations, which inhibit any social scientist's ability to comprehend complex social systems, what is to be done? Short of diverting most of the world's resources to the endeavor, or, alternatively, surrendering or becoming twentieth-century dilettantes, how ought a finite, mortal anthropologist proceed? The answer must be: directly to the main objective.

The strategy of this book
Our goal is to offer a current assessment of the nature and causes of cultural evolution in Mesoamerica. In order to accomplish this in a reasonably sized volume, we shall restrict ourselves in several ways. First, we only briefly discuss social systems

that existed prior to the earliest ceramic-using villagers, about 1500 B.C. This is admittedly an arbitrary beginning, and we do not mean to imply that earlier periods are unimportant for evolutionary studies. However, we are severely limited in our ability to study changes in scale, integration, complexity, and boundedness in the earlier periods because of the paucity of data and the difficulty of locating and then dating sites within reasonable limits. It was only with the advent of the widespread use of pottery that people began leaving behind the kind of remains that archaeologists find most useful for easily locating, then dating, sites with a reasonable degree of accuracy. We end our discussion with the arrival of the Spaniards in the sixteenth century. That too is an artificial barrier in time, but the colonial period is presently beyond our competence. Thus we are restricted to a consideration of changes in "pristine" Mesoamerica, during the time when its civilization was uninfluenced by interaction with the Old World societies.

This time span, from the period of the earliest pottery-using villagers to the arrival of Europeans, will involve us in a consideration of some of the most important kinds of evolutionary changes that human societies have manifested anywhere. Included is the rise of complex governments, cities, market systems, and highly stratified social systems. Changes of this sort occurred throughout Mesoamerica, but again in the interest of grappling with such important and complex issues in a modestly sized volume, we restrict ourselves further by focusing primarily on three of Mesoamerica's most important "nuclear" zones, the valleys of Oaxaca and Mexico, and the eastern Mesoamerican lowlands (Fig. 1.2). These were all focuses of change, and areas of massed political and economic power. Controlled comparison and contrast of them can illustrate very well some of the critical features pertinent to the dynamics of early complex societies. Too, the three areas are all well known archaeologically, at least by contrast with most other Mesoamerican regions. Our strategy is to summarize and offer explanations for change in these three areas separately, but always to keep in mind the possibility of making broad generalizations and conclusions through the comparison and contrast of the separate archaeological sequences. In the final chapter we relate what happened in these three areas to developments in the rest of Mesoamerica, and we offer some conclusions about the role of population, the rise of the state, the evolution of market systems, and the nature of Mesoamerica as a world system.

Special topic 1. The origins of a market system in the Valley of Oaxaca

Much has been written about how and why market systems originate, but little work using archaeological evidence has been done on the problem. This is not surprising, because archaeological indications of market activities are difficult to come by. In Mesoamerica, for instance, we know of no particular artifact categories that can be directly associated with actual marketplaces. The evidence we bring forth here is indirect, but still highly suggestive.

Market systems are an important kind of human institution. Of the major areas of the world that witnessed the early development of civilization (which include China, the Indus Valley, Mesopotamia, Egypt, and the Central

Andes), Mesoamerica, in particular, has been identified as an area in which markets were an especially important mode of economic exchange. Although market systems developed in these other areas, their earlier periods are often associated with managed or "redistributive" economies, in which governments provide the major channels for the exchange of goods. In a market system, by definition, suppliers and consumers of goods and services participate freely, in the sense that they retain, as economic actors, choices regarding transactions, marketing destinations, production sites, and so forth. They are thus able to minimize costs and maximize returns (see Special topic 2). The actual degree of freedom of choice will depend on a variety of factors, as we discuss in later sections of this book, but market systems provide at least some level of choice.

The notion of market systems implies the exchange of specialized goods. These items can be difficult to identify from archaeological data, with only a few exceptions. Specialized ceramic production is usually the easiest to locate and date. We shall thus depend heavily on the ceramic information, while keeping in mind that the market system no doubt involved other classes of production specialties that might have been organized rather differently.

One indication that a market system developed in the Valley of Oaxaca during Monte Albán I is that this is the first period in which there is obvious and substantial evidence for specialized ceramic production (for example, concentrations of "kiln wasters" and unusual concentrations of a ceramic type). Specialized production alone, however, is not sufficient proof that a market system was the medium through which exchange occurred. We reasoned, though, that if marketing choices existed, this should be reflected in the way specialized producers were distributed over the landscape. Presumably, producers would have distributed themselves in such a way as to maximize their access to potential customers, and to minimize costs. As the clays needed for ceramic making were available essentially everywhere, potters should have therefore tended to locate themselves close to the marketplace or marketplaces where their goods would be sold, to minimize their costs of moving the pottery. The distribution of ceramic production sites, then, should provide a kind of faint image of the structure of the region's system of marketing places.

In a market system, a range of goods is available, not only in terms of the kinds of items, but in terms of the costliness of items within a single category such as pottery. More costly pots are presumably those that have taken more energy to produce. (They are better fired, better finished, have more decoration, and so forth.) Consumers will prefer the more costly types, probably because they are better made, and because having them confers prestige. Normally, however, the less expensive varieties are purchased, because most families can't afford the costly ones, at least not very often. This is supported by our surface collections. Most sites will have some evidence indicating use of the costly categories, but by far the bulk of most assemblages consists of the cheaper pots. (To see how we evaluated the relative costliness of different pottery types, see Special topic 3.)

A market system and its specialized producers can't be supported if the producers can't make a living. They have to be able to supply a sufficiently large number of households that are willing and able to consume a sufficiently large quantity of their goods. The point at which demand in a region becomes sufficient to support specialized producers is referred to as the "demand threshold." Below it, specialized suppliers are not supported; above, they are. A marketing system in a region consists of a variety of marketing localities. Each has the range of products whose sale can be supported in that particular locality. For example, costly items that are desirable but relatively infrequently consumed cannot be supplied in every market location, because suppliers must have a large number of consumers in order to be supported. The more frequently consumed goods are available in more places because sufficient demand is present even if the area serviced (and therefore the number of households) is small. Also, people will not be willing to travel long distances to a market to buy frequently consumed, inexpensive products, so such goods have to be made available in many localities, scattered around to service the population maximally. People are willing to travel further, however, on those rare occasions when they are able to purchase a costly good. These factors give rise, in market systems, to a hierarchy of marketplaces, in which one or only a few places in a region have a wide range of items available, including the very costly goods. A large number of lower-order marketplaces supply a narrower range, primarily the more mundane, frequently consumed objects.

The data on ceramic production sites in the valley conform to these expectations very nicely as early as about 500 B.C. (Early I). Only one site contained evidence for production of the most costly Early I types, and this is located in the center of the valley. This would have maximized the producer's opportunities to supply the population of the entire valley. A number of production sites of the less costly types were found scattered around the valley, each apparently supplying a small local area. Too, families living farthest away from the suppliers of the costliest types used them the least. Their pottery costs include travel costs, so they are less often able to buy the more expensive products.

Special topic 2. Was there a profit motive in prehispanic Mesoamerica?

Market systems, as we know them ethnographically and historically, are arenas of exchange in which, to a marked degree, participants try to minimize costs and maximize returns (that is, they exhibit a "profit motive"). The degree to which these aims are realizable depends, of course, on a number of factors, including the extent to which governments impinge on exchange transactions. But it should come as no surprise that in an organizational sphere such as market system people should behave in this way – even in "precapitalist" societies. And yet, recently, some anthropologists have stated that there was no profit motive in prehispanic Mesoamerica, and that therefore the phenomena we have been calling markets were really just "redistributive points." It is not clear how they arrived at this conclusion, as no supporting evidence from prehispanic sources is mentioned by them. Evidently, though, they must feel they are mirroring the sentiments of the so-called substantivist anthropologists, whose argument is that the assumptions and methods of formal Western economics are not applicable to precapitalist economic systems. But they have misinterpreted the substantivists. Although nobody would want to try to argue that capitalist institutions such as banks, multinational corporations, or stock markets were present in prehispanic Mexico, even the most vociferous substantivist would point to the fact that in certain situations exchange transactions, even in primitive societies, are carried out with gain in mind. These are transactions that take place beyond the realm of kin ties and community solidarity, involving instead exchanges with nonkin and strangers in broader regional or interregional spheres. This is precisely the context within which most market transactions are likely to occur. As expected, then, we can bring forth abundant evidence for a profit motive in the realm of market exchanges in prehispanic Mesoamerica. Why, for instance, would cacao-bean money have been counterfeited? Judges in the markets punished those who committed fraud in transactions. "Good" merchants were distinguished from "bad" ones. The latter profited excessively by selling fake stones as precious stones, or bad-tasting, old tamales as fresh ones, and so on. This sort of thing sounds very much like "business as usual," and certainly provides overwhelming evidence for a profit motive.

Special topic 3. A measure of ceramic production steps (see Fig. 1.3)
It is not difficult to see, intuitively, that G-3M bowls and polychrome pots were more carefully made than G-35s. (These designations for ceramic types were established by A. Caso, I. Bernal, and J. Acosta, whose ceramic study is mentioned in the Bibliographical essay.) To quantify this, an index was devised to reflect the number of steps required to produce a finished vessel. The G-35, G-12, and G-3M bowls were the most popular, "everyday" serving dishes of their day. Polychrome, on the other hand, was a "fancy" ware. Here are the basic production steps for each, beginning after the first shaping of the vessel:

G-12, Monte Albán Late I and II
1   interior wiped
2   exterior wiped
3   interior burnished
4   two wide lines incised on interior rim

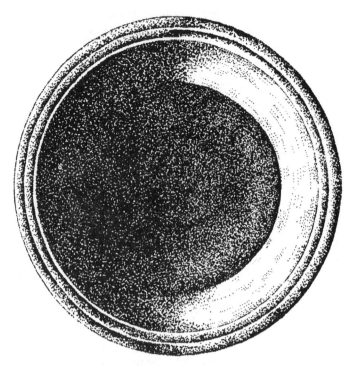

A

B

Figure 1.3. (A) G-12 bowl, four production steps; (B) G-35 bowl, two production steps; (C) G-3M bowl, seven production steps; (D) polychrome pot, eleven production steps.

G-35, Monte Albán III and IV

1 interior wiped
2 interior burnished
   (the exterior is unfinished)

G-3M, Monte Albán V

1 interior wiped
2 exterior wiped
3 interior highly burnished

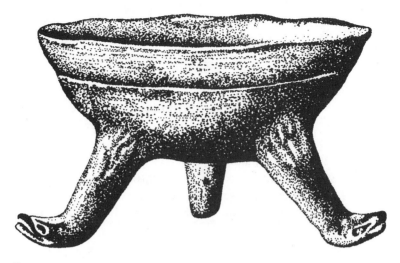

C

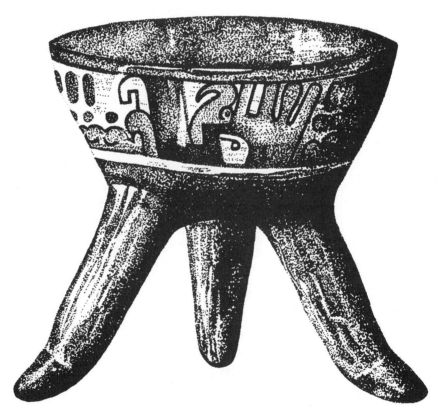

D

4   exterior highly burnished
5   snake head molded and formed into a support
6   finished snake support attached after initial drying of vessel
7   long firing time required due to absence of temper

Polychrome, Monte Albán V

1 interior wiped
2 exterior wiped
3 interior burnished
4 exterior burnished
5 supports attached after initial drying of vessel
6 interior painted red
7 exterior painted red
8 exterior painted cream
9 exterior painted orange in intricate design
10 exterior painted red in intricate design
11 long firing time required due to absence of temper

Preceramic Mesoamerica

Introduction

Mesoamerica was first colonized by humans probably 10,000 years ago. These earliest inhabitants survived by hunting and trapping animals, gathering and collecting wild plant foods, and perhaps fishing and collecting shellfish. No doubt, their lives were rich with ritual and ceremony that bound small, family-based groups together during the more plentiful times of year, but of these activities we have little archeological evidence. By 8,000 years ago, the nomadic occupants of Mesoamerica had begun experimenting with wild plants in a way that altered them, increasing their utility for human use. Out of these experiments, thousands of years later, an agricultural way of life was born. Domesticated plants that, with sufficient human care and intervention, could provide basic foodstuffs for entire villages of people year-round, had a profound impact on the subsequent course of human history in the prehispanic New World. In this chapter, we provide a background to our discussion of three nuclear regions by briefly examining the archaeological evidence for when humans first reached and colonized Mesoamerica, for the subsequent Archaic period, and for processes by which agriculture, or a food-producing economy, came to predominate over food collecting.

The earliest Mesoamericans

According to the available evidence, biologically modern humans migrated to the New World from the Old thousands of years before the voyages of Christopher Columbus. Archaeologists agree that the route of these human migrations crossed a now-submerged, broad land mass called Beringia. At times of low sea levels in the past, when glaciers tied up large amounts of water, Beringia linked modern-day Alaska with easternmost Siberia. Arctic-adapted hunters could have moved easily across what is now the Bering Sea, probably in pursuit of migratory game, not realizing that they were entering a "new world" never before inhabited by humans. It is also possible that human groups, accustomed to traveling in boats and capturing sea mammals in shallow coastal waters, gradually moved eastward along the southern coast of Beringia and then Alaska, moving southward along the Pacific coast. Any archaeological trace that might allow us to determine which of these alternatives actually occurred, however, has long since been destroyed as sea levels rose to their present position.

Archaeologists agree that humans reached North America by way of Beringia, but there is enormous debate about when this happened, and when people first

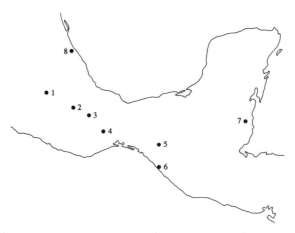

Figure 2.1. Locations of some preceramic sites. Basin of Mexico sites (1), Valsequillo (2), Tehuacán Valley sites (3), Valley of Oaxaca sites (4), Santa Marta cave (5), Chantuto Complex sites (6), Lowe Ranch sites (7), Santa Lucia (8).

moved into Mesoamerica. A detailed discussion of all purportedly early Mesoamerican sites and their different interpretations is beyond the scope of this book. It has long been accepted that humans had not only crossed Beringia to reach Alaska but had migrated southward, penetrating as far as South America, by 11,000 years ago. From Canada to Chile are found distinctive projectile point types, often in obvious association with the remains of animals that became extinct at the end of the Pleistocene epoch 9,000–12,000 years ago. Archaeologists are divided about whether these clearly dated remnants are those of the earliest inhabitants of the New World, or whether people had followed similar paths 20,000 or more years ago, bringing with them a simpler technology that lacked projectile points.

It is no small wonder that controversy and disagreement are so rife concerning when people first arrived in the New World. As humans moved southward, populating the hemisphere for the first time, the numbers of people would have been very small and their lifestyle highly mobile. Few traces of their presence could be expected to remain after the intervening centuries. It is entirely possible that very early migrations failed, leaving no descendants and no apparent relationship between the earliest tool technologies lacking projectile points and the late Pleistocene technologies that are so widespread and well dated.

Among the better-known, purportedly very early sites in Mesoamerica are Tlapacoya and Tequixquiac in the Valley of Mexico, and a series of sites near Valsequillo, Puebla. The site of Tlapacoya lies on what was the shore of the former Lake Chalco (Fig. 2.1). Between 1965 and 1973, eighteen different localities on ancient beaches, on the former lakeshore, and in rock shelters were excavated. Among the finds were several features identified by the excavators as hearths on a Pleistocene beach, bones of now-extinct animals, small numbers of flakes of both obsidian and local chipped stone, and several bones bearing signs of having been modified by humans. Two radiocarbon samples from hearths suggest an age of about 21,000–24,000 years, but many others give much more recent dates.

At Tequixquiac in the Basin of Mexico, in 1870, an animal's head carved in camel bone was found twelve meters beneath the ground surface. The context is not reliable and the act of carving, which is the indicator of human presence, need not be the same age as the camel bone itself. Even if it were, this find need not indicate a human presence earlier than the Paleo-Indian period. More recently, chipped stone tools have been recovered from the base of fossil-bearing deposits dated to 9,000–16,000 years old. Projectile points are absent from the lithic assemblage of Tequixquiac, and lithic artifacts in general are few in number. To date, no evidence from this site compels us to accept an age older than 9,000–12,000 years, which is comparable to Paleo-Indian sites known throughout North America.

At several sites near Valsequillo, Puebla, stone artifacts and flakes are associated with the bones of extinct animals (horse, camel, and mastodon). Two radiocarbon dates taken from mollusk shell in the deposits give widely disparate ages of about 9,000 and 22,000 years. Despite the well-known fact that freshwater shell provides notoriously unreliable radiocarbon dates, the excavators have accepted the older age for this flake-tool complex. Other archaeologists are skeptical and point to the conflicting and confusing results that have arisen from independent efforts to determine the age of the deposits using a battery of different techniques.

Apart, perhaps, from the Tlapacoya finds, there is no persuasive evidence that humans had inhabited Mesoamerica before about 9,000–12,000 years ago, an age that is consistent with the most widely accepted age for earliest occupations elsewhere in the New World.

Paleo-Indians in Mesoamerica

The Paleo-Indian period in North American prehistory is known principally by its projectile points, forms that are called Clovis and Folsom, which bear a distinctive flute or channel along their long axes. Points from sites of comparable age in South America lack flutes, and fluted point finds in Mesoamerica have been rare. During the Paleo-Indian period, at the end of the Pleistocene, people coexisted with very large animals that became extinct as glaciers retreated and modern climates were established. Mammoth, mastodon, horse, camel, and giant sloth, among others, occasionally fell prey to humans, and apparently failed to adapt to the warmer, generally drier climates of modern times. To a great extent, our knowledge of this period in Mesoamerica is biased toward localities where humans did indeed succeed in bringing down a mammoth, but does this mean that mammoths and their other very large contemporaries were the predominant prey of late Pleistocene Mesoamerican hunters? Probably not, although the data are still too scant to say so with any degree of certainty. As Richard MacNeish has remarked, most Paleo-Indians probably killed one mammoth in their lives and never stopped talking about it.

Surprisingly, relatively few sites in Mesoamerica can be dated securely to the Paleo-Indian period. In addition to Tequixquiac and the Valsequillo Reservoir sites already mentioned, Paleo-Indian sites are known at few localities in the Valley of Mexico. Among the strongest candidates for sites of this period is Santa Isabel Iztapan, where stone tools, including projectile points, have been found associated with the remains of two mammoths. A radiocarbon date from organic material associated with these remains suggests a date of 7000 B.C. More dubious examples include Tepexpan and Atepehuacan, both sites of mammoth finds, but in the first case accompanied only by a single obsidian flake that may or may not be of human production. In the second, the age of associated lithic artifacts is confused badly by the presence of several potsherds indicating obvious, much later intrusion.

Elsewhere, a single fluted point has been recovered from Tlaxcala, just east of the Valley of Mexico. At Lake Zacoalco, Jalisco, the skeleton of a mammoth is associated with a single obsidian flake that may or may not be an artifact. At Chimalacatlan Cave in Morelos, the remains of extinct animals are numerous but the indications of human presence are at best vague and their association with these ancient bones is uncertain. While several mammoth remains have been found in the Valley of Oaxaca, they are not accompanied by any traces of contemporaneous humans. A single projectile point found in isolation on the surface on the Valley of Oaxaca may be fluted, but this artifact alone cannot be taken as definitive evidence of occupation during the Paleo-Indian period.

Five Paleo-Indian sites with fluted points are known from highland Guatemala. These included an isolated fluted point found near Guatemala City. At Los Tapiales in the Quiche Basin, leaf-shaped projectile points, blades, burins, and other artifacts are dated to 10,000–11,000 years ago. A more recent survey in the Quiche Basin recovered at least 117 sites with remains suggestive of Paleo-Indian and/or Archaic period occupations.

The small number of known sites and scant material remains at these sites are the result of a number of factors. Most Mesoamerican archaeologists are concerned with later prehispanic periods and the vast majority of research undertaken reflects this concern. We have already mentioned the problems of recovery and preservation that plague archaeologists studying the societies of Mesoamerica's earliest occupants. However, another important factor is the small scale of Paleo-Indian social systems themselves, at least in terms of group sizes; spatially, scale was undoubtedly substantial. Social interaction must have occurred over very large areas, linking together widely spaced, small foraging groups. Although slender, all of the evidence is consistent with social systems consisting of small, mobile groups based on kin relations. We presume that these small groups coalesced into larger ones upon occasion, as is known to have been the case among mobile hunter-gatherers of this century elsewhere in the world. Taking place during times of relative abundance, larger encampments would have provided opportunities to visit friends and relatives, arrange marriages, perform rituals, and perhaps exchange rare materials. Although no archaeological evidence speaks directly to the existence of larger encampments, we know that small groups would not have been demographically viable over the long term. Intermarriage among groups must have occurred and such encampments would have provided the obvious mechanism through which it could be arranged.

Integration and complexity, as we have defined them in Chapter 1, were limited in the Paleo-Indian period. Numerous social groups existed, but these groups did not perform different functions or roles in a broader system. Instead, the system was relatively undifferentiated and the communities represented by individual sites would all have tended to play very similar roles.

The paucity of data makes it impossible at present to do much more than speculate about boundaries. The existence of a number of complexes or traditions, based on projectile point and other lithic artifact styles as well as the frequencies of artifact types, has been posited. These traditions distinguish the central and southern highlands and the Gulf of Mexico coast. But until a great deal more research is carried out, their existence must be viewed as tentative. However, the very fact that the systems themselves are so difficult to identify in the lithic data suggests that boundaries were very open and that people interacted in networks that covered vast areas composed of diverse resource zones.

The Archaic period

The period from 9000 to 2000 B.C. was one of seemingly slow but very important change. It shares with this period elsewhere in North America a mixed hunting, gathering, and collecting economic orientation. What sets Mesoamerica apart from the same time in the remainder of North America is the beginnings of plant domestication. The earliest inhabitants of Mesoamerica hunted, snared, and collected wild animals and gathered wild plants for food. During the Archaic people began interacting with some species of plants in ways that produced genetic changes in the plants: they became domesticated. For many of these plants, as we will discuss in greater detail below, the genetic changes meant a greater reliance on human intervention if they were to survive, and a greater degree of intervention on the part of people if the plants were to continue to be useful to them.

Compared to the Paleo-Indian period, known Archaic sites are relatively numerous and some have produced considerable data. But information varies considerably for different areas and for different times. Geological and preservation factors have contributed to this variety, making some preceramic sites nearer modern ground surfaces, and archaeologically richer, in marginal environments like the Tehuacán Valley and the Valley of Oaxaca. In the more environmentally productive lowlands, Archaic period sites are known from the Pacific and Gulf of Mexico coastal plains as well as in Belize. For a number of different reasons, though, it is difficult to piece together a coherent picture of change over the thousands of years of the Archaic period in most of the lowlands. Generally, the number of known sites is very small. The depth of deposits at many has meant that excavations cannot uncover the broad areas that are needed to locate settlement features and get datable and other archaeological material from a variety of different contexts. Plant remains have not been preserved or analyzed and reported where they have been sought, and in other cases, appropriate methods to collect them were not employed.

The earliest evidence for plant domestication comes from the comparatively arid environments of the southern and central highland valleys and precedes the first permanently settled villages by several thousand years. It has long been thought that richer environments such as the lowlands would have permitted sedentary life well before the adoption of full-scale agriculture. However, as we will see below, the archaeological evidence in support of this view is at best scant. Nor is there evidence that plant domestication first took place, or developed independently, in the environmentally richer areas of Mesoamerica.

Domesticated plants

Corn, beans, and squash formed the backbone of subsistence in much of prehispanic Mesoamerica, and continue to form an important part of the diet in much of rural Mexico and Guatemala today. These three plants are often grown together in a single field called a *milpa,* the beans creeping up the corn stalks while the squash plants catch along the lower leaves of the corn plants. While growing corn takes great quantities of nitrogen from the soil, beans replace this nutrient, thus reducing soil depletion. Together, corn, beans, and squash make a nutritionally balanced diet that no one plant alone can supply. Dozens of other plants were domesticated in prehispanic Mesoamerica, including chile peppers, avocados, and cotton. The bottle gourd, a member of the same botanical family as squashes and pumpkins, has never been used for food but continues to be used, after drying and hollowing out, as a container for carrying water. This natural canteen may have been the first plant to undergo domestication in Mesoamerica.

Ancestral wild species of most of the domesticates with which we are concerned still exist in some areas of Mesoamerica. Corn is a possible exception, and its origin continues to be a contentious issue. Some botanists believe that domesticated corn is descended from a now-extinct wild maize. Others believe that its ancestor is a wild grass called teosinte, which still grows in areas of the Mesoamerican highlands. The weight of the present evidence favors a teosinte origin for domesticated corn. Today, in abandoned fields, teosinte, wild runner beans, and squash grow together, just as the domesticated species do in milpa fields. Today's milpa, with maize substituted for teosinte, is thus modeled on a natural predecessor. Supporters of wild corn point out that no existing archaeological data document a gradual genetic change from teosinte to maize. However, such a change may have occurred too rapidly to be detectable archaeologically. Recent reexamination of the earliest known examples of domesticated maize, from Coxcatlán Cave, Tehuacán, supports a teosinte origin. The specimens already are fully domesticated and exhibit the form one would expect had they evolved very rapidly from teosinte.

Because the known ancestors of domesticated plants are found in the highlands, research over the years concerned with the origins of agriculture in Mesoamerica has focused on the highlands as the probable location where domestication first took place. The presence of preserved plant remains in the archaeological record, and the development in the 1960s of methods for recovering them, have been instrumental in forming our current understanding of plant domestication and its impact on the Archaic period systems. While it is possible, even probable, that some plant species were first domesticated in the Mesoamerican lowlands, circumstances make it unlikely that this can ever be demonstrated. Rising sea levels since the end of the Pleistocene have submerged ancient coastlines where some early lowland inhabitants may have lived, and have elevated water tables, thus inundating the

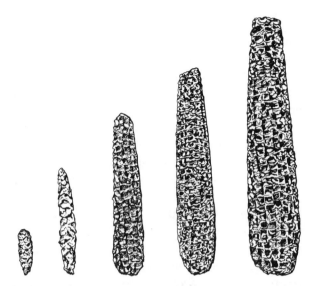

Figure 2.2. Changes in corncobs from about 5000 B.C. (left) to A.D. 1500. Largest cob is 13 centimeters long. Redrawn from Mangelsdorf, MacNeish, and Galinat (1967: fig. 122).

earliest levels at many lowland sites. Heavy alluviation along the major river courses as they carry silt from the mountains has buried their former banks under deep deposits, making locating preceramic sites very difficult and hampering efforts to excavate them.

The Archaic sequences

Large, multidisciplinary projects in the valleys of Tehuacán and Oaxaca were designed and carried out in the 1960s to study the history of plant domestication and the processes by which agriculture developed in Mesoamerica. Both projects surveyed the valleys to locate preceramic sites, tested sites to determine which ones had suitable, stratified deposits and good preservation of plant remains, and then carried out excavations at those that met these criteria.

These valleys are good examples of marginal environments in Mesoamerica. Both are semiarid. Rainfall is not abundant and lakes, major rivers and other large, year-round sources of water are lacking. There may be numerous different environmental zones within the valleys, but none of them is highly productive for humans all year, and the seasonal variation in the availability in resources tends to be marked. The long dry season is a time of true scarcity.

The work of Richard S. MacNeish and others in the Tehuacán Valley yielded some of the earliest evidence for plant domestication in the New World. In levels dating to 5050 B.C. at Coxcatlán Cave (toward the end of the El Riego phase), eighteen tiny carbonized corncobs measuring only a few centimeters in length were found (Fig. 2.2). Dozens of other specimens turned up at other localities in the Tehuacán Valley dating between 5000 and 3000 B.C. during the Coxcatlán phase. Other clear domesticates in Coxcatlán times, between 5000 and 3000 B.C., include the avocado, chile pepper, and a species of squash (*Cucurbita mixta*). A few rinds of bottle gourd are suggestive of its cultivation but inconclusive.

Artifacts and other archaeological remains indicate small groups of humans who relied on a changing mix of animals, wild plants, and cultivated plants. Archaic artifact assemblages at the Tehuacán Valley sites include projectile points of different types, manos, scrapers, stone bowls, mortars and pestles, and pebble choppers. Animals hunted included deer, peccary, and many others. The bones of cottontail rabbits appear in such large numbers that they may have been hunted in large, communal drives. Reconstructions based on the archaeological record suggest a gradual change in the proportions of the diet accounted for by meat, wild plants, and cultivated plants. Prior to 5000 B.C., meat predominated. In the El Riego phase, meat and plant foods each accounted for about half of the diet, with cultivated species forming only a small proportion of plant foods consumed. During the Coxcatlán and Abejas phases (ca. 5000–2300 B.C.), meat continued to make up about half the diet, but cultivated plants accounted for a much larger share, perhaps nearly half, of the plants eaten. A different analysis that examines trace elements left in human bone by different food groups suggests that a heavy reliance on grains, presumably maize, began in the Coxcatlán phase and may have remained unchanged for 5,000–6,000 years.

In Oaxaca, preceramic sites are known primarily from the eastern part of the Valley of Oaxaca, although another in the Nochixtlán Valley has been recorded and several probable Archaic sites have been located in the mountains between these valleys. The earlier part of the Archaic period is revealed in some detail, but several gaps exist and information about the last several millennia is sketchy. The earliest Archaic level in Oaxaca is found at Cueva Blanca, dated to 9050–8780 B.C., but preservation is poor. It appears to represent a brief occupation by a small group that left behind only a few tools and presumably hunted modern animal species.

Guilá Naquitz, a cave located high in the hills on the north boundary of the Valley of Oaxaca, gives a much more detailed and lengthy picture of Archaic life. At least six fall season "microband" encampments (i.e., encampments of from two to five individuals, probably consisting of families) took place during the Naquitz phase (8900–6700 B.C.). People moved into Guilá Naquitz in late summer but continued harvesting resources in the mesquite forest below in the alluvium. In late fall, they began to harvest the resources of the oak-pine and thorn-scrub-cactus forests, while continuing to hunt and trap animals. The most abundant food remnant dating to these levels is acorns, which probably were ground into a flour and eaten as a staple component of the diet. The second and later occupants of the cave grew and ate domesticated squash, and the latest Archaic inhabitants may have attempted to cultivate a species of wild runner bean. Although abundant in the deposits, this particular species was never domesticated. At Guilá Naquitz is found the earliest clear evidence for the domestication of squash (*Cucurbita pepo*), in levels dated at 7400–6700 B.C. A single seed may indicate an even earlier date for the domestication of this species, between 8750 and 7840 B.C. Fragments of bottle gourd rind, perhaps also domesticated, occur by 7400–6700 B.C.

Following the abandonment of Guilá Naquitz in the seventh millennium B.C., there is a gap in the archaeological record of the Archaic period until the Jícaras phase, dated indirectly to approximately 5000–4000 B.C. This phase is known only from the open-air site of Gheo-Shih, situated in the lower reaches of the valley near several stream beds. Like most other open-air sites of great antiquity, Gheo-Shih lacked preserved plant remains, and also animal bone. However, it has a number of unusual features that suggest that it was not a microband encampment like the cave sites. Its size (about 1.5 hectares) and a series of stone alignments suggest to Flannery that Gheo-Shih was an area where related microbands that foraged in the hills during late summer and fall gathered together, probably during the relatively plentiful summer season (a "macroband camp").

The Blanca phase in Oaxaca (3300–2800 B.C.) is known from levels at Cueva Blanca. Contemporary with the Abejas phase in the Tehuacán Valley, it has similar projectile point styles. The Martínez phase, dated to about 2000 B.C., is known from a level at the Martínez Rock Shelter in the Valley of Oaxaca and Yuzanú, an open-air site in the Nochixtlán Valley. Unfortunately, neither site has yielded any direct evidence of subsistence, in the form of either plant or animal remains, for this phase that precedes the transition to settled farming villages.

The Archaic in richer environments

Some highland areas of Mesoamerica were much richer than the marginal valleys just discussed. They were better watered and offered a broader range of rich micro-environments. Some of these offered various resources that, combined, would have meant less pronounced seasonal variation in productivity. A survey in the Quiche Basin of highland Guatemala has yielded some interesting, if very tentative, results that would indicate contrasts with the Archaic patterns in the highland Mexican valleys. The number of sites attributed to Paleo-Indian and/or Archaic occupations is 117. If these temporal assignments are supported by more detailed investigation, a higher population density than elsewhere is Mesoamerica at the time is suggested. It must be underscored, however, that the chronological placement of these sites is tenuous. These data may indicate a general trend through the Archaic toward a higher degree of sedentism, perhaps with some settlements occupied year round, very likely without agriculture. Agriculture may have been consciously resisted for several centuries. While the data upon which these speculations are based are tenuous, they are supported by excavations at Santa Marta Cave in nearby Chiapas where the late Archaic economy lacked agriculture, relying instead on the hunting of animals and collecting of wild plants.

Zohapilco, on the former shore of Lake Chalco in the southern Valley of Mexico, provides stronger, if still tentative, evidence of more permanent habitation in a rich environment. Archaic period occupations date to 6300–5300 B.C. (Playa I phase) and 5300–4500 B.C. (Playa II phase). Three environmental zones would have been available for exploitation: pine, oak, and alder forests, fertile alluvial soils, and the shallow, fresh waters of Lake Chalco. The forests yielded wild fruits, mammals, and important resources like wood. Wild grasses such as teosinte, amaranth and chenopodium thrived in the alluvium. In the lake itself, or on its shores, were freshwater fish, mollusks, reptiles and amphibians, and migratory waterfowl. In stark contrast to present times, the southern Basin of Mexico was an optimal environment, containing numerous plant and animal species that were easily exploited. Many of these species were productive year round, while the periodic ones tend to be distributed fairly evenly between the rainy and dry seasons. Such an environment contrasts markedly with the more marginal environments of the Tehuacán Valley and the Valley of Oaxaca. At Zohapilco, the environment could have supported year-round occupation, but the direct evidence for sedentary settlement is not overwhelmingly strong. The presence of bones of migratory waterfowl (dry-season residents) and of a reptile that can only be caught easily during the rainy season provide some evidence that, between 6300–4500 B.C., sedentary occupation had developed in the absence of any obvious cultigens. However, there are no traces of storage pits, structures, or shelters of any kind in these early levels.

Lowland sites dating to the Archaic period are known from the Pacific and Gulf of Mexico coastal plains as well as inland, along rivers and on the Caribbean coast of Belize. The lowlands share the same general characteristics as the richer highland environments. Although most specific resources peak at particular times of year, those times vary considerably so there are no pronounced seasons of scarcity. Research conducted over several decades at five sites in estuarine wetlands on the Pacific coast of Chiapas reveals part of late Archaic (ca. 3000–2000 B.C.) adaptations in coastal areas. In one case, sites consist of tiny artificial islands made of alternating layers of burned and unburned clam shell. Despite their abundance, analysis of the shells and of other archaeological evidence reveals no sign whatsoever that clams were harvested for their meat. Clams may have been collected to build the small islands which would facilitate harvesting some other estuarine resource, probably shrimp.

The only evidence of Archaic period structures in the lowlands comes from one of these coastal Chiapas sites. Because the floor and associated features were more than four meters below the present surface, only a small proportion of the entire area could be uncovered. Combined with the paucity of artifacts, this has made interpretation very difficult. A ramadalike, oval structure without walls lacks apparent traces of domestic use. Other features may have included racks for net-making, windbreaks, drying racks or a simple hut, and areas to support containers or delineated work areas of unspecified function. Alternatively, some or all of these other features may have had to do with ceremonial activity, but of this there is no direct evidence. However, this floor and the associated features reflect an atypical use of the island, since it is unique in the stratigraphy of those tested.

The Santa Luisa site on the shore of the Río Tecolutla in the modern state of Veracruz has an Archaic component. A single radiocarbon date of 2930 B.C. ± 100 suggests an age approximately equal to that of the lowest levels at the Chiapas shell sites. The earliest occupation at Santa Luisa lies at and below the modern dry-season water table, and four to six meters below the modern ground surface. The environmental setting is similar to that of the Chiapas sites, an estuary with abundant shellfish. A major difference is the absence of any features including hearths. The deposits consist predominantly of oyster shell together with cracked river cobbles, stone tools, and mammal and fish bone, although bone preservation was poor. Artifacts and shell tended to occur together in concentrations, of which some were excavated. Unlike contemporaneous (or earlier) Archaic sites in the highlands, Santa Luisa lacked the ground stone tools associated with agriculture or a heavy reliance on wild plant foods, although the data on this are poor. Three environmental zones easily exploited from this location may have attracted the sites' occupants. These were the estuary, with its abundant shellfish, the adjacent river with its fish, and nearby hills where hunting would have been the primary economic activity. The original investigator has suggested that these lines of evidence point to a permanent pre-agricultural or nonagricultural village occupation whose economy focused on exploiting the resources of these three relatively abundant environmental zones. However, no settlement or other feature evidence, or analyses to determine seasonal exploitation of different faunal resources, support this interpretation.

Belize is the only region of the lowlands to have been the subject of a large-scale effort to locate and study Archaic sites, comparable to the efforts made in the highland valleys of Tehuacán and Oaxaca. However, the survey was not undertaken in an intensive manner, and much reconnaissance focused on the Caribbean coast and the major rivers. Known site locations may not reflect the range of environments actually inhabited in Archaic times. At the end of three field seasons, about 150 sites with possible preceramic components had been located, but only a handful of these had been excavated. A tentative chronological sequence for preceramic Belize suggests a transition from the exploitation of edible wild plants and Ice Age herbivores at the end of the Paleo-Indian period (ca. 9000 B.C.) to a focus on a wider range of environments, including the Caribbean coast, in the early Archaic. The use of seed and plant foods increased. By 5000–4000 B.C., some settlements in especially favorable locations may have accommodated large (multiband) encampments for several months at a time. The succeeding millennium saw a continuation of a trend toward greater utilization of littoral resources. At least one site dating to this time may represent a long-term or permanent settlement. This site is located in an environmental setting much like that of the Santa Luisa site in Veracruz, near the coast where a number of aquatic and terrestrial environments adjoin. Analyses that would support this interpretation of permanent occupation, based only on site size and environmental location, have yet to be published. The final millennium of the Archaic in Belize (3000–2000 B.C.) is the only one dated by an absolute method. The greater preference for riverine, deltaic, or estuarine environmental settings may have set the stage for the predominantly agricultural economies of Formative villages some centuries later. Confirmation of these trends awaits completion of analyses.

Archaic trends

Although rich in many ways, the preceramic data are much more uneven and far less complete than one might wish when embarking on an effort to identify long-term trends in scale, complexity, integration, and boundedness. The existing data suggest that a reliance on domesticated plants developed very gradually, over a period of thousands of years, in environmentally marginal highland valleys. The delayed development of permanent villages contrasts with certain areas of the Old

World, where settled communities preceded plant and animal domestication. The possibility of a sedentary settlement pattern in the richer environments of the lowlands and of some highland areas is suggested, but there is too little supporting evidence to draw firm conclusions.

With the possible exception of Belize and coastal Chiapas, the lowlands are known from only a few sites representing fairly short periods late in the Archaic period. Information is sketchy for richer highland environments, as well, where interpretations are based on the analysis of a single site or on undated surface finds. The semiarid highland valleys, especially the Tehuacán Valley and the Valley of Oaxaca, have yielded the most comprehensive data. But even there major gaps persist. In the Tehuacán Valley, most Archaic phases are represented in the archaeological record with occupations in most seasons, although the methods for determining seasonality, at least in some cases, are problematic. In the Valley of Oaxaca, only late summer-fall habitations are represented. In both valleys, sites dating to the last millennia immediately prior to the emergence of permanent farming villages in the Early Formative are extremely rare.

In the Valley of Oaxaca, the seasonal round involved moving between the uplands and low-lying areas, as people took advantage of resources that became available in different zones during different seasons. We have seen from Guilá Naquitz in Oaxaca, for example, that fall subsistence was oriented toward resources in the oak-pine and thorn-scrub-cactus forests. Acorns were harvested by the basketload, and smaller amounts of piñon nuts and other upland products also played a role in the diet at this time of year. But we have no direct evidence of Archaic peoples' whereabouts and activities during the long, dry winter or the summer. In summer, people were presumably down on the alluvium, collecting the resources of the mesquite forest and, later, planting a few crops along the streamsides. The open-air site of Gheo-Shih may represent a summer occupation. Winter, when plant foods would have been scarcest, remains a blank page.

An increasing reliance on cultigens eventually would have kept people down in the low-lying riverine areas for longer periods, probably well into the fall. Perhaps the abandonment of Guilá Naquitz in the seventh millennium B.C. is partly attributable to a need to stay lower down longer in order to reap the benefits of cultivated crops. Generally, however, the data are frustrating with respect to such questions. Initially, at least, at Guilá Naquitz these changes did not have a noticeable effect on the late summer–late fall portion of the annual cycle. By the time it did, the effect was so profound that major shifts in many aspects of life are apparent.

The available archaeological evidence suggests that the earliest efforts to result in plant domestication occurred in marginal highland environments where the dry seasons are long and severe and drought is a recurrent but unpredictable threat. The Tehuacán Valley data suggest gradual change through the Archaic toward increased population overall, larger group size, reduced group mobility, and greater reliance on domesticated plants. But nowhere in Mesoamerica are the Archaic period data adequate to address systematically the causative interrelationships of demographic change, plant domestication, sedentarization, and agriculture. It is apparent that populations grew between 10,000 and 2000 B.C., but it seems unlikely that population levels anywhere were high enough to force an economic shift from hunting and collecting to potentially more productive cultivation. Even if estimated Archaic populations are off by an order of magnitude, and they almost certainly are, it is difficult to accept that overpopulation had become a problem by the time domestication is first apparent in the archaeological record.

The selection of storable plants figured prominently in the process of plant domestication. Squash seed, for example, will keep for months, as will corn dried on the cob. Early meddlings with plants may have involved attempts both to increase and diversify the availability of storable foods, and to augment supplies of wild storable foods such as acorns and mesquite pods. Food storage would have been one important strategy for dealing with the risk and hardship of the long, lean dry season. Efforts to even out the variability in available foodstuffs by selecting plants that would store well may have been important in the beginnings of cultivation and the origins of plant domestication in the environmentally marginal highland valleys of Tehuacán and Oaxaca.

East of the Isthmus of Tehuantepec, highland Guatemala and Chiapas may contrast markedly with this highland Mexican temporal trend toward a gradually increasing reliance on cultivated plants, but additional research is sorely needed. If the contrast is genuine, agriculture may have been adopted later in these richer highland environments in part because the variation in moisture and wild plant productivity between the winter and other seasons was not as pronounced. But the data do not reflect the complete settlement and subsistence systems. And the absence of pollen or other direct evidence of plant use in the Quiche Basin makes any conclusions there highly speculative.

Data from Zohapilco in the Basin of Mexico point to a very different conclusion. The rich environment may have permitted year-round habitation before plants had been domesticated, as may have been the case in the Quiche Basin. Palynological and other evidence indicates that wild grains, including teosinte and amaranth, were abundant in the immediate vicinity of the site and presumably were harvested. Comparison of plant remains from middle and late Archaic levels indicates changes in the plants that probably were the result of human selection. Although the Zohapilco data are far too incomplete to draw firm conclusions, they suggest that the intensive harvesting of some plants by permanent occupants may have led to their domestication.

The picture for the lowlands is even less complete. In Belize, the Archaic period may have been characterized by trends very similar to those in the Tehuacán Valley, including increasing overall population, larger group size, and more permanent occupation. The growing importance of domesticated plants documented for the Tehuacán Valley is not found in Belize, but an increasing reliance on littoral resources is posited. Whether these postulated trends are adequately supported by excavation and analysis remains to be seen. Elsewhere in the lowlands the data are inadequate for a discussion of even tentative temporal trends. The only well-known Pacific coast sites date to late in the Archaic period and were specialized localities oriented toward the exploitation of coastal resources. Collecting shrimp or shellfish, perhaps only during the winter, presumably would have been only one element of a more diverse economy, but it is at present the only one for which there is archaeological evidence. Shrimp collecting would not have conflicted with cultivating crops during the rainy season, but agricultural settlements dating to the Archaic period have yet to be found. The Santa Luisa site on the Gulf of Mexico coast is comparable in age and appears to represent a settlement at which economic activities were more diversified. Agriculture apparently was not among them although the data may be inadequate to draw this conclusion. Since estuarine, riverine, and terrestrial resources all were collected, Santa Luisa may represent a multiseasonal occupation. But without any features or seasonal indicators, it is impossible to say whether the site's size is the result of a large, permanent occupation or of repeated reoccupations of approximately the same locality.

Over the millennia of the Archaic period, the effective unit for many economic and social activities, at least in marginal environments, would have been a microband, a small group of two to five individuals related through kinship. Some economic activities, such as communal rabbit drives, as well as certain social activities would have been carried out by macrobands, composed of five to ten related microbands. The present evidence is very sketchy, but suggests no change in these basic group sizes or organization through the Archaic in most of the areas of Mesoamerica examined, although the number of microbands and macrobands probably did increase. As would have been the case during the Paleo-Indian period, larger organizational units linked macrobands to form effective breeding populations of at least 175 to 400 individuals. Even in the marginal highlands where preservation is good, sites are accessible, and extensive surveys have been done, estimated populations remained well below these levels throughout the Archaic, suggesting that social systems involving marriage exchanges occupied spatial scales larger than regions like the Valley of Oaxaca or Tehuacán. From 8000 to 5000 B.C., for example, it is likely that one language, Proto-Otomanguean, was spoken over a large area extending from the central highlands to the southern highlands. In subsequent periods, as families became more sedentary and population grew, the scale of long-distance interaction was reduced. A result of this was that Proto-Otomanguean gradually fragmented into the twenty different languages of later prehispanic times, representing eight major language groups.

During the Archaic, long-distance contacts to arrange marriages may have involved exchanges of gifts and raw materials. The little available evidence of raw material exchange suggests links between the highlands and the lowlands. Marine shell has been recovered from one Valley of Oaxaca site, and obsidian was abundant on both Chiapas and the Gulf of Mexico coast sites. We have no way of knowing whether marriage partners moved in the same circles as shell and obsidian, but clearly raw materials and perhaps people too moved over great distances.

Throughout the Archaic period, complexity and integration were minimal. In marginal environments, specialized settlements included hunting camps, plant collecting camps, maguey roasting camps, and so on. But these were occupied sequentially by small, mobile groups rather than by food-collecting specialists. In richer environments shrimp-collecting and processing, shellfish-collecting, fishing, and hunting settlements may have been occupied sequentially or on a seasonal basis by the inhabitants of more permanent communities. The Archaic systems lacked a division of labor in food collecting or food production beyond the division of labor by age and sex within local groups. Integration was forged through social mechanisms, such as special rituals and feasts, that linked local groups together into an effective biological population whose members shared a common language over a large territory.

Integration may have increased somewhat as reliance on food storage increased and the degree of mobility declined. In good years when storables were plentiful, macrobands may have persisted for longer periods of time to share in both the labor and the bounty of the harvest. Sharing in times of localized drought may also have increased. And as domesticated plants became more dependent on humans for their successful germination and growth, cooperative efforts may have become more important at planting, but these are only suggestions, given the limited data.

Population growth and moves toward more sedentism throughout the Archaic period may have been associated with an increase in boundedness of social systems, although boundaries probably continued to be open and fluid compared to later prehispanic times. Distinctive projectile point and other artifact styles and frequencies may reflect the distributions of social systems. But at present, stylistic data for major phases of the Archaic period are inadequate to posit the locations of such boundaries.

3

The Valley of Oaxaca

Today the largest and busiest city in the Valley of Oaxaca is Oaxaca City, the administrative, marketing, and educational capital for the valley and for the surrounding territory that makes up the state of Oaxaca. Despite its modern appearance, one cannot overlook the valley's signs of continuity with the past. The most visible skyline in the Valley of Oaxaca is not modern, but ancient. From miles away, the silhouettes of ruins covering the mountains in the center of the valley still dominate the landscape. These are the archaeological remains of Monte Albán, the capital of the valley from 500 B.C. until A.D. 700. From any point in the valley, it is impossible to walk very far in any direction without encountering other remains of ancient communities. Broken pottery, stone tools, and building rubble litter many modern cornfields. Mounds loom from the centers of fields or the backyards of modern houses. Even on remote, high, piedmont ridges, today traversed only by grazing cattle and goats, ancient inhabitants left remains of farms, towns, and cities. In fact, an archaeologist with many decades of Oaxaca experience once wrote that the whole valley ought to be considered an archaeological site.

This rich record of occupation attests to the importance of the first of our three case areas in prehispanic Mesoamerica. Often the Valley of Oaxaca was at (or near) the forefront of cultural change. The early sedentary agriculturalists were among the first people in Mesoamerica to erect public buildings, low platforms that were the forerunners of the impressive pyramids that dominated many later Mesoamerican sites. Carved-stone glyphs from the Valley of Oaxaca represent some of the earliest writing known from Mesoamerica. Monte Albán was Mesoamerica's first city, and long remained one of its larger settlements. Even at times when cultural change in other areas of Mesoamerica caught up to or superseded the Valley of Oaxaca, the valley remained a focus of political, demographic, and economic power.

Environment, resources, and main strategies
The Valley of Oaxaca sits roughly in the center of a large rugged mountainous zone called the southern highlands (Fig. 3.1). The Valley of Oaxaca's position as a nuclear area of Mesoamerican civilization cannot be explained without reference to its agricultural advantages relative to any other part of this highland block. Although other small valleys occasionally break the tumultuous mountain topography of this part of Mexico, the Valley of Oaxaca's roughly 1,500 square kilometers of arable land easily make it the largest single expanse. Slope and soil conditions permit farming almost everywhere within the valley, and with the valley floor lying at only 1,500

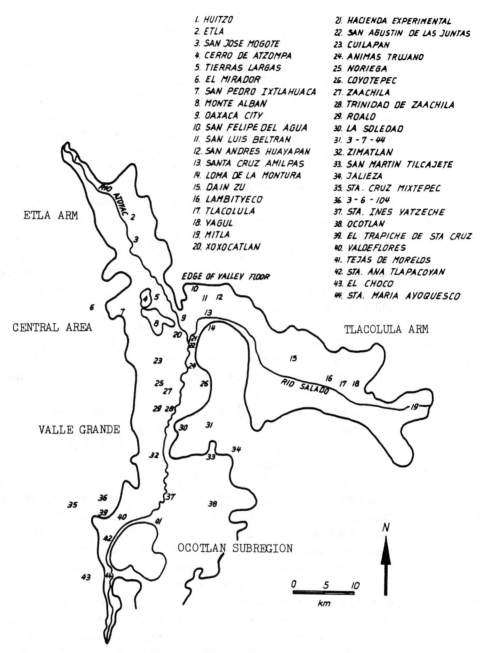

1. HUITZO
2. ETLA
3. SAN JOSE MOGOTE
4. CERRO DE ATZOMPA
5. TIERRAS LARGAS
6. EL MIRADOR
7. SAN PEDRO IXTLAHUACA
8. MONTE ALBAN
9. OAXACA CITY
10. SAN FELIPE DEL AGUA
11. SAN LUIS BELTRAN
12. SAN ANDRES HUAYAPAN
13. SANTA CRUZ AMILPAS
14. LOMA DE LA MONTURA
15. DAIN ZU
16. LAMBITYECO
17. TLACOLULA
18. YAGUL
19. MITLA
20. XOXOCATLAN

21. HACIENDA EXPERIMENTAL
22. SAN AGUSTIN DE LAS JUNTAS
23. CUILAPAN
24. ANIMAS TRUJANO
25. NORIEGA
26. COYOTEPEC
27. ZAACHILA
28. TRINIDAD DE ZAACHILA
29. ROALO
30. LA SOLEDAD
31. 3 - 7 - 44
32. ZIMATLAN
33. SAN MARTIN TILCAJETE
34. JALIEZA
35. STA. CRUZ MIXTEPEC
36. 3 - 6 - 104
37. STA. INES YATZECHE
38. OCOTLAN
39. EL TRAPICHE DE STA CRUZ
40. VALDEFLORES
41. TEJAS DE MORELOS
42. STA. ANA TLAPACOYAN
43. EL CHOCO
44. STA. MARIA AYOQUESCO

Figure 3.1. Map of the Valley of Oaxaca showing places mentioned in the text.

meters above sea level, frost is relatively rare. In the semiarid climate, water is the critical determinant of maize yields. (In our discussion of agriculture, we focus on maize because it was by far the most important aboriginal cultigen.) Only 400 to 800 millimeters of rain fall each year. In a good year, the rains will support a single crop grown during the June-to-October wet season. Supplementary water sources are critical both for preventing crop failure and for allowing more than one crop to be planted in a single year. The Valley of Oaxaca is fortunate to have a number of water sources in addition to rainfall. In some places on the valley floor the high water table supplies extra water to plants through capillary action. The high water table also can be exploited by pot irrigation, which involves digging a shallow well and pouring the water on the plants by hand. The valley's many tributary streams can be tapped with simple irrigation techniques, and with adequate organization, more ambitious, larger-scale agricultural projects can be carried out to drain and control flooding in the freshwater marshlands. These two factors – the overall availability of fairly flat farmland and the variety of supplementary water sources – combine to make the Valley of Oaxaca more agriculturally productive and more attractive to farmers than any other area in the southern highlands.

In fact, the valley's food-producing lands are its most distinctive natural resource. Most of its other resources – such as wood, pottery clay, decorative mica, cane for baskets, building stone, copal for incense used in religious ceremonies, chert and quartz for chipped-stone tools, and other types of stone for corn-grinding implements – are commonly found throughout the southern highlands. Salt deposits, of which the valley has eight, are less evenly distributed, but these were probably not sufficient to meet the needs of the local population in some periods. The only other significant mineral deposits in the valley are of low-quality marble, onyx, and magnetite. When gold-hungry Spanish conquerors reconnoitered the Oaxaca region, they found an important gold mine in the mountains just beyond the northwestern edge of the valley. At that time, however, it was outside the territory controlled by valley rulers: the source may never have been under valley control. Most cotton had to be imported from the lowlands, where growing conditions are more suitable. All obsidian, the volcanic glass that is more easily worked and that produces sharper cutting edges than chert or quartz, had to be imported. So did many exotic goods prized by the elite, such as cacao, brilliantly colored bird feathers, marine shells, turquoise, and jade. The Valley of Oaxaca's relative poverty in other exportable resources reinforces the significance of its potential for producing a wealth of food.

Up to this point we have treated the valley as a unit in order to show how it is distinct from the surrounding landscape for 200 kilometers or so in any direction. But as a key to understanding the dynamics of its settlement history, one must also be aware of the geographical variation among its parts. The valley is shaped like a Y, with the right arm bent down (Fig. 3.1). The northern, Etla arm is narrow and fairly dry; however, in proportion to its land area, it has the best possibilities for irrigation. Compared to the other two arms of the valley, Etla has the highest proportion of irrigable land with access to reliable sources of water. Where the three arms join is the series of 500-meter-high hills on which Monte Albán was built. Because this area was most influenced by the capital, we often refer to the zone within ten kilometers of Monte Albán as a separate "central" area (Plate 1). To the south lies the most extensive part of the valley, the Valle Grande or southern arm. Typically it receives more rainfall than the other valley areas, so dry farming is somewhat more productive. The Valle Grande also has more land (than other arms of the valley) that can be farmed through the use of irrigation strategies, drainage works, or tap-

Plate 1. The Valley of Oaxaca's central area, as seen looking north from Monte Albán. The hill in the center is Cerro Atzompa. Note the cluster of mounded buildings sitting atop the hill.

ping the high water table. But because of its greater size, the proportion of arable land that is irrigable is smaller than in Etla. The eastern, Tlacolula arm has an irrigation potential that is less than in the other two arms, and its rainfall is usually the poorest. On two-thirds of the cultivated land in Tlacolula, farmers can expect an adequate harvest only one year out of every three, compared to a two-out-of-three-year success rate in the Valle Grande.

In the Valley of Oaxaca the availability of water determines the relative success or failure of maize harvests. The average rainfall is marginally adequate for farming corn, but because the rains vary considerably and unpredictably from year to year and from place to place, and because more than two-thirds of the land depends on rain, how to deal with local variation and how to manage the supplementary water sources were basic, system-shaping problems (although these were by no means the only problems valley residents were concerned with).

The specific solutions to these problems adopted by ancient Oaxacans changed over time because circumstances changed. Here we anticipate what will be discussed in more depth later by drawing a few broad generalizations. During the long period of small villages prior to the founding of Monte Albán, both the matter of how to deal with local variation in rainfall and the problem of how to manage the land that had water resources were handled by maintaining a human system of relatively small scale and little vertical complexity. The valley system in these times operated with a small population that had little tendency to grow. (Some growth occurred, but it was minimal by comparison with some of the post-Monte Albán periods.) Most families lived on or near land that had water resources in addition to rainfall. Depending on the high water table and on very simple, small-scale irrigation meant that local variation in rainfall had a limited effect on farm production. Shortfalls in what households wanted or needed easily could have been made up by simple horizontal exchanges based on kinship.

As we shall see (and try to explain below), there was a thousand-year trend toward increased vertical differentiation in the social system, but from our long historical vista these early social differences were not nearly as marked as those that occurred later on. Keeping the vertical complexity to a minimum meant that there was a less intensive demand (compared to later in the sequence) for agricultural production or household reproduction. Thus, the system was small in scale and agricultural problems were manageable primarily at a local level. This lifeway was maintained until a regional capital was established, about 500 B.C. After that, a new, more volatile, and more dynamic set of stresses and conditions came to pass. To address these shifts, novel strategies were devised and implemented – and these were revised continually during the rest of the valley's history. In general, the cumulative response to local variation in rainfall was exactly the opposite of the pre-Monte Albán solution – instead of staying small, the system became larger, both in terms of area and in numbers of participants. Vertical complexity was amplified, not minimized. A greater volume of material and information was sent through a variety of regularized channels such as tax systems, markets, and elaborate commemorative and funerary rituals that signified large-scale, system-wide integration.

In Chapter 1 we touched on the transformation in this society that occurred as a consequence of the formation of the new political capital. This set of changes resulted in a need to support a large number of urban residents – sometimes composing as much as a third of the society's population – meaning, in turn, that the previous solutions to agricultural problems would no longer work. More production was needed, and under the new regime, this led to a larger labor force, sometimes imported, sometimes the consequence of more rapid demographic growth. The low-lying humid lands, however, were usually not extensive enough to produce the subsistence needs of both a large rural labor force and the urban center. Too, this land was probably under the rather tight control of territorial entities that had existed for hundreds of years. Their populations, we can guess, were not always willing to support the new capital. Furthermore, some of the largest patches of fertile alluvial land were rather distant from the regional center. For the elite at Monte Albán, encouraging farming in the drier and more rugged piedmont, in places with the aid of canal irrigation, was one solution. This more marginal land that had been only sparsely settled was also probably less tightly controlled by the old corporate groupings, so the proceeds from its development could be exploited more easily by the new political institution.

The piedmont strategy, however, is precisely where the difficulty of local variation in rainfall comes to the fore. If not for that fact, Monte Albán might have encouraged piedmont farming only in the convenient five kilometers or so surrounding the urban center. But the failure rate there for rainfall farming is 50 percent, far too risky for the long-term maintenance of an urban population. A better strategy would be to tap the production of a large number of dependent peasant farmers who were dispersed over many different parts of the valley. The risks of failure to provide a surplus are thus much reduced, and local losses are covered by the increased scale. This was essentially the agricultural regime that was in place during the remainder of the Monte Albán sequence. The high water table and valley-floor canal-irrigated lands traditionally remained under the control of local lords. Through its district administrators, the central government encouraged, occasionally managed, and reaped some of the benefits of farming the piedmont. But, although productive, this strategy resulted in increased instability. For a variety of reasons, including deforestation, erosion, and changing political conditions, the foci of intensive piedmont development shifted dramatically from one part of the valley to another.

This repeated pattern of growth and decline in piedmont exploitation became an essential feature of the region's dynamics, powerfully constraining and shaping many aspects of the Valley of Oaxaca system and its trajectory of long-term change. During the prehispanic sequence, as the population and patterns of resource exploitation shifted, the specific constraints and parameters of the Monte Albán polity and its component segments and interest groups also varied.

This discussion of the geography of our Oaxaca study area allows us to delineate the main features of how the ancient inhabitants extracted the energy necessary for survival, and to outline some of the major consequences of production strategies. Given this omnipresent background, we are now ready to examine the evolution of the valley system, in detail and in a narrower time scale, beginning with the period of the initial settled villages of the Early Formative.

The Early Formative Period (Tierras Largas phase, 1500–1150 B.C., and San José phase, 1150–850 B.C.)

By 1500 B.C., the beginning of the Tierras Largas phase (see Table 3.1), sedentary farming villages were located throughout the Valley of Oaxaca. These, with one exception (San José Mogote), were small communities, containing ten or fewer wattle-and-daub (cane-and-mud) houses, each of which was associated with outdoor cooking and storage facilities (see Fig. 3.2). Most of the settlements were located on low, well-drained piedmont ridges or spurs adjacent to both the fertile zone of high alluvial soils and the major river channels.

The remains from house floors and storage pits suggest that domesticated plants (maize, avocados, beans, and squash) composed the main part of the inhabitants' diet. Most households, however, continued to rely on wild plants and animals as important dietary supplements. The reliance on maize as well as the other cultigens suggests that these settlements were occupied for most of the year, as maize farming would have required continual labor inputs between April and October. As ancient Mesoamericans were without beasts of burden, patterns of transhumance typical of some parts of the Old World were never established in Mesoamerica.

Table 3.1. *Chronology of the three Mesoamerican regions, and their relationships to the overall Mesoamerican chronology*   Table : Chronology

Radiocarbon Years	Major Mesoamerican Period	Valley of Mexico Ceramic Phases	Valley of Mexico Neutral Terminology	Valley of Oaxaca Ceramic Phases	Eastern Lowlands Major Archaeological Periods
– 1400	Late Postclassic	Late Aztec	Late Horizon	Monte Albán V	Mayapan
– 1200		Early Aztec			Chichén Itzá
– 1000	Early Postclassic	Mazapan	Second Intermediate		
		Coyotlatelco		Monte Albán IV	Puuc
– 800	Late Classic	Metepec	Middle Horizon	Monte Albán IIIB	Tepeu
– 600	Early Classic	Xolalpan			
– 400		Tlamimilolpa		Monte Albán IIIA	Tzakol
– 200	Late Preclassic or Formative	Miccaotli	First Intermediate	Monte Albán II	Floral Park
A.D. / B.C.		Tzacualli			
		Patlachique			Chicanel
– 200		Ticoman		Monte Albán Late I	
– 400	Middle Preclassic or Formative			Monte Albán Early I	Mamom
– 600				Rosario	
– 800		Zacatenco		Guadalupe	Xé
– 1000		Ixtapaluca	Early Horizon	San José	
– 1200	Early Preclassic or Formative			Tierras Largas	Swasey
– 1400					
– 1600			Initial Ceramic		

Though Tierras Largas phase settlements have been found in all three arms of the valley, they were most frequent in the northern, Etla arm. Eight occupations of the phase were located in this northern part of the region, an area of about 340 square kilometers. Seven of these were less than three hectares in area, although the eighth, San José Mogote, covers approximately seven hectares. By comparison, only ten small (less than two hectares) villages were dispersed across a roughly 1,050-square-kilometer area in the central and southern parts of the valley. Few Tierras Largas phase communities have been found in the eastern, Tlacolula arm of the valley, and none were located in the Ejutla Valley, a small (522-square-kilometer) region that lies to the south of the Valley of Oaxaca.

Not only was San José Mogote twice the size of any contemporaneous settlement, but it is also the only occupation of this period in which nonresidential, public constructions have been found. The earliest sedentary occupation included an unusual open area, perhaps seven meters wide, that was set off from the residential portion of the site by a staggered double line of posts reinforced in some spots by a row of heavy stone slabs. This partially enclosed area contained no architecture and, when investigated, was almost totally free of artifacts. The feature was oriented slightly west of true north, an alignment that characterized public architecture in the Valley of Oaxaca for centuries. In several respects this feature resembled a cleared area that was found at a preceramic site in the valley (dating to about 5000 B.C.) called Gheo-Shih. Both of these areas appear to be very much like the open dance grounds at base camps of the mobile aboriginal populations that inhabited the Great Basin of the western United States.

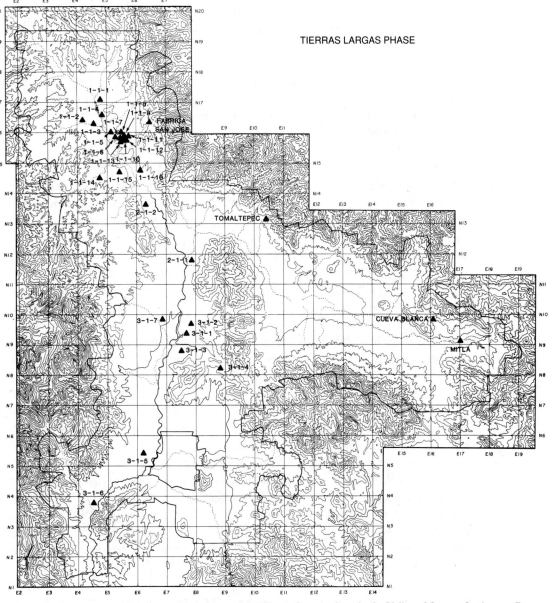

Figure 3.2. Settlements of the Tierras Largas phase in the Valley of Oaxaca Settlement Pattern Project survey region. The dark lines indicate the survey boundary.

Not long after the transition to sedentism, the population at San José Mogote ceased using this open area, and a second kind of Tierras Largas phase nonresidential feature was constructed. These features were small one-room (roughly four by five meters) structures that had crushed bedrock foundations and interior walls that were lime-plastered. Generally, they also had a low, rectangular, altarlike platform that ran along the southern interior wall. Although only one of these structures was in use at any particular time, eight very similar buildings were erected. Each of these constructions was built almost directly above previously used structures. All were oriented 8° west of north. No domestic features or refuse were associated with any of them.

The changes in the nature of nonresidential architecture suggest that the organization of public or ritual activities shifted during the Tierras Largas phase. This change may indicate that the access to ritual activities became more restricted. However, if the access to ritual activities was indeed more restricted, these limitations may have been determined either by age and sex differences or by individual achievements. Based on the analyses of the Tierras Largas phase burials, houses, and storage pits, there is presently no indication that either ranking or socially determined inequality or stratification existed at this time. The small sample of known burials contained single individuals who were interred without elaborate grave offerings, and a very similar array of artifacts was found in most houses.

The relatively dense distribution of Tierras Largas phase population in the Etla arm may have in part been due to the concentration of very productive agricultural land adjacent to San José Mogote. However, this factor alone cannot account for the demographic concentration, as an equally rich agricultural zone in the valley's southern arm, near Santa Ana Tlapacoyan (see Fig. 3.1), was only sparsely inhabited.

Although the causes of this initial spurt of development at and adjacent to San José Mogote are difficult to pinpoint, the demographic growth in this part of the valley may have been related to a centering of ritual activities at the site. Elders or other individuals associated with ritual or public functions may have encouraged individual households to reside close to them by providing services (for example, increased opportunities for exchange, protection, matchmaking, and feasting) less frequently available in other parts of the valley. At the same time, it seems likely that individuals who organized these ritual functions would have encouraged the concentration of population around them, as it would have increased their potential supply of labor and agricultural produce. The ability to tap surplus labor and its fruits would have been necessary both to build and maintain the nonresidential structures and to support the feasts or other activities associated with these civic-ceremonial features. Among many ethnographically known populations characterized by relatively simple, largely achieved leadership positions, the relative importance and renown of a leader were largely a function of the number of his followers and his ability to extract surplus from his supporters. These leaders thus spent considerable time and energy building and maintaining a network of ties and associations with their relatives and followers.

The development of this kind of simple organizational structure during the Tierras Largas phase also is suggested by the changes that took place between the Tierras Largas and San José phases. During that time, demographic growth in the

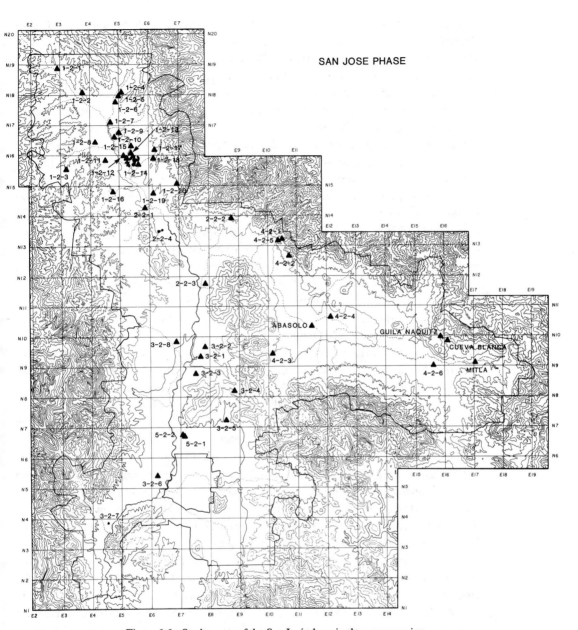

Figure 3.3. Settlements of the San José phase in the survey region.

valley was neither uniform, nor was there a gradual "filling in" of unoccupied areas. Rather, the most rapid growth occurred at San José Mogote, which expanded to ten times its Tierras Largas phase size. In addition, most of the population growth noted for the valley as a whole occurred in the Etla arm. Although there was a net increase of ten sites in Etla, only five San José phase settlements were founded in the central and southern parts of the valley and six in the Tlacolula arm (Fig. 3.3).

This pattern of growth did not fit expectations based solely on an examination of the distribution of agricultural land in the valley. During the San José phase, a

considerable increment in corncob size almost doubled the extent of potentially productive farmland, because the newer, more productive maize allowed farmers to
plant in previously marginal areas. Though the Valle Grande contained twice as
much of this potentially productive farmland as did Etla, a substantially larger population resided in the latter arm. The differential rates of population growth were
associated more closely with the organizational variation between the different arms
of the valley than with the distribution of arable land. Leaders and influential families at San José Mogote may have encouraged people to live in Etla in order to take
advantage of services and opportunities available only there, but these same leaders
would have placed labor and tribute demands on those households adjacent to
them. These increased demands may have encouraged increased household size
to aid in production and to build a larger social network. The selection for larger
households over generations would have promoted population growth in the Etla
area. As the leaders at San José Mogote may not have had as much sway over
households located in the central and southern portions of the valley, and as there is
no evidence of equivalent Early Formative Period ritual or public activities having
taken place in those areas, it is likely that labor demands and the consequent population growth rates may have been lower in the rest of the valley.

Organizational differences between the Etla arm and the rest of the valley during
the San José phase have been suggested by both surface surveys and excavations.
Whereas the San José phase occupation at San José Mogote was roughly 70 hectares in size, all but one of the other contemporaneous settlements in the region
were two hectares or smaller. Several different kinds of public buildings were found
at San José Mogote, whereas the earliest public structures at other valley sites do
not date until the very end of the San José phase.

The one-room public structures at San José Mogote were still being erected during the initial part of the San José phase. However, a larger nondomestic building
was also constructed at the site. Built in several tiers of stone and adobe, this building included two carved stones, which originally may have stood on an upper tier.
The stones depict a jaguar head and a raptorial bird and currently represent the earliest examples of the Oaxacan carved-stone tradition.

Several factors suggest that San José Mogote was economically prominent during
the San José phase. The small, flat, magnetite mirrors, found in the valley and as far
away as San Lorenzo Tenochtitlan on the Gulf Coast, were made only in a small
cluster of houses at San José Mogote. Examples of finished mirrors have been found
at four other valley settlements, but no evidence of mirror production has been
located at any of these other sites. Interestingly, four stratigraphically superimposed
house floors in this residential cluster at San José Mogote contained evidence of
mirror polishing and manufacturing, suggesting that this economic specialization
had a long history. Clearly, some households at San José Mogote also were tied
somewhat more closely to other areas of Mesoamerica than were households at
other valley sites. Nonlocal goods (including Gulf Coast ceramics, stingray spines,
shells, and jade) are found more frequently at San José Mogote than at other sites in
the region. These differences in size, public construction, and economic importance suggest that San José Mogote was the center or "head town" in a settlement

system that by the end of the San José phase integrated at least a portion of the valley in a nonegalitarian sociopolitical system. This sociopolitical unit may have been akin to ethnographically known chiefdoms or ranked societies. This was a society in which access to goods and positions of power were restricted according to social factors in addition to age, sex, and lifetime achievements.

The residential and burial data from San José phase occupations indicate some of the dimensions of these emerging status differences. At San José Mogote, most of the houses were small (fifteen to twenty-four square meters) and made of wattle and daub; however, several houses were much larger and built on low platforms of stone and adobe. These bigger houses, which often had their exterior walls whitewashed with lime, usually contained larger concentrations of marine products, high-quality chert, mica, magnetite, and deer bone than were found in the simpler residential structures. Thus, high status appears to have been related to better access to nonlocal goods and to venison, the best source of animal protein.

Burials dated to the San José phase show marked social differentiation. Certain individuals were buried without any grave goods, whereas others were interred with jade labrets and earspools, well-made ceramic vessels, and magnetite and shell ornaments. Most males were buried with ceramic vessels that bore Olmec-style motifs depicting either the fire-serpent or the were-jaguar (see Fig. 3.4A). Each burial contained vessels characterized by only one of the motif sets, indicating that males were apparently affiliated with only one of these "supernatural entities." As infants also were buried with pots bearing these motif sets, it seems likely that at least males were assigned group membership at birth. In the archaeological remains associated with different residential units, the distribution of the two motif sets was just about mutually exclusive; households with high frequencies of were-jaguars have a negative association with fire-serpents, and vice versa. Hamlets tended to have only one of these motifs. Larger San José Mogote was divided into residential wards, each of which was associated with one of the two mytho-religious entities.

Explaining Early Formative change

The San José phase developments of social inequality and a hierarchical political organization are not easily explained. Some archaeologists have suggested that these developments were the consequence of direct contacts between Oaxaca and the people of the Olmec Heartland of the Gulf coast. Yet the early public buildings in the valley are not similar to contemporary Gulf coast constructions (Fig. 3.4B). Instead, these valley buildings show a direct continuity with Archaic period constructions from Oaxaca. Also, the earliest stone carvings in the region were not stylistically Olmec. San José phase utilitarian ceramics and house construction show great continuity with the earlier Oaxacan Tierras Largas phase traditions and are not similar to Gulf coast styles.

Olmec-style motifs and Gulf products like marine shell were more prevalent in San José phase than in Tierras Largas phase artifact assemblages, but this appears to have reflected the involvement of individuals from the valley in a pan-Mesoamerican exchange sphere and not the one-way intrusion of people or ideas from the Gulf coast. Magnetite mirrors and pottery from Oaxaca have been found in Gulf coast

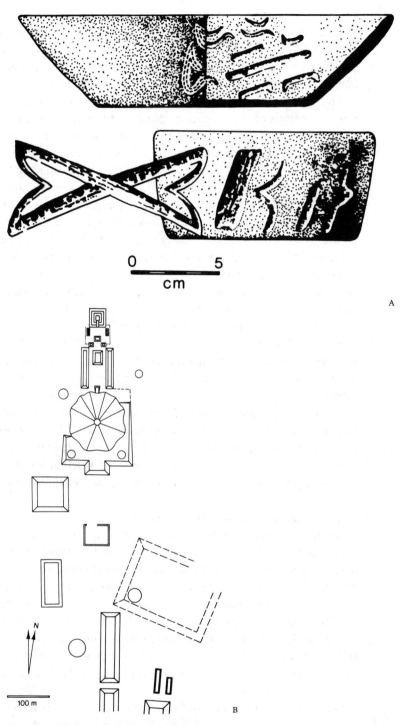

0   5
cm

A

B

Figure 3.4. (A) Pottery serving vessels from San José Mogote, Oaxaca. Top: a variant of the "fire-serpent" motif on a gray bowl. Bottom: a variant of the "were-jaguar" motif on a clouded black-and-white cylinder. Redrawn from Pyne (1976: figs. 9.8 a,b). (B) The mound-and-plaza complex at the head town of La Venta in the Olmec Heartland. Redrawn from Coe (1968:64).

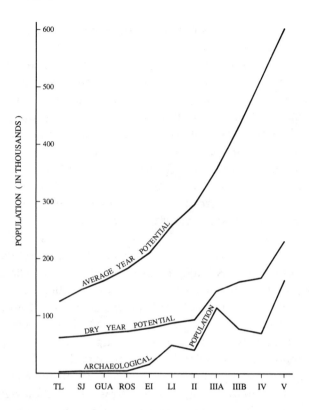

Figure 3.5. Population change in the prehispanic Valley of Oaxaca (based on archaeological estimates) compared with potential population. The population estimates are derived primarily from archaeologically determined site areas. The potential population figures are based on maize productivity increases over time.

settlements. The specific fire-serpent and were-jaguar motifs found on San José phase ceramics actually were more prevalent in collections from San José Mogote than in the collections from San Lorenzo Tenochtitlan, the largest site in the Olmec Heartland. Perhaps these motifs should be viewed as Oaxacan or Zapotec variants of a pan-Mesoamerican iconographic system. The widespread distribution of these symbols conceivably could have reflected the iconographic conventions and underlying sacred beliefs that were shared across Mesoamerica. Similar exchange or interaction networks, marked by widespread similarity in designs on high-status goods, also have been found in highland South America (Chavín), pre-Columbian Panama, and the eastern United States during the Hopewell and Mississippian periods.

Sociopolitical development in Oaxaca cannot be understood solely in terms of the patchy or uneven distribution of prime agricultural land. As stated above, the largest expanse of agricultural land was in the Valle Grande, yet evidence of Early Formative Period mounded architectural construction was almost absent there. Population densities were comparatively low in that part of the valley. The San José phase developments cannot be understood as a simple function of "population pressure." The potential agricultural productivity during the Early Formative Period greatly exceeded the regional population (Fig. 3.5). Even the number of people inhabiting the Etla arm was substantially smaller than that which could have been supported through agriculture.

Although as yet we do not have a totally satisfactory explanation for San José phase developments in the Valley of Oaxaca, we can offer several tentative hypotheses. Most importantly, we suggest that to understand this transition the analytical scale must include the entire southern highlands. At this scale, the differences between the wide, fertile Valley of Oaxaca and the adjacent mountain slopes and tiny valleys are dramatic. These environmental differences are significant given the nature of the Early Formative economy. The transition from foraging to planting and harvesting required both increased sedentism and a revised yearly work schedule. The foraging populations of Oaxaca stored small amounts of food, so they worked at a more or less regular pace throughout the year. Planting and harvesting, in contrast, require a period of intensive work during the agricultural season followed by a relatively slack time once the harvest is in. This doesn't necessarily imply more leisure time for the farmers – if anything, they probably worked more hours per year in subsistence than did their foraging ancestors – but their scheduling was different. One consequence of this shift may have been the transition from the ad hoc rituals characteristic of many hunters and gatherers, which are carried out pretty much whenever food supplies are sufficient to feed larger groups, to the seasonally scheduled rituals more characteristic of settled agriculturalists. The latter usually occur after harvesting, during the agricultural off-season. In the Valley of Oaxaca, this shift may be related to the change in the Tierras Largas phase public buildings.

Sedentary populations probably increased the nature and frequency of two other activities during the nonagricultural season: long-distance trading and raiding. Agriculturalists, unlike foragers, cannot easily pick up and move in response to low yields. Thus, to buffer harvest fluctuations, they often engage in exchange, and agricultural time budgets allow for such activities. Exchange is an efficient means for "banking" temporary surpluses. Trade goods and the social capital built up in hours and days of visiting can be exchanged for food in lean years. Under some conditions, long-distance raiding with the goals of theft and abduction could have served the same purposes by adjusting temporary imbalances between populations and their food supplies. Warfare thus was probably a much more salient feature of the Mesoamerican cultural landscape after the transition to sedentary farming, even though there is no evidence of competition over resources due to population pressure. Warfare would have been an important strategy for coping with unpredictability even though the human populations were substantially below potential densities.

Both raiding and trading were ways of transferring people, information, and goods over long distances under conditions of year-to-year perturbations in harvests, and highly dynamic, weakly defined social system boundaries. Both raiding and trading created conditions that we think would have favored evolutionary change in the southern highlands macroregion. Given the unequal distribution of agricultural resources over this zone, the population of the Valley of Oaxaca would have had a special role to play in interregional interaction. Extreme agricultural deficits would have been more frequent in the marginal mountain valleys than in the Valley of

Oaxaca. This would have had two consequences favoring secular change following the shift to sedentism: (1) a net accumulation of "wealth" in the form of items exchanged for food by the Valley of Oaxaca groups (the possible significance of which is discussed in connection with bride price in a later paragraph), and (2) more frequent exposure of residents of the Valley of Oaxaca to raiding pressure. The latter perhaps promoted the development of more elaborate strategies than would have been required elsewhere to cope with military problems. These strategies, we might guess, could have involved developments such as the formation of alliances among villages and the promotion of war leaders to more permanent positions of power.

Another dimension of macroregional inequality pertains to population dynamics. Sedentism at the extremely low population densities found in Mesoamerica during the Early Formative raised a new problem: the high probability that local populations did not reach the size at which they would have become self-contained demographic entities. Computer simulations show that human populations must include at least several hundred people in order to withstand random imbalances in the sex ratio of successive generations. Theoretically, such random fluctuations can lead to extinction in small, closed populations. And, as the likelihood of extreme fluctuations is inversely proportional to population size, the small, localized population aggregates inhabiting the rugged southern highlands outside the Valley of Oaxaca would have been at higher risk of extinction than the valley population. These marginal populations thus would have been forced to participate in macroregional social networks in order to assure themselves of marriage partners.

To an extent, abduction could have been a mechanism for supplementing local populations, but people probably spent a great deal of time on interregional social exchange and on forming marriage alliances too. And the most desirable alliances they could make would have been with the valley population, which was the largest population and therefore the most dependable source of marriage partners in lean times. Fluctuations would have characterized all Early Formative populations, given their very low densities, but again, when viewed macroregionally, the seriousness of fluctuations would not have been evenly distributed. On the average, the larger, somewhat denser population of the Valley of Oaxaca surely was favored. The flow of people through the network would have taken the form of a donor–recipient system with the Valley of Oaxaca more often in the position of donor and the marginal populations more often the recipients.

Generally, in similar mating networks (or circulating connubia), people-donors have higher status than people-receivers. People-donors accumulate wealth (for example, bride-price payments) and prestige, because both circulate in the direction opposite to the flow of people. As the prestige and wealth of donors increase, greater bride prices are expected to be given to them, because the price is supposed to reflect the status of the donors. Wealth accumulated by donors (or accumulated in food exchanges, as we discussed in earlier paragraphs) can be used to further enhance prestige through feasting and other activities. Now, if prosperity and fertility are considered to be under the control of supernatural forces (as they were in Formative Period Mesoamerica), then the donor populations (which also have the greatest wealth and the most secure agricultural production) are considered to have closer ties with the supernatural. Donor groups can thus come to be seen as mediators with the supernatural, and this becomes a source of increased prestige and power for them.

This set of propositions for explaining the emergence of a hierarchical system out of a "flat" egalitarian one has a number of limitations when applied to the Valley of Oaxaca. Most noticeably, it cannot account for the fact that most of the changes that we can detect during the Early Formative in the valley occurred in one place only, San José Mogote. Nonetheless, the advantage in considering interregional differences in population sizes and inequalities in the distribution of agricultural resources is that it enables one to explain why development occurred in some areas but not in others. For example, in an area containing populations that interact in a circulating connubium, but without a single group that can more often serve as the donor population, secular changes in the direction of rank and wealth differentials are less likely to occur. Indeed, this may have been one reason why ranked systems were not developed until several hundred years later in Mesoamerica's eastern lowlands. As we shall see in Chapter 5, the eastern lowland environment is more finely grained (that is, its resources are found in small, closely grouped patches) than the southern highlands, thus offering fewer opportunities for the development of permanent demographic inequalities.

This model for Formative Period social change does not rely on population pressure as a causal factor. Throughout the Formative Period the population level of the Valley of Oaxaca was markedly below the regional agricultural potential. Our argument has instead considered how people cope with unpredictability, and how in the context of low population densities and the uneven distribution of large patches of farmland, macroregional interaction provides the impetus for change. Indeed, whereas macroregional interactions may have been handled most frequently by each individual household during the Tierras Largas phase, such extra-valley exchanges of goods, mates, and information may have become somewhat more the purview of a subset of influential individuals and families during the later San José phase. At this point we turn to an examination of the Middle Formative Period, when more vertically complex political hierarchies probably evolved in the Valley of Oaxaca.

The Middle Formative (Guadalupe phase, 850–600 B.C., and Rosario phase, 600–500 B.C.)

Etla continued to be the most densely settled area of the valley through the Rosario phase (Figs. 3.6, 3.7), with roughly half of the valley's total population. San José Mogote remained the largest settlement, several times the size of the next largest occupation. Public construction at the site also increased in monumentality and diversity. Nevertheless, in the Rosario phase, the regional population was somewhat more evenly distributed across the arms of the valley than it had been during the Tierras Largas, San José, and Guadalupe phases.

The total population of the roughly seventy known Rosario phase settlements was still substantially smaller than the potential population that could have been sup-

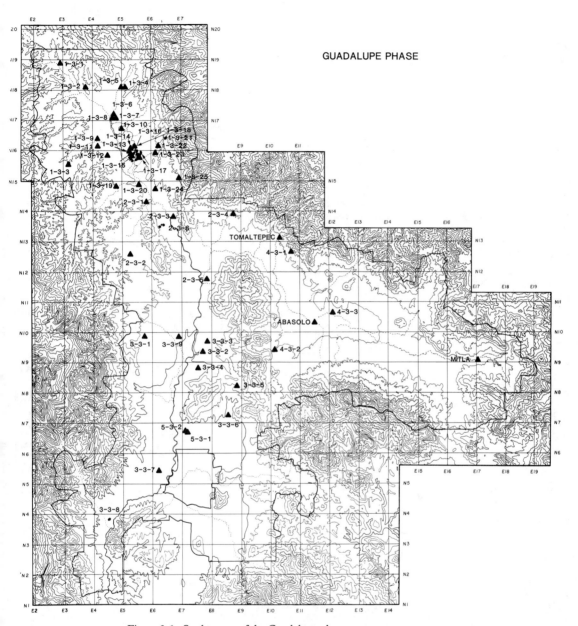

Figure 3.6. Settlements of the Guadalupe phase.

ported through maize farming. Moreover, as in the Early Formative Period, the demographic changes from phase to phase were not simple responses to variability in agricultural potential. Although the largest expanse of excellent cultivable land lay within the Valle Grande, the population growth in this area was extremely slow in comparison with growth in the Etla area.

Fewer than ten occupations in the valley contain definite evidence for civic-ceremonial structures during the Middle Formative. These sites can be divided into

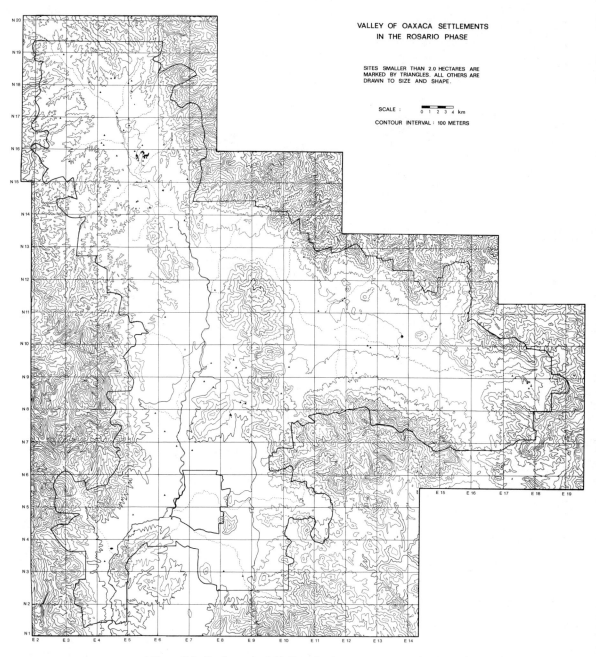

Figure 3.7. Settlements of the Rosario phase.

two tiers. The top tier consists of only San José Mogote, which was tens of hectares in extent and had a wide array of different nonresidential structures. The second tier was composed of several sites (Huitzo, San Martin Tilcajete, Tierras Largas, Tomaltepec, Yegüih) that were less than ten hectares in size and that featured more modest public architecture. All other sites were three hectares in size or smaller, and contain no evidence of public architecture that can be dated securely to the Rosario phase.

As yet we lack a full comprehension of the Middle Formative sociopolitical system in the Valley of Oaxaca. Looking at the Rosario phase settlement pattern map (Fig 3.7), it appears that the valley was divided into at least three settlement clusters, one in Etla and one south of the central area, with most of its sites in the Valle Grande. A third cluster was located at the center of the Tlacolula arm. We do not know the degree of integration among these clusters. As in the Early Formative Period, San José Mogote served certain high-order administrative and economic functions, but the specific size of the area that it integrated remains to be determined. Was it the total valley, the entire Etla arm, or possibly just the southern part of the Etla area?

Although the organization of the valley underwent several major transitions during Monte Albán I, some of the changes that characterize this period were foreshadowed in the earlier Rosario phase. San José Mogote may have served, for at least part of the region, some of the same functions that were carried out at Monte Albán beginning in Monte Albán I. Evidence for this is a carved stone (Fig. 3.8), called a *Danzante,* that was uncovered at San José Mogote and that resembles the *Danzantes* from Monte Albán. This monument depicts a man, naked and in a contorted position, who appears to be a slain or sacrificed captive. The monument was positioned at the threshold of a corridor running between two large public buildings, so that anyone passing through the structure would tread on it. It thus seems likely that similar sacrificial and/or military activities were commemorated at the valley's largest centers in both the Rosario phase and Monte Albán I. The efficient coordination and management of these activities at the regional level may have been one important factor fostering the development of a valley-wide political institution centered at Monte Albán.

Monte Albán Early I (500–350 B.C.)

The founding of Monte Albán in the Early I phase capped the previous two-level administrative system with a new hierarchical level, a regional capital. The establishment of this centrally situated hilltop site coincided with the marked increases in the spatial and demographic scale of the Valley of Oaxaca socioeconomic system. As we discussed in the first chapter, these changes were destined to have profound effects on demography, settlement distribution, subsistence activities, local administration, and exchange.

Monte Albán's original colonizers probably came from a number of valley communities as well as, perhaps, from outside the valley. A neutral location was chosen for the capital, an unoccupied zone within the valley's central area – an area that, in general, had been sparsely settled throughout the preceding phases (Fig. 3.9). Clearly, a sizeable number of the residents of this new community were not oriented primarily toward farming. The site's hilltop position is removed from the largest patches of the region's prime land that would have been most suitable for

Figure 3.8. *Danzante* from San José Mogote, dating to the Rosario phase. Drawing by Mark Orsen, courtesy of Joyce Marcus.

maize cultivation at that time, and an Early I irrigation system on the hill's eastern slope would have provided food for only a small fraction of the site's population. Even most drinking water probably would have had to be laboriously hauled up the mountain, as there are no dependable, substantial water sources at the site. However, the hilltop is an excellent observation point, providing sweeping views of the valley in all directions. Its centrality is ideal for mediating communication among communities in all three arms of the valley. Given the new capital's agriculturally marginal location, it must have depended heavily for its support on other existing valley settlements.

Historically, one of the situations in which a new, neutrally located capital is founded arises when a group of autonomous societies forms a confederation, often for defense against a common threat. Thucydides' comments on early Athens give an illuminating description of such a case:

> Most of them had been always used to living in the country. . . . From very early times this way of life had been especially characteristic of the

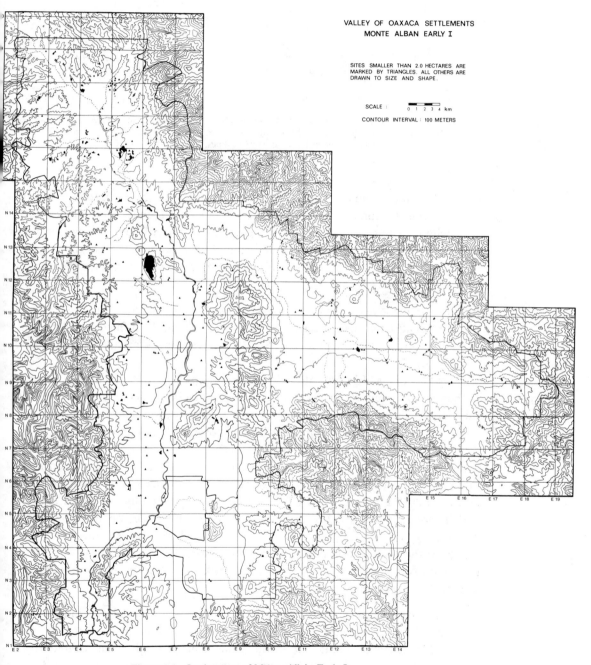

Figure 3.9. Settlements of Monte Albán Early I.

Figure 3.10. *Danzante del Museo.* Presently located in the Museo Nacional de Antropología, Mexico City. Originally recovered by Leopoldo Batres at Monte Albán near Mound M. To date, 320 *Danzantes* have been found at Monte Albán. Drawing by Mark Orsen, courtesy of Joyce Marcus.

> Athenians. From the time of Cecrops and the first kings down to the time of Theseus the inhabitants of Attica had always lived in independent cities, each with its own town hall and its own government. Only in times of danger did they meet together and consult the king of Athens; for the rest of the time each state looked after its own affairs and made its own decisions. (Warner 1954: 106)

In such circumstances, a neutral location may be chosen for common decision making, because no existing center is willing to augment the influence and prestige of another center at its own expense. Such considerations, we think, were operative during Early I.

Early I residents of Monte Albán lived in three spatially discrete *barrios,* or neighborhoods. The Main Plaza was a special area that lacked general habitation even in this period, although most of its monumental construction dates to later periods. Only one definite Early I building has been exposed by the Main Plaza excavations. This is a sloping wall fragment about 2.5 meters high, which is unlike any building exposed in excavations of ordinary Early I residential areas. A second Main Plaza building that may date to as early as Early I is the *Danzantes* gallery of carved-stone monuments (Fig 3.10 and Plate 2). These monuments, dating to Monte Albán I and II, portray human figures in grotesque poses, often accompanied by glyphs. The gallery contains only a fraction of the 320 such monuments that have been found on the Main Plaza; many others were recycled in the construction of later buildings. Although numerous interpretations of the *Danzantes* have been proposed, Coe's is the most convincing:

> The distorted pose of the limbs, the open mouth and closed eyes indicate that these are corpses, undoubtedly chiefs or kings slain by the earliest rulers of Monte Albán. In many individuals the genitals are clearly delineated, usually the stigma laid on captives in Mesoamerica where nudity was considered

scandalous. Furthermore, there are cases of sexual mutilation depicted on some *Danzantes*, blood streaming in flowery patterns from the severed part. To corroborate such violence, one *Danzante* is nothing more than a severed head. (Coe 1962: 95, 96)

Danzantes are absent at other valley sites dating to Early I or later (including San José Mogote, where a Rosario phase *Danzante* was found). Conversely, carvings at other sites depict activities of a ritual nature that are not depicted on Monte Albán monuments dating through IIIA. This supports the idea that Early I Monte Albán functioned primarily as a regional center for offense-defense activities. A frightening display of terror tactics at the capital, and at no other place, may have helped to legitimize the early polity's authority.

Monte Albán grew more rapidly than any other valley site, as its population burgeoned from zero to over 5,000 in less than 200 years. This annual growth rate, 6 percent, is two to three times higher than the growth rates of modern industrializing countries such as Mexico in the 1970s. Such an extremely rapid increase probably surpasses the upper limit of a human population's ability to reproduce, indicating that Monte Albán was initially colonized by a rather large population, or that it attracted many immigrants after its founding. The organization and support of such a large center, and of a new hierarchical level of administration, posed problems that people in Mesoamerica rarely (if ever) had encountered before. Increased requirements for surplus to support an expanding nonagricultural population placed new demands on the labor and time of the rural populace and thereby helped to promote Early I population growth. One response by families was to increase their

Plate 2. Buildings along the west edge of the Main Plaza, Monte Albán. The freestanding stones in the center of the photograph are in the vicinity of the *Danzantes* gallery.

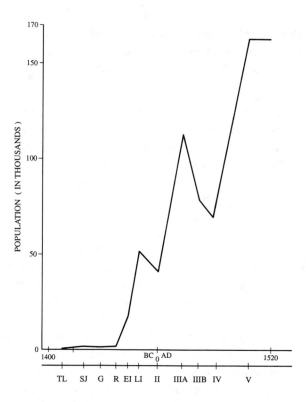

Figure 3.11. Demographic change in the prehispanic Valley of Oaxaca. The line represents the archaeologically estimated population totals for the survey region (including Monte Albán) for all prehispanic periods after 1500 B.C.

households' working capacity by having more children. The total population of the valley swelled to nearly 15,000 (Fig. 3.11), with most of the increase outside of Monte Albán occurring within eighteen to twenty kilometers of the capital. Beyond roughly thirty kilometers of Monte Albán, growth was minimal. The new capital's influence on its immediate surrounds was considerable.

The impact of Monte Albán also is reflected in the beginning of a trend toward greater occupation of the agriculturally risky piedmont. As was true for population growth, the move to more marginal topographic zones was not a region-wide trend. Occupation of the piedmont tended to occur within eighteen to twenty kilometers of Monte Albán. It is also in this zone that we see the initial archaeological evidence of piedmont irrigation systems, dating to Early I, which implies a move toward planting two to three crops per year. Meanwhile, the predominantly piedmont zone in the south of the valley was virtually uninhabited. The new capital's influence on changing agricultural strategies thus also is evident.

Finally, even seemingly trivial aspects of the archaeological record reflect the extent of Monte Albán I changes on valley households. We mentioned in the last chapter that Early I ceramics differed from ceramics in earlier periods, in part reflecting increased indications of larger-scale production by full- or part-time specialists supplying a newly developing regional market system. Another example of change at the household scale is the first appearance of *comales*, pottery griddles still used today to cook the piles of corn tortillas consumed daily by the average Mexican family. Tortillas are a "convenience food" – relatively imperishable and easily carried out to the fields by farmers. Even when stale they are not wasted, because they can be combined with other ingredients and then eaten. By "convenience food" we mean to imply a form of food that would have allowed farmers to work more efficiently for more hours in their fields as they intensified production; but tortillas were not labor-saving for men or women. In the home, they require much time to prepare (particularly to grind the corn into flour). Thus, the use of *comales* (and so tortillas) signifies a change in food preparation habits, which in turn implies a shift in household time budgets and the sexual division of labor.

Also, valley residents in Early I lived in adobe houses rather than in the wattle-and-daub houses that were used prior to that time. Adobe houses were more time-consuming to build, but they were also more durable. The shift to adobe construction suggests a willingness to invest in more permanent structures. This trend may have been related to the increased security of life in the valley after the establishment of Monte Albán made boundary maintenance more effective. Administrators also may have encouraged the building of more permanent residences to facilitate control over the population. Residents of mud-brick houses were less likely to move frequently, so census taking and taxation were made easier.

In summary, we have approached explaining the changes that took place between the Rosario phase and Early I as follows. The foundation of a new regional institution and its center of operations at Monte Albán was both a cause and consequence of other societal transformations. Population grew, especially in and around the new center. Household time budgets and production strategies were altered. And a market system became a key means of furthering regional economic integration. The new capital emerged as a city whose functions became increasingly varied and more important regionally in response to an increasingly complex set of organizational problems that were faced by the settlement's elite population. These included a developing regional economy, agricultural intensification, increasing economic specialization, and population growth, especially the growth of an urban population that necessitated the dependable production of more and more surplus by rural producers. This set of suggestions, however, does not constitute a complete and satisfactory explanation of the Rosario to Early I metamorphosis. For one thing, the establishment of a military confederation among a group of autonomous but cooperating societies need not always have the transformational consequences we think it had in the Valley of Oaxaca. Look, for example, at the famous League of the Iroquois. This was a voluntary confederacy of five Iroquois tribes, with the stated purpose of minimizing intra-Iroquois warfare. As a unit, the league was very successful militarily. But this by-product aside, it is evident that the formation of the new structure had a minimal impact on the conjoining tribes. The Onondaga tribe, the most centrally located of the five, was the focus of many league affairs. And yet the Onondaga villages did not become urbanized. No Iroquois market system ever developed, and no changes occurred in household production strategies or fertility in any of the villages.

To understand the differences between the Valley of Oaxaca and the Iroquois region in these regards, two factors need to be noted. First, by Rosario times the organizational segments in the Valley of Oaxaca already had more complex political institutions than were present among the preconfederation Iroquois. Iroquois villages were highly egalitarian, governed by councils made up of representatives from the constituent matrilineages. Politically, villages were highly autonomous. In contrast, during Rosario times, Valley of Oaxaca societies had head towns that governed territories perhaps equivalent to whole arms of the valley. These communities had public architecture and the elaborate residences of an elite that was thought to be descended from powerful supernatural beings through venerated, deceased ancestors. Therefore, politically, the Early I changes in Oaxaca were important, but not altogether revolutionary.

A second point we can make in comparing the Valley of Oaxaca and the Iroquois region has to do with the "interaction potentials" of communities in the respective regions. Presumably, the level of political and economic complexity that developed during Early I in the Valley of Oaxaca was associated with a rather high degree of interaction among communities. The emergence of a state, for example, implies a steady flow of communication and materials between capital centers and lower-order administrative places and between the state as a whole and the general population. Market systems, too, imply the presence of some minimal level of movement of people from their villages to marketing destinations – otherwise, specialized producers supplying villagers cannot be supported (see Special topic 1).

We are not in a position to test these hypotheses or to identify what minimal levels of interaction are required for complex political and economic institutions to develop. To our knowledge, no research has been done along these lines. We suggest, however, that the Valley of Oaxaca in the Rosario phase was characterized by more potential intercommunity interaction than occurred in the Iroquois region, and that with the foundation of Monte Albán there was even greater potential for interaction. This dissimilarity between the two regions had cultural-evolutionary consequences.

Many variables are related to intercommunity interaction, but perhaps the single most important factor is distance between communities. And in this regard the two regions are highly dissimilar. Although the population of the seventeenth-century Iroquois League amounted to roughly 12,000 people (compared with the 2,000 or so people we think resided in the Valley of Oaxaca in Rosario times), the Iroquois villages were scattered over some 50,000 square kilometers, implying a population density of only 0.24 persons per square kilometer. As the Valley of Oaxaca covers roughly only 2,100 square kilometers, the Rosario population density was almost four times the Iroquois density, at 0.95 persons per square kilometer. And during Early I, the population of the Valley of Oaxaca increased to several thousand more than the seventeenth-century Iroquois. These density values suggest that communities in the Valley of Oaxaca, in that they were more densely packed, would have had more potential for interaction. With higher population densities and more interpersonal interactions, the requirements for dispute mediation and resolution would

Plate 3. A portion of Monte Albán's major defensive wall. This is the section of the wall located in grid squares N6–7 × E8 in Fig. 3.13. The wall extends northeast, starting in the left center of the photograph, crosses a drainage, then continues up the hill, crossing the photograph left to right.

have been greater. This in turn may have been one factor that prompted the establishment of more hierarchical institutions.

We are not trying to argue that growth in complexity is favored in higher-density situations due to population pressure. Valley of Oaxaca populations were comfortably below the region's agricultural potential, in both Rosario and Early I. The argument, instead, is that at higher densities, the increased interaction potentials make possible the growth of certain kinds of institutions that depend on a relatively intense movement of information, goods, and people. Evidently, the friction of distance between the widely scattered Iroquois communities was so great that, in concert with other factors, the growth of such institutions was precluded.

Monte Albán Late I (350–200 B.C.)

Many of the trends that were initiated in Early I continued into Late I. Monte Albán's population more than tripled to 17,000, making the city larger than most modern valley communities. House plots covered most of the main hill by the end of the phase, and sizeable neighborhoods grew up on adjoining hills (Fig. 3.12). Massive construction was carried out at the North Platform, the site of the small Early I building on the north edge of the Main Plaza. Leveling of the Main Plaza may have begun in this phase, although the eastern and southern edges were not yet enclosed by monumental buildings. The number of *Danzante* carvings in the grisly military showcase grew, approaching the final total of at least 320. Excavations show that work probably also began at this time on a large defensive wall that defines part of the northern, northwestern, and western boundaries of the city (Fig. 3.13 and Plate 3).

Population growth outside the capital also continued during Late I, where the increase amounted to about 24,000 people. As in Early I, most (75 percent) of the growth occurred within about twenty kilometers of the capital, with the rate of expansion in this rural hinterland even more rapid than at urban Monte Albán.

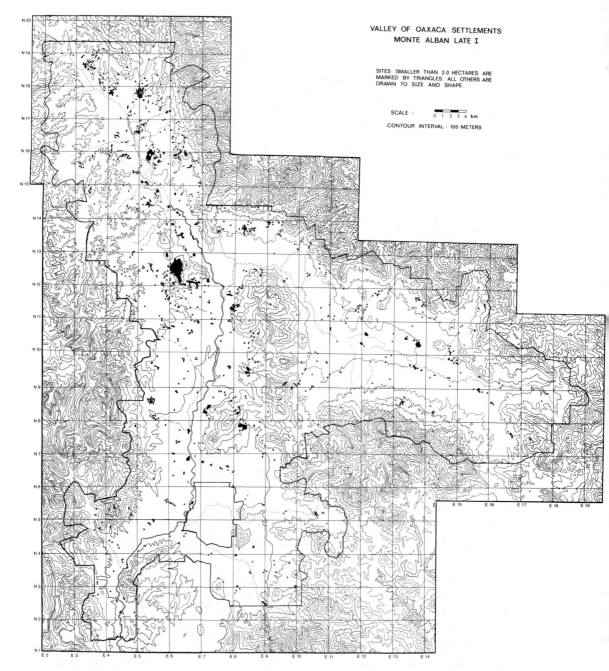

Figure 3.12. Settlements of Monte Albán Late I.

Thus proximity to Monte Albán continued to be a more important determinant of settlement location than the availability of prime agricultural land. Although the largest tract of prime farm land in the valley lies south of Zaachila (Fig. 3.1), this area experienced relatively slow growth. Meanwhile the expanding population of the central area spread into more and more marginal piedmont areas, as the available alluvium in this zone was now crowded with people and as there were not enough permanent tributary streams to allow everyone access to a dependable source of irrigation water.

The Late I regional system was not just a larger version of the Early I system. As we discussed in our first chapter, growing administrative structures experience diminishing returns to scale. This implies that administrative complexity and administrative costs will increase at a rate faster than the growth rate of the system, assuming that the amount of administration does not decrease. The proliferation of Late I administrative centers and of nonresidential construction on the valley landscape attests to a rapid growth in administrative activity. The number of centers with civic-ceremonial construction (such as platforms, mound groups of various sorts, and possibly ball courts) increased from fifty-one in Early I to eighty-six in Late I. New buildings were added at many former Early I centers, and existing buildings were renovated or capped with new construction. With the establishment of many new centers and the growth of others, at least one new intermediate administrative level was created. By this time, the Monte Albán state was well established.

Even though the number of small rural communities increased substantially from Early I to Late I, 75 percent of the population growth between these phases occurred at larger settlements (with populations greater than 100). Many of these larger communities also had civic-ceremonial structures. These findings suggest the growth of a more complex and costly administrative infrastructure in the valley. Funding this construction boom and the associated activities no doubt created problems for the valley elite. A key strategy they evidently employed to alleviate these problems already has been mentioned: more concentrated agricultural development of the piedmont, especially in and around the valley's central zone. The concentration of population in rural areas near Monte Albán began in Early I, but this trend greatly intensified during Late I. Because of the large increase in the rural labor supply, much greater amounts of food surpluses could have been produced in this central zone of the valley in most years.

Nevertheless, due to variation in precipitation, not all farmers in the central zone or other piedmont areas would have been able to produce a successful crop each year. At the same time, intensified agricultural production left families with less time to engage in other production activities. Perhaps, in response, a more tightly integrated regional production and exchange system was established. These changes were accompanied by increases in the scale of craft production. Larger-scale specialized production, particularly when centered near state functionaries, affords more opportunities for meddling, manipulation, and control by politico-religious authorities. Thus, the economic shifts during Early and Late I may have been both stimulated by, and provided opportunities for, the increasingly complex Monte

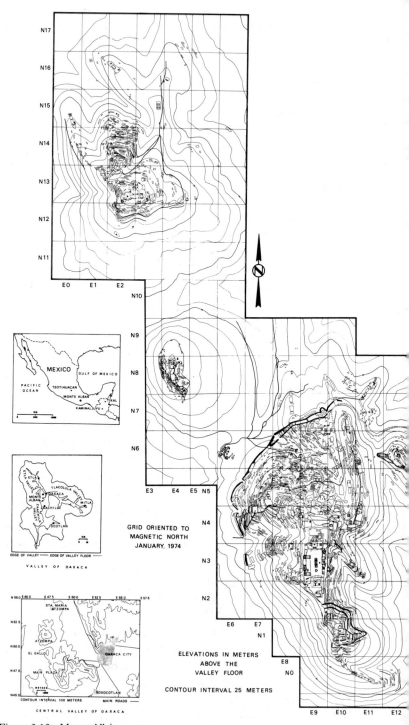

Figure 3.13. Monte Albán.

MONTE ALBAN

OAXACA, MEXICO

ARCHAEOLOGICAL AND TOPOGRAPHIC MAP

KEY

1. NORTH PLATFORM
2. SOUTH PLATFORM
3. BUILDING OF THE DANZANTES
4. SIETE VENADO SYSTEM
5. TOMB 7
6. EL GALLO
7. ATZOMPA
8. TOMB 104

LEGEND

RESIDENTIAL TERRACES _ _ _ _ _

MOUNDED BUILDINGS _ _ _ _ _

EXCAVATED BUILDINGS _ _ _ _

STONE WALLS _ _ _ _ _ _ _ _

DEFENSIVE WALLS _ _ _ _ _

ANCIENT ROADS _ _ _ _ _ _ _

MODERN PAVED ROADS _ _ _ _

MAP SHOWS MAXIMUM EXTENT OF THE SITE CA. A.D. 600.
INTERPRETATIONS OF BUILDINGS IN THE MAIN PLAZA AREA ARE BASED
ON PLANS PUBLISHED BY THE INSTITUTO NACIONAL DE ANTROPOLOGIA E
HISTORIA, MEXICO, AND INTERPRETATIONS MADE BY MEMBERS OF THE
VALLEY OF OAXACA SETTLEMENT PATTERN PROJECT. ALL OTHER
INTERPRETATIONS ARE BASED ON SURFACE REMAINS MAPPED BY
MEMBERS OF THE VALLEY OF OAXACA SETTLEMENT PATTERN PROJECT.

0   1

KILOMETER

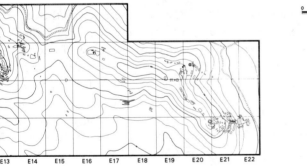

E13   E14   E15   E16   E17   E18   E19   E20   E21   E22

VALLEY OF OAXACA SETTLEMENT PATTERN PROJECT
RICHARD BLANTON, DIRECTOR
HUNTER COLLEGE, CITY UNIVERSITY OF NEW YORK

DRAFTED BY JILL APPEL

SUPPORTED BY GRANTS FROM THE NATIONAL SCIENCE FOUNDATION
AND THE CITY UNIVERSITY OF NEW YORK RESEARCH FOUNDATION

WORK DONE IN CONJUNCTION WITH CONCESION ARQUEOLOGICA NO.
5/71, GRANTED BY THE INSTITUTO NACIONAL DE ANTROPOLOGIA E
HISTORIA, MEXICO.

Albán state. In either event, greater political complexity and enhanced economic integration in conjunction with population expansion and nucleation led to marked shifts in the production and distribution of at least one common good, pottery.

For example, a higher proportion (seven of eight) of Late I ceramic production locations were situated in administrative centers than had been the case in Early I, when only three of seven ceramic manufacturing sites were so located. At the same time, the Late I ceramic complex was more standardized, less decorated (see Special topic 3), and more evenly distributed than the Early I ceramic complex. Early I and Late I decorated grey wares dramatically illustrate the change. The Early I vessels show a variety of intricate, finely incised designs. Most of the Late I grey wares, on the other hand, simply have a circular pattern raked with a comb on the bottom of the vessel, and two plain lines encircling the rim. Undecorated grey bowls and jars became common in almost every Late I household, whereas grey wares had been quite rare in Early I, and no type or types had dominated Early I assemblages.

Overall, Late I administrative centers averaged two and a half times as many ceramic types as nonadministrative sites had. In comparison, in Early I, they had just under two times as many. At the household level, this implies that families in sites with monumental architecture were able to obtain a greater variety of ceramics, including more decorated wares and more special-purpose vessels, than families in nonadministrative centers. Modern equivalents might be the use of certain dishes for entertaining and others for everyday meals, or the use of a variety of dishes, like butter dishes and casseroles, instead of the same plates and bowls for all purposes. Thus, access to ceramics (and possibly other goods) appears to have been associated somewhat more closely with politico-religious activities in Late I than had been the case earlier in the period.

The growth cycle of Monte Albán Early and Late I, which depended on the heavy utilization of the area immediately surrounding Monte Albán, was not maintained. Perhaps the valley's rather delicate piedmont zone began to show signs of wear and tear. Alternatively, extraregional factors, such as the growth of small, agricultural populations in outlying regions, may have provided opportunities for tribute and conquest for the Monte Albán polity. Whatever the exact cause or causes, the resulting Monte Albán II Valley of Oaxaca system was somewhat smaller in population size and in several respects more heterogeneous. However, these internal shifts were coincident with the tributary expansion of the Monte Albán state outside the physiographic boundaries of the Valley of Oaxaca.

Monte Albán II (200 B.C.–A.D. 300)

To refer to the Late I–II transition as an episode of collapse would be misleading. True, the valley's population declined (Fig. 3.14), and Monte Albán's intraregional importance was somewhat decreased (as we outline in this section). On the other hand, phase II was the only time in Monte Albán's history in which it embarked on significant imperial ventures outside the Valley of Oaxaca. Whereas Late I pottery rarely is encountered beyond the Valley of Oaxaca and adjacent regions (such as the neighboring Ejutla Valley), select Monte Albán II types (particularly the distinctive

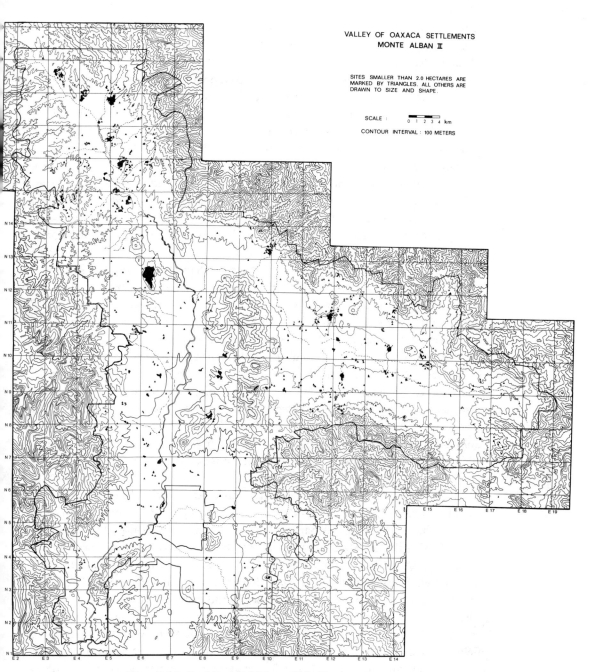

VALLEY OF OAXACA SETTLEMENTS
MONTE ALBAN II

SITES SMALLER THAN 2.0 HECTARES ARE
MARKED BY TRIANGLES. ALL OTHERS ARE
DRAWN TO SIZE AND SHAPE.

SCALE : 0 1 2 3 4 km

CONTOUR INTERVAL : 100 METERS

Figure 3.14. Settlements of Monte Albán II.

cremas or cream paste wares that were made near Monte Albán) can be found in several distant places in the southern highlands macroregion. One such site, near Cuicatlán, some 100 kilometers northeast of Monte Albán, has been identified as a military outpost of Monte Albán, indicating that perhaps the spread of pottery from this time may be related, at least in part, to the formation of a tributary domain.

Closer to the Oaxaca capital, in the Ejutla region to the south, *crema* pottery was rare in Monte Albán I, but more abundant at the region's largest settlements in Monte Albán II.

Additional evidence that Monte Albán was more externally oriented during phase II comes from a remarkable arrow-shaped structure (Structure J) added to the south part of the Main Plaza during this time (Fig. 3.15). Although the building has at times been identified as an astronomical observatory, closer examination reveals that it was the Monte Albán II version of the earlier military showcase. Set into the sides of the building are forty carved slabs commemorating military conquests. Some of these have been identified, and they refer to places outside the Valley of Oaxaca.

The content and frequency of the Monte Albán II conquest glyphs give further clues to the dynamics of Monte Albán's imperial ventures. The numerous carvings dating to Early and Late I depict captured leaders who had been brought back to the capital to be humiliated and slain. In contrast, the fewer phase II slabs show the conquests of particular places or centers rather than individuals. We suggest that the *Danzante* monuments indicate that other people of the southern highlands, during Early and Late I, were organized into many small, autonomous polities. The monuments may indicate that Monte Albán carried out punitive raids in response to military threats, or that Monte Albán conquered these polities in an attempt to gain access to their resources. But it is unlikely that empire formation would have been successful at that time, because of the difficulty of trying to incorporate so many diffuse, separate units into the state. By phase II, however, the processes of centralization and formation of larger regional polities were proceeding in other areas, creating stable "subassemblies" that made the formation of larger tributary domains feasible. (See the section on scale in Chapter 1.) It is these larger territorial units, rather than numerous individual leaders, that are shown on the phase II conquest slabs.

In the context of Monte Albán's extra-regional expansion, the valley itself underwent significant changes. Total valley population dropped by 19 percent, to roughly 40,000 (Fig. 3.11). Monte Albán, with a 16 percent population decline (to 14,492), was only slightly less affected. Monumental construction at the capital continued, though. By the end of phase II, the site had begun to look more as it appears to visitors today. Construction of the large defensive walls had been completed during the beginning of the period. Laborers began the task of flattening the entire Main Plaza, "a titanic feat which required the leveling of enormous rock outcrops and the filling of deep concavities" over an area large enough to encompass six football fields. Structure J now stood near the south end of the plaza, and a new phase II structure defined the plaza's east edge. Finally, by the end of the phase, an early version of the Main Plaza ball court also had been added (Fig. 3.15).

As this construction activity indicates, phase II Monte Albán remained an important center. It was still the largest and architecturally most elaborate central place in the Valley of Oaxaca. However, as the rulers of Monte Albán turned their attention to the tasks of administering and collecting revenue from a much larger area, their direct influence in valley affairs apparently lessened. A sizeable phase II population

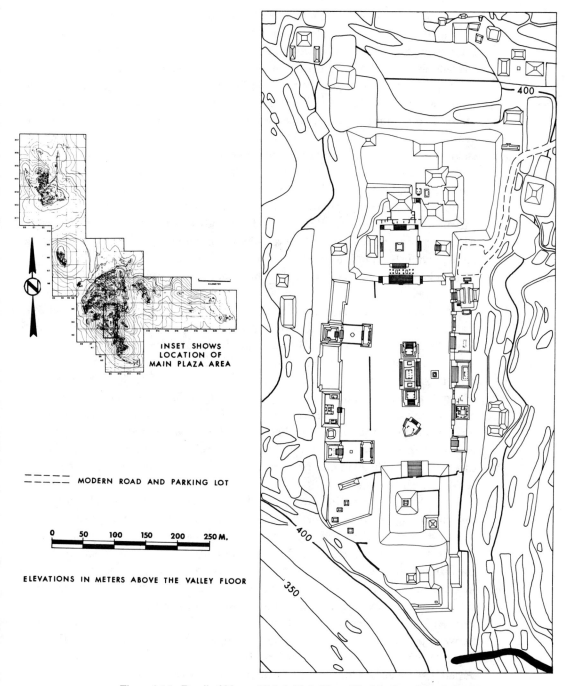

INSET SHOWS
LOCATION OF
MAIN PLAZA AREA

– – – – – MODERN ROAD AND PARKING LOT

0   50   100   150   200   250 M.

ELEVATIONS IN METERS ABOVE THE VALLEY FLOOR

Figure 3.15. Detail of Monte Albán's Main Plaza. The North and South platforms are the buildings at either end of the large open plaza. The ball court is located just to the southeast of the North Platform.

decline occurred in the area immediately surrounding Monte Albán, the same area in which the greatest population growth had taken place in Early I and Late I. Heavily exploited in Late I, much of the previously inhabited piedmont zone was virtually abandoned during phase II, indicating a curtailment of the piedmont development strategy that had figured so prominently before. Correspondingly, a much higher proportion of the total phase II population resided on the alluvium. With the deemphasis on piedmont agricultural development, many of the piedmont administrative central places were abandoned. Many of these centers apparently were replaced by small centers established in the alluvial zone.

State revenues were now drawn from a larger domain that extended beyond the physiographic limits of the Valley of Oaxaca. Concomitantly, there was no longer a substantial piedmont population that required support in poor years, and the stable agricultural system on the alluvium yielded mostly consistent surpluses. The regionwide exchange network that Monte Albán had evidently promoted and manipulated previously would no longer have been as critical to the state.

Details of Monte Albán phase II architecture at San José Mogote in the Etla arm seem to bear out the rise in the power of local authorities. There, excavators discovered that the first substantial palace structure appeared in phase II, and that it stands on a plaza whose dimensions and structural arrangement closely copy the Main Plaza at Monte Albán. Although ball courts and temples had a uniform plan in the Valley of Oaxaca, the orientation and layout of structures at Monte Albán II centers showed more variation than had existed in Late I. Besides San José Mogote, ambitious (and distinctive) construction efforts were enacted at several other large valley centers in Monte Albán II. This elaboration of secondary centers, occurring at the same time that Monte Albán was actually declining in population, indicates that lower-level elites had relatively more resources at their disposal. Probably a smaller proportion of their total revenues had to be diverted to Monte Albán.

As we found for architecture, phase II pottery was marked by elaboration and diversification. A variety of new, highly decorated ceramic types appeared (several of which were restricted largely to a single subregion or valley arm), and a yellow paste that was very rare in Late I became more common. The design florescence, the promotion of a fourth paste type, and an overall increase in the amount of labor invested in pottery (Table 3.2) all suggest greater ceramic diversity and elaboration during Monte Albán II. In part, these changes may reflect a more open and less centralized exchange system in which there would have been increased competition between producers. The concentration of some highly decorated phase II ceramic wares in different valley arms suggests an increase in the degree to which ceramic varieties signaled the local ethnic or political identities of social segments that were only loosely linked to the regional system centered at Monte Albán. Evidently, even the average phase II household benefited from these changes. Although residents of administrative centers still had greater access to ceramic types than residents of nonadministrative sites, the gap was narrowed in phase II.

According to the available carbon-14 dates, Monte Albán II was evidently a long phase, lasting relatively unchanged for some 400 to 500 years (Table 3.1). During

Table 3.2. *The production-step measure: mean number of production steps of ceramic categories, by phase*

Phase	All types	All bowls	Rank
Early I	4.39	4.80	3
Late I	4.10	4.54	4
II	5.06	5.50	2
IIIA	3.82	4.07	5
IIIB	2.68	2.90	6
IV	2.45	2.58	7
V	5.14	5.88	1

Note: For a discussion of the production-step measure, refer to Special topic 3.

this time, the intense pressures to increase levels of household production and reproduction that had characterized the Valley of Oaxaca in Early and Late I were reduced. Based on our ceramic observations, more highly decorated goods apparently were produced, and they were distributed somewhat more equitably. Population levels were far below potential capacities everywhere, and fewer communities were located in the agriculturally risky piedmont. The apparent longevity of phase II lifeways contrasts with those of Late I, a time of rapid change that could be sustained for only a century or two.

We know of few internal reasons why the phase II arrangement in the valley could not have persisted even longer with only minimal change. Perhaps internal contradictions between the central Monte Albán state and outlying elite led to difficulties. Alternatively, the end of phase II may have been brought about by factors unrelated to the valley's regional organization: specifically, a powerful new force on the Mesoamerican scene – Teotihuacan, in the Valley of Mexico – that was expanding militarily and forging new macroregional economic arrangements on a scale never before seen anywhere in the Mesoamerican world. The reaction in the Valley of Oaxaca was the initiation of a growth cycle in some ways reminiscent of Early and Late I, but on a far grander scale.

Monte Albán IIIA (A.D. 300–500)

In Monte Albán IIIA, major shifts took place in the nature of the relationship between the Valley of Oaxaca and the rest of highland Mesoamerica, and these changes co-occurred with marked shifts in the organization of the valley and at Monte Albán. Once again, the population of the valley hilltop center grew, reaching 16,500 people. The leveling of the Main Plaza continued, and more buildings were erected along the sides of the plaza. The Main Plaza ball court was modified, and the South Platform was built (Fig. 3.15). Military themes persisted on Monte Albán monuments, which were now freestanding stelae. But only six (out of a total of nine) IIIA stelae depict bound captives associated with place glyphs. Although these places have not yet been identified, they differ from those subjugated in phase II. The extent of Monte Albán's military conquests decreased drastically. In fact, the Monte Albán state apparently lost territory and influence as the powerful central Mexican state of Teotihuacan expanded. By IIIA, the indications of a Monte Albán presence in and near Cuicatlán had ceased. Several areas outside the valley that previously had Monte Albán-style pottery in phase II show heavy Teotihuacan influence in their Early Classic Period ceramics.

The situation was rather different in neighboring Ejutla, where Valley of Oaxaca-style pottery was retained. For the first time, a network of centers ran unbroken from Monte Albán to the Ejutla site. The settlement growth in Ejutla appears to be an extension of the population buildup that occurred in the southern arm of the Valley of Oaxaca. A ring of hilltop terrace settlements dotted the periphery of the southern and eastern arms of the Valley of Oaxaca, extending south into the Ejutla Valley. Thus, while more distant northern parts of the phase II tributary domain were apparently lost, Monte Albán's integration of the Ejutla region solidified.

The specific nature of the relationship between Monte Albán and Teotihuacan was complicated and multifaceted, and so difficult to discern with archaeological data alone. In contrast to many highland areas to the north, Monte Albán IIIA ceramics are stylistically very different from other Mesoamerican pottery of the time, and display little Teotihuacan influence. While the valley seems to have avoided direct incorporation into the Teotihuacan political domain, special ties linked Monte Albán and Teotihuacan. An enclave of Oaxacans resided at Teotihuacan itself; they seem to have been one of the few groups of foreigners that were accorded this status. At Monte Albán four monuments at the base of the South Platform depict foreign, perhaps diplomatic, relations between individuals clothed in Teotihuacan style and others in Zapotec dress. An additional carved-stone slab found at Mound X on the northeast side of the Main Plaza also commemorates an important political meeting between emissaries from the two cities. Still, the distinctiveness of IIIA ceramics implies that overall contacts between the valley and other areas of Mesoamerica were minimal. The Monte Albán polity apparently was unable to compete with Teotihuacan for political and economic access to most other regions.

The retraction of Monte Albán's tributary domain and the decline in interregional contacts were associated with a major reorganization within the valley. Monte Albán's population growth was minor compared to the much more rapid expansion that occurred at secondary and tertiary centers in the region (Fig. 3.16). Great population concentrations emerged at Jalieza (grid squares N7 × E8–9 on Fig. 3.16), in the piedmont, about twenty kilometers southeast of Monte Albán, and in the Tlacolula arm near the contemporary communities of Dainzu, Macuilxochitl, and Tlacochahuaya (grid squares N11 × E11–12). Both of these sites grew to 70–80 percent of Monte Albán's population. Jalieza boomed practically overnight from 0 to 12,000 people. Unlike the three prior phases, the region in Monte Albán IIIA was not dominated demographically by a single center.

Despite the more even population distribution of the valley's top centers, several factors suggest that Monte Albán retained its preeminent political position in the Valley of Oaxaca, and that the region's population was more integrated than it had

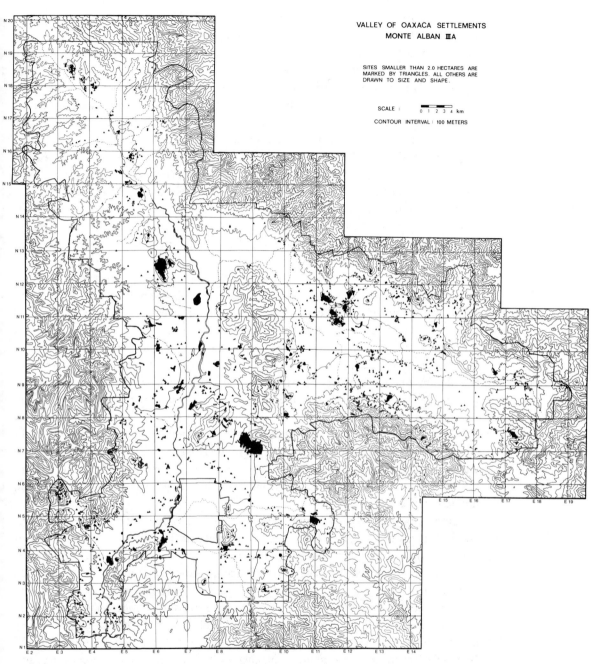

VALLEY OF OAXACA SETTLEMENTS
MONTE ALBAN IIIA

SITES SMALLER THAN 2.0 HECTARES ARE
MARKED BY TRIANGLES. ALL OTHERS ARE
DRAWN TO SIZE AND SHAPE.

SCALE :   0 1 2 3 4 km

CONTOUR INTERVAL : 100 METERS

Figure 3.16. Settlements of Monte Albán IIIA.

been in Monte Albán II. The volume and elaboration of monumental architecture
on the Main Plaza at Monte Albán far exceeded that found at any other valley site.
The layout and orientation of public construction was generally more uniform than
it had been earlier. For the first time in the history of the valley, stone monuments

outside Monte Albán were carved in the same style as monuments at the capital – indicating that other valley centers were more strongly integrated than they had been previously. Monte Albán's role, therefore, appears to have been more strongly differentiated from other valley centers and more powerful at the same time. Its functions were probably restricted to coordinating the activities of lower-level administrators, organizing military activities, and handling trade and diplomatic contacts.

Settlement patterns in the rest of the valley reflect this change in Monte Albán's regional role. In the Valley of Oaxaca outside Monte Albán, population more than quadrupled. The total regional population climbed to approximately 115,000, higher than in any prior prehispanic period (Fig. 3.11). Both high alluvium and piedmont zones underwent population expansion, but the heaviest growth was concentrated in the piedmont, especially in southern Valle Grande. In certain respects, the intensity of piedmont settlement was reminiscent of what had occurred in Early and Late I. However, during phase I, development had centered in Monte Albán's immediate area. In IIIA, large settlements with sizeable nonresidential structures were situated in the central part of the valley, suggesting that the capital was less directly involved with the development and administration of its immediate hinterland. As in the prior phase, the countryside in the central part of the valley remained sparsely settled.

The rate of population for the Valley of Oaxaca between phases II and IIIA was more rapid than the average rate for the entire prehispanic sequence, but slower than the tempo of Early and Late I demographic change. Internally, the pattern of population changes was neither simple nor uniform. Etla, containing some of the region's richest land, actually declined in population. In contrast, rapid growth occurred in the southern Valle Grande and Tlacolula. Much of this settlement expansion was focused on the higher and agriculturally more risky piedmont and mountain zones. Previously almost unexploited, these areas were an open agricultural niche whose development was fostered by the foundation of new secondary and tertiary centers. Settlement tended to be heaviest in the immediate vicinity of these centers, including Jalieza.

Factors that may have prompted renewed and intensified state concern with agricultural development are: (1) the external threat of Teotihuacan, (2) the loss of extraregional sources of tribute (that may have prompted the placement of greater demands on the valley populace), and (3) the possible depletion of soils in the Etla arm, an area that was substantially depopulated for the first time in IIIA. In the wettest years, IIIA piedmont farmers could have produced huge quantities of surplus maize. Yet, at the same time, the agricultural system was somewhat more susceptible to periodic droughts and localized agrarian risks than it had been for centuries (Fig. 3.5). Expanded efforts in intraregional economic integration were necessary, and so it is not surprising that the ceramic complex was distributed more evenly than in any prior or subsequent phase. In contrast to Monte Albán II, there was much less decorative variation in the pottery found in different parts of the region.

Identified pottery workshops were located in larger centers, which generally were situated in the triangular-shaped area between the region's three largest sites. Highly standardized, widely distributed ceramic types reappeared – most typically, a carved grey bowl and a crudely made grey utilitarian bowl. The amount of labor invested in pottery manufacture decreased even more than it had in Late I (Table 3.2), and grey wares again dominated the ceramic assemblages, as they had in Late I. The scale of ceramic production appears greater than ever before, and this seems to correspond with increases in the specialized production of chipped stone tools, ground stone implements, and other craft items.

In a sense, the Early Classic shifts that we have discussed were complicated. At the same time that Monte Albán's influence beyond its immediate valley system (that is, outside the Valley of Oaxaca and associated tributary valleys like the Ejutla Valley) seemed to wane, the population of the region grew to an unprecedented level. During IIIA, the volume of monumental construction more than doubled. This expanded system scale coincided with greater economic and political integration. Yet the increases in scale and integration coincided with a decline in the valley's demographic centralization as the centers at Jalieza and Dainzu-Macuilxochitl-Tlacochahuaya approached Monte Albán in size (and experienced more rapid growth). Thus, the changes in the Early Classic Period Valley of Oaxaca were very different from the contemporaneous shifts that were occurring in and around the primate center of Teotihuacan in the Basin of Mexico to the north, which are discussed in the following chapter.

Monte Albán IIIB (A.D. 500–750)

The two-century IIIA growth cycle persisted longer than the Late I cycle, which had lasted only a little more than a century or so. The IIIA breakdown, however, was different from that of Late I in two major respects. First, the result was a IIIB regional system that was more highly centralized and more focused on Monte Albán. This differed from the Late I–II transition during which secondary and tertiary centers became more autonomous. Second, at least in the southern and eastern arms of the valley, the collapse was more profound. The piedmont development strategy in these zones appears to have failed almost totally. In parts of the valley more than eighteen kilometers south of Monte Albán (Fig. 3.17), there was a 95 percent decline in population, including a virtual abandonment of Jalieza, which had become the valley's second-largest city during IIIA. The magnitude of the IIIA–IIIB transition is indicated in another respect. A site called Santa Inés Yatzeche, located in the alluvium in the southern Valle Grande (in grid square N5 × E6, Fig. 3.16), had been an important district center for hundreds of years. Over these hundreds of years it had persisted, even prospered, relatively unaffected by the various changes that had been brought about by the formation of Monte Albán and by all that happened in the valley after that time. The collapse of the southern valley in IIIA, however, was so complete that even this venerable center lost roughly 75 percent of its population.

By contrast, the valley's central area experienced massive growth in IIIB, as much of the region's population was pulled toward Monte Albán. The capital's population grew to nearly 25,000 people, its highest level ever, making the city five times the size of the next-largest center in the valley. Architecturally, it was far more massive and complex than any other valley center.

As IIIB was the final period of major construction at Monte Albán, it is for IIIB that we have the best picture of the appearance and layout of the capital. By this

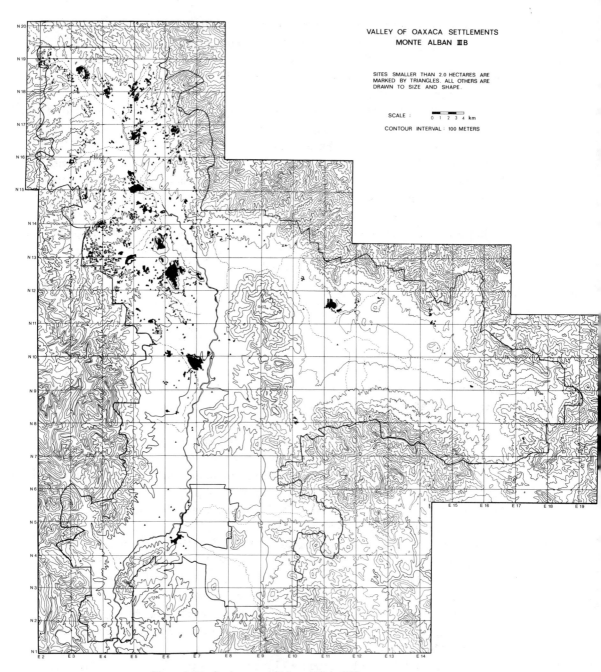

VALLEY OF OAXACA SETTLEMENTS
MONTE ALBAN ⅢB

SITES SMALLER THAN 2.0 HECTARES ARE
MARKED BY TRIANGLES. ALL OTHERS ARE
DRAWN TO SIZE AND SHAPE.

SCALE : 0 1 2 3 4 km

CONTOUR INTERVAL : 100 METERS

Figure 3.17. Settlements of Monte Albán IIIB.

time, buildings nearly completely enclosed the Main Plaza (Plate 4). Along the sides are a ball court, some probable residences, and a number of buildings whose functions are unknown. An elongated temple stood in the center of the plaza, adjacent to Structure J. The towering South Platform at the south end of the plaza supported mounded structures. At the opposite end was the North Platform (Fig. 3.15). Topping this platform was the "ruler's palace," a grandiose complex consisting of colonnaded halls, a vast sunken patio surrounded by pyramids (Plate 5), and (accessible only through a maze of easily guarded stairways, narrow passageways, gates, and small rooms) the most secluded residence at Monte Albán, no doubt home to its succession of ruling families. Major roads bypassed the Main Plaza, and the entire plaza complex could be entered only through three narrow, easily guarded openings – which strongly suggests that it was open to only a select group of people. The average citizen of Monte Albán in IIIB probably had no more opportunity to view the interior of the Main Plaza than the average American of today has to view the innermost interior of the CIA headquarters. Although we do not know what "traffic control" features, if any, regulated access to the Main Plaza in earlier periods, its seclusion in IIIB clearly signifies a rigid formalizing and differentiation of the highest level of decision making.

Fifteen site subdivisions have been identified for IIIB, including the Main Plaza and its surrounding area. Most of the subdivisions have evidence for some craft production, including manos and metates, pottery, celts, shell and obsidian, chert, and quartzite tools. The area immediately north of the Main Plaza contains many elaborate residences. Each of the other subdivisions centers on one or more elite residences, plus one highly accessible single-mound or double-mound group that has been interpreted as a civic building. These proposed civic complexes are easily reached by major roads, and may have functioned as neighborhood marketplaces, ritual spaces, or meeting places. Surrounding each cluster of elite residences and civic buildings are ordinary residential terraces that now lack standing architecture (Fig. 3.18). Excavations at three of these terraces have shown that low- or middle-status IIIB households consisted of rooms partially or completely enclosing a central

Plate 4. Monte Albán's Main Plaza. Photo taken from the top of the North Platform, looking south.

Plate 5. Sunken patio on the North Platform, Monte Albán.

patio. IIIB residential architecture also was characterized by its compactness and formal use of space; all features except ovens were inside the houses, and rather elaborate walls and stairways defined the relationship between residences. These traits may be related to greater crowding at the site and perhaps to more administrative regulation of the use of space; in contrast, residences from phases I through IIIA had tended to be broader, more open clusters of features.

During IIIB the total population of the valley dropped to less than 80,000. This decline coincided with key shifts in the population distribution within the valley. Considerable growth occurred in the Etla arm (relatively sparsely settled in IIIA) and at Monte Albán. On the other hand, the Valle Grande and the Tlacolula arm experienced dramatic losses, possibly up to 80 percent. Generally, areas farthest from Monte Albán had the steepest declines. South of Zaachila only one site – possibly a military outpost – contained more than a thousand people. Almost 60 percent of the IIIB inhabitants of the survey area were crowded into an area within twelve kilometers of Monte Albán. As in Late I, the high population of the central area dwelled mainly in the piedmont. However, in Late I the absence of other administrative centers in the central zone suggested that Monte Albán directly administered its hinterland population. In IIIB, piedmont settlers seemed to have been primarily administered through a number of second- and third-ranking centers located in or immediately adjacent to the piedmont. As in IIIA, five levels of administrative hierarchy can be identified. Thus the regional system in IIIB was in some respects as

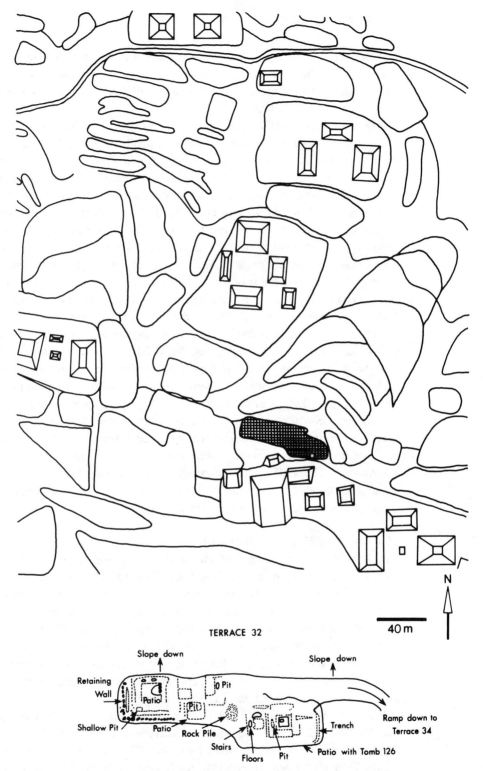

TERRACE 32

40 m

N

Slope down

Slope down

Retaining
Wall

Patio

0 Pit

Pit

Shallow Pit

Patio

Rock Pile

Stairs

Floors

Pit

Trench

Ramp down to
Terrace 34

Patio with Tomb 126

Figure 3.18. Bottom: Two Classic Period houses on a terrace at Monte Albán. Residences consisted of rooms arrayed around central patios. Top: The same terrace (no. 32) is shown with its neighboring house lots. Note the groups of pyramid mounds on several terraces, and the ancient road to the north. Redrawn from Blanton (1978: figs. A.X–14, site map).

vertically complex as in IIIA, but it was packed into a smaller, congested area adjacent to the capital. With the growth of Monte Albán (and the loss of population at Jalieza and Dainzu), the organization of the IIIB system was more centralized and more primate than in IIIA.

The economy in IIIB seems to have been tightly intertwined with the region's political organization. Virtually all ceramic production was located in large centers with monumental construction. In fact, for the first time Monte Albán itself became an important center of pottery manufacture. Pottery was even more standardized than in IIIA, and the amount of labor invested in it was low compared to other phases in the Monte Albán sequence (Table 3.2). Utilitarian grey wares dominated assemblages to an extent previously unseen. All IIIB occupations in the valley are littered with fragments of heavy, mass-produced bowls and jars that the uninitiated might easily mistake for rocks. Their extraordinarily rough surface finish and porosity suggests that use-life was short, as they must have broken and cracked easily, and leaked more often than the better-made pottery of other periods. Again, as in Late I and IIIA, the sites closest to Monte Albán seem to have been keyed most directly into a system of production and distribution that supplied them with a small number of standardized types. Most IIIB households outside Monte Albán but within twelve kilometers of the capital evidently could obtain only low-quality pottery, and even then only little more than the minimum of ceramic types needed for everyday cooking, storing, and serving. Typically, such an assemblage consisted of plain grey bowls, plain grey storage jars, and perhaps an incense burner or a plain grey bowl with supports. On the average, even residents of lower-level administrative centers had access to only a few more types than represented in this minimal assemblage. The IIIB system of production and distribution was such that only select segments of the population of the hilltop center itself could obtain much more than a marginal number of ceramic types.

Monte Albán IV (A.D. 750–1000)

The Main Plaza, the symbol of Monte Albán's power for over 1,200 years, stood empty by the end of phase IV. The loss of Monte Albán's valley-wide sovereignty may have been accompanied by security threats, as the site had precincts defended by walls dating to this time, and occupation was confined within the main defensive wall. With a population of about 4,000, phase IV Monte Albán was probably just one of several large, competing centers (Fig. 3.19). A renewal of contacts with areas outside the valley was another feature of this reorganization; pottery virtually identical to ceramics (based on surface appearance) from southeastern lowland Mesoamerica is present, though rare, at many phase IV sites.

Following the breakup of the IIIB system, the valley population dropped to about 70,000. Most of the decline occurred at Monte Albán as well as in the Etla arm and the central area. Much of the core of the IIIB settlement system was abandoned or largely depopulated. In contrast, settlement in the Valle Grande and Tlacolula expanded, as several large communities were founded. Almost 50 percent of the region's inhabitants resided in the dry Tlacolula arm. However, the largest site on

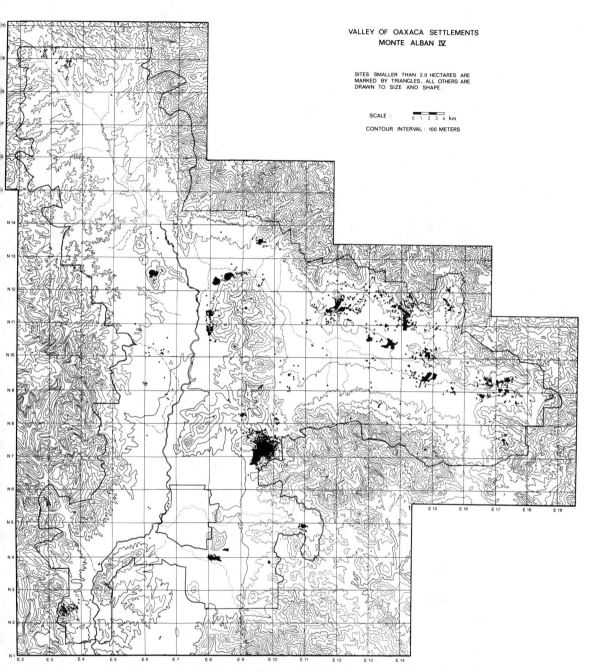

VALLEY OF OAXACA SETTLEMENTS
MONTE ALBAN IV

SITES SMALLER THAN 2.0 HECTARES ARE
MARKED BY TRIANGLES. ALL OTHERS ARE
DRAWN TO SIZE AND SHAPE.

SCALE :   0 1 2 3 4 km

CONTOUR INTERVAL : 100 METERS

Figure 3.19. Settlements of Monte Albán IV.

the phase IV landscape was Jalieza (in the Valle Grande), which was reoccupied in
a slightly different location than the large IIIA site. With 16,000 people, Jalieza was
more than twice the size of any other valley site. Although Jalieza's size is reminiscent of the region's former capital (Monte Albán), other evidence shows that it was
a different type of center. Jalieza lacked the functional equivalent of the Main Plaza,

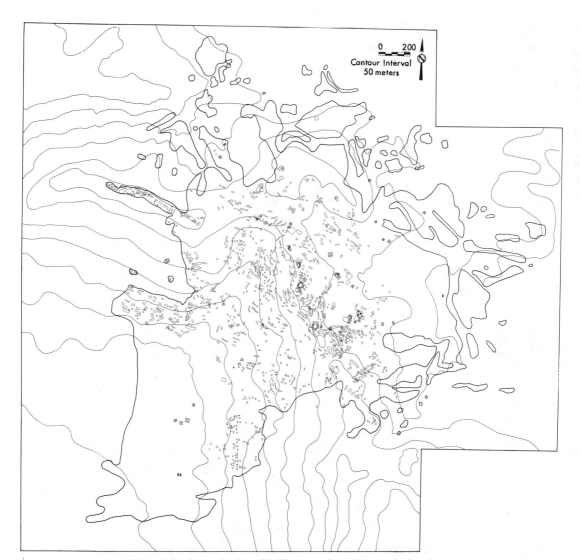

Figure 3.20. Jalieza in phase IV. The heavy lines show the limits of the sherd scatter. Mounds and residential terraces are indicated.

a central plaza surrounded by public buildings. Instead, at Jalieza, several small elite residences were scattered along the occupied ridges at fairly regular intervals (Fig. 3.20). The phase IV structures totaled less than one-third the volume of mounds at the IIIA occupation of the site. In fact, compared to IIIB Monte Albán, the non-residential building at IV Jalieza was practically negligible. The volume of civic-ceremonial building at Jalieza apparently was less massive than that found at several contemporaneous sites. The hegemony of Jalieza's rulers likely did not extend far beyond the immediate surrounds of the site.

The comparison of Monte Albán and Jalieza, in conjunction with regional settlement pattern analysis, suggests profound differences between the political organization of the Early Postclassic and that found in all preceding periods. The site of Jalieza itself was atypical in size. Yet, in a regional context, the settlement with its surrounding villages and hamlets resembles five other settlement clusters in the southern arm of the valley. Each of these smaller concentrations (with individual populations of several thousand) was composed of at least one nucleated town (with monumental architecture) and small surrounding sites. As in the case of Jalieza, several of the central settlements were located in high, rugged, defendable settings. Broad tracts of unoccupied land separate these clusters.

In Tlacolula, the IV settlement pattern was rather different. There, three major population clusters dominated. Each of these clusters included several large settlements, often with massive civic-ceremonial construction. In contrast to the Valle Grande, some of the Tlacolula centers were located in lower, alluvial terrain, and there was less unoccupied space between the concentrations of settlement. At a number of these Tlacolula towns, including Lambityeco and Macuilxochitl, evidence for economic specialization was recovered in quantity. These findings, along with the spatial differences in settlement patterns, suggest that the Tlacolula towns may have been more interconnected (particularly through economic links) than those in the southern valley.

Nevertheless, overall, phase IV seems to have been a time of considerable decentralization and competition among semiautonomous political units or "petty states," with a correspondingly low degree of formal political integration in the region. Generally, the IV settlement clusters covered only 25–50 square kilometers, and the nature of the links between these settlement units varied among valley subregions. In the Valle Grande, the threat of military activities may have had an important role in settlement location, whereas in agriculturally risky Tlacolula, craft specialization and commercial exchange took on added importance with the collapse of the valley's central political institution at Monte Albán.

Monte Albán V (A.D. 1000–1520)

During phase V, regional boundaries were less strictly defined than ever before, as political, social, and economic ties linked valley communities into broad interregional networks. Ethnohistoric sources speak of marriages between the Zapotec nobility of the valley and lords from the neighboring Mixteca Alta, immigration of Mixtecan nobility and peasants into the valley, the conquest of the coastal market center of Tehuantepec by valley and Mixtec armies, the entrance of Aztec traders, and the establishment of an Aztec colony. Ceramic traces of such intensive interaction include Aztec vessels found at Monte Albán and Yagul, similarities between painted red on cream wares found in the valley and those found in the Mixteca Alta, the presence at many valley sites of the elaborately decorated polychromes found across Mesoamerica in the Late Postclassic, and the abundance of Oaxaca-style utilitarian bowls at both Ejutla and Miahuatlán (south of the valley) and in the Mixteca Alta. Obsidian, considered to be a useful marker of interregional trade because it had to be imported into the valley, was more common in phase V than in other periods. Even the physical boundaries of the valley no longer isolated the regional system, as settlements stretched across the previously sparsely occupied piedmont and mountains that separate the valley from other areas of the southern highlands.

Within the valley, the population grew to over 160,000 – greater than in any prior phase – although, due to increases in maize plant productivity, it remained below the region's agricultural potential. Since Monte Albán V was a very long phase (nearly six centuries), the rate of growth was slow, less than it had been in either I or IIIA. The Monte Albán regional settlement system had a rural as well as urban character. The rural aspect is clear as over a thousand small isolated residences, many more than in any prior phase, have been found. Settlement was dispersed across all environmental zones and geographical sectors (Fig. 3.21). While no Monte Albán V center dominated the regional landscape politically or demographically, in the manner that Monte Albán and Jalieza had earlier, twenty-five settlements did have average populations of greater than 1,000. The region's two largest communities, Sa'a Yucu (meaning "at the foot of the mountain" in Mixtec), which ran from Cuilapan to the southern slopes of Monte Albán, and Macuilxochitl-Teotitlán (located in grid squares N11 × E11–12 and N12 × E12, Fig. 3.21), were nearly equivalent in size (ca. 14,000). Mitla, a third large site, also located in the Tlacolula arm, had over 10,000 people and was associated with the most massive public architecture in the region.

Ethnohistoric documents describe the division of the valley into approximately twenty small, internally stratified polities at the time of the conquest. Each consisted of a large head town and several small, supporting villages or hamlets. At least one high-ranking lord, who resided in the head town, governed each kingdom. Aiding him or her were lower-ranking members of the nobility who were appointed as administrators of each neighborhood or subject community. In local affairs, the highest-ranking nobility were semiautonomous. They were independently responsible for levying tribute on the local commoners, mediating disputes, and organizing the military forces of the kingdom.

As elsewhere in Mesoamerica in the Late Postclassic, the valley was organized politically as a series of petty states, with an average of around 8,000 inhabitants. As noted above, this patchwork extended in all directions into adjacent areas, such as Ejutla to the south and the mountains to the north and west. Although the population and polity density were not even everywhere in Oaxaca, these petty states formed a macroregional system that erased the boundaries of the earlier centralized states of the Classic era. The organization of the Late Postclassic Oaxacan landscape was complicated by an apparently continuous cycle of federations, marriage alliances, military escapades, and fragmentations that grouped and regrouped the component states. These groupings did not always follow ethnic lines in any simple manner. Mixtecs warred against Mixtecs, Zapotecs against other Zapotecs, and petty states associated with noble speakers of the two languages fought between themselves. At times, Zapotec and Mixtec lords also allied with each other against the Aztec. Elite marriages also often crossed ethnic and linguistic lines.

Based on certain readings of sixteenth-century native accounts, it has been suggested that the ruler of Zaachila (located in grid square N9 × E6 of Fig. 3.21) was recognized as the overlord of the valley up until the last years before the conquest. Excavations have confirmed the association of important phase V rulers with Zaachila – two tombs at the site yielded unusually rich offerings of jade, gold, turquoise, onyx, obsidian, shell, carved-bone objects, and polychrome vessels. Yet, even though some of the V occupation lies buried under the modern town, it

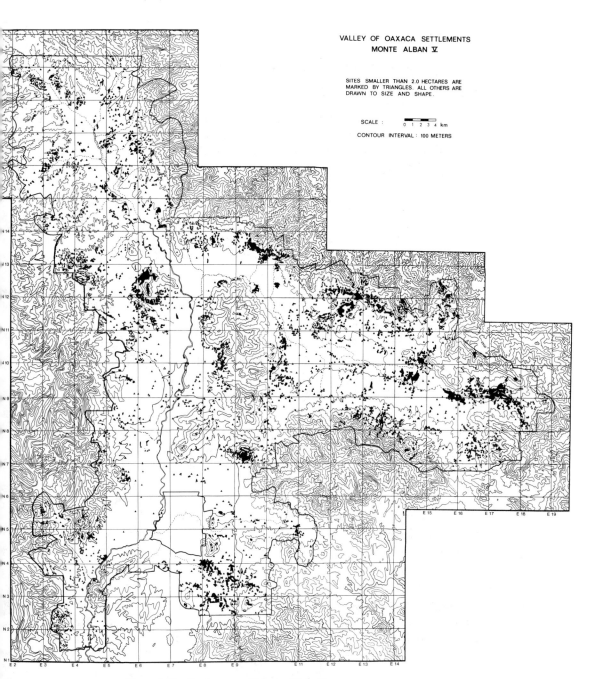

VALLEY OF OAXACA SETTLEMENTS
MONTE ALBAN Ⅴ

SITES SMALLER THAN 2.0 HECTARES ARE
MARKED BY TRIANGLES. ALL OTHERS ARE
DRAWN TO SIZE AND SHAPE.

SCALE : 0 1 2 3 4 km

CONTOUR INTERVAL : 100 METERS

Figure 3.21. Settlements of Monte Albán V.

appears that Zaachila was not a major population center during the Late Post-classic. Furthermore, the site's population peak evidently had occurred during IIIB, not V, and most of the pyramids at Zaachila were built before V. The remarks of a priest who lived at Zaachila in the 1600s corroborate archaeological evidence for this site's relatively small size and lack of architectural complexity. He commented:

"I have been unable to discover any signs of large buildings [dating to late prehispanic times] or continued occupation such as one finds in other places that persist since ancient times." Based on the archaeological evidence, it appears doubtful that Zaachila was as important a center as earlier studies suggested.

In spite of the political decentralization, there is excellent evidence for economic interaction and interdependence among petty kingdoms. Production of ordinary goods appears oriented toward exchange. The way the population was distributed over the land indicates a potential to produce large agricultural surpluses, as the late prehispanic tribute requirements, demanded by Aztec conquerors, suggest. This pattern contrasts to the Classic Period and earlier times when defensive or administrative concerns were more important factors in site location. There is more evidence of craft production for phase V than for any earlier time. Craft production sites are especially common in the drier Tlacolula arm. Etla, while rather densely settled, has comparatively few craft production sites. This subregional difference has some historical depth, as for much of the sequence Etla tended to specialize in agricultural production. An obvious implication is that such subregional specialization and segmentation required integration, perhaps through the market system, as it has been accomplished historically.

Monte Albán V had more ceramic workshops than did other periods, and manufactured pottery that was the most costly (measured in terms of the average amount of labor invested in its production) in the Monte Albán sequence (Table 3.2). The majority (ten out of sixteen) of ceramic workshops were situated in places without civic-ceremonial construction (for the first time since Early I). At the same time, households in nonadministrative sites participated more heavily in exchange than in IIIB or IV. Although they still had fewer ceramic types than did households in administrative sites, the disparity was less than it had been since the establishment of Monte Albán. In sum, nothing here indicates political control or redistribution as a force restructuring the economy. Attempts by rulers to mobilize production through tribute had little effect on settlement patterns or the distribution of craft producers. Perhaps the most significant force in Postclassic Oaxaca was not the lords of the prehispanic codices, but the workings of a commercial market system.

The Postclassic was distinguished from the earlier Monte Albán phases by the absence of an architecturally dominant center on the order of Monte Albán. Another important break between V and earlier phases in the valley was the significant decline in the amount of monumental construction; only thirty-one settlements have at least 5,000 cubic meters of public architecture, compared to fifty-one settlements dating to Monte Albán IIIA. These figures do not reveal the degree of difference in building activities between the phases, as many mounds that were used in the Late Postclassic were actually constructed earlier and modified only slightly with reoccupation. In addition, phase V centers are distinct from those of prior phases in that very few have dominant plazas. Instead, Late Postclassic centers with multiple mounds tend to have many plazas, none of which is especially dominant in size. The paucity and dispersed nature of phase V monumental construction would seem to signal a shift in civic-ceremonial activities or a change in the abilities of the elite to mobilize labor for construction projects.

The overall picture of phase V is one in which the hierarchically shallow, fluctuating, and weakly integrated political system was not the major source of regional integration. During the period of Monte Albán's hegemony, most economic, political, and ritual transactions evidently were channeled primarily through a single hierarchy, a primarily political one centered at Monte Albán. Phase V, on the other hand, featured separate functional hierarchies – economic and political – that only partly overlapped spatially and structurally.

Conclusion

We have proposed that to best understand cultural-evolutionary processes in the Valley of Oaxaca in Early and Middle Formative times, a vantage point should be taken that encompasses all of the southern highlands, or perhaps an even larger area, as an analytical unit. Exchanges of various sorts among those small, widely scattered populations would have been critical for survival, especially in the context of the kinds of demographic risks inherent in small population size. Throughout Mesoamerica's prehistory, interregional exchanges were important, but with initial sedentism these interactions were likely to have been consequential at a very basic, household-to-household level. Later in time, interregional exchanges tended to involve primarily elite-to-elite contacts (a topic we discuss more fully in our concluding chapter), as regional boundary definition began to be rigidified and as nonelite households were engaged primarily in intraregional interactions. In fact, in the Valley of Oaxaca, region-wide political integration tended to be most extensive when the state controlled an area no larger than the valley itself, and when valley boundaries were relatively closed. Under these conditions, Monte Albán promoted economic integration as a means of funding the governmental institutions centered in the capital, and of supporting the large urban population associated with these institutions. The valley's size and topographic situation facilitated strong central control by hindering competition from more peripheral centers. Monte Albán, at the center of the valley, had a hinterland roughly equal in size to the valley itself. The potential hinterlands of outlying centers lacked a comparable agricultural and demographic capacity, as they were composed mainly of rugged, less densely settled mountains. The valley is also small enough that almost all communities lie within a one to two days' walk of Monte Albán. This meant that activities in other centers could be subjected to direct scrutiny and regulation, and that the energy costs of integrating the valley from the capital were relatively low. Finally, communities near the valley peripheries were in the most vulnerable position militarily; thus they had much to gain from supporting a regional capital that had as one of its most important functions the coordination of military activities.

Although the region's political organization tended to be most centralized when its area was small, it was at these times that it relied primarily on locally produced surpluses for support. Stepped-up production demands on valley residents stimulated population growth, as families sought to increase the working capacity of their households by having more children. Valley elites also may have encouraged or forced immigration into the region in order to boost the supply of labor. However, in the long run, population growth increased administrative costs. First, it involved supervision of greater numbers of people. Second, the agriculturally riskier pied-mont absorbed the growing population and yielded surpluses that were more easily exacted by central authorities. But piedmont development also promoted inte-grated regional networks that families could plug into in poor years (and that also were a source of basic goods such as pottery). Third, greater crowding, scarcity of the best land and water resources, and the use of piedmont irrigation systems created pressures for more adjudicative mechanisms. These factors all tended to in-crease the growth and complexity of the administrative apparatus, which, in turn, cycled back into greater demands on producers.

Thus, through the Classic Period, population growth, enhanced vertical com-plexity of the administrative hierarchy, and expanded political meddling in ex-change and production all tended to be associated in the Monte Albán sequence. Phases I and III (both marked by a strong central institution) illustrate these dyna-mics. At the end of each of these phases (in II and IV) there were major changes in the distribution of settlements and in administrative organization. These changes suggest that there were ceilings to the cycles of intensification. In the early stages of growth, piedmont productivity would have been high because the lands brought under cultivation were essentially virgin farmland and because at low population densities administrative costs were relatively low. But as growth continued, produc-tion would have declined because of the degradation of piedmont soils, while admin-istrative costs would have continued to increase. When production declined and increased adjudicative costs reached a critical point, reorganization occurred.

Phase II represented a reorganization within a regional system that was still headed and integrated by Monte Albán. Political, economic, and demographic changes in the valley were related to the fact that support for the state was drawn from a region that had been vastly enlarged through conquest, thus decreasing the burdens on local valley producers. When Teotihuacan expansion forced the con-traction of regional boundaries in IIIA, Monte Albán returned to the phase I strat-egy of instigating growth within the valley. But the Classic Period was not a simple repetition of phase I. During the Classic, populations were larger and society was more highly integrated politically (and in part through these channels, economically as well). Administrative hierarchies were more strongly differentiated than had been the case in phase I. In IIIA and IIIB, Monte Albán specialized in regional administrative coordination, boundary maintenance, and diplomacy, relinquishing direct control over agricultural production to local administrative districts.

Though enormous change had occurred from Early I to IIIB, a hierarchy of administrative central places capped by Monte Albán persisted throughout the time span. The IIIB-to-IV transition marked a crisis for this mode of regional organiza-tion. With the reorganization that followed IIIB, numerous local administrative units emerged as nearly autonomous polities. This decentralized regional adminis-trative structure characterized the Valley of Oaxaca for the next 800 years, through phases IV and V. But by V, commercial transactions, independent of centralized administrative control, made a stronger contribution to local and regional integra-tion than they had in any previous period, as the amount of specialization and the volume of commercial activity reached unprecedented levels. The trends toward local control of commerce and less political meddling in economic relations may have begun during IV, perhaps as valley residents attempted to maintain access to goods following the collapse of the IIIB state. We discuss this problem further in our concluding chapter. In phase V, with a larger population creating greater aggregate demand for goods, with the resettlement of the alluvium so that steady surpluses could again be produced by a sector of the population, with lowered governmental demands on producers, and with expanded contacts with other areas of Mesoamerica creating further potential for trade, commercial networks became much more fully developed.

A strict neoevolutionist might look at the prehispanic Valley of Oaxaca and focus exclusively on the long-term trend toward growth and increases in scale (as measured by regional population size and the more widespread distribution of communities across the valley landscape). Yet the prehispanic pattern of growth in the Valley of Oaxaca was more cyclical than linear, marked by relatively rapid episodes of increment punctuated by phases of relative stability and decline. Significantly, through this sequence, neither settlement sizes nor patterns of public building maintained a monotonic relationship with increasing scale. The Classic Period not only had the largest central place, but it also had the highest percentage of population residing in urban centers. Phase V was largest in total population, but the distribution of the population was more rural than it had been during the Classic Period. Similarly, the scale of public architecture failed to track increasing system size in any simple way; more people did not automatically translate into more labor employed in construction. The Late Postclassic, in fact, had less mound construction than even the Late and Terminal Formative, though the population of these earlier periods was only roughly one-fifth that of the later period. Looking at the entire scope of the prehispanic era, regional population, degree of urbanization, and volume of public construction were interrelated in more complicated fashion than many theorists have presumed.

4

The Valley of Mexico

Introduction

Modern Mexico exhibits the kind of primacy in city-size distribution that was characteristic of the Valley of Oaxaca in some of its prehispanic periods. A single center – Mexico City – is vastly larger than any other Mexican community (with over 15,000,000 inhabitants, it is the largest city in the New World), and it is the nation-state heartland of industry, commerce, government, and arts and letters. Mexico City overlies the ruins of an earlier capital – Tenochtitlan-Tlatelolco – which, until it was reduced to rubble by the Spaniards under Cortés, was Mesoamerica's most important city. Tenochtitlan-Tlatelolco, the seat of the expansionist Culhua Mexica, was the center of a loosely organized but substantial empire that extended from the Gulf coast in what is now the state of Veracruz to the Pacific coast of Guatemala, and included the Valley of Oaxaca. Earlier capitals situated in or near the Valley of Mexico had exerted their influence over sizeable portions of Mesoamerica. Tula, Hidalgo, located just beyond the valley's northern limit (Fig. 1.2), was the capital of the legendary Toltecs prior to Tenochtitlan's rise to prominence. Earlier, during phases IIIA and IIIB in the Valley of Oaxaca, a Valley of Mexico center called Teotihuacan had been Mesoamerica's largest and most influential capital. Obviously, for the anthropologist curious about the evolution of large-scale political and economic systems, the Valley of Mexico has much to offer.

Since 1960, when the plan to carry out a total, systematic archaeological surface survey was first agreed upon, more area – 3,500 square kilometers – has been covered in the Valley of Mexico than anywhere else in Mesoamerica. These survey data, in combination with surveys in and around Tula, studies based on ethnohistoric and archival sources, and excavations, provide an unprecedented amount of information from a region that was one of the most important in the New World during prehispanic times.

Environment

Like the Valley of Oaxaca, the Valley of Mexico sits atop a highland block – the central highlands of Mexico (Fig. 1.2). Prehispanically it was an internal drainage basin, involving an area of roughly 7,000 square kilometers (measuring close to 120 kilometers north–south by 70 kilometers east–west). The floor of the valley is at roughly 7,000 feet above sea level, which results in a generally cool climate. Frost can be a severe problem for farmers in the fall, winter, and spring. A late spring or early fall frost can interfere with even a one-crop agricultural cycle. The rainy season comes during approximately the same period as in Oaxaca, from May through October, and the amount of rainfall is comparable. Rainfall in the northern part of the region ranges from a low of about 450 millimeters per year, but as you move south there is a gradual increase to 1,000 millimeters or so along the southern slopes. Throughout the valley, irrigation is crucial for long-term agricultural success, though it is especially critical in the north. Even in the wetter south, however, the unpredictability of rain makes irrigation a plus for minimizing risk. Irrigation is often a dry-season strategy utilized prior to planting, to augment the moisture in the soil as a precaution against insufficient rain.

High mountains surround the valley (except for the northern boundary, which is less clearly defined topographically), projecting far above the altitudinal limits of maize cultivation. Before the Spaniards engineered a drainage canal, the valley was a closed hydrographic unit. Water flowing down from the mountains fed a series of shallow, marshy, interconnected lakes (Fig. 4.1). The central and lowest of these, Lake Texcoco, was saline. To the north was the higher and less salty Lake Xaltocan-Zumpango, and to the south was the freshwater Lake Chalco-Xochimilco. These lakes covered an estimated 1,000 square kilometers and represented a resource unique in Mesoamerica for hunting, collecting, certain kinds of intensive farming, and transportation.

Given the system of lakes, the environment of the Valley of Mexico contrasts with that of the Valley of Oaxaca, even though the two regions are generally similar in elevation and aridity. In the Valley of Mexico, instead of a riverine, alluvial plain, there is the lake and its surrounding lakeshore plain. Resources here included such lacustrine products as fish, insect larvae, reeds, and waterfowl. The lakeshore plain was probably rather swampy and subject to floods in the absence of water control and drainage projects, but no doubt some parts of it were usable for cultivation with simple forms of high-water-table cultivation, as in parts of the Oaxaca alluvium. Toward the end of the prehispanic sequence, much of the valley's lake system and some of its lakeshore plain zone were developed for farming. In part this involved the drainage of low-lying areas, but most of this activity involved the creation of thousands of small, consolidated agricultural plots in the shallow parts of the lakes (except where the salinity of the water could not be eliminated), called *chinampas*. Coupled with a system of dikes for regulating lake levels, the *chinampa* technique "irrigates" by keeping the water table within reach of the crop's roots. By the time the Spanish arrived in the 1520s, the Valley of Mexico *chinampa* system was one of the most complex, labor-intensive, and productive agricultural strategies in the New World.

Above the lakeshore plain is a zone of piedmont similar to the transition zone between the alluvial valley floor and the mountains in the Valley of Oaxaca. Not all of the surface above the lakeshore plain in the Valley of Mexico is sloping piedmont, however. Some expanses of flat alluvium can be found – for example, the floor of the Teotihuacan subvalley. Near the center of this small valley is a group of springs (Fig. 4.1) that today supports the irrigation of some 3,000 hectares. Much of the piedmont is suitable for agriculture, especially in the lower and middle ranges. A

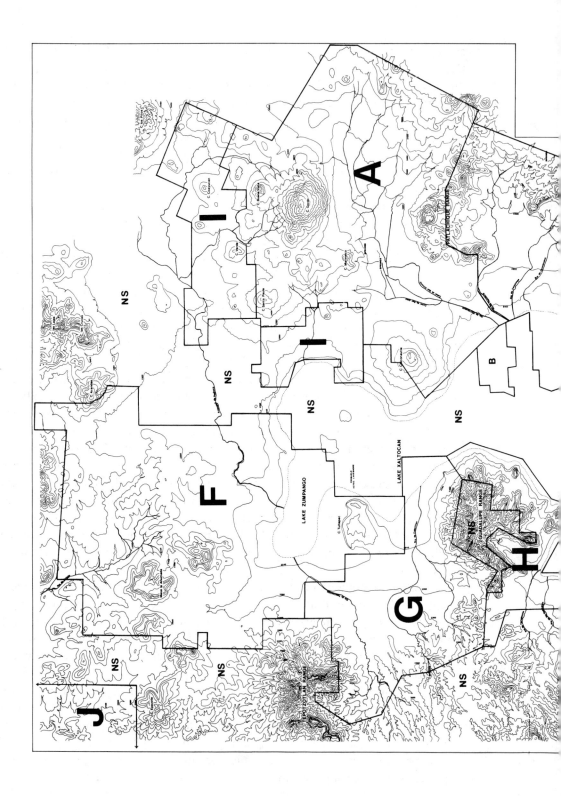

Figure 4.1. Valley of Mexico, showing the survey regions. This and Figs. 4.2–4.6, 4.8, 4.9, 4.11, 4.13, and 4.14 are from Sanders, Parsons, and Santley (1979).

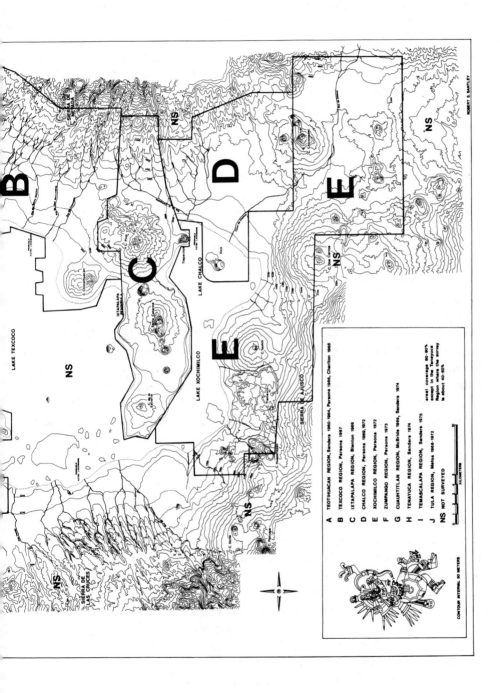

variety of techniques can be used, including dry farming, floodwater irrigation, and canal irrigation using the water either from springs or from rivers and streams that flow down from the surrounding mountain ranges. Above the upper piedmont zone rise the steeper, high slopes of the Sierra. This area is too high for cultivation, but is useful as a source of forest products and game.

In spite of the environmental differences embodied in the distinctions made between lake and lakeshore plain zones, on the one hand, and different kinds of piedmont, on the other, basically the valley as a whole can be considered a single, large environmental "patch" from the point of view of prehispanic cultivation. Although each environmental zone may require a distinct set of techniques and strategies for cultivators, still the basic crop complex (dominated, of course, by maize) can be grown almost anywhere in the region.

These two highland nuclear zones – the valleys of Oaxaca and Mexico – are thus, in some key respects, similar environmentally. Both are high and semiarid, with a marked seasonality and high degree of unpredictability in rainfall. Irrigation is therefore of considerable importance. Both valleys contain environmental subdivisions, but not to a degree prohibiting the cultivation of the basic crop complex almost everywhere. Farmers in the Valley of Mexico do have a problem that is not a serious concern in the Valley of Oaxaca – a short growing season due to frost – but in other respects Mexico presents certain kinds of opportunities not available in the other Mesoamerican highlands. The lake system was an important source of raw materials and food, and, as developed during the final centuries of prehispanic times, it was a highly productive agricultural zone. Too, the Valley of Mexico has an important resource not found in the Valley of Oaxaca – volcanic glass, or obsidian. Several sources are present, including one in the vicinity of Teotihuacan (at Otumba; see Fig. 4.12 later in this chapter), and three some fifty kilometers northeast of Teotihuacan, just outside the valley proper. These were some of the most important obsidian sources in all of prehispanic Mesoamerica. This is an important point, as obsidian was a highly desired raw material for cutting tools and decorative items in pre-Spanish times.

Chronology

As we have seen, Table 3.1 shows the correspondences between the ceramic chronologies of the valleys of Mexico and Oaxaca. (All dates are in radiocarbon years.) Due to the paucity of carbon-14 dates, these correspondences could change slightly when more information is available, but probably not in a significant way. Along the left side of the Valley of Mexico column in this table are found the local names for the ceramic complexes for each phase. Further subdivisions of the ceramic complexes of some of these phases have been identified, but they are of little interest for our purposes here. In most cases the ceramic differences that have been noted by the excavators who have done this subdividing are so minor they cannot be readily detected in surface-collected samples.

The phase names like "First Intermediate," and so forth, refer to the neutral terminology recently proposed for the Valley of Mexico sequence. The purpose of this new terminology was to replace value-laden terms like "Classic" and "Formative." This is an admirable goal, but in our opinion the change is not needed. The new scheme does little but add to the confusion and proliferation of phase designations. In this book we will therefore use the existing set of names. Admittedly, names like Patlachique, Tzacualli, and Coyotlatelco are not easy to remember (or pronounce), but they have the advantage of having been in the literature for some time, and they could never become value-laden. We do find the new term "Early Horizon" a convenient way to refer to the ceramic phases that pertain to the period roughly equivalent to the San José phase in the Valley of Oaxaca. We will also make use of the new term "Middle Horizon" to refer to the set of ceramic phases during which the settlement pattern associated with Teotihuacan at its height developed.

Settlement pattern history of the Valley of Mexico

The following pages contain brief descriptions of the major changes in human society in the Valley of Mexico as these can be inferred from the results of the settlement pattern surveys, and as they can be substantiated where appropriate by information from excavations and historical sources. As we mentioned previously, the survey data are substantial, representing the coverage of some 3,500 square kilometers. The area surveyed represents the bulk of the valley below the Sierra zone, except for a large portion of ancient Lake Texococo and the adjacent lakeshore and piedmont to the west. This latter belt cannot be surveyed because it is largely underneath the asphalt and concrete of modern Mexico City. Figure 4.1 shows the limits of the surveyed zone and the names of the subdivisions of the surveyed area, and indicates the person or persons responsible for the survey of each of the subdivisions.

The Early Horizon (1400–900 B.C.)

The Early Horizon incorporates the earliest well-defined ceramic assemblages in the valley. These ceramics include types with Olmec motifs of the sort encountered at San José Mogote in the Valley of Oaxaca, indicating that the Valley of Mexico villagers at that time participated in the same interaction sphere. Only nineteen sites of this period have been located (not all were necessarily occupied contemporaneously), indicating a very low population density, even in the southern valley, where virtually all the sites are located (Fig.4.2). Most Early Horizon sites are the remains of small villages or hamlets, each containing no more than a few hundred persons.

Recall that in the Valley of Oaxaca San José phase one community, San José Mogote, grew to regional prominence, indicating that even during that early time there was a degree of centralization of functions in a single head town. We cannot be sure that a similar degree of centralization had developed during the Early Horizon in the Valley of Mexico. There is a site that has fragmentary evidence of regional prominence, Tlatilco (Fig. 4.2), where excavations have produced an impressive array of elaborate grave goods. As the site is now largely buried under a suburb of Mexico City and a cement factory, however, we will probably never know its population size, or be able to assess its regional significance in political or economic

PATLACHIQUE RANGE

LAKE ZUMPANGO

LAKE XALTOCAN

C. Tultepec

GUADALUPE RANGE

EL ARBOLILLO

LOMA TORREMOTE

TEPOTZOTLAN RANGE

112

Figure 4.2. Settlements of the Early Horizon.

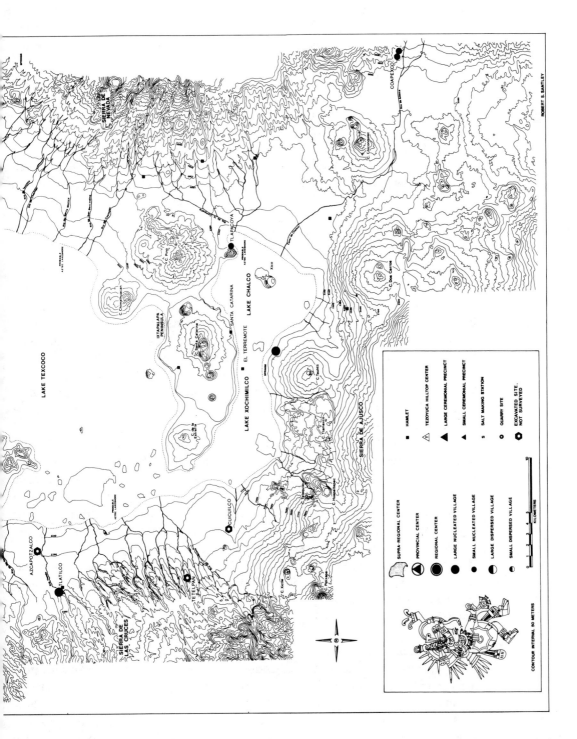

113

terms. A site located on a high plateau at the very southeastern corner of the region, at Coapexco, was one of the largest communities of the Valley of Mexico Early Horizon. Although it persisted for no more than a century, it probably had a population of 1,000, covering an area of 44 hectares. Excavated evidence indicates lithic production and trading at the site, particularly involving exotic obsidian from distant sources; it is located near what was later to become an important trade route connecting the valley to points south and east. Coapexco illustrates the probable importance of long-distance trading connections in the growth of the larger communities of the Early Horizon.

One other site, we can guess, may have had regional importance in Early Horizon times. The community of Cuicuilco (Fig. 4.2) became one of the valley's most important centers later, during the Ticoman and Patlachique periods, but its early history and settlement layout are poorly understood. Sometime during the Middle Horizon it was covered by a lava flow from the volcano Xitli, which turned the site and its surrounds into a barren lava plateau now known as the Pedregal. Excavations suggest the presence of Early Horizon materials, but no data are available on the population size or function of the site at that time.

The Zacatenco phase (900–600 B.C.)

The Zacatenco ceramics mark the cessation of the use of Olmec decorative motifs, but design similarities with ceramics from other parts of Mesoamerica persisted, especially indicated by the various cream-slipped vessels with incised designs. Sites identified as Zacatenco are much more numerous (seventy-five) (Fig. 4.3) than those linked with the Early Horizon (nineteen). The population estimate for the Valley of Mexico, based on the size and density of occupations, is close to 20,000. Several of these Zacatenco settlements were much larger than any of the earlier sites, ranging up to 50 hectares. A site this size would suggest a community of 1,000 to 2,000 or more people. Although Cuicuilco is poorly known, it probably fell within this latter size range. As during the previous phase, the valley's southern half tended to be favored for settlement. Tlatilco, we know, continued to be occupied, but again we know nothing of its size or importance.

The fact that some Zacatenco sites are considerably larger than others cannot be explained at this time. It is possible that the larger communities were central places, but no evidence exists to support this suggestion. None of the sites has any clear evidence for public architecture. This fact alone seems to indicate important differences between Zacatenco times in the Valley of Mexico and the contemporaneous Guadalupe and Rosario phases in Oaxaca, where, at least at San José Mogote, substantial public works existed.

The Ticoman phase (600–150 B.C.)

This phase was characterized by a continuation in growth in numbers of sites (to a total of 154) and population (to an estimated 90,000) (Fig. 4.4). Too, the larger Ticoman sites (regional centers in Fig. 4.4), which covered as much as 100 hectares, were larger than any of the Zacatenco sites. Ticoman is the first phase in which one can definitely distinguish sites with central-place functions in the Valley of Mexico. Several sites in the southern valley have mounds up to five meters high. However, by Ticoman times the Valley of Mexico had still not yet developed a sociopolitical system with the vertical complexity of the contemporary Valley of Oaxaca system. In Early I, Monte Albán's dominant position at the top of the administrative and settlement-size hierarchy was already established. No such system had evolved in the Valley of Mexico. In fact, the larger Ticoman sites in the Valley of Mexico are about the same size as the Oaxaca secondary centers, except for Cuicuilco, which toward the end of Ticoman may have reached a population of between 5,000 and 10,000 people, or roughly 30 percent to 60 percent of the contemporary population of Monte Albán.

A group of sites referred to as "Tezoyuca hilltop centers" may date to Ticoman times as well. Their locations, however, are indicated on the Patlachique map (Fig. 4.5) for the sake of convenience, as their actual chronological placement is in doubt. Excavations and carbon-14 dates are needed before a secure placement in time can be made, but other evidence indicates that the Tezoyuca hilltop centers may date to Ticoman times. If so, they suggest a move in the northern valley, especially in the vicinity of the Teotihuacan subvalley and the northern Texcoco region, to a peculiar form of site hierarchy in which administrative centers were segregated from agricultural villages and located on isolated hilltops. All of these Tezoyuca centers had platform mounds ranging up to about four meters high, and their hilltop locations were quite distinct from those of the Ticoman sites. Too, the ceramic assemblages on the Tezoyuca sites consisted largely of small, highly decorated serving vessels, whereas the Ticoman sites contain many fewer decorated types and more large vessels, including storage vessels that are nearly absent from the Tezoyuca sites. These data make sense if the Tezoyuca sites were elite centers, supported agriculturally by the surrounding sites with the Ticoman ceramic assemblages.

Not until the succeeding phases are the data and our understanding sufficient to begin to comprehend the ancient Valley of Mexico as a dynamic regional system. From the Early Horizon to the Ticoman phase – a period of time well over a millennium – we know of sites and a few patterns, but explaining how those sketched-in patterns came to be and why they existed and changed is a challenge that to date has not been met. Many key sites (for example, Cuicuilco and Tlatilco) have been destroyed, adding to the difficulties. Nevertheless, the drawing up and testing of new interpretations about the Formative Valley of Mexico could perhaps still yield constructive and interesting findings for students of cultural evolution.

The Patlachique phase (150 B.C.–A.D. 1)
Settlement patterns indicate a much more complex regional organization in the Patlachique phase than in prior times (Fig. 4.5). Several major trends can be recognized. First, there is some evidence for more vertical differentiation in the hierarchy of sites. Two centers, Teotihuacan and Cuicuilco, grew during the period to cover larger areas than had any communities previously. Again, a precise estimate is not possible for Cuicuilco, but a reasonable estimate is that it extended over 400 hectares and had perhaps as many as 20,000 people. Several very large platforms were constructed at Cuicuilco that were so high that much of the construction was never

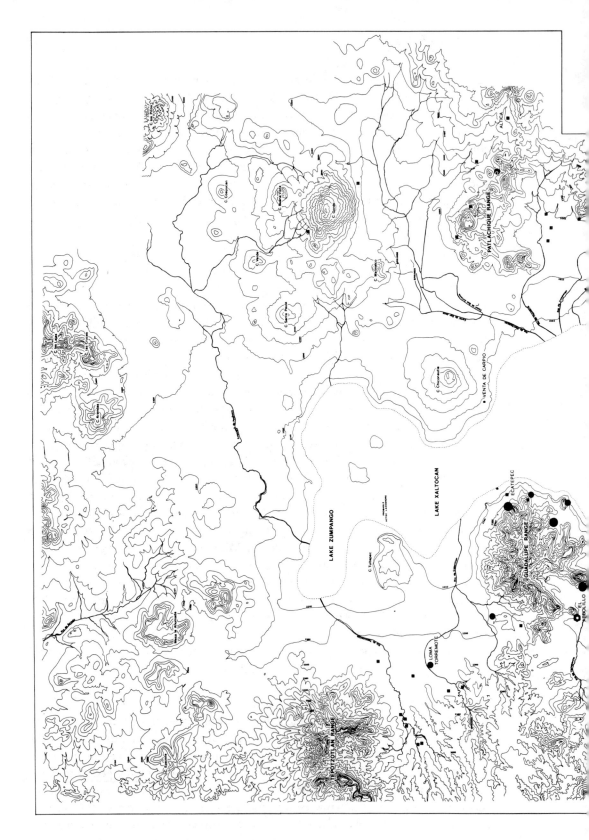

116

Figure 4.3. Settlements of the Zacatenco phase.

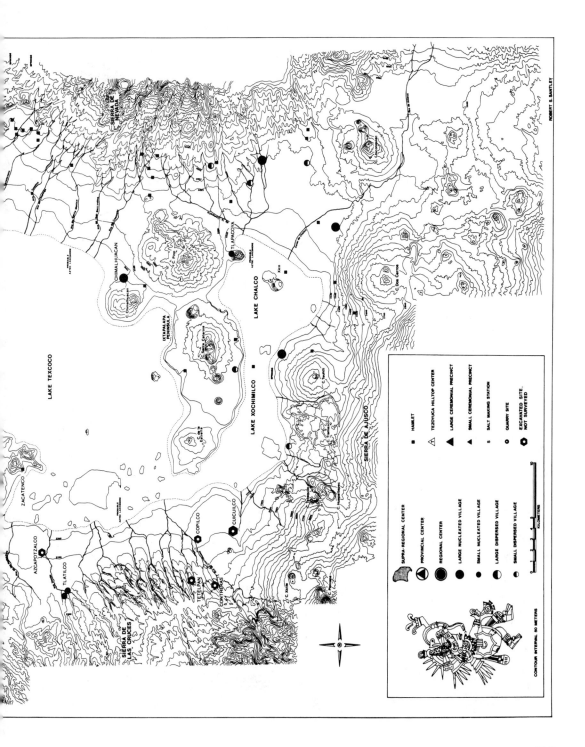

Figure 4.4. Settlements of the Ticoman phase.

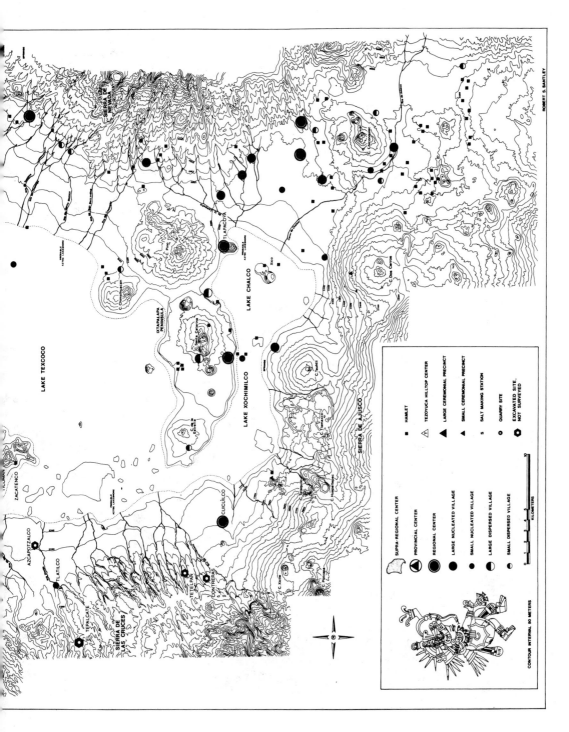

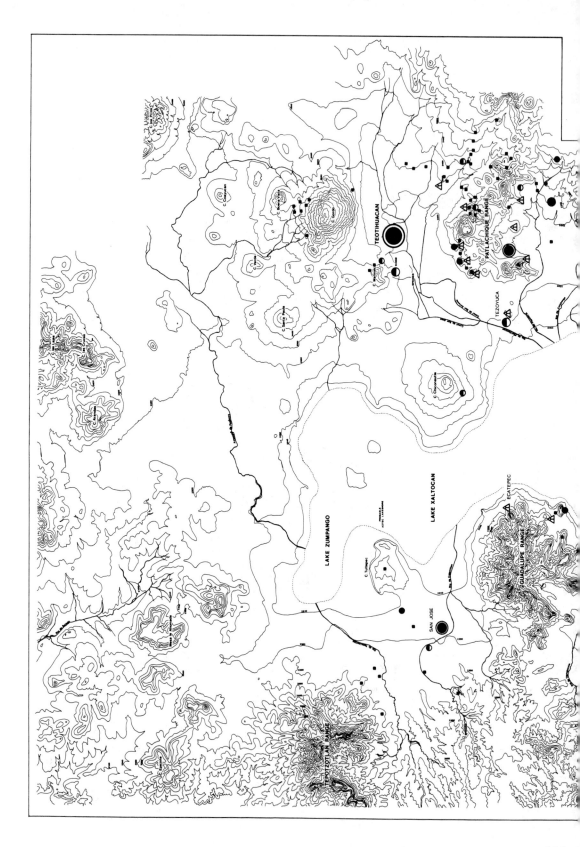

TEOTIHUACAN

TEZOYUCA

PATLACHIQUE RANGE

C. Chiconautla

LAKE ZUMPANGO

LAKE XALTOCAN

C. Tultepec

GUADALUPE RANGE

ECATEPEC

SAN JOSE

TEPOTZOTLAN RANGE

Figure 4.5. Settlements of the Patlachique phase.

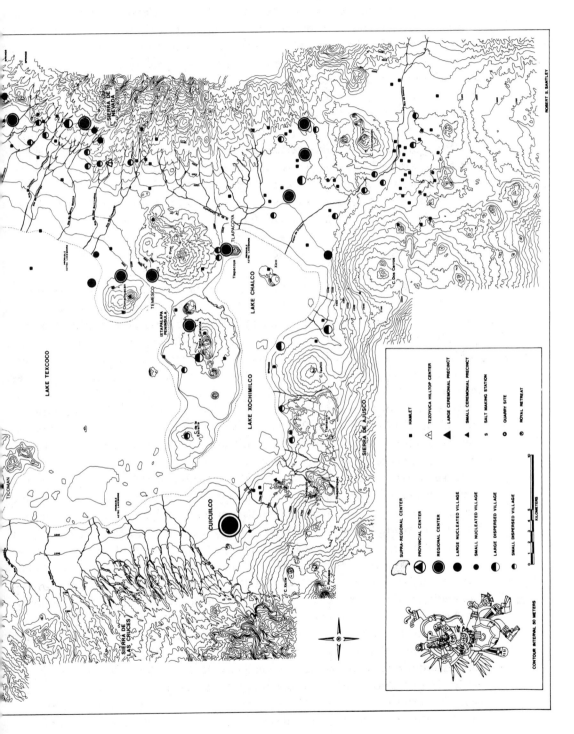

covered by the lava blanket. The largest of these is twenty meters high and eighty meters in diameter.

At the opposite end of the valley from Cuicuilco is the city of Teotihuacan, which has Patlachique sherds over roughly eight square kilometers, thus suggesting a population of probably well over 20,000. Although much of the Patlachique center at Teotihuacan is buried under the cultural debris of later periods, there are suggestions of large-scale Patlachique public architecture. Studies of obsidian at Teotihuacan indicate that by this time specialized obsidian working was already an important activity. Teotihuacan was located at the head of an important group of springs whose flow could have been used for irrigation, a decided asset in the dry northern part of the valley. Evidently, however, as the obsidian analyses suggest, farming was not the sole factor involved in the placement of this regional capital for the northern Valley of Mexico. Yet Teotihuacan's location near prime agricultural land suggests a situation very different from that in the Valley of Oaxaca, where a new regional center at Monte Albán was established with total disregard for local agricultural resources. Note that Cuicuilco, similarly, was located in an alluvial and probably at one time irrigable plain.

Several clusters of Patlachique sites elsewhere in the valley may reflect the coexistence of several sociopolitical units of smaller scale than those focused on Teotihuacan and Cuicuilco. Examples are the clusters in the very southeastern corner of the valley and in the Texcoco region (Fig. 4.5). One of these clusters, along the Ixtapalapa peninsula, is right along what might have been the dividing line between the spheres of influence of the larger capitals. A number of Ticoman sites along this peninsula were abandoned and replaced in Patlachique times with hilltop centers obviously placed with defense in mind. In another respect this peninsula looks as though it was along a contested boundary. Although there had been a general increase in population over the valley as a whole, from 90,000 in Ticoman times to an estimated 175,000 in the Patlachique phase, the population of the Ixtapalapa peninsula suffered a moderate decline. Perhaps mortality was exceptionally high in the buffer zone, or people emigrated to avoid conflict.

In sum, the region in the Patlachique time period of 150 B.C. to A.D. 1 was divided between at least four competing sociopolitical units, which are quite visible on the settlement pattern map as fairly distinct clusters of sites around a larger capital or head town. Between these clusters of settlements were less densely occupied areas, buffer zones that offered little in the way of the central-place services of the head towns, and, perhaps, not much security. In much later times, too – for example, in the Aztec phases – the Valley of Mexico was also divided up among many competing polities. But beyond the fact of disunity there is not much to compare. In Aztec times the whole valley was tightly integrated by great volumes of movement across the political boundaries. People in different polities were economically interdependent. Unoccupied buffer zones, if they existed at all, were so quickly obliterated that they are now largely undetectable archaeologically. In contrast, the scale of a Patlachique person's economic and social connections was most likely the same as the territorial extent of his or her political citizenship. The infrequent connections that might have been made among units – elite interaction and markets in addition to warfare? – are topics that need more research.

The coexistence of two large centers in the Valley of Mexico was short-lived. By the following phase, the Tzacualli, Teotihuacan had emerged as the region's dominant city. Cuicuilco's fall to relative insignificance was evidently due to the eruption of the volcano Xitli, which poured lava over a portion of the city's sustaining zone. Several hundred years later, another eruption completed the job, burying the city completely.

The Tzacualli phase (A.D. 1–100)

Over a large portion of the Valley of Mexico, away from the Teotihuacan subvalley and nearby stretches, Tzacualli pottery cannot be found in significant amounts (Fig. 4.6). This might imply the continuation, for a century or more, of the Patlachique complex in areas far from Teotihuacan, the newly dominant center. Or it might mean a vast movement of people to Teotihuacan. If the latter is true, then the total population outside Teotihuacan was probably only 15,000 or so, suggesting that 80 percent to 90 percent of the valley's total population resided in the capital during the Tzacualli phase. It is unfortunate that we face this serious problem in ceramic chronology at such a critical juncture in the valley's history. This was the time when Teotihuacan first became Mesoamerica's premier city, and the time when a kind of integrated valley-wide regional organization first began to develop. The apparent unification of the entire Valley of Mexico beginning in the Tzacualli phase was a mode that was to persist for some 600 years. It involved a high degree of concentration of power and wealth in the one city.

Three features of Tzacualli Teotihuacan indicate the magnitude of change in the Valley of Mexico capital. The city's population jumped quickly, to an estimated 80,000 or more. Archaeological materials of the period are found over an area of twenty square kilometers. The Pyramid of the Sun, the largest platform mound ever constructed in the Valley of Mexico and one of the ancient world's greatest buildings (at one million cubic meters), was built almost entirely during this phase (Plate 6). The building of a second very large structure, the Pyramid of the Moon (Plate 6), was also begun. During this time the city began to assume the cruciform layout that it maintained during its long history as Mesoamerica's largest city (up to roughly A.D. 750) (Fig. 4.7). In this highly planned configuration, a major north–south avenue, now called the Street of the Dead, divided the city. (The orientation is actually a version of north–south, at 15°30′ east of astronomic north, called "Teotihuacan north.") Arrayed along the north portion of this street in Tzacualli times were some twenty temple complexes, in addition to the Sun and Moon pyramids. It is possible that the major east and west avenues were laid out at this time also (Fig. 4.7). Another very large building, called the Ciudadela, was completed during the subsequent short ceramic phase (Miccaotli), but possibly was initiated during the Tzacualli phase. Its location at the intersection of the main east–west and north–south avenues (grid square N1 × E1 on the Teotihuacan map, Fig. 4.7) indicates this structure's importance in the hierarchy of public buildings in the city. It is a massive structure, covering 16 hectares, with a construction volume (700,000 cubic meters) equal to 70 percent of that of the Pyramid of the Sun. It consists of four elevated platforms enclosing a massive open plaza, that, according to one esti-

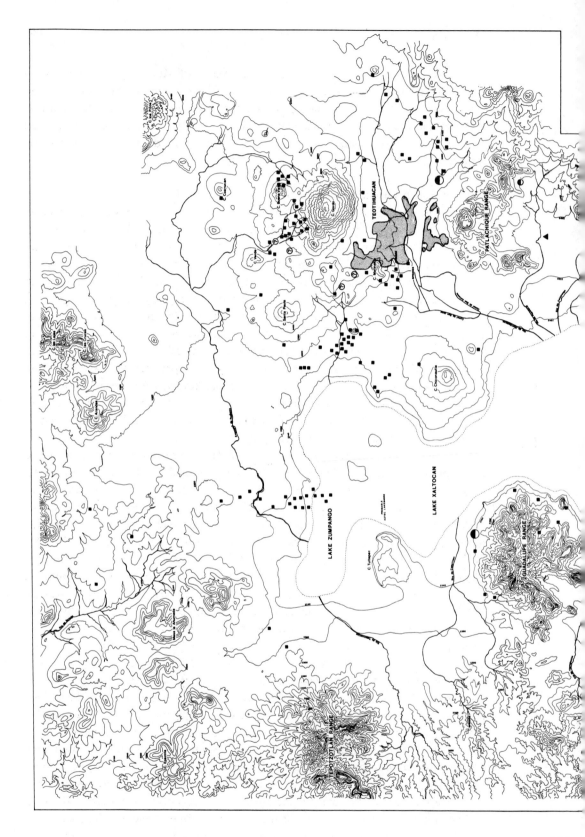

TEOTIHUACAN

PATLACHIQUE RANGE

LAKE XALTOCAN

LAKE ZUMPANGO

C. Tultepec

GUADALUPE RANGE

TEPOTZOTLAN RANGE

124

Figure 4.6. Settlements of the Tzacualli phase.

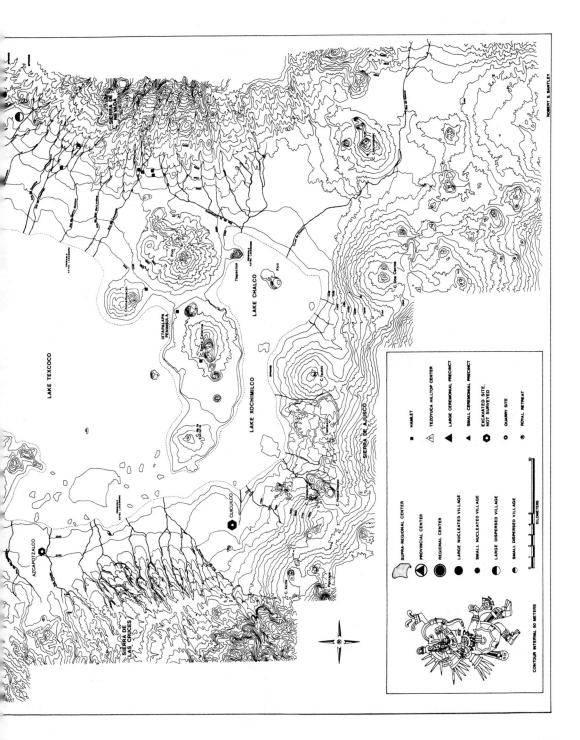

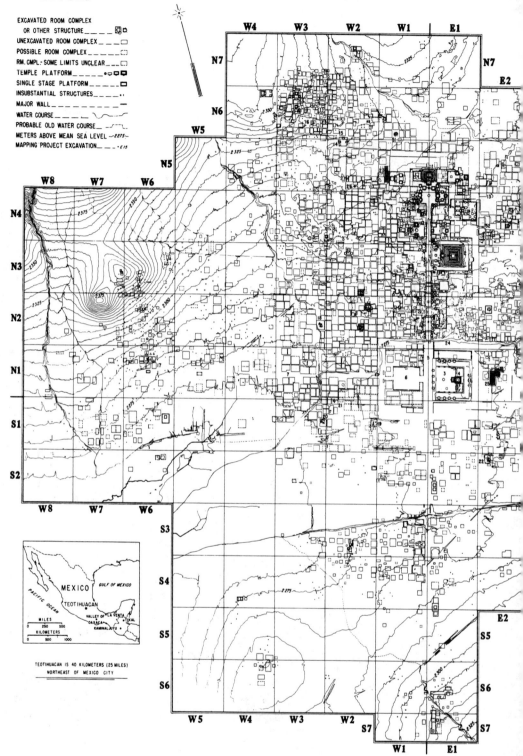

LEGEND

EXCAVATED ROOM COMPLEX
OR OTHER STRUCTURE _ _ _ _ _

UNEXCAVATED ROOM COMPLEX _ _ _

POSSIBLE ROOM COMPLEX _ _ _ _ _ _

RM. CMPL.: SOME LIMITS UNCLEAR _ _ _

TEMPLE PLATFORM _ _ _ _ _

SINGLE STAGE PLATFORM _ _ _ _ _

INSUBSTANTIAL STRUCTURES _ _ _ _ _

MAJOR WALL _ _ _ _ _ _ _ _ _ _

WATER COURSE _ _ _ _ _

PROBABLE OLD WATER COURSE _ _ _

METERS ABOVE MEAN SEA LEVEL _2275_

MAPPING PROJECT EXCAVATION _ _ _ •E15

MEXICO
GULF OF MEXICO
PACIFIC OCEAN
TEOTIHUACAN
VALLEY OF LA VENTA TIKAL
OAXACA
KAMINALJUYU

MILES
0   250   500
KILOMETERS
0   500   1000

TEOTIHUACAN IS 40 KILOMETERS (25 MILES)
NORTHEAST OF MEXICO CITY

Figure 4.7. Map of Teotihuacan. From R. Millon, *Urbanization at Teotihuacan, Mexico*, vol. 1:
The Teotihuacan map, part 1: *Text.* Copyright © 1973 by René Millon.

126

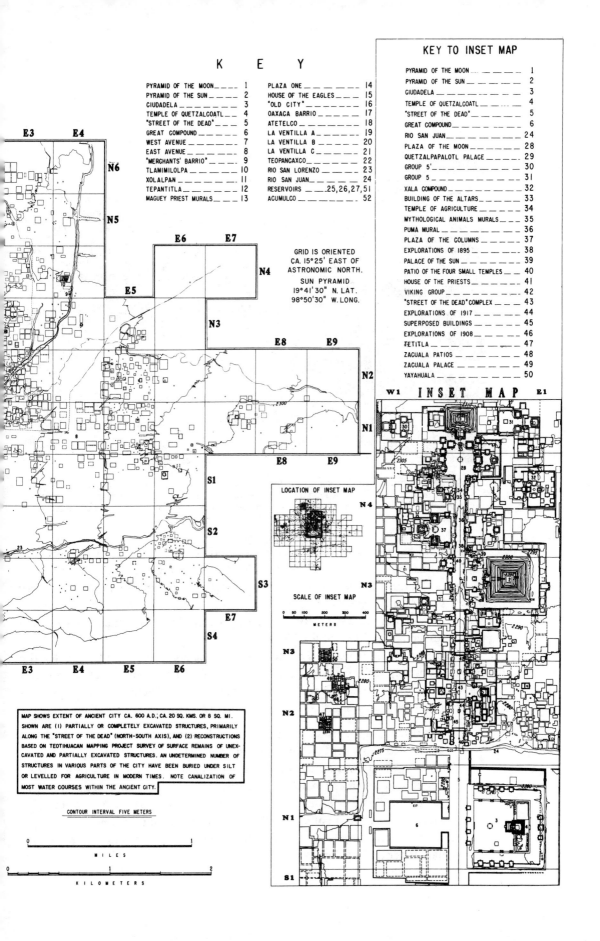

K E Y

PYRAMID OF THE MOON — — — — 1
PYRAMID OF THE SUN — — — — 2
CIUDADELA — — — — — — 3
TEMPLE OF QUETZALCOATL — 4
"STREET OF THE DEAD" — — — 5
GREAT COMPOUND — — — — 6
WEST AVENUE — — — — — 7
EAST AVENUE — — — — — 8
"MERCHANTS' BARRIO" — — 9
TLAMIMILOLPA — — — — — 10
XOLALPAN — — — — — 11
TEPANTITLA — — — — — 12
MAGUEY PRIEST MURALS — 13

PLAZA ONE — — — — — 14
HOUSE OF THE EAGLES — 15
"OLD CITY" — — — — — 16
OAXACA BARRIO — — — — 17
ATETELCO — — — — — 18
LA VENTILLA A — — — — 19
LA VENTILLA B — — — — 20
LA VENTILLA C — — — — 21
TEOPANCAXCO — — — — 22
RIO SAN LORENZO — — — 23
RIO SAN JUAN — — — — 24
RESERVOIRS — — 25,26,27,51
ACUMULCO — — — — — 52

GRID IS ORIENTED
CA. 15°25' EAST OF
ASTRONOMIC NORTH.

SUN PYRAMID
19°41'30" N. LAT.
98°50'30" W. LONG.

KEY TO INSET MAP

PYRAMID OF THE MOON — — — — 1
PYRAMID OF THE SUN — — — — 2
CIUDADELA — — — — — — 3
TEMPLE OF QUETZALCOATL — — 4
"STREET OF THE DEAD" — — — 5
GREAT COMPOUND — — — — — 6
RIO SAN JUAN — — — — — 24
PLAZA OF THE MOON — — — — 28
QUETZALPAPALOTL PALACE — — 29
GROUP 5' — — — — — — 30
GROUP 5 — — — — — — 31
XALA COMPOUND — — — — — 32
BUILDING OF THE ALTARS — — 33
TEMPLE OF AGRICULTURE — — 34
MYTHOLOGICAL ANIMALS MURALS — 35
PUMA MURAL — — — — — 36
PLAZA OF THE COLUMNS — — — 37
EXPLORATIONS OF 1895 — — — 38
PALACE OF THE SUN — — — — 39
PATIO OF THE FOUR SMALL TEMPLES — 40
HOUSE OF THE PRIESTS — — — 41
VIKING GROUP — — — — — 42
"STREET OF THE DEAD" COMPLEX — — 43
EXPLORATIONS OF 1917 — — — 44
SUPERPOSED BUILDINGS — — — 45
EXPLORATIONS OF 1908 — — — 46
TETITLA — — — — — — 47
ZACUALA PATIOS — — — — 48
ZACUALA PALACE — — — — 49
YAYAHUALA — — — — — 50

INSET MAP

LOCATION OF INSET MAP

SCALE OF INSET MAP

0 50 100 200 300 400
METERS

MAP SHOWS EXTENT OF ANCIENT CITY CA. 600 A.D.; CA. 20 SQ. KMS. OR 8 SQ. MI.
SHOWN ARE (I) PARTIALLY OR COMPLETELY EXCAVATED STRUCTURES, PRIMARILY
ALONG THE "STREET OF THE DEAD" (NORTH-SOUTH AXIS), AND (2) RECONSTRUCTIONS
BASED ON TEOTIHUACAN MAPPING PROJECT SURVEY OF SURFACE REMAINS OF UNEX-
CAVATED AND PARTIALLY EXCAVATED STRUCTURES. AN UNDETERMINED NUMBER OF
STRUCTURES IN VARIOUS PARTS OF THE CITY HAVE BEEN BURIED UNDER SILT
OR LEVELLED FOR AGRICULTURE IN MODERN TIMES. NOTE CANALIZATION OF
MOST WATER COURSES WITHIN THE ANCIENT CITY.

CONTOUR INTERVAL FIVE METERS

0   1
M I L E S

0   1   2
K I L O M E T E R S

Plate 6. Teotihuacan, looking south. The Pyramid of the Moon is in the foreground, at the head of the Street of the Dead. The larger Pyramid of the Sun is to the left of this main avenue. From R. Millon, 1973, *Urbanization at Teotihuacan, Mexico,* vol. 1: *The Teotihuacan map.* Copyright © 1973 by René Millon.

mate, could have held 100,000 people gathered for ritual occasions. On the east edge of this plaza is a structure that is the third-largest pyramid mound at Teotihuacan, the Temple of Quetzalcoatl. Apartmentlike compounds on both sides of the Temple of Quetzalcoatl may have been the residences of ruling families or other high-ranking officials, although there are other elaborate residential areas further north along the Street of the Dead.

"Audacious" is the word used by René Millon, the archaeologist who directed the systematic survey of the city's ruins, to describe the monumentality of planning and construction in Tzacualli Teotihuacan. Imagine the motivation behind the construction of the Sun Pyramid: As Millon expressed it, the structure's

> very existence is unmistakable evidence of the vigor and power of the city as a sacred and ritual center. No doubt the population of Teotihuacan could have built the pyramid unaided. But it seems likely that the attraction of the pyramid as a testament to a faith that transcended Teotihuacan itself would have involved others from the Teotihuacan Valley and beyond in its construction. Teotihuacan already must have been exerting the powerful attraction that it continued to have throughout the rest of its history as a great religious center. (Millon 1973:54)

The Middle Horizon (A.D. 200–750)

The long period referred to by the Valley of Mexico archaeologists as the First Intermediate ends with the change from the transitional Miccaotli phase to the ceramic forms of the Tlamimilolpa phases, around A.D. 200. The time span that followed, the Middle Horizon, lasted into the eighth century A.D. Although there were ceramic subdivisions of the Middle Horizon, the long span is itself a meaningful unit, for it was beginning with the Tlamimilolpa phases (and then persisting until the end of the Middle Horizon) that two highly distinctive features of Teotihuacan society developed: an expansion of Teotihuacan political, economic, and stylistic influence well beyond the borders of the Valley of Mexico, and a residential pattern within the city in which most people resided in multifamily walled apartment compounds.

Looking at the Valley of Mexico during the Middle Horizon, one's attention naturally tends to continue to focus on Teotihuacan (Fig. 4.8). Outside the capital relatively little can be found other than villages and hamlets – especially in the valley's southern zone – although there was clearly a resettlement of areas that had probably been largely abandoned during the Tzacualli phase. The only areas of significant rural settlement were located along the north edge of the Guadalupe range and along the north slopes of Cerro Gordo. Rural sites regarded as "provincial centers" were at most no more than one-twentieth the size of Teotihuacan, and their civic-ceremonial architecture does not even approach the scale of Teotihuacan's. Little in the way of surface or excavated evidence for specialized production has been found outside the capital (other than for the sorts of activities that produced things destined for consumption in the capital – for example, limestone mining). The lack of much activity outside the capital – as evidenced by the low population densities, very small centers, and little specialization – shows how underdeveloped was the region's hierarchy of central places. Virtually all of the Valley of Mexico's political, commercial, and religious activity was very clearly concentrated in the one center. Thus the capital was vastly larger, more complex, and wealthier than other communities.

A serious problem with such unicentered "primate" regional systems is that, due to transportation costs, more distant rural families are poorly serviced. They lack choices, because they are by the structure of the system forced to make the one center their only important marketing destination. This produces a marked dichotomy between the affluent, well-serviced families within and near the center, and the poorer, disadvantaged families at more of a remove from the main central place. This rural–urban dichotomy is abundantly evident in the Middle Horizon Valley of Mexico. Within an area of roughly thirty kilometers of the capital (a distance easily traveled in a day), the Middle Horizon population grew vigorously from what it had been in prior periods. The rural population alone grew to 65,000 (up from 18,000 for the Patlachique phase). Generally, surface archaeological deposits are reported to be dense in this area close to the capital. Often sites had the complex residential architecture typical of the center itself. Beyond a thirty-kilometer radius, Middle Horizon population density was actually less than it had been earlier. (The population total was 15,000, as compared with 90,000 for the Ticoman and Patlachique phases.) In addition, artifact assemblages were more meager, and residential architecture was far simpler and less costly.

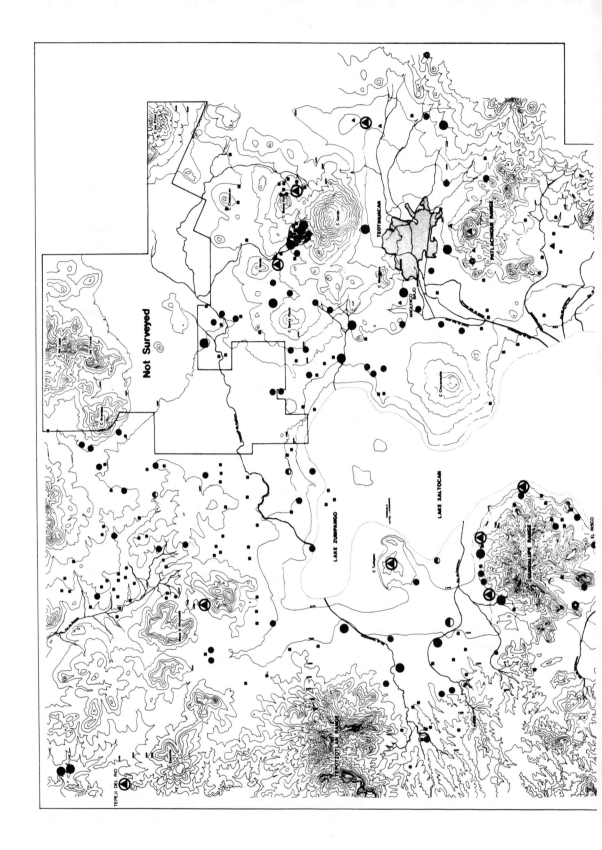

Not Surveyed

TEOTIHUACAN

PATLACHIQUE RANGE

MALINCO
BAJO

LAKE ZUMPANGO

LAKE XALTOCAN

GUADALUPE RANGE

EL RISCO

TEPOTZOTLAN RANGE

TEPEJI DEL RIO

Figure 4.8. Settlements of the Middle Horizon.

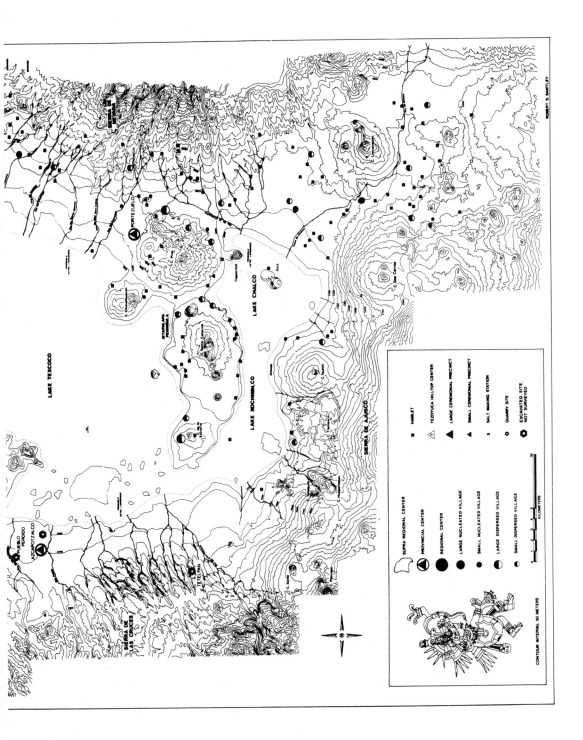

131

In the capital, monumental construction continued at a rapid pace. Miccaotli ceramics have been found in association with impressive buildings along the Street of the Dead, including, as we mentioned, the Ciudadela. Again, in the words of Millon:

> It is difficult to escape the conclusion that by the Miccaotli phase, if not earlier, there was a self-conscious attempt on the part of the architects of Teotihuacan's "Street of the Dead" to overwhelm the viewer by the sheer size and monumentality of conception of both the avenue and of the pyramids and temples along it. . . . For this monumentality and the rituals we may infer were performed in such a setting, must have had a profound effect on many – Teotihuacano and outsider – charging the religion of Teotihuacan with emotional and aesthetic qualities which help to explain at least in part the appeal which it so clearly had for so long a time. (Millon 1973:55)

Several additional changes in Teotihuacan's form – occurring primarily during the Tlamimilolpa phase – brought the city to essentially the form it was to have up to its collapse around A.D. 750 (see Fig. 4.7). One of these involved the construction of the so-called Great Compound, a building that covers an area larger than any other structure in the city (Fig. 4.7, grid square N1 x W1). Evidence excavated (but not yet fully reported) here suggests this was the city's major marketplace. If it was a marketplace, its monumental size gives testimony to the magnitude of Teotihuacan's commercial endeavors. The extensive construction activities of the Tlamimilolpa phase included the beginning of a major commitment to the elaboration of residential architecture. It was during this phase that the distinctive Teotihuacan residential pattern – the walled, multifamily compound that we mentioned before (see Fig. 4.9) – developed. A considerable degree of central planning in the city is evidenced by the fact that all of these compounds are carefully oriented the same way as the major avenues. The compounds themselves, however, would have provided a considerable degree of privacy to their occupants, as they were surrounded by high, heavy walls, and access to them was often through easily watched entryways. The interior arrangement of spaces in the compounds was highly variable, indicating the absence of any standardized cognitive model of ideal house layout in Teotihuacan culture. Most, however, were probably multifamily compounds, housing on average 60–100 persons, with family living spaces arrayed around a common central patio which in some cases contained a temple mound. The common central patios and temples indicate that the residents occupying many of the compounds constituted corporate groups (perhaps centered around agnatically related males) whose members participated in common rituals and coordinated everyday activities. In some cases they engaged in a common craft-production specialty.

Above the level of the residential compounds, speaking in organizational terms, Teotihuacan may have had *barrios* or residential wards that were perhaps in some manner analogous to the site subdivisions noted at Monte Albán. These Teotihuacan *barrios* were groups of contiguous residential compounds oriented around temple complexes larger than those normally found within the individual compounds. In some cases the *barrios* were also units of occupational specialization.

In general the relationships between the residential compounds and the state are poorly understood. Some evidence along this line, however, comes from the analysis

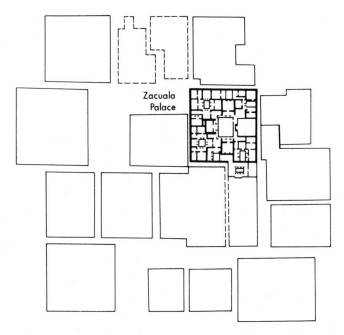

Figure 4.9. A Teotihuacan residential compound called the Zacuala Palace. Note how the large, central patio is surrounded by the smaller family apartments, each consisting of several rooms. Adjacent compounds, not excavated, are shown in outline. Redrawn from Millon, Drewitt, and Cowgill (1973: 57).

of the city's obsidian-working sites. Most of the obsidian production seems to have been carried out in the residential compounds, which were relatively autonomous, or free from state control insofar as their economic specializations were concerned. But a few workshops have been found located adjacent to public buildings. These latter places were not residential, suggesting that obsidian workers may have been required to pay a kind of tax by working in these "state shops" periodically. Does this indicate state control of the obsidian industry? Probably not. The state shops are so small that they couldn't have accounted for any more than a small proportion of the total output. The most satisfying scenario is one in which the state and the obsidian workers maintained a kind of symbiotic relationship, wherein the state managed some aspects of the mining and distribution of the raw materials. In addition, the Teotihuacan state acted to minimize competition that might have faced its obsidian workers by suppressing the growth of other obsidian-working localities in the Valley of Mexico. The manufacture of finished obsidian products was largely confined to the city.

Due to the paucity of analyses of other categories of craft production – for example, ceramics, ground-stone working, and so on – we cannot be sure that this proposed symbiotic pattern was a general one between the state and craft producers. In the course of the settlement pattern surveys outside the city, however, little evidence for craft production has been found suggesting the existence of a broad Teotihuacan monopoly. If the specialized production of durable goods had been a common practice at sites other than Teotihuacan, the surface survey teams undoubtedly would have found and noted it.

The city never grew much beyond the size it attained early in its history, in the Tzacualli phase. It reached an area of 23.5 square kilometers in the Xolalpan phase, and a best-estimate population of 125,000 people (although a value closer to 200,000 might not be too high). The size of the urban area and the city's population size were maintained, for the most part, until Teotihuacan's collapse around A.D. 750, although a slight decline occurred during the last ceramic phase, the Metepec. Many of the city's residents – probably at least 33 percent – were nonagricultural specialists of various kinds. Obsidian production was by far the largest industry, involving some 12 percent of the total population by the Xolalpan phase. Some of this production was destined for export. In fact, it is likely that Teotihuacan was the single most important supplier of obsidian in the central highlands, and perhaps over an even broader area. The city's orientation to obsidian working is reflected in its empire building outside the valley, which seems to have been engaged in partly to extend control of the Mesoamerican obsidian industry. Near one of the most important Guatemalan obsidian sources is the site of Kaminaljuyú (Fig. 1.2) (now largely covered by modern Guatemala City), where buildings were constructed in the unmistakable style of Teotihuacan, and where some elite were buried with offerings of Teotihuacan-style pottery and mosaics. Architectural evidence of Teotihuacan control of a major center was also found at Matacapan, in what is now the state of Veracruz (Fig. 1.2).

Research in places like Kaminaljuyú and Matacapan is helping to clarify the nature of the Teotihuacan presence outside the Valley of Mexico, but the picture is by no means clear as yet. In some places, such as Monte Albán, there is a Teotihuacan presence of sorts, but it is stylistically diffuse and clearly does not indicate conquest. For example, Monte Albán's Main Plaza buildings were built in a modified Teotihuacan style, and some of the fancy IIIA ceramic types were obviously inspired by Teotihuacan styles. Tomb 105 at Monte Albán was decorated with mural paintings that are unmistakably Teotihuacano in fashion. More direct evidence concerning the nature of the relationship between these two cities exists in the form of several carved-stone monuments found on and around Monte Albán's Main Plaza, depicting Teotihuacan emissaries to Monte Albán. And on the western outskirts of Teotihuacan, a "Oaxaca *barrio*," which has Oaxaca-style pottery (made at Teotihuacan) and Oaxaca-style funerary urns (carried from Oaxaca), was discovered by Millon's crew. The role of these "foreigners" at Teotihuacan is unclear. Their quarters were not very close to either the market or the government center; the *barrio's* people were neither very well-off nor dirt poor. No complementary Teotihuacan or other foreign *barrio* was located at Monte Albán.

Recent settlement pattern research in the central highlands is beginning to show the outlines of a Teotihuacan "domain," an area outside the Valley of Mexico but controlled directly from the capital. This area – and the valley itself – is estimated by Millon to have covered some 25,000 square kilometers (10,000 square miles), extending from eastern Morelos to the south, up to Tula in the north, and then eastward into what is now southern Hidalgo and Tlaxcala. The population of this tightly controlled core was perhaps 500,000.

Teotihuacan was thus a city unlike any other in Mesoamerica. Almost all the leading Mesoamerican urban centers were mainly administrative places, but Teotihuacan was that and much more. It was a commercial center, with by far more evidence of craft specialization (some 600 workshops) than any other city. It was the seat of an empire that extended much further beyond the bounds of its own region than any other contemporary imperial enterprise Mesoamerica. In all likelihood its economic and political uniqueness was reinforced by its role as Mesoamerica's leading center of sacred power.

The collapse of Teotihuacan

After A.D. 600, Teotihuacan influence was no longer present at Kaminaljuyú. At Teotihuacan itself, though, the decline did not occur that early, although some changes are evident. There was an increase in the frequency of the portrayal of armed figures in Teotihuacan murals toward the end of the Middle Horizon. Like Monte Albán's Main Plaza in IIIB, architectural modifications to the Ciudadela made it more closed and defensible just prior to the city's collapse. During the Metepec phase, the city's population declined slightly. Economically, Teotihuacan continued to be active up to about A.D. 750.

After the Metepec phase, though, collapse must have been rapid. The population of the Coyotlatelco phase city was only about 30,000, representing a loss of perhaps as much as 80 percent of its prior population. Substantial evidence exists for major fires, destruction of buildings and religious effigies, and even slaughtered persons, particularly among the civic-ceremonial buildings along the Street of the Dead. It is not known whether this destructive frenzy was carried out by invaders or by irate Teotihuacanos perhaps motivated by an internal schism or by a desire to overthrow the state and its cults. The fact that the subsequent occupants of the city carefully avoided reusing the major civic-ceremonial buildings does suggest an internal revolt by groups who wanted to disassociate themselves from these buildings and their political and religious symbols. Whoever was responsible carried out the task in the form of a giant ritual of political destruction. Millon writes:

> Our evidence shows that the fires that destroyed the city center were deliberately and systematically set. The destruction was ritual destruction and cannot be understood if thought of purely in terms of pillaging, looting, and burning. . . . To destroy Teotihuacan politically was itself a monumental undertaking, in some ways matching the energy that went into its building. Destroying it politically apparently required destroying it so thoroughly ritually, that it never again rose to a position of political preeminence. Those who burned it succeeded in their objective. (Millon 1981:70–2)

The Coyotlatelco phase (A.D. 750–950)

For a time after the collapse of Teotihuacan, the Valley of Mexico was not the dominant center of political or economic power in the central highlands and beyond. After Teotihuacan's collapse, no single valley community developed to take up its domineer-

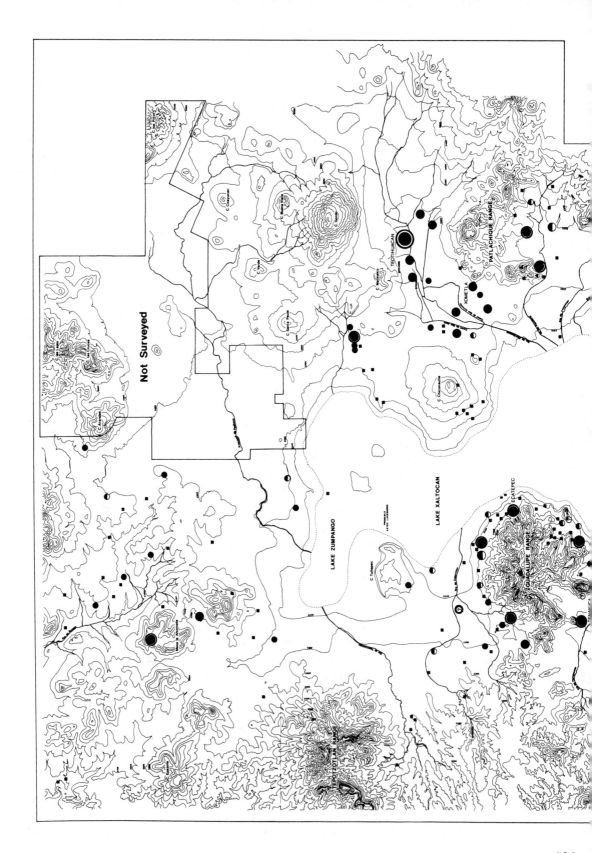

Figure 4.10. Settlements of the Coyotlatelco phase.

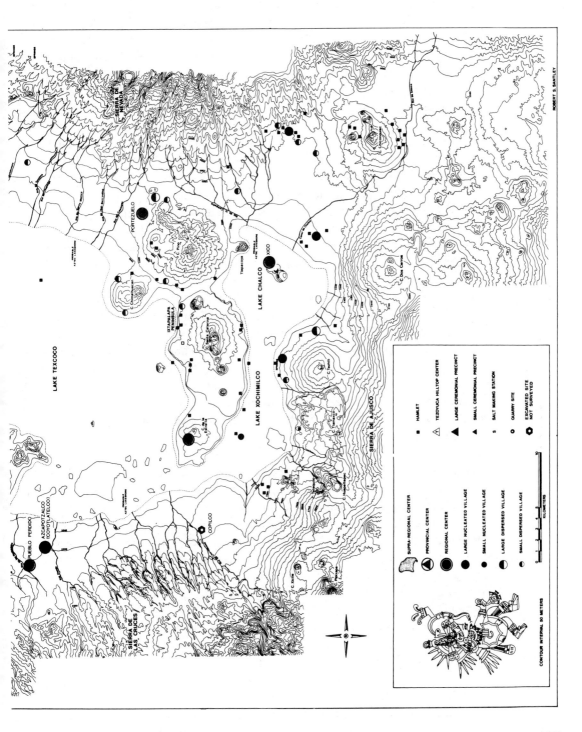

ing role (Fig. 4.10). New centers that evidently led large regions gained ascendance just outside the valley, especially at Xochicalco and Cholula (Fig. 1.2). Whether the valley itself was under the control of one or both of these centers is not known. Most probably the Coyotlatelco phase was one of political fragmentation in the Valley of Mexico, with no overarching political authority to integrate the whole region. Instead, the valley had perhaps six independent, warring political units in Coyotlatelco times, each consisting of clusters of sites ranging in total population from 5,000 to over 60,000 people. Each cluster focused on one or more central places with civic-ceremonial architecture. The clusters can be easily discerned in Fig. 4.10. They are referred to as the clusters of the Teotihuacan Valley, Guadalupe, Portezuelo (southern Texcoco region), Cerro de la Estrella (Ixtapalapa peninsula), Mesa la Ahumada, and Xico (in and around the east end of Lake Chalco). None of the centers had mounded buildings that even approached the scale of antecedent Teotihuacan. Interestingly, the largest of the capitals was Teotihuacan (with 30,000 people).

The 200 years of the Coyotlatelco phase were times of intense warfare among these six local political units. A number of the centers that dominated the clusters are located on defensible hilltop positions. Large, unpopulated areas between the clusters can be seen in the settlement pattern map (Fig. 4.10). These areas had perfectly fine land, occupied and farmed in prior periods, but they no doubt were insecure "shatter zones" between competing political entities in Coyotlatelco times.

The population transitions that occurred after Teotihuacan's fall give some clues as to the influence the venerable city had exerted in the Middle Horizon. After A.D. 750, the population of the Teotihuacan Valley declined due to the losses at the center. The population of those areas nearby that had been closely tied into Teotihuacan's own economic system also declined after the collapse. Elsewhere in the Valley of Mexico, however, populations grew. The result was some loss of population from the Middle Horizon to the Coyotlatelco phase (Fig. 4.11) in the valley as a whole, but the decline was not as dramatic as one might expect given the tremendous declines at the capital.

The parallel with the Valley of Oaxaca is striking. In both regions, at almost the same time, large-scale states that had integrated whole behavioral regions broke up; their capitals lost 75 percent of their inhabitants and became simply other (though more venerated) centers among a number of equals; their personnel founded new, flourishing, and independent realms in what had been the state's home provinces. These changes in both areas happened rather quickly – the key actors probably knew just what they were doing, and they undoubtedly saw the consequences. That such profound changes occurred in both areas in the same way at the same time certainly indicates that the actors were performing in a drama of Mesoamerican, not just regional, scale. We will have more to say about this transition in the concluding chapter. For now, the subject is broached, and we return to our history of changes in the Valley of Mexico settlement pattern.

The Mazapan phase (A.D. 950–1200)

To a much greater degree than prior periods, the Mazapan phase is known for both its archaeology and its native history. Ethnohistorians can begin to decipher bits

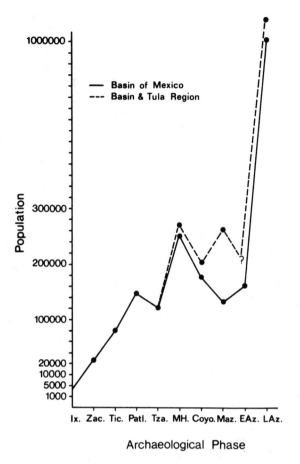

Figure 4.11. The archaeologically estimated populations for the Valley of Mexico from the Early Horizon to the Spanish conquest. Modified from Sanders, Parsons, and Santley (1979: fig. 6.1).

and pieces of a rich and complex, but often obscure, aboriginal history. Even this late in the sequence, however, historically related events have been so greatly reinterpreted or drawn out of proportion that, as Nigel Davies, the author of the most recent synthesis of this period's history, notes, interpretation is "tortuous and tiring." The dominant theme in all of these histories is a political capital – Tula – and its residents, the legendary Toltecs. Virtually everyone interested in this period now agrees that the legendary Tula is the archaeological site of Tula, Hidalgo, located just north of the Valley of Mexico proper (Fig. 1.2).

In several respects, the ascendancy of Tula to political dominance in the Valley of Mexico (and over a broader area, though the limits of its empire are not precisely known) represented the reassertion of a Teotihuacan-like regional system. Tula's rise to power coincided with the abandonment of the independent Coyotlatelco capitals and a return to a settlement pattern nearly identical to that of the Middle Horizon, except that the focus was shifted northward (Fig. 4.12). Over much of the valley, villages and hamlets were virtually the only kinds of communities. Especially in the southern valley, few public buildings were constructed or used. And, in the south,

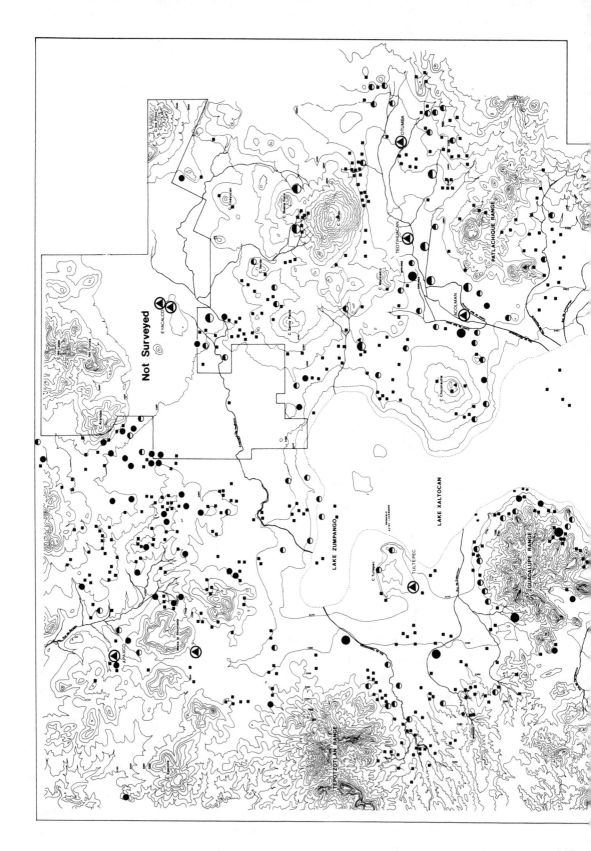

Figure 4.12. Settlements of the Mazapan phase.

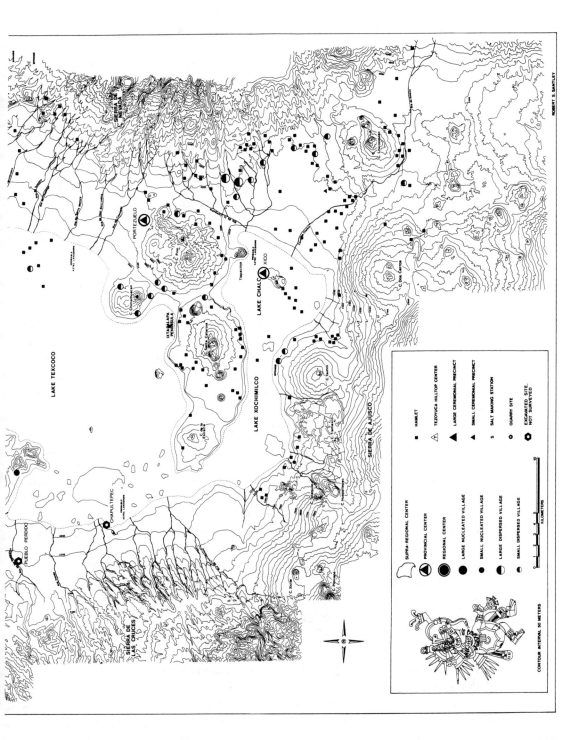

141

the Mazapan phase was again a time of reduced population levels. Surveys around Tula show a different pattern. Within a radius of about twenty kilometers of the site, Mazapan phase settlement was dense. Many of the sites had elaborate residential architecture not found at all farther south in the valley. All of this very strongly argues for the reimposition of the policies of extreme nucleation of political and economic functions in one overbearing primate center. As in the Middle Horizon, a sharp rural–urban dichotomy was a basic, conditioning feature of the Valley of Mexico cultural reality.

In another respect the Tula state seems to have followed policies very much like those of its Teotihuacan predecessors. Recall that a Maya site – Kaminaljuyú – had been partially rebuilt in the style of Teotihuacan. In Mazapan times, a similar east–west axis was created, this time involving the Maya site of Chichén Itzá in the Yucatan peninsula (Fig. 1.2). Tula and Chichén Itzá rose to macroregional political prominence together and at the same time. A number of writers have commented on the similarity in architecture between the two cities. Likewise, architectural parallels can be drawn between Tula and a site in lowland Veracruz called El Tajín (Fig. 1.2). The Teotihuacan/Kaminaljuyú/Matacapan connection we discussed earlier seems to have been repeated by the Tula/Chichén Itzá/El Tajín trio.

So much for the Tula and Teotihuacan parallels. The Mazapan phase was not a simple reconstitution of the Teotihuacan pattern. Tula never equaled Teotihuacan in scale or architectural grandeur. During its period of maximum population, Tula extended over twelve square kilometers (compared with over twenty for Teotihuacan), and had a population variously estimated from 40,000 to 60,000. Although there is evidence of city planning, there are no features that match the great avenues that defined the quadripartite city plan of Teotihuacan. The major cluster of public buildings (Fig. 4.13) was quite small by comparison with Teotihuacan's massive construction projects along the Street of the Dead.

Perhaps these differences can be attributed in part to the fact that Tula was a major center for not much more than a century or two at most. Evidently the degree of regional control that Teotihuacan enjoyed and exploited over some 700 years could not be maintained in Tula's time, even for 200 years. But remember, on the other hand, that Teotihuacan had achieved its ponderous size and already had its reputation for architectural grandeur very early in its history as a regional capital. If Tula had simply been cycling back to an earlier evolutionary form, it too should have attained Teotihuacan-like proportions within the time span of the Mazapan phase – but it did not. The Postclassic world was a context more complex and more intricately and subtly integrated than the Mesoamerica of the first states and their primate capitals of more than a millennium earlier. These Mesoamerica-wide trends are a subject we wish to treat more fully when, in the concluding chapter, we discuss the transition from the Classic to the Postclassic.

The Early Aztec phase (A.D. 1200–1400) and the Late Aztec phase (A.D. 1400–1520)

By the convention of repeated use, the term "Aztec" has come to mean, in a loose sense, the various Nahuatl-speaking people Cortés and his soldiers encountered in the Valley of Mexico in the sixteenth century. The people themselves thought more

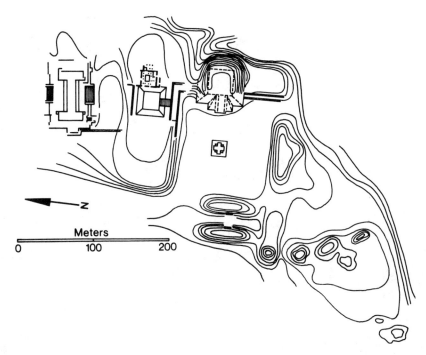

Figure 4.13. Central civic-ceremonial center of Tula. Modified from Marquina (1964: Lámina 45).

in terms of the plethora of distinct ethnic groups (for example, Chalca, Tepaneca, Acolhua) that occupied the region, none of whom referred to themselves as "Aztec." Although the people cognized local, ethnic distinctions, they also recognized that all of the people of the region participated in a regional social system in the valley and even beyond. At least by Late Aztec times, common ritual, diplomatic, and military behavior, and, important for the nonelite masses, an integrated market system, provided integration into a wider, "Aztec" society.

Tula's hegemony was brief; its collapse as a political power was thorough but is not at all well understood. Historians are faced with a welter of conflicting, superficial accounts of events and personalities, but the root causes of the center's perdurable political and economic problems and strategies remain unknown. Archaeologically, the Early Aztec phase is similar to the immediately post-Teotihuacan Coyotlatelco phase in that there was a series of local centers, each dominating a small part of the valley and each separated from its neighboring polities by a frontier of contested, not well-inhabited borderland (Fig. 4.14). By Late Aztec times, these centers still existed, but new ones had been established, most notably at Tenochtitlan-Tlatelolco and Texcoco, and the contested borderlands were being repopulated (Fig. 4.15). Politically, the Late Aztec phase was more unified and consolidated than the Early Aztec. The Culhua Mexica of Tenochtitlan, along with their allies in Texcoco and Tacuba (Tlacopan in Fig. 4.15), worked to incorporate the various local systems into one large unit focused primarily, as it turned out, on Tenochtitlan. This renewed round of political integration in the valley, however, was unlike the prior periods under Teotihuacan and Tula. Local centers were incorporated

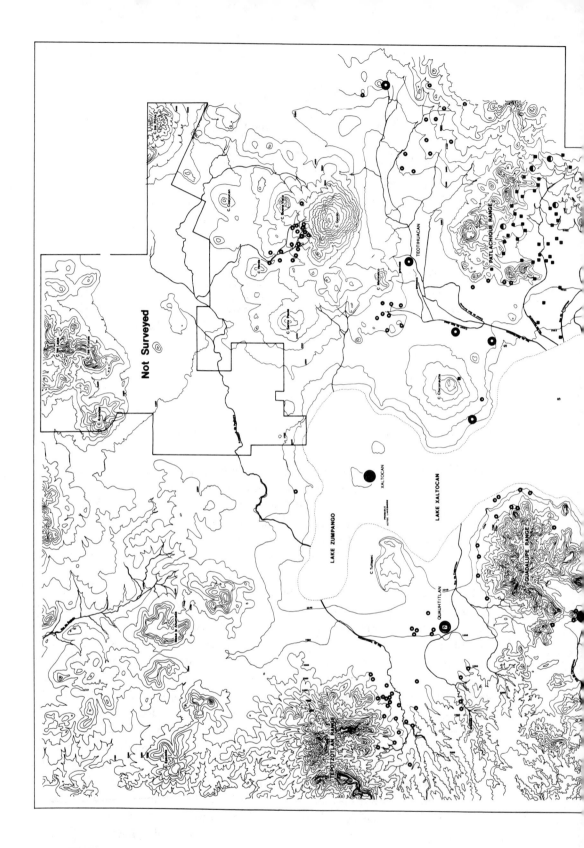

Not Surveyed

Figure 4.14. Settlements of the Early Aztec phase.

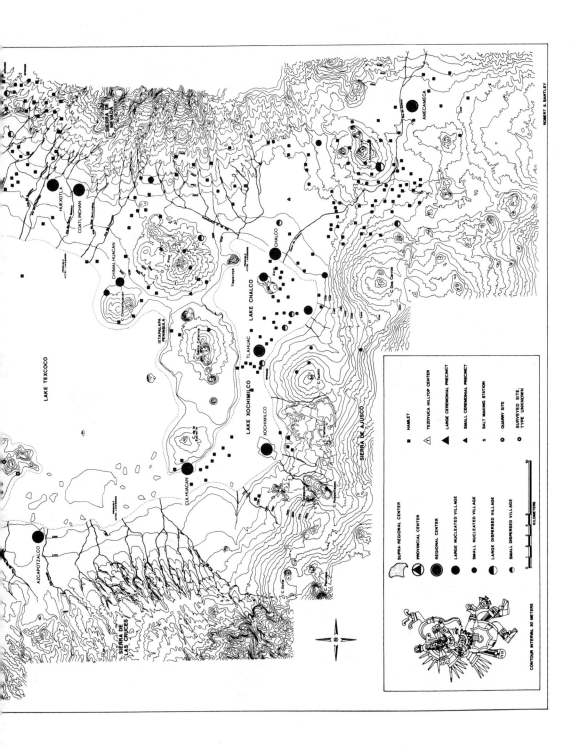

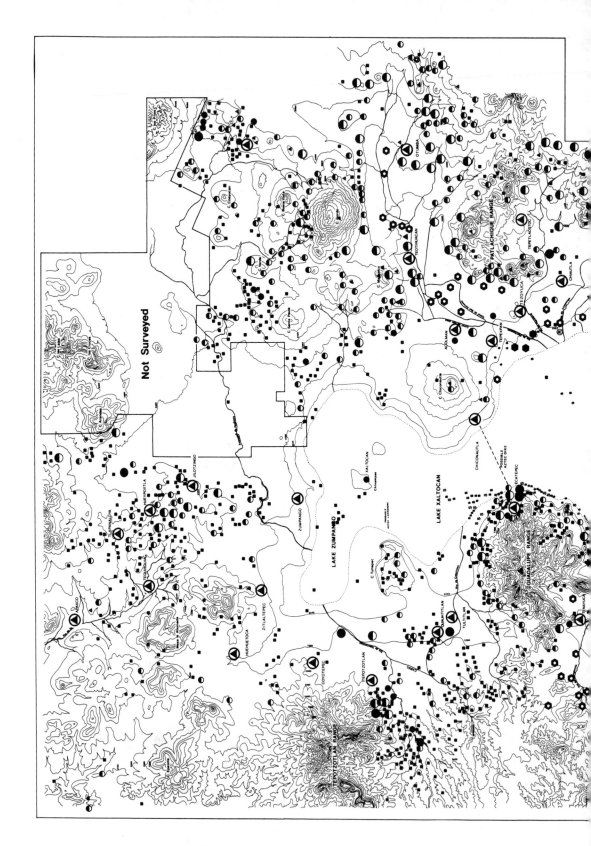

Not Surveyed

Figure 4.15. Settlements of the Late Aztec phase.

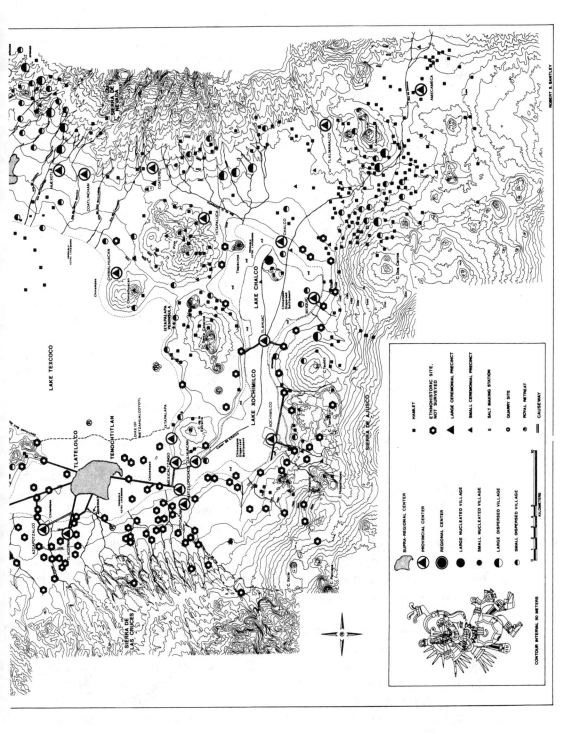

into an expanding unitary structure, but were not always in the process vastly restructured or eliminated. Local centers not only persisted during the Late Aztec phase, but also grew substantially in population (with few exceptions), and local feelings of ethnic identity remained strong. Some of these local groups claimed legitimate genealogical ties back to Tula, whereas others were in-migrating "Chichimecs" or members of other non-Toltec groups.

According to the histories, the Chichimecs had their origins along Mesoamerica's barren northern frontier, and they were supposed to have brought with them some of the ruggedness and backwardness of a peripheral, relatively uncivilized people. They rapidly adopted the behavior and technology of the valley's more urbanized dwellers, however, and soon rose to political prominence. The story of one of these immigrant groups – the Mexica – is one of the greatest tales of epic progress from rags to riches ever recorded. The Mexica were originally considered to be so undesirable that they were forced to live on a series of low, swampy, bug-ridden islands in the middle of brackish Lake Texcoco. They survived by exploiting the meager lacustrine resources, by selling themselves as mercenaries, and by establishing a marketplace that gradually grew in importance. Through cunning and generally shabby behavior they eventually established themselves and their island city of Tenochtitlan as a force to be reckoned with. The city was an independent political entity within about a century after its foundation in 1325. From 1427 until the Spanish conquest in 1519, Tenochtitlan carried out an aggressive policy of political expansion. As it turned out, their location in the lake, although marginal with respect to agricultural resources on the mainland, eventually proved to be a blessing. Not only could the shallow lakes be developed for *chinampa* cultivation, but the location, central to the valley as a whole, gave economic advantages. Too, transportation into and out of the city was easy because goods and people could move cheaply by boat.

Early in their history the Mexica split into two often antagonistic groups. The Tlatelolca tied themselves to a western Valley of Mexico group called the Tepanecs, and formed a twin city, Tlatelolco, just a stone's throw to the north of Tenochtitlan. It was Tlatelolco, not Tenochtitlan – a matter of some jealousy – that became the preeminent commercial city, holding the valley's major marketplace. The Tenochca, on the other hand, married into a Toltec lineage from Culhuacan, and through political intrigues and military exploits made the city of Tenochtitlan into the valley's political capital. They are sometimes referred to as the Culhua Mexica, and they allied with Texcoco and Tacuba, conquered the Valley of Mexico, and went on to establish an empire that extended from the coast of what is now northern Veracruz to Chiapas and Guatemala (Fig. 4.16).

A comparison of Tenochtitlan-Tlatelolco and Teotihuacan
The following brief description of the Aztec capital of Tenochtitlan-Tlatelolco is offered in the form of a comparison with Teotihuacan, and with Tula where the data permit, in order to illustrate some features of long-term change in the Valley of Mexico. Information on the size, layout, and organization of Tenochtitlan-Tlatelolco comes from several sources, especially early Spanish descriptions and maps, and from

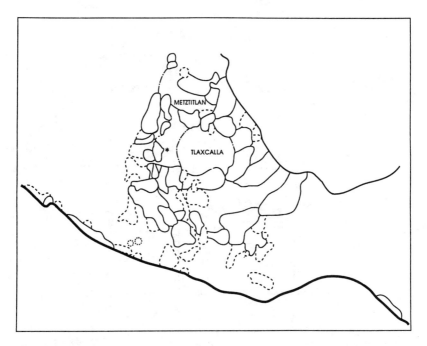

Figure 4.16. Extent of the Aztec empire. Solid lines demarcate major provinces conquered for tribute collection. Dashed lines indicate strategic provinces along contested borderlands, conquered for military value. The asterisk is Tenochtitlan-Tlatelolco. Tlaxcalla and Metztitlan are major unconquered domains. From Berdan et al. (in press).

research among the early colonial archives. Very little can be derived from survey or excavation, as the city now lies buried under Mexico City. A few glimpses have come to light as a result of the construction of tunnels for a new subway system, and excavations have recently been carried out at the main pyramid mound, the "Templo Mayor."

A major difference between the Aztec capital and Teotihuacan is that the former was, as we mentioned, a dual city (Fig. 4.17). The Tenochca conquered Tlatelolco after a brutal civil war in 1473, but that catastrophe never really erased the dual focuses – political and commercial – of the community, or the mutual enmity felt by the two groups. As there were really two cities, there were two clusters of civic-ceremonial structures. Associated with Tlatelolco's was the major marketplace (although by no means the only marketplace) in the Valley of Mexico, which, according to one Spanish observer, serviced 25,000 to 50,000 people per day. Tenochtitlan's market plaza was smaller; but benefiting the center of decision making for a wide-ranging empire, its cluster of civic-ceremonial buildings was the most impressive in the valley. Interestingly, though, in spite of the fact that Tenochtitlan's population (at between 150,000 and 200,000) was probably larger than Classic Period Teotihuacan's, the Aztec capital's major temple pyramid was smaller, measuring roughly 74 meters along each side of the base, with a volume of close to 240,000 cubic meters. Teotihuacan's Pyramid of the Sun measured over 200 meters and had a volume of close to 1,000,000 cubic meters. This may mean two

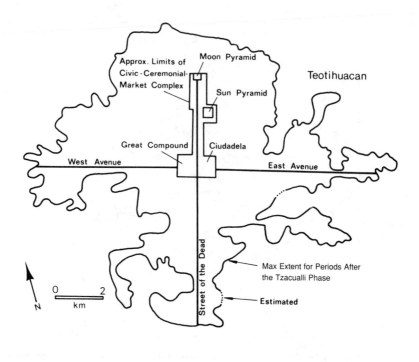

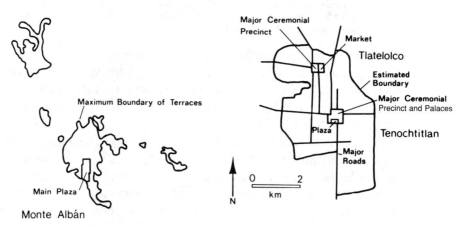

Figure 4.17. The cities of Teotihuacan, Monte Albán, and Tenochtitlan-Tlatelolco, drawn to the same scale. From R. Millon (1973: Map 1), Blanton (1978: fig. 1.3), and Calnek (1972: fig. 3).

things: (1) Religious ritual was less important as an integrating factor in the Aztec center than it had been at Teotihuacan, and (2) the Tenochcan rulers had less labor available for major public construction projects. We feel that both of these factors may have been operative. The evidence seems to favor a more secular orientation in the Late Aztec capital, as compared with Teotihuacan's strong religious orientation. More energy was expended on the construction of rulers' palaces in Tenochtitlan than had been expended in the Middle Horizon city. Teotihuacan's Ciudadela is a massive structure that combined high-level governmental and religious functions, but its residential area is comparatively small. Also, there is no evidence that it or any other elite residential compound at Teotihuacan had been the residence of any particular ruling family or dynasty. The Tenochcan rulers' palaces were large and elaborate to say the least, and each new ruler built himself a new palace. As Edward Calnek puts it:

> No palace thus far identified at Teotihuacan approaches the size and independence of Motecuhzoma's [the last ruler] palace, as described by early chroniclers as Cortés. . . . This structure occupied an area of about 2.4 ha – approximately double the combined areas of three closely related residential complexes adjoining the Temple of Quetzalcoatl in the Ciudadela of Teotihuacan (R. Millon, personal communication). (Calnek 1976:295)

These observations support our first hypothesis – that by Aztec times the state was more secular in its orientation. Our second hypothesis can be supported if we compare the central civic-ceremonial complexes of the two cities. Teotihuacan's cluster of temples, palaces, and plazas is not equaled anywhere in Mesoamerica. Excluding from consideration the massive Great Compound (market), the rest of the complex of buildings stretching from the Ciudadela northward along the Street of the Dead, and including the massive Sun and Moon pyramids, covered an area of roughly seventy-seven hectares. Tenochtitlan's central cluster, including the various rulers' palaces, covered only about half that area, at close to thirty-six hectares (Fig. 4.17). (Tula's main complex, in comparison, covered a paltry eleven hectares.) These differences are especially striking when we consider that the total population of the valley during the Middle Horizon was only around 250,000, whereas the Late Aztec population was probably four times that figure. So, per capita, the Tenochcan public buildings, manifesting the power of the pinnacle of the state hierarchy, were even less impressive than Teotihuacan's. Evidently the elite at Teotihuacan had vastly more labor at their disposal for such construction projects (even in the first couple of centuries of its climb to power, when the Pyramid of the Sun was built) than did the rulers of the Aztec empire. Below we consider the implications of this for understanding long-term change, but now we conclude tentatively that during the Late Aztec phase the valley's regional system had less centralized control than during the Middle Horizon.

Another difference between the Middle Horizon and Late Aztec capitals is instructive of how groups of households were interrelated. From the Tlamimilolpa phase onward, the walled apartment compound was the basic residential unit at Teotihuacan. No such structures existed in Tenochtitlan (or in Tula). According to reconstructions of residences in the Aztec center, houses were small, and each was typically inhabited only by a married couple and perhaps some of their married children. According to Edward Calnek:

> The Tenochtitlan household compound most closely resembles the individual apartments within the Teotihuacan apartment compounds in scale . . . but it was an architecturally free unit, in the sense that each compound at Tenoch-

titlan enjoyed direct access to streets and canals, and was related to neighboring sites mainly by physical juxtaposition rather than by assimilation to large unitary structures of the Teotihuacan type. This, in turn, may reflect a greater freedom in the organization of production activities and interpersonal or interhousehold bonds, as well as greater possibilities for upward mobility based on wealth or personal achievement than was characteristic of Teotihuacan society. Even commoners could achieve high rank through military service or the acquisition of great personal wealth. . . . The architectural segregation of relatively small residential compounds permitted the public display of status markers – most commonly architectural ornamentation – to distinguish individual compounds from even their immediate neighbors. (Calnek 1976:300)

This is what one would expect from a comparison of two societies if one (the Aztec) was less vertically integrated, and, as we will argue below, had a less administered economy in which there was more possibility for freedom of choice in economic transactions. The Teotihuacan residential pattern, which can be called the introvert pattern, is a common product of the growth of powerful, highly centralized governments. In such cases, the state exercises its power to prevent the growth of merchant, proprietary, or other independent forms of leadership. Thus the tendency, in order to avoid the wrath of the state, is "to hide luxurious courtyards and dwellings behind a noncommittal facade" (Wittfogel 1957:86). Recall that in the IIIB phase in the Valley of Oaxaca, a period of highly centralized control, residential architecture at Monte Albán became more formalized and introverted (although not to the degree seen at Teotihuacan). Extrovert architecture, such as that in Tenochtitlan-Tlatelolco, is associated with weaker governments, but stronger nongovernmental institutions.

One other statistic can be brought to bear in our comparison to help evaluate the extent to which regional central-place functions were centered in the respective capitals. As we mentioned, during the Middle Horizon, some 50 to 60 percent of the total population of the valley resided in the capital. By Late Aztec times, only 20 percent of the total resided in the main center itself, although the total valley population had grown steeply. This reflects the fact that although Tenochtitlan and its allies exerted their political muscle over the entire valley, local centers persisted and most retained considerable numbers of people along with variable mixes of local governmental, religious, and commercial functions. The Late Aztec phase was, in short, less of a "primate" system than was the one headed by Teotihuacan.

A multicentric marketing system of the sort that was in operation in the Valley of Mexico during the Late Aztec phase was advantageous in that more producers, merchants, and consumers had access to conveniently located buying and selling points, and that people had more marketing choices. This limited the extent to which monopoly pricing could occur, assuring the marketing participants of competitive prices and high-quality goods. Thus, the Aztec system, more than any previous valley economy, approached something like "full commercialization." In Aztec

times no vast differential in wealth between urban and rural settings developed –
unlike what occurred in the highly primate systems. To date the Valley of Mexico
researchers have not published the data that would make possible a more quantitative
assessment of the degree of commercialization in the Teotihuacan system versus the
Late Aztec system. One of us (Blanton), however, who has done a Valley of Mexico
survey is impressed with the generally high quality of the Late Aztec phase ceramics
(which, like the Monte Albán V assemblages, are generally well burnished and
fired), and with the extent to which Late Aztec assemblages, even on small rural
sites, contain a good representation of the decorated types. Still, this point needs
testing through statistical analyses of the surface ceramic collections from all over
the valley.

Regional organization in the Late Aztec phase was unique for the Valley of
Mexico – nothing like it, evidently, had ever developed during the thirty centuries
since the valley was first occupied by village-dwelling farmers. This unique organization resulted from a delicate balance of unified regional control, exercised such
that local systems were not totally destroyed by the system's political center.

Evidently this pattern contained certain possibilities for change that had never
before been allowed free reign. The two major manifestations of change were massive population growth and agricultural development. Populations reached levels
higher than in any prior phase, by a substantial margin. The Late Aztec total, roughly
1,000,000, is four times the highest number reached in prior times (Fig. 4.11), and is
a figure that was not equaled by the valley population after Late Aztec times until
this century. Agricultural production developed and intensified over the valley as a
whole more fully and dramatically than during any other prehispanic phase. This
involved the employment of a complex and interrelated variety of techniques, ranging from extensive terracing of slopes for soil and water control to large-scale irrigation enterprises. According to several experts,

> the massive buildup of [Late Aztec] occupation on the low-lying lakeshore
> alluvium and lakebed indicates a transformation of this previously marginal
> swampy terrain to highly productive agricultural land by means of large-scale
> drainage and flood control technology. Particularly significant was the expan-
> sion of agricultural activity in the Zumpango, Cuautitlan, Texcoco, and
> Chalco plains. The [ruler] of Cuautitlan actually redirected the Rio Cuautitlan
> northward to irrigate lands west and north of that center and to regulate
> flooding in low-lying areas. . . . The massive channels that collect and direct
> the piedmont floodwaters east of Lake Texcoco almost certainly date to
> [Late Aztec]. Drainage agriculture reached its maximal expression, of course,
> in the conversion of the vast swamps of Lake Chalco-Xochimilco to culti-
> vated fields – the famous *chinampas*. This was truly a monumental hydraulic
> enterprise, involving the construction of massive drainage ditches, the imple-
> mentation of an elaborate flood control apparatus of dikes and sluice gates
> that closely regulated water levels over a wide area, and a huge outlay of
> labor in the construction of fields by piling up masses of soil and vegetation.

> We estimate that some 10,000 ha of chinampa fields were thus created in the
> southern [valley], and there may have been a few thousand additional
> hectares in the walled-off southwestern corner of Lake Texcoco, around
> Xaltocan in the north and Chimalhuacan on the southeast shore of Lake
> Texcoco. . . . The production of the agricultural land newly created during
> the [Late Aztec] by means of massive hydraulic engineering in swampy land
> and lakeshore areas would probably have been sufficient to supply at least a
> half million people with basic food staples. (Sanders, Parsons, and Santley
> 1979:176–7)

Nothing could equal the contrast between these advances in the Late Aztec and
the situation in the Middle Horizon, when the foremost manifestation of massed
labor expenditure was the temple-pyramid building in the region's capital. During
Late Aztec times far less energy was expended in the glorification of the capital and
far more in agricultural development projects, some at the bidding of Tenochtitlan,
but many underwritten and coordinated by local-level, semiautonomous governmental units.

Summary of population trends in the Valley of Mexico

The population of the valley grew from only a few thousand people in the Early
Horizon to roughly one million by the end of the Late Aztec. This is an impressive
expansion in size, but actually represents only a modest growth rate considering
that the time span involved was roughly thirty centuries. This increase can be accounted
for by only nine doublings of the base population, the equivalent of a doubling every
three centuries or so. (The modern world's growth rate amounts to a doubling of
the population total every seventy to eighty years.) Of course the valley's growth
trend was neither uniform over time nor spatially uniform. Only certain time periods (or subareas) contained the peculiar mix of social, political, and economic conditions that favored sustained growth in numbers through increased family sizes,
reduced mortality, or immigration.

The earliest conjuncture of such conditions took place in the southern valley
from the Early Horizon through the Ticoman phase. Growth in that area accounted
for most of the valley's total population increase (from a few thousand up to 75,000),
as the northern reaches tended to remain fairly stationary. The explanation for this
intraregional differential may have to do with the fact of higher rainfall in the south,
but a more satisfying explanation is that the southern valley was favorably situated
near the rest of a developing Mesoamerican system that included the Olmec area,
Morelos, and Oaxaca.

In the southern valley after Ticoman, population first reached a plateau, then was
reduced during the Middle Horizon. Beginning with Teotihuacan's explosive growth
in the Patlachique phase, the Teotihuacan Valley and areas adjacent to it became the
new center of demographic change. For several hundred years this area was consistently the most demographically vigorous, until the long period of population stasis
that commenced with the Middle Horizon began.

Clearly, the highly primate Teotihuacan and Tula systems did not induce population growth, at least beyond a certain point, and the more fragmented Coyotlatelco and Early Aztec systems were not conducive to demographic expansion. Thus the valley's population remained stationary, pegged at roughly 200,000 to 250,000 or so, for some 1,000 years (Fig. 4.11). The valley's outstanding growth episode occurred simultaneously with the Late Aztec unification which, as we have seen, transformed society in so many other respects. This growth was from some 175,000 people to roughly a million people in perhaps two and a half centuries, a 0.7 percent annual increase, indicating a doubling every 100 years. This is a growth rate equivalent to that of Europe during the early part of the industrial revolution. We lack a full understanding for this period of transition in numbers. One possibility is that the expanding, commercially active economy and opportunities for social mobility not only encouraged household reproduction but also attracted immigrants from other regions, where perhaps comparable economic opportunities had been lacking.

Although we lack anything near a full understanding of the various social, economic, and political conditions that affect population densities and population change, one feature of the Valley of Mexico is clear. Throughout the valley's prehispanic history, its human population underused the valley's agricultural resources. The numbers of people never approached the levels that could have been supported through full and sustained use of agricultural resources. Whatever were the factors that determined the numbers of people during various periods, they evidently operated to keep total population comfortably below the maximum potential levels. The calculated potential population values (even assuming no use of irrigation) for the Early Horizon, Zacatenco, Ticoman, and Patlachique phases, for example, are 150,000, 220,000, 220,000, and 250,000, respectively. But the actual populations based on observed remains are a few thousand, 25,000, 75,000, and 150,000, respectively. The potential values should be even higher than these figures, as it is unreasonable to assume that during these phases no irrigation agriculture was practiced at all. Abundant evidence for irrigation activities exists for highland Mesoamerica, even from the earliest periods. Irrigation this early is understandable, as it would always have been critical for reducing unpredictability. Consider the potential population value for the Patlachique phase, 250,000 people. Even without any irrigation, that figure is equal to the approximate size of the region's actual prehispanic population during the long plateau that started with the Middle Horizon. Some mix of Middle Horizon through Early Aztec social, political, and economic factors, a nexus of causes still not fully understood, held the population to levels far below what the valley could have supported. Surprisingly, even the very high population levels of the Late Aztec phase did not equal the valley's potential. The estimated carrying capacity at that time (considering the development of the lakebeds, and so forth) has been calculated at roughly 1,250,000 people. The actual population reached only somewhere between 65 percent and 88 percent of this value.

We conclude that the pressure of human populations on agricultural resources was never a driving factor in cultural evolution in the prehispanic Valley of Mexico.

If anything, especially during the periods of demographic stasis that started with Teotihuacan's dominance, a major problem faced by valley elites may have been labor shortages, rather than a surplus of people, especially in the poorly serviced and disadvantaged peripheries of the primate systems, exacerbated by unhealthy living conditions in the capital itself, at least among the poorer residents.

In the absence of evidence for "population pressure," are we left without a viable explanation for the growth of complex societies in the Valley of Mexico? By no means. Unfortunately, however, most of the Valley of Mexico researchers have paid so much attention to this one variable that they have failed to propose and test hypotheses that are more viable. We shall return to this issue in our concluding chapter.

The Valley of Mexico: primate versus nonprimate systems

The Middle Horizon (Teotihuacan) and the Mazapan phase (Tula) represent vast increases in the scale of regional systems in the valley, as previously autonomous local political entities were dismantled and incorporated into the larger entities. These were also periods of high levels of regional vertical integration, as the dominant capitals evidently exerted strong economic and political control over broad areas. In each case, however, the extremely poor development of secondary centers vis-à-vis the tremendous growth in size and complexity of the capitals indicates that in spite of high levels of regional integration and large scale, these were systems with attenuated regional central-place hierarchies. Evidently the policy of the Teotihuacan and Tula administrators was to build large and highly integrated systems by "washing out" the complexity of their respective regions, and, in effect, by concentrating that complexity in the primate centers. This is quite different from the Valley of Oaxaca, where increases in scale and integration (for example, in the Late I and IIIA phases) were accompanied by increased vertical complexity in the region's administrative central-place hierarchy. Explaining these divergent growth patterns will not be easy, but there are several variables that may be worth considering in this regard. We shall discuss these in our concluding chapter.

Whatever favored the growth of such large, highly integrated systems, once developed they would no doubt have experienced certain kinds of problems. Among the difficulties would have been a disgruntled and uncooperative rural periphery, depressed due to poor access to the economic opportunities concentrated in a few hands in the capital, and a declining demographic situation in which growth would be hard to stimulate. It is somewhat difficult, at first glance, to understand how such an organizational mode could be viable. Tula obviously was not, at least not for long, but Teotihuacan persisted in spite of its policies for some hundreds of years. The secret of their success, if we may judge from descriptions of analogous systems found ethnographically ("solar" marketing systems and some modern nations), may have been their use of massive and overwhelming force, and perhaps more successfully, over the long run, their primacy in the sphere of religion. In the contemporary solar marketing arrangements, an important component of the services and goods supplied by the primate center to the periphery involves ritual and ritual items. Perhaps such organizations cannot operate for very long unless rural peasants are dependent on the capital as their main link to the supernatural, and rely on the center for the kinds of items that are used in ritual observances. Although it is not clear how this type of reliance develops, it seems evident that this aspect of control was very important in Teotihuacan's history. More resources – expertise, time, labor, materials – were expended there in the construction of temple-pyramids than anywhere else in the valley at any time. Recall from René Millon's conclusions that an important component of Teotihuacan's greatness was the fact that it served as a "repository of symbols." In the design of the temple complex, the goal was to induce awe in the viewer and thus reaffirm Teotihuacan's position as the preeminent religious center in the region. Vertical integration in primate systems is thus maintained by strong ideological ties between the highest-level center and each low-level unit.

Under the Aztec phase Tenochtitlan hegemony, the valley was integrated, but more decentralized in the three senses of ritual, marketing, and decision making. This is reflected in the complex regional hierarchy of central places (and their associated temples), which existed in spite of the overall control by Tenochtitlan and its "Triple Alliance" friends in Texcoco and Tacuba. Looking at the distribution of mounded buildings and elite residences in the valley in Late Aztec times, a hierarchy of places that contained at least the following levels can be identified: (1) local units involving on the order of magnitude of 1,000 people, focused on a small complex of mounds and usually one or more elite houses (these local units have been identified as the *calpultin*, the aboriginal corporate descent groups that were the basic Aztec social, economic, and political units); (2) the semiautonomous "city-states," each focused on a local center (at the time of the conquest, some fifty of these existed); and (3) "supraregional" centers at Tenochtitlan-Tlatelolco and Texcoco.

Additional complexity was certainly present, as some of the city-state centers and the supraregional centers had internal subdivisions, and because in some cases adjoining city-states had grouped together to form minor leagues. At any rate, ritual events were performed in association with temple-pyramids located in the *calpultin*, city-state, and supraregional centers. Each of these was also a unit of administrative decision making and jurisprudence. The city-state and supraregional centers had marketing functions as well. This was anything but a "flat" hierarchy, and no single place was the region's only "repository of symbols."

Tenochtitlan, evidently, was less able to meddle in religious, political, and economic affairs in the region than was its Teotihuacan predecessor. This is reminiscent of the pattern we discussed in connection with phase V in the Valley of Oaxaca, where, in the Postclassic Period, a two-thousand-year-old system of regional dominance by a primate center gave way to a more complex, more horizontally integrated kind of society. In our concluding chapter we consider this phenomenon in a more comparative and explanatory perspective.

5

The eastern lowlands

Our third area of study is the eastern Mesoamerican, "Maya" lowlands (Fig. 5.1). A great deal of archaeological effort has been expended in this area on finding "lost cities," excavating temples and tombs, recording carved-stone commemorative monuments, and constructing architectural and pottery sequences. Ethnohistorians have published commentaries on the principal chronicles and surviving native manuscripts. Art historians and epigraphers have described ancient styles, gods, calendrics, and dynastic texts. Culture history, the study of the genius and accomplishments of supposed ethnic groups or civilizations, has been developed to an unquestionably dominant position among scholars of "the Maya."

The setting

In practice, when one speaks of the Maya area one refers to the highland and lowland areas of Mesoamerica east of the Isthmus of Tehuantepec that were inhabited by speakers of the various languages of the Maya family at the time of the Spanish conquest. In the sixteenth century all the people of Yucatan spoke one language, Maya; and those of Tabasco spoke a related tongue, Chontal, not always understood by Maya speakers. In the southern lowlands were speakers of Chol, Mopan, and Chorti, which together probably formed a single language. Intruding into the southern lowlands in later times were the speakers of Itzá and Lacandon, dialects of Yucatecan Maya, and Kekchi from highland Guatemala. The latter area is linguistically much more diverse than the lowlands; its many languages are localized and mutually unintelligible, but all are still of the Maya family.

One should not presume that any particular cultural patterns are necessarily correlated with Maya speech. Indeed, in the sixteenth century there were ethnic cleavages among speakers of the same Maya language. Thus in this book we do not assume that there are any special cultural practices associated with speaking a Maya language.

Nonetheless the linguistic situation of eastern Mesoamerica is interesting from the point of view of the social processes that created it. For our view of this area it is pertinent that the population of the entire eastern lowlands spoke only two languages – Yucatecan or the Chol group – and these two languages are very similar. Thus in Classic times the area was linguistically perhaps more uniform than it is today. This would of course leave room for ethnic or other cultural distinctions regionally, and from time to time there were probably intrusive Nahuatl speakers. But on the whole

Figure 5.1. The eastern lowlands, with names of places mentioned in the text.

the lowland Maya area may almost be considered a single, large, interacting speech community.

Here we concentrate on the lowlands, because compared to some other areas of Mesoamerica there is a fair amount of information covering a long period of time, and because the area was the scene of spectacular and theoretically interesting cultural elaborations. In many respects the eastern lowlands provide a marked contrast with the highland valley systems of western Mesoamerica.

The eastern lowlands, an area of 250,000 square kilometers, extend from the Gulf of Campeche to the Gulf of Honduras, and from the northern tip of the Yucatan peninsula to its base along the mountain front of Chiapas and Guatemala. Geologically the area is a low, gently folded limestone shelf, 300 meters above sea level in the Department of Petén, Guatemala, and about sea level in the north. In Belize, the Maya Mountains, trending northeast–southwest, are of volcanic origin, with their highest peak at about 1,200 meters. In the north, lines of low (300-meter-high) ridges, such as the Puuc hills, are the only major relief. Elsewhere the lowlands are not completely flat, but are usually composed of continuously undulating hills, knobs, and ridges on the order of fifty meters high.

Rainfall varies from the dry northwest (450 millimeters a year) to Petén (1,800 millimeters), and reaches up to 3,800 millimeters at the base of the highlands. Year-to-year variation is significant. In 1902 Mérida received 400 millimeters of rain, not enough for corn; but in 1916 the rainfall was over 1,600 millimeters. Even in Petén, where yearly variations are not so critical, rainfall in successive years has fluctuated from 890 millimeters to 2,360 millimeters. There is a marked dry season in the early spring (February through April), when shallow lakes may disappear and even water for drinking is scarce. Surface water is virtually nonexistent in northern Yucatan, where no rivers flow. But the countryside has cenotes, natural openings in the limestone that give access to abundant water. Wells can be dug by hand in some places, but over much of the lowlands the water table is generally low, usually too low for agricultural purposes except where there are rivers and swamps.

The central and southern lowlands are drained by rivers, such as the Pasión, the Usumacinta, the Belize, and the Candelaria. But central Petén, the heart of the Classic development, is an interior drainage basin, dotted with *aguadas* or swamps whose only outlet is down, through the cracked and pitted basement limestone. Water would have then been a problem, though not an insurmountable one, for prehistoric populations in northern Yucatan and in Petén, especially during the dry season. In the north use was made of the cenotes, and in Petén reservoirs were constructed.

Soils in the lowlands tend to be naturally fertile but thin and easily exhausted and eroded, except along the rivers. Soil depth and fertility increase from north to south. Vegetation consists of developed, climax rain forest with a high canopy in the south, and tropical deciduous forest, often thorny, in the central and northern parts, grading into open savanna in the dry northwest. Temperatures in the lowlands are tropical, reaching 38°C in the daytime at the height of the dry season, and rarely going below 10°C at night.

The eastern lowlands have few sharp ecological boundaries. Biotic communities tend to grade into one another, and most economically important plant and animal species are found widely distributed over the lowlands. Although this environment may appear forbiddingly dense and difficult to outsiders, families with traditional knowledge and experience have many ways to make a good living. The knowledge and technology developed by prehistoric people – common sense centuries ago – are only now beginning to be relearned (see Special topic 4). The secret was close attention to the behavior of plants and animals and to the details of microenvironments. Basically, people learned how to obtain substantial yields by replicating the diversity and complexity of the natural environment.

The preceding paragraphs present a very generalized, broad-scale picture of the eastern lowlands environment. When the scale of observation is changed, different patterns of environmental diversity emerge. The choice of scale depends on the human behavioral questions one is asking. For comparing the eastern lowlands and other areas as stages for the evolution of regional societies and macroregional systems, a "large-block" scale of 250,000 square kilometers is instructive. At this scale, for example, the eastern lowlands are topographically less diverse than areas of similar size in western Mesoamerica, but the lowlands' net primary productivity, the amount of material produced by plants each year, is roughly three times as large. The number of plant species is probably on the order of five to ten times greater in the eastern lowlands than in the Mexican highlands.

For the amount of land that a family or group of cooperating families would use in a sedentary, agricultural subsistence system, a scale focusing on blocks of between five and ten square kilometers is appropriate. Within a given area of this size in the eastern lowlands there was usually a series of many small niches, side by side in space (Fig. 5.2), each with its own potential for producing varying crops, each with its different growing seasons and requirements for labor. If one imagines moving from one five-to-ten-square-kilometer unit to a neighboring one, many of the potential niches will be repeated, a few new ones will be available, and a few kinds might not be present. What this means for human systems is that horizontal differentiation and specialization in economic production may often be the strategy of choice. Increasing horizontal differentiation in economic pursuits may have been the most obvious way to increase production in the short run (and in the long run, too). Although in the highland valleys the surest way of producing a large surplus was to plant maize everywhere, over most of the lowlands this was not necessarily true. Such "monoculture" would displace valuable crops, would require a large initial labor investment in forest clearing, would degrade soils, and would not in fact result in very good yields on much of the land. In the highlands maize can be grown with very little special skill or variation in technique over extensive areas. In the eastern lowlands even adjacent milpas can be treated differently. This is one reason (along with poorly developed markets) why, in this century, highland colonists have at times not fared as well as expected in the rain forests.

It would be wrong to say that monocropping was not practiced in some lowland areas (it was, with at least maize and cacao), but here more than in the highlands the alternative strategy of horizontal specialization had great advantages. Economic exchange within and between regions in the eastern lowlands was based partly on natural resource diversity over a small spatial scale, but one must also remember that a great deal of commercial activity is quite artificial. That is, much exchange depends on differences in prices not at all fostered by microenvironmental variation,

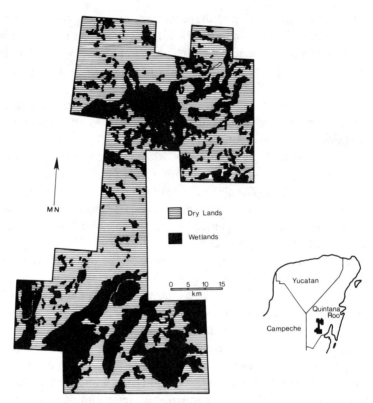

Figure 5.2. A diversity of niches: landforms in southwestern Quintana Roo. Wetlands include lakes (permanently standing water), *bajos* (seasonal or temporary water), and semi-*bajos* (occasional *bajos* overflow). Dry lands include permanently dry ground and high, hilly ground. Redrawn from Harrison (1977: fig. 3).

but created by the history of human decisions to specialize in one thing or another. For example, a hypothetical eastern lowlands farmer decides to devote 80 percent of his labor and land to the growing of cacao for sale or exchange. He might just as well have opted to plant maize on the same land – or, as can often be done in this environment, on land a scant fifty meters away. But once he decides on either of these courses or on some other potential strategy, a basis for exchange is created. As one can see, reasons other than natural resource diversity may underlie exchange systems.

To anticipate what follows, the potential for horizontal specialization had a determining effect on the evolutionary trajectory of eastern lowlands social systems. This is a hypothesis, not a fact, but it can be investigated by detailed surface and subsurface sampling of house areas in adjacent habitats. We suggest that from the earliest times people employed a wide and diverse spectrum of production techniques. The diversity entailed coordination in matters such as access to resources, allocation of time and labor, and exchange of products. Economic institutions facilitating exchange on the local and regional scales thus developed early, and consistently provided the basis for survival throughout the area's history. The evolutionary problem was thus what is known as the "organization of diversity," whereas the "replication of uniformity" was the main task of highland valley systems. The term "organization of diversity" refers to the basic problem of horizontally complex systems – how to keep the components doing their jobs even though they have very different roles and interests. The "replication of uniformity," on the other hand, is a continual preoccupation in systems with comparatively little horizontal complexity – the vast majority of parts are alike, and they tend to stay that way. The replication of uniformity is usually accomplished by means of strong vertical differentiation – a powerful hierarchy manages most affairs. The distinction should not be considered absolute, but to an extent it generally characterizes a salient difference between the eastern lowlands and the highland valleys.

Another feature of evolutionary significance in the eastern lowlands is the area's size. At 250,000 square kilometers, it is between forty and one hundred times the size of our other two study areas. But no subarea of the eastern lowlands (for example, comparable in size to the Valley of Mexico) ever had an autonomous, basically self-determined development. Instead, the eastern lowlands were an interacting whole. This presents a different set of problems for social systems. Highland valleys are naturally set off from their neighbors by mountains, which offer relatively little for agriculture and pose communications barriers. No such naturally bounded areas exist in the eastern lowlands.

An idea of the implications of the size and unbounded character of this area can be conveyed by the map of imaginary territories in Figure 5.3. Each of the units depicted may be considered a sociopolitical territory of one sort or another. They are drawn as hexagons because that shape leaves no in-between or contested area, as circles might, while it retains a fairly even, minimal distance from center to boundary. The size of the units we have set by the average distance one would travel in the lowlands in a day by foot or canoe, which in the sixteenth century was about thirty-three kilometers. Societies of mobile hunter-gatherers, such as the first inhabitants of the eastern lowlands, needed far more area. But as we will see, state polities in the Late Classic Period could have had territories about the size used in our hypothetical example. The *provincias* encountered by the Spanish in Yucatan varied from roughly the same size to five times as large.

The eastern lowlands typically had many sociopolitical systems in close juxtaposition. Either the boundaries of the sociopolitical units were very permeable, or a great deal of energy had to be expended to regulate the flow of things and people across boundaries. Too, the nearness of so many political neighbors may have at times meant intensive competition, and undoubtedly the evolution of sociopolitical organizations was conditioned by that fact. In respect to the nearness of so many social units, the eastern lowlands resemble the Mesopotamian "cradle of civilization," sub-Saharan Africa, and Southeast Asia more than they do the western Mesoamerican highlands. In this respect the controlled comparison of the eastern and western Mesoamerican evolutionary trajectories should be quite instructive.

Problems relating to the size, juxtaposition, and boundedness of social integrations in the eastern lowlands remind us that the social scientist must be theoretically and empirically equipped to deal systematically with scale factors. He or she must

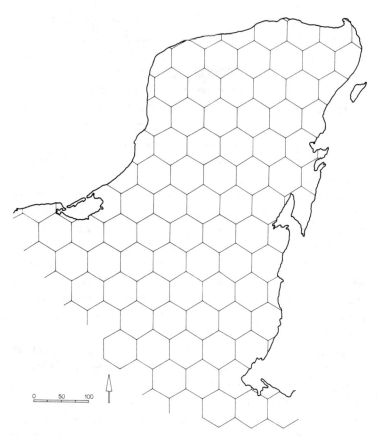

Figure 5.3. Hypothetical eastern lowlands territories. Each unit has a radius of thirty-three kilometers, roughly a one-day journey on foot. The eastern lowlands probably had many more juxtaposed territorial units than the Mexican highland valleys.

be able to detect relationships among variables operating at the household level, through the local and regional levels, up to the 250,000-square-kilometer macro-region, and in Mesoamerica as a whole. One must see how actions at one level might accumulate into stresses that are dealt with (or not) at the next level. One must be able to specify how many households, over what area, were altered because of higher-level changes.

Special topic 4. Agriculture in a finely grained, tropical environment
   Prehistoric Indians of the eastern lowlands grew not only corn but also beans, squash, pumpkin, camote, tomato, tomatillo, chile, chaya, ramon, cashew, zapote, edible palms, mamey, avocado, papaya, anona, guanabana, guava, cocoyol, balche, and cacao – to name a few of the important food crops of the over 200 crops used for food and other purposes.
   Today the most common farming technique is slash and burn. Usually, good yields can be obtained only in the first year or two after clearing. After that, farmers must clear new fields, and allow the old milpa to lie fallow for

fifteen to twenty years. Fertilization, crop rotation, and crop diversity – making the milpa into a complex garden, like the forest it replaces, instead of just a cornfield – can preserve soil quality and allow the milpa to be used almost continuously.

Terracing was a means of preventing soil erosion and slowing the movement of water. Bottomland soils were sometimes used as fill for hillside agricultural terraces. This technique was used extensively in ancient times, particularly in the central area.

Like the *chinampas* of the Valley of Mexico, the raised fields of the eastern lowlands represented a labor-intensive but very productive farming method. Artificial canals between the fields, and the nutrient-rich swamp soils would have permitted year-round cultivation. Cash crops, maize, or a variety of "garden" species could have been grown. Raised fields were confined to river floodplains and interior swamps with slow-moving water. This would have constituted a very small portion of the total land area, unless the *aguadas*, clay-filled natural depressions common in Petén and the central areas, were used.

These land- and labor-intensive techniques, producing many crops, generally require exceptionally well-interconnected networks for horizontal exchange. The changing circumstances – prices, state demands, security, soil degradation – that influenced farmers' decisions to use one or a combination of these strategies at one time or another are not at all known for the eastern lowlands.

The Early Preclassic Period

Given the environmental richness of the eastern lowlands, there is no reason to believe that sedentary villages were not established there as early as anywhere else in Mesoamerica. In what became an important area for growth in the Classic Period in northeastern Petén, few artifactual remains have been found dating to earlier than 650 B.C. Possibly this is because earlier living floors have been removed or covered by massive later construction. But in the northern lowlands, too, there is little evidence of sedentary occupation prior to 500 B.C. Pollen cores from Lakes Petenxil and Eckixil (Quexil) in Petén clearly show human disturbance of the tropical forest, and evidence of maize, in the third millennium B.C. From the period from 1000 to 600 B.C. there are indications of sedentary people, with pottery and domesticates (at least jack beans) along the Pasión River (the Xé phase).

The most complete early archaeological remains are those of the Swasey phase of northern Belize, equivalent in time to the Xé phase, or a little later. At the Cuello site several structures were excavated. These consist of lime-plaster floors and postholes, along with hearths. Artifacts include pottery bowls with flat bottoms, tecomates (neckless jars), and cooking and storage jars. Decorative techniques on pottery include painting in several colors, burnishing, slipping, incising, and appliqué modeling. There is no obsidian (which would have had to come from 350 kilometers away), but jade and greenstone for ornaments were imported from at least that distance.

Other lithics include manos and metates (from perhaps 150 kilometers away), and a fairly wide variety of tools made of regionally available chert. Subsistence remains include evidence for maize, root crops, deer, turtle, dog, armadillo, rabbit, agouti, fish, and mollusks. The terrestrial fauna are those preferring a disturbed vegetation habitat rather than deep forest.

We may conclude that at least the lake and river country of the southern part of the lowlands was inhabited by sedentary people relying on horticulture, hunting, and collecting. Occupations are inferred prior to 2000 B.C., and known archaeologically after that date. How people came to be sedentary and how their societies were organized no one can say with confidence.

We suggest one model for early social organization in the Maya area, a model that grew out of the question of why there was no "Olmec Horizon" in the eastern lowlands. "Olmec," as discussed in the two previous chapters, refers to a distinctive set of motifs, including feline symbolism and "baby-face" human figures, executed in bas-relief and fully three-dimensional stone sculpture, and seen in pottery, jade, and other exotic materials. The style had its peak between 1000 and 800 B.C., and it occurs in one form or another all over western Mesoamerica, through the Isthmus of Tehuantepec to the Chiapas highlands and the Pacific slopes of Chiapas and Guatemala. But the distinctive Olmec features do not occur in the eastern lowlands, even though the area had sedentary village inhabitants.

To understand why the people of the eastern lowlands did not use Olmec-style objects, we must examine how these distinctive items functioned in those societies where they are found. The details of the significance of Olmec objects remain somewhat obscure, but the outlines are becoming apparent. The biggest, most prominent Olmec objects were probably employed in signaling or displaying the state of the regional society – its existence, territory, and power. This display was intended for internal spectators (the society's own members) and for visitors from neighboring and more distant societies. Its content concerns the most mysterious and powerful forces known, and thus in some way the makers of these objects may have been seen to gain in power by their linkage to the highest orders of the supernatural realm. Highly visible, public artifacts like pyramid mounds, formal plaza arrangements, and the carved-stone monuments were well suited for displaying social cohesion. Public events such as corvée labor projects or conspicuous consumption may also be inferred from the archaeological remains.

Also involved in the Olmec Horizon style were many small, portable objects, some of great value, such as jade ornaments and magnetic mirrors, and some of lesser value and more universal distribution, such as cups and bowls incised with the "flaming eyebrows," or "paw-wing" motifs of the fire-serpent or were-jaguar (see Fig. 3.4A). Used in household contexts, these portable items seem to have signaled the status, specifically the rank status, of individual people within the society.

The personal ornaments of exotic materials figured prominently in an individual's display of his or her status to the rest of the world. Most of the Olmec pottery vessels and figurines have been found in contexts that suggest that their "messages" were conveyed by feasts, burials, and other rituals – for example, among families and individuals – although these rituals did not necessarily involve all members of a participating group at once. Among many other North American Indian groups known ethnographically, society consisted of clans (groups of related families), which were ranked by a traditional order of ritual precedence. Individuals' statuses were in large part determined by hereditary clan membership. The fact that some of the Olmec pottery motifs have a complementary distribution among households in Oaxaca might suggest that some of the portable objects were associated with particular social segments, such as clans.

The Olmec motifs, where their occurrence can be brought together with settlement pattern, house-cluster, and burial data, are associated with ranked societies, whose bounds, where known, would appear to be discrete and more or less confined to the area of a highland valley or a smaller tract. The artifacts that are distinctively Olmec are those that signal the power of these regional societies and their leaders, as well as the rank status of social segments and individuals.

We suggest that the reason there is no known Olmec Horizon in the eastern lowlands is that the lowland populations were not organized into regional societies with strongly defined boundaries and had little in the way of institutionalized, clanlike ranking of persons or social segments. This model is hypothetical, but it can be checked using archaeological data, though, admittedly, remains of villages from 1000 B.C. are hard to find in the eastern lowlands. According to this model, the people of the eastern lowlands were organized in flat, open-network social systems. "Flat" means that the societies had little institutionalized hierarchy. "Open network" means that the boundaries of societies were weakly defined, so that in going from place to place it might have been difficult to say whether one was in the same society or had entered a different one. This is somewhat like a segmentary, tribal society, but without a very clearly defined, persistent unit that one could call a tribe. In some respects, though not in all, especially considering the effects of Western contact, the ethnographic parallels are with New Guinea, Amazonia, and the Tiv and the Nuer of Africa.

Early villages in the eastern lowlands were not autonomous in any perdurable sense. No household, lineage, or village could carry out all its necessary tasks over a period of even a few years in isolation. All of the well-known ethnographic cases of acephalous, segmentary societies show considerable flows of people and material items among places. What *may not* have developed were the fixed, dominant central places like the head towns common in the highlands and Veracruz from the earliest of Preclassic times.

A flat, open network is a viable organization in an environment such as the eastern lowlands, with its open, relatively uniform topography and productivity. For early sedentary populations who could not or would not invest much labor in public works, only the seasonally waterless areas might look unattractive. Everywhere else there were adequate resources. This may figure in explaining why larger head towns (apparently) did not exist. Support for single, fixed central places required a regular surplus production from a known number of households. Where the constituent households were able to channel surplus production and labor to a number of points in the social system, then none of the potential or incipient central-place institutions could count on support all the time. If time and energy demands placed on households were excessive, moving somewhere else or allying with other people was a practical option.

In fact it may have been more advantageous for households to have invested "surplus" only in activities that served to emphasize the flatness (and the vastness) of the social network. In relatively flat, open social systems known ethnographically, such activities include rituals of intensification emphasizing rather temporary groupings, celebrations of the fusion of allies or the fission of villages, ceremonies recognizing kin ties, and personal rites of curing and passage. The emphasis is usually on short-run personal or group prestige, but this does not translate into formal institutions for authoritative decision making. Fission is the preferred solution to conflict, but the seeking of allies over large areas and the wide exchange networks keep people in contact. All of these mechanisms would have the effect of dispersing and equilibrating population densities.

Finally, we may note a theoretical point. Discrete, bounded social systems have internal hierarchies, and systems that are hierarchical have well-defined boundaries. Probably the processes that produce hierarchies form boundaries at the same time, and vice versa. Thus the forces preventing hierarchy formation in eastern lowland social systems probably helped keep the system "open."

Our answer to why the Olmec Horizon is not seen in the eastern lowlands is that the ritual emphasis was on maintaining broad, open networks and flat exchange systems. Ritual paraphernalia associated with the opposite goals of societal closure and ranking would have had little meaning or acceptance.

The Middle Preclassic Period

By 500 B.C. no major region of the lowlands was left unoccupied. The ceramics of this time were ubiquitous and distinctive, sharing broad similarities in design. These similarities suggest to some archaeologists a rapid spread of colonists into new lands, perhaps from a common origin along the rivers of the southern lowlands. According to this view, regional style differences developed as groups began to drift farther apart. But these changes were slight, all occurring within the same basic tradition, called Mamom.

At Altar de Sacrificios, on the Pasión River, evidence of public architecture dates only to the late Mamom phase. Burials show little evidence of ranking. The neighboring site of Seibal had no public buildings until the Late Preclassic. To the east, in Belize, villages dating to López Mamom occupied the northern part of the country, but none yet known had public architecture. In central Belize, along the Belize River at the site of Barton Ramie, eighteen of the sixty-five house mounds excavated had Jenny Creek (the local manifestation of Mamom) occupations, but none of this looks like public architecture. Tikal, in Petén, had Mamom occupation, but it was scant, and there is no evidence of public architecture. The situation was similar at Uaxactún, Becan in the central lowlands, and Dzibilchaltún in the north.

Overall, the existing archaeological data suggest that all or most areas of the eastern lowlands were occupied by sedentary villages, with agriculture and pottery, by no later than 500 B.C. Social ranking and political institutions requiring large, permanent buildings, at least insofar as one can tell from burials, houses, and the lack of public architecture, were absent from these early village settlements. Yet the pottery was remarkably uniform over the entire lowlands, indicating broad exchange patterns, perhaps maintained by marriage, or rapid spread from a single source.

The latter interpretation would be favored in a model hypothesizing a spread of farming colonists from wetlands into the interior. This interpretation is similar to that for the spread of neolithic farming into Europe in the fifth and sixth millennia B.C. Land-devouring slash-and-burn maize agriculture, thought to be relatively easy and initially productive, has been suggested as the main subsistence technique, itself partly responsible, along with population growth, for the spread of the sedentary way of life. So far, however, this model has received almost no empirical support, and very little is actually known about the period. Therefore, at the present time the idea that the lowlands were colonized by slash-and-burn farmers must be considered speculative and suspect. An identical posture of doubt ought to be taken regarding the mechanism – rapid spread from a single source – behind the broad Mamom pottery similarities.

The Late Preclassic and the Terminal Preclassic

The period from 300 B.C. to A.D. 300 saw the establishment of complex, hierarchically organized chiefdoms throughout the eastern lowlands. Three features of these chiefdoms stand out: They developed later in time than did similar political organizations in the highlands, they were relatively unstable, at least over the long, archaeological time scale, and they rose and fell within a rather uniform cultural matrix. Toward the end of this period the distinctive characteristics and material accoutrements of "Classic Maya" elite culture were established over most of the lowlands. These traits (see Plates 7, 8, 9, and 10) include polychrome pottery, jade jewelry, carved stelae and altars, elaborate masonry architecture with corbeled vaults, causeways, supernatural concepts such as the bacabs (sky bearers) and chacs (lightning deities), ancestor veneration, painted bark-paper manuscripts and the bark beaters to make the paper, the writing system, place-value notation, and the calendar. Most of these Classic practices were firmly in place in the A.D. 1–250 Protoclassic Period.

Altar de Sacrificios and Seibal, on the Pasión River, developed into town-sized centers of several thousand people during the Late Preclassic. At both sites public buildings were larger and more numerous than before, and there is clear evidence of personal rank-status differences in burial goods. Some high-ranking people were buried in "public," nondomestic places. Seibal declined somewhat in the Protoclassic, although Altar increased in size, thus leading to speculation that there may have been some political consolidation along the Pasión at that time.

A considerable population increase (350 percent) is suggested from the Middle to Late Preclassic periods in northern Belize, though at Barton Ramie, on the Belize River, the most pronounced growth did not occur until the Protoclassic. Public architecture achieved rather massive proportions at Los Cerros, a center on the

7

8

Plates 7–10. Examples of fancy material culture from the Classic Period. Plate 7: A four-inch-high jade figure found in a dedicatory cache on the North Acropolis (a temple complex) at Tikal. Plate 8: A narrative scene from a polychrome pot included in a Tikal burial. Plate 9: Stela 22 and Altar 10, from Twin Pyramid Complex Q, Tikal. Plate 10: The arch at Labná, in the Puuc area, restricted access to an enclosure of public buildings. Plates 7–9 © copyright by the University Museum, University of Pennsylvania.

northern Belize coast. In a study area of 1.5 square kilometers at Los Cerros, 178 mounded features were recorded. A sample of these was excavated that suggested that 90 percent had their major construction episodes in the Late Preclassic. A large ditch dating from this period encloses a 37-hectare area of the site. Perhaps this feature was used for defense and to define a boundary; certainly it was constructed with a massed labor force.

At both Uaxactún and Tikal public structures representing a considerable social investment were built. The bulk of Tikal's North Acropolis dates to the Preclassic. Another pyramid, Structure 5C-54, had almost 40,000 cubic meters of construction

9

10

fill, and some of the other projects at Tikal were equally massive. The layout of the public areas during the Preclassic at Tikal and Uaxactún gives the impression of openness and rather easy access to broad plazas, with small buildings on top of high platforms. These buildings apparently involved rituals meant to be visible to large numbers of people, but carried out by just a few persons physically removed from ground level by great height. These Late Preclassic architectural layouts are reminiscent of Mississippian temple platforms and plazas in the southeastern United States, and similar structures from other complex chiefdoms and early states. In chiefdoms elsewhere the political leader has the religious duties of seeing to the spiritual welfare of his whole society and representing it to the rest of the supernatural order. Although often the ruler may be ritually separated from his people and his person may be sacrosanct, this does not prevent usurpation, rebellion, treachery, secession, or other ordinary political unpleasantnesses aimed at shortening his tenure in office. In short, in complex chiefdoms known ethnographically, chiefs are theoretically omnipotent, and they often have monumental architectural displays to prove it, but their rule is quite unstable. The Late Preclassic eastern lowlands were probably organized into a series of polities similar to these.

The site of Becan, in the central Yucatan peninsula, has a similar arrangement of a few large public structures built facing an open pavement. About nineteen hectares of this site are surrounded by a five-meter-deep, ten-meter-wide ditch, which, with its embankment imposing a twelve-meter-high barrier, was a formidable obstacle. Seven causeways gave access from the outside to the site center.

Late Preclassic occupation, often rather dense, is found at most archaeological sites in northern Yucatan. Prior to 50 B.C. Dzibilchaltún featured several public architectural groups, including a 1,600-square-meter paved plaza with five probable ceremonial structures arranged around its sides. The site was the center of the north's largest, most densely packed regional population, a situation that lasted perhaps 300 years at the most before Dzibilchaltún collapsed.

Although little is known about regional demographic patterns anywhere in the lowlands during the Preclassic, there is a general consensus that, overall, populations were markedly higher in the Late Preclassic. In some areas, like Barton Ramie, the increase is not spectacular; in others, like the northern plains, regions experienced a population boom, even reaching levels not met until the Late Classic, if then. Based on ten carefully mapped survey tracks around Lakes Yaxhá and Sacnab in Petén, it is thought that population densities may have increased from ten persons per square kilometer in 500 B.C. to seventy persons per square kilometer in A.D. 250. Thus some regions grew faster than others, and some, like the Puuc area which in the Late Classic experienced a population boom, were downright undeveloped. On the whole, however, at the scale of the entire eastern lowlands, a long-term addition to population by means of more births than deaths is indicated. For this area no accurate population estimates are possible, but the figure of two to five million in 100 B.C. is consistent with the surveys done so far and may give some idea of the magnitude.

Furthermore, these ancient people were in regular contact and interaction with each other across the entire eastern lowlands. This was not only a large population, but also an integrated one. Emerging regional elite participated in a prestige system that involved the Classic Maya traits mentioned above. But on a more ordinary level there was considerable interaction as well. Two lines of evidence suggest frequent, everyday interaction. One is linguistic, in that the present linguistic uniformity might have been maintained since nomadic hunting-and-gathering times. This is a strong but circumstantial argument.

The other line of evidence suggesting commoner-level integration is ceramic. Recall that pottery of the previous Mamom phase showed great similarities throughout the Maya lowlands. The pottery of the Late Preclassic is called the "Chicanel ceramic sphere." These ceramics are characterized by certain vessel forms, surface finishes, slips, painting, and even gross paste appearance. They are much more standardized than the previous Mamom pottery, and consistently uniform all over the lowlands from Yucatan to Petén. This remains true throughout the three or four centuries of the Late Preclassic, even though at most well-studied sites the pottery styles are progressive and dynamic over time, so that archaeologists are able to make finer temporal subdivisions with relative ease. This perhaps indicates two things about the organization of craft production. First, it was in the hands of specialists. Technologically the pottery required assembly of too many special materials to be handled by every household. Secondly, it was specialized in such a way that design changes, production, and distribution of the finished products were not greatly interfered with by the political hierarchies that periodically closed boundaries and brought tighter political control to some regions. Instead of marking sociopolitical boundaries, pottery seems to have ignored or transcended them. Because this general ceramic uniformity lasted for many hundreds of years, and because pottery styles changed over time while retaining macroregional uniformity, we doubt that the sphere can be explained by a rapid spread of colonists from a single source. As indicated by the linguistic evidence, too, the pottery distributions suggest strong economic integration maintained on local, regional, and macroregional scales.

A Protoclassic ceramic complex called Floral Park followed the Chicanel phase ceramics, and it can be readily identified at some but not all sites throughout the lowlands. The complex is characterized by serving bowls with tripod or tetrapod mamiform supports, by certain kinds of painting, including polychrome, and by Usulatan ware – all rather attractive, "flashy" traits. On present evidence the spatial distribution of Floral Park pottery might best be called "selective" – some sites have it, others do not. It is not simply a matter of elite versus commoner goods, though undoubtedly Floral Park pots were fairly expensive. And it is not a marker of migration, either, because the style was in vogue even as far west as Oaxaca, where there is certainly no evidence of "new peoples." Lacking detailed distributional studies, the significance of the Floral Park ceramic sphere cannot yet be determined. The key would seem to be in the organization of craft production and distribution, about which little is known.

On the basis of the Late Preclassic/Protoclassic pottery distributions we suspect that many of the fundamental integrations had to be those of basic commodity production and exchange on the local and regional scales. We suspect, but cannot prove, that families relied for their day-to-day needs on specialized production of agricultural and craft goods for exchange through strong local and regional economic institutions. We suspect that this production and exchange system was well developed in the Middle Preclassic, that it developed further until the end of the Late Classic, and that it persisted in the north until the conquest. The economic system was usually flatter and more open, but more stable and enduring than the typically fragile political formations of the eastern lowlands. Finally, if our suspicions are correct, the eastern lowlands production and exchange system was usually more complex than the market systems of the highlands, until the Late Postclassic.

The Classic Period

Between A.D. 300 and 900 many areas of the eastern lowlands saw their most intensive development ever. Especially in the southern and central parts of the lowlands, ancient populations reached levels unattained even today, and construction, both monumental and on an ordinary scale, boomed as never again.

During the Classic Period populations were ruled by state-level governments. Exactly how and why states were created in the eastern lowlands is still not well understood. But certainly the presence of many contiguous and distant neighbors must have been a major concern to the rulers of complex chiefdoms and early states in the area. "Foreign" affairs in the lowlands, in that they involved dealings with multiple polities of similar scale and complexity, would have been different from the policies pursued by the highland hegemonists.

We present in the following pages an outline glimpse of the eastern lowland world in the Classic Period. The intention is to describe the richness of the information that potentially can be obtained. Within the limits of the scope of this book we attempt to emphasize that the eastern lowlands were not all of a piece, and that considerable variation existed at every scale. This variation undoubtedly holds the key to understanding how the ancient systems worked.

Examples of a few classic Period houses are shown in Figure 5.4. Apparently, hard plaster floors and at least some masonry construction were typical of most houses known archaeologically. In many areas houses were built up on still-visible earthen or stone mounds, though ground-level houses of perishable materials were built in some contexts. Outdoor activity areas were essential. One such activity involved storage in underground cisterns called *chultuns*, used possibly for storing the breadnut (ramon) and other foods in the south and for water in the north. Houses can occur singly, but are often found in groups arranged around small courtyards. That the people living in a single courtyard group were closely related kin is certainly possible.

Unfortunately for archaeologists, the ancient people swept their floors clean, so artifacts are not usually found exactly where people kept or dropped them. An idea of the material goods of households can be obtained, however, by examining nearby refuse deposits. An impression of the kinds of things found in household contexts is given in Table 5.1, which is a partial inventory of objects found in household contexts in the vicinity of Barton Ramie in Belize (Willey et al. 1965). Variation in the occurrences of these items, among households and over time, should be of great interest. Households in the agriculturally marginal savannas that dot central Petén,

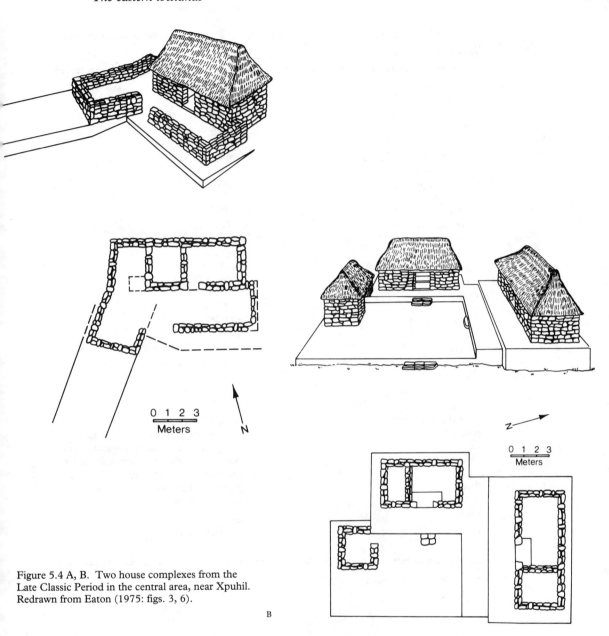

Figure 5.4 A, B. Two house complexes from the
Late Classic Period in the central area, near Xpuhil.
Redrawn from Eaton (1975: figs. 3, 6).

for example, had meager artifactual inventories and very poorly fired pottery in contrast with the richer possessions of the Barton Ramie households. Some house sites
can be shown by their repeated renovations to have been occupied virtually continuously for several archaeological phases; others may have been lived on for only a
generation or so. At Nohmul in northern Belize, modest houses built at ground
level without the telltale masonry platform were concentrated in specific sectors –
which changed through the town's history. Many poor dwellings were situated near
the raised fields at the edge of the swamp.

Table 5.1. *Partial inventory of objects found in household contexts in the Barton Ramie area of Belize*

pottery vessels	manos
cooking	hammers
serving	grooved stones
storage	bark beaters
other pottery objects	celts
moldmade figurines and whistles	pendants
figurine molds	beads
spindle whorls	spindle whorls
disks	disks
pendants	mirrors
ear ornaments	*bone objects*
chipped-flint objects	awls
projectile points	spatulas
knives	fishhooks
chippers	tubes
adzes	rings
gouges	needle cases
chisels	needles
drills	pendants
scrapers	perforated animal teeth
cores	*shell objects*
blades	pendants
eccentrics	beads
waste	ornaments
obsidian objects	*animal remains*
points	deer, brocket, peccary, tapir, dog,
knives	rabbit, howler monkey, agouti, opossum,
cores	ocelot, pocket gopher, armadillo, turtle,
blades	crocodile, chachalaca, turkey; fourteen
flakes	marine shellfish species, seven freshwater
eccentrics	and land species
waste	*plant remains*
ground-stone objects	maize, beans, cacao, nuts
metates	

Source: Willey et al. (1965).

The comparative lack of *comales* in the lowlands, by contrast with highland areas like Oaxaca, is interesting. At the very least we may infer a difference in cooking styles, but perhaps it signals a contrasting tempo and organization of work. Differences in economic activities and status among households show up in the size and degree of elaboration of the houses themselves, in access to exotic resources, in the sheer quantity of goods, and in burial treatment. Everywhere, wealth differences among households vary widely along a continuum. Where wealth and economic activities are concerned this was a far more complex situation than simply "elite" and "commoners," whatever the legal social statuses might have been.

In the Classic Period, obsidian, an imported item, was used in higher-status residential and public ceremonial contexts at the major centers. In places it was also used in small sites and at the residences of farmers.

In the species-rich, fine-grained, tropical environment of the eastern lowlands, we would expect considerable variation among households or groups of households in activities involving plants. Although there has been little systematic research on this, archaeologists could easily obtain three kinds of information relevant to the economic use of plants: chemical traces and residues in soils, pottery (form, function, and use-wear), and the plant remains themselves. In fact, excavations at a single patio group of Cobá found at least nineteen different plant taxa, almost all of which were economically useful. Test excavations at Pulltrouser Swamp in northern Belize recovered macrobotanical remains of at least forty-one taxa.

And there was variation in the placement of human burials and the quantities of exotic trade goods and crafted items included in human burials. Veneration of family ancestors is apparent in burial treatments, a practice that cross-culturally usually means intergenerational, kin (often father-to-son) control of estates. The wide variation in the richness of burial ritual and furnishing may reflect wide variation in the size, prestige, and power of kin groups and the relative sizes of their estates.

House sites in the eastern lowlands tended to be dispersed rather than aggregated into settlements with distinct boundaries. Concentrations of buildings can be observed, however (see Fig. 5.5). In eastern Petén clusters of around five to twelve house ruins sometimes occurred within a radius of between 200 and 300 meters. In some cases such a cluster was spatially isolated from the next, but in other instances closer inspection shows that the clusters ran together. Such clusters often but not always contained a larger house or a shrine.

Above the level of clusters of houses, some survey evidence suggests that for every 50 to 100 (or more) houses there may have been a minor center – a group of buildings consisting of one or several pyramidal structures, probably for temples, at least one "vaulted" range structure (a "palace"), and several paved plazas. Groups of this size need not have had stelae, altars, or ball courts. One such group excavated near Copán, Honduras, had two plazas and a total of nine buildings. One of the buildings, on the east side of the larger plaza, was probably a temple. Other buildings were associated with domestic as well as special elite functions, including obsidian knapping and use, incense burning, and burial rituals.

Major centers were larger, internally more complex, and less frequent. They had formal arrangements of plaza groups and causeways, "acropolises" or mazelike complexes of palaces and courtyards, towering temple pyramids, ball courts, stelae, and altars. Furthermore, the major Classic centers had population muscle – Tikal in Late Classic times had between 65,000 and 80,000 people. This city (see Figs. 5.5 and 5.6) was surrrounded on the east and west by dense, swampy, logwood *bajos*, and on the north and south by artificial earthworks consisting of a formidably deep ditch with a rampart on the inner side. These boundaries encompass an area of 120.5 square kilometers, which indicates a density of 538 people per square kilometer – which is considerably lower than the density at Teotihuacan or Monte

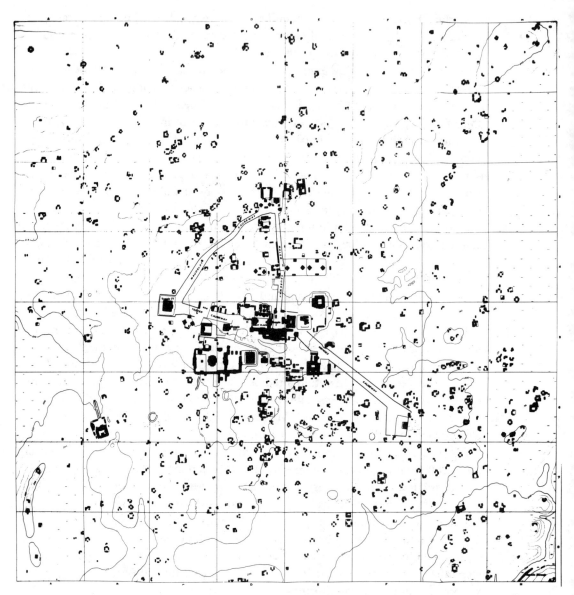

Figure 5.5. Map of the central sixteen square kilometers of Tikal. Each grid square is 500 meters on each side. The grid is oriented to magnetic north (at the top of the map). From Carr and Hazard (1961).

Albán. Low within-site house densities such as these from the Classic Period in the eastern lowlands are generally in Mesoamerica associated with intensive agriculture concentrating a lot of labor on small plots of land.

Households in the cities of the eastern lowlands thus had space around them for kitchen gardens and orchards (Fig. 5.7). At Tikal each house had an average of between 0.59 and 0.82 hectares of cultivable land. A survey of trees now growing on the ruins of Cobá, in the northeastern Yucatan peninsula, shows that in Classic times tree culture may have been similar to that described for Yucatecan towns in the sixteenth century:

> The natives lived together in towns in a very civilized fashion. They kept the land well cleared and free from weeds, and planted very good trees. Their dwelling place was as follows: in the middle of the town were their temples with beautiful plazas, and all around the temples stood the houses of the lords and the priests, and then [those of] the most important people. Thus came the houses of the richest and of those who were held in the highest estimation nearest to these, and at the outskirts of the town were the houses of the lower class. And the wells, if there were but few of them, were near the

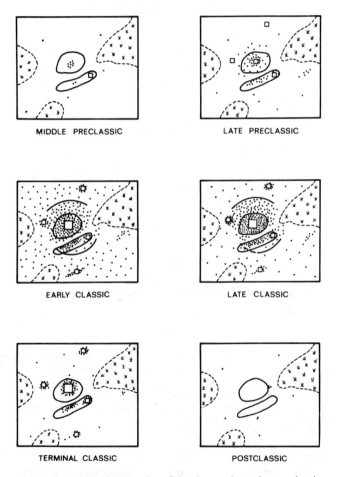

MIDDLE PRECLASSIC   LATE PRECLASSIC

EARLY CLASSIC   LATE CLASSIC

TERMINAL CLASSIC   POSTCLASSIC

Figure 5.6. A visual impression of the changes in settlement density around Tikal from Middle Preclassic to Postclassic times. These drawings are based on the 500-meter-wide survey strips (*brechas*) running out from the center of Tikal. The dots represent relative density of habitation and the squares symbolize major clusters of civic-ceremonial architecture and, in periods later than the Middle Preclassic, elite residential architecture. The contour lines show the main ridges of high ground. Earthworks are depicted in heavy line. Major *bajos* are represented by the vegetation symbols. The area is about thirty by thirty-three kilometers, or roughly 1,000 square kilometers. Redrawn from Puleston (1973: figs. 28–33).

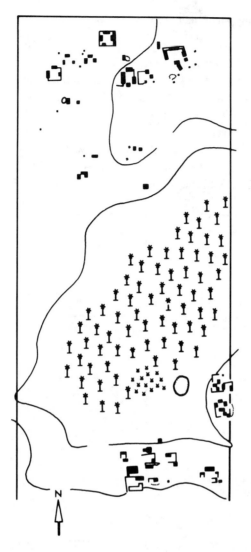

Figure 5.7. A section of a survey strip five to six kilometers south of the Tikal site center. Houses were built on the higher ground, often in clusters of "courtyard groups." The strip is 500 meters wide, and the contour interval is 10 meters. The swamp in the center is *corozal* and *pital bajo*. *Corozal* palm is rich in food oil, and *pital* was used for cordage. Such stands may be remnants of ancient orchards. The solid dots mark *chultuns*. Redrawn from Puleston (1973: plate 2g).

houses of the lords; and they had improved their lands, planted with wine trees and they sowed cotton, pepper and maize. (Tozzer, ed. and trans. 1941:62–4)

At Cobá the ceremonially important *balche* trees, used to make wine, *pom*, used for incense, and several different fruit trees (ramon and guayas, especially) were planted only in the civic-ceremonial and adjacent elite residential zones. In fact all of the economically important trees used for fruit, fiber, bark, and resin were grown mainly by people living between one and a half and two kilometers from the site center. This was also the part of the site with the greatest frequency (10 to 50 percent) of elaborate vaulted architecture. Landa's description of the sixteenth-century town thus seems to apply to Cobá, a Classic Period center in the more humid part of the northern lowlands.

The Classic Period cities supported craft specialists, including flint and obsidian workers, potters, woodworkers, "dentists" who provided people with decorative inlays for their teeth, stoneworkers or monument carvers, textile weavers, human carriers, feather workers, leather workers, musicians, manuscript painters, merchants, basket makers, bark-cloth makers, and so forth. How were these specialists supported and their products distributed? How did households acquire things they did not grow or make themselves, and how did they dispose of their staple, garden, and orchard surpluses? Both tribute and markets are possibilities, but a detailed study of the pottery from collections within and outside the Tikal earthworks sheds some light on the question. At Tikal, the large utilitarian pots had discrete, small (five-kilometer) areas of distribution, indicating manufacture near the place of use. This could mean either very localized markets or purchase directly from the manufacturer. Serving vessels, on the other hand, were distributed more widely, in a pattern

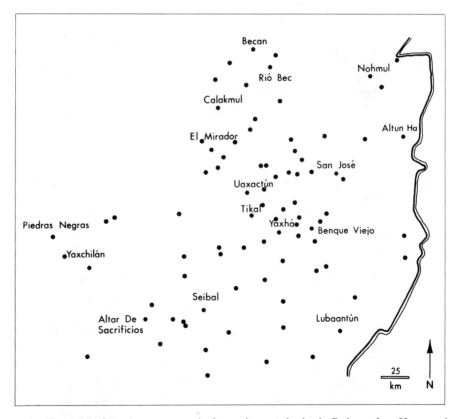

Figure 5.8. Some known centers in the southeastern lowlands. Redrawn from Hammond (1974: fig. 2).

Table 5.2. *Surveyed areas and structures per square kilometer, selected eastern lowlands sites*

Site	Zone of site	Surveyed area (sq. km.)	Structures per sq. km.	Peak period
Mayapán	center & periph.	4.2	986	Late Postclassic
Dzibilchaltún	center & periph.	19.0	442	Terminal Classic
Chunchucmil	center & periph.	6.0	400	Terminal Classic
Sayil	center	2.4	324	Terminal Classic
Copán	center	0.6	1449	
	periphery	24.0	99	
	rural	37.7	28	
	total	*62.3*	*72*	Late Classic
Tikal	center	9.0	235	
	inner periph.	7.0	181	
	outer periph.	8.5	112	
	rural	11.5	39	
	total	*36.0*	*133*	Late Classic
Nohmul	center	4.0	58	
	periphery	18.0	26	
	total	*22.0*	*32*	Late Classic
Yaxhá-Sacnab	rural	10.0	59	Late Classic
Macanche-Salpetén	rural	6.0	68	Late Classic
Petenxil-Quexil	rural	5.5	39	Late Classic
Belize Valley	rural	5.0	118	Late Classic
Uaxactún	center	2.0	112	
	periphery	2.3	32	
	total	*4.3*	*70*	Late Classic
Tayasal	center	4.0	221	Late Classic
Becan	center & periph.	3.0	222	
	rural	1.0	80	
	total	*4.0*	*187*	Late Classic
Tikal-Yaxhá	rural	3.2	65	Late Classic
Caracol	center	2.3	300	Late Classic
Albion Island	center & periph.	2.3	444	Early Classic
Seibal	center	1.6	275	
	periphery	0.7	144	
	total	*2.3*	*235*	Late Preclassic

Sources: Culbert and Rice, eds. (1990: esp. Table 1.1); Pyburn (1991).

indicating a complex marketing exchange system. At least for pottery, Tikal had both a central market and local markets.

Pottery making at Quirigua was dispersed, not concentrated, and sometimes it has been found together with the evidence of more-than-usual chipped-stone tool reduction at elaborate residences. Activities involving chipped-stone tools have a regionally complex distribution in those areas where they have been studied (especially northern Belize). The town of Colhá was a production center for hoes and bifacial tools and cores (they look like hand axes); people living around Pulltrouser, thirty kilometers away, were the consumers – the worn tools and reduced end-products are found around their houses.

Thus far we have discussed aspects of the Classic Period in the eastern lowlands detectable with "site-centered" methods. Definitive statements about these and other phenomena must await the application of regionally oriented approaches. Clues about what could be learned are available from studies of small tracts between known centers, and from maps showing the distribution of known centers over large areas (even if poorly known).

In the first place it is clear that on a regional scale populations were high (see Table 5.2). If highland-valley average regional population density during the Classic was around 40 to 80 people per square kilometer when city and rural populations are considered together, it appears that the *rural* densities in the southern part of the eastern lowlands were often on the order of 150 to 200 people per square kilometer. (In the centers density climbs to 500 to 1,000 persons per square kilometer; on the other hand, perhaps a third of the area is uninhabitable *bajo*.) Figure 5.8 shows the locations of eighty-three known centers in part of the southern lowlands, and Figure 5.9 suggests a breakdown of some known sites in northern Belize into major- and minor-center categories.

These data suggest that when regional methods are applied in the future, the results may be both large in scale and complex. If we may extrapolate from the

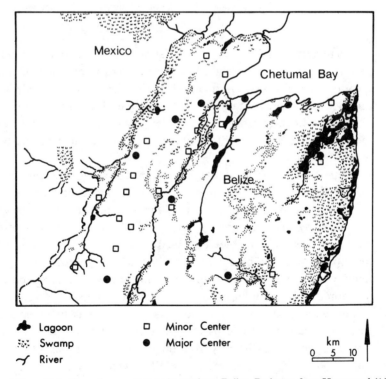

Figure 5.9. Some known centers in northern Belize. Redrawn from Hammond (1975: fig. 1).

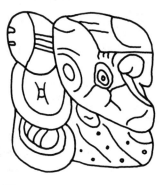

Figure 5.10. Two variations of the Palenque emblem glyph. Redrawn from Marcus (1976b: figs. 4.21 c,d).

intersite surveys in the Tikal area, subtracting the uninhabitable zones, the area covered by Figure 5.1 might have had a rural population of seven to ten million people in the Classic Period. This is not to claim that it actually did, as the area has not been surveyed, but one should be prepared for that magnitude. The landscape must have been organized in complex ways – both vertically, with hierarchies of dependent centers, and horizontally, with territorial divisions between centers of equivalent function.

Regional-scale political integrations are known for the eastern lowlands because of the Maya writing on stone monuments. Students of Maya hieroglyphics are able to "read" a considerable portion of the ancient texts, most of which speak of the events of dynastic histories. Many political centers had an "emblem glyph" that functioned as its name (see Fig. 5.10). On carved-stone monuments of small centers, only the name of a nearby major center appeared – not the names of other, more distant major centers. Elite persons of low rank arranged marriages with the daughters of high-ranking lords at the major centers.

Given these patterns, several territorial polities can be reconstructed. These consisted of a capital in the center of the territory, a ring of about four to six secondary centers spaced equidistantly from the capital (known cases vary from about twenty to fifty kilometers), and rings of smaller, tertiary centers grouped around the primary and secondary centers (see Fig. 5.11).

In Mesoamerica the substance of the very first writing from the Early Preclassic had to do with legitimizing the authority of political sovereigns, and this concern, along with portents and prophecies, was the principal subject of the writing that has been preserved for us through the Classic to the Spanish conquest. The Maya texts had little to do with economic transactions or tribute lists. This contrasts sharply with other early writing systems, such as that of Mesopotamia, where writing seems to have been developed as an aid to the management of large quantities of tribute. What this might suggest for the eastern lowlands is that economic integration was not supplied by political authorities who collected and redistributed tribute, but by less vertically integrated, "hidden-hand" mechanisms operating outside the state apparatus.

On the other hand, having to carve one's ancestry in stone and having to extol personal greatness by erecting magnificent buildings do not seem like practices befitting serene and secure authority. Such a flurry of stelae construction as went on in certain Petén sites (like Uaxactún) in the Early Classic and over much of the southern part of the lowlands between the Maya dates 9.10.0.0.0 and 9.18.0.0.0 (A.D. 633–790) makes one wonder whether the lords were not self-proclaiming overmuch. Dynastic discontinuities, succession struggles, and political instability seem to have been common, although Palenque claims to have had an unbroken succession of rulers lasting 300 years. Major-center commemorative activities were sporadic, not constant. Of the nineteen dated monuments at Cobá, sixteen were carved in one eighty-year period (A.D. 613–92), and most of the well-known commemorative architecture at Palenque was built at the end of the seventh century.

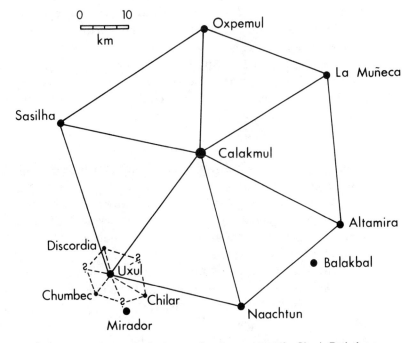

Figure 5.11. The capital, secondary, and tertiary centers of a Classic Period state, as reconstructed from the glyphic evidence. Redrawn from Marcus (1976b: fig. 1.15).

Uaxactún, twenty kilometers north of Tikal, had a dozen stelae dating to the earliest two centuries of the Classic, whereas Tikal had only three. In the Late Classic Uaxactún became a political dependency of Tikal. Inside the vaulted-masonry palaces of Bonampak are polychrome murals celebrating apparently violent and chaotic scenes surrounding a ruler's accession to the throne. We take this fragmentary information to mean that the lords of the Classic Period states sought legitimate authority but did not retain it for very long.

The trend throughout the Classic, however, may have been toward a gradual accumulation of political power in more complex and more extensive states. Tikal's domain in the Late Classic included at least 2,500 square kilometers and 360,000 people – and it might have been larger (note that this is about the area of the Valley of Oaxaca, with three times the contemporary population). The demand for labor for military purposes, basic production, and construction, uneven as it was given the up-and-down fortunes of competing states, would have had a profound effect on regional demography. If states were assuming more and more of the tasks involving the employment and management of greater numbers of people, one might expect even greater than proportional outlays for administrative costs.

More energy input in administration in fact did occur in the Late Classic. Structure A-V at Uaxactún (Fig. 5.12) illustrates the change from the Early Classic Period's open "temple courtyard" to a closed administrative complex in the Late Classic centers. Figure 5.13, a ground plan of the Central Acropolis at Tikal, shows buildings for public purposes (the structures facing outward, and Court 5D-1, for example) and secluded space with highly restricted access (Court 5D-3) for the ruler. When the region around the Puuc hills was developed around the end of the Classic, the most characteristic buildings were long, multidoorway structures, sometimes forming closed quadrangles, that probably served state administrative functions (see Plate 11). Another indication of increasing administrative expense are the *sacbeob*, elevated causeways that linked main centers to their secondary satellites. These roads would have decreased travel times, thus facilitating control of boundaries.

Regional states in the eastern lowlands may have been organized at a still higher, interregional level, with four capitals integrating the central and southern zones. And the spatial patterning of political centers suggests somewhat larger regional states than the emblem glyph territories. This integration was not complete by any means, as style differences in elite material culture (pottery, stone carving, architecture) occurred on a regional scale throughout the Classic. Distinctive styles, nevertheless, were expressed within the same cultural and linguistic medium, a commonality preserved by constant interaction and exchange.

Indeed, a reasonable explanation for the origin and elaboration of the calendar for which this ancient society is justifiably famous might have been the need for a uniform way of scheduling long-distance exchanges. Farmers usually do not need to be told when to plant, as they can observe the rains and the field weeds. But traders must know delivery dates and when to meet their connections, events quite independent of nature's rhythms.

Direct evidence of macroregional distribution exists for many kinds of items. Highland-mined jade and obsidian were carried to elite centers throughout the eastern lowlands. Volcanic ash temper for pottery had a long history of being traded as far as northern Yucatan. Salt and fish from the coasts were moved inland. The famous Fine Orange pottery was made only in Tabasco, but was traded widely throughout the eastern lowlands beginning before A.D. 700. Fine Orange was mass-produced and easily transportable, but available in many shapes and designs suited to high- and low-income consumers.

In sum the Classic world of the eastern lowlands was one of many people – probably over ten million, perhaps two or three times that, given the fact that every tract that is carefully mapped produces abundant numbers of houses. This was not only a large population, but also an interacting, integrated one. Culturally, socially, and linguistically, the area in the Classic Period was a single sphere in many respects distinct from the rest of Mesoamerica, but it was internally a meaningful unit. Integration on this scale was not provided by the institution of the state, but by the elite prestige system and strong economic ties.

The collapse and the Early Postclassic Period

The world of the southern part of the lowlands fell apart between A.D. 800 and 900. The collapse of the south fundamentally altered the surviving system in the north. The universal impact of the collapse shows, if nothing else, that the whole area had been tightly interdependent.

The Classic way of life began to come apart first in the west, in the area around Palenque. Building in that area boomed until early in the 700s, tapered off, and ceased by 800. The last long count dates (dates in the Maya calendar) at big centers on the Usumacinta (Piedras Negras, Bonampak, Yaxchilan) were recorded before A.D. 840. Altar de Sacrificios on the Pasión River had Petén-style elite material until about 770, when fine-paste ceramics first began to show up. Major construction ceased by 910, and the site was abandoned by 950. After a similar style shift about 790, the site of Seibal actually expanded, and monument building continued until about 930, when the center and its environs were deserted. Tikal's population may have stayed about the same from the Early to the Late Classic, but the intersite area, to the north at least, declined in density, and central Tikal experienced a gigantic construction spree between 690 and 750. After that new construction slowed down, and stopped completely by 830. By 910 more than 90 percent of the population was gone. In the Belize Valley the major center of Benque Viejo was abandoned by 830, and the politically less important Barton Ramie settlement was deserted by 900. But people continued to build at Lamanai, in Belize, through the Early Postclassic. In central Yucatan a distinctive architectural style apparently had waxed and waned between 690 and 830, but from the Puuc hills to the north coast, the period from 800 to 1000 saw florescence and growth rather than decline.

In the southern part of the lowlands the collapse was not simply a cessation of elite activities, though elites may have been in a better position to desert the sinking ship first. Nor was the collapse simply a breakup of the state, as in the highland

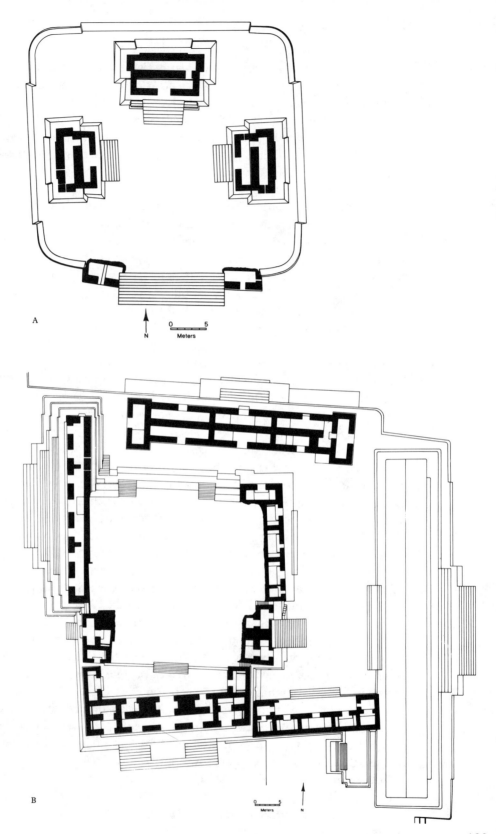

A

N

0 5
Meters

B

0 5
Meters

N

188

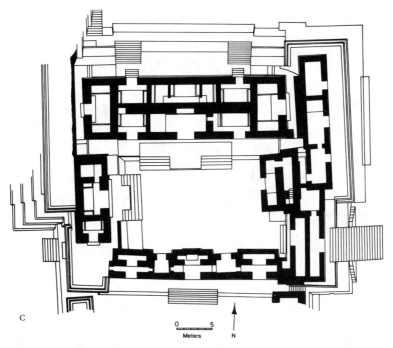

Figure 5.12. Structure A-V, Uaxactún. (A) The group consisted of temples in the Early Classic Period. (B) and (C) The main and upper stories of the structure in its near-final form. By the Late Classic Period, temple functions were overwhelmed by the administrative offices of the state. Redrawn from A. L. Smith (1950: figs. 60, 69, 70.)

Classic–Postclassic transition. In the eastern lowlands the destructive forces were powerful enough to prevent ordinary people from subsisting. We suspect that this could have happened only if households were already very dependent on one another for most "subsistence" needs. Whatever forces caused the collapse, they were powerful, thoroughgoing, and subtle enough to dismantle the entire basic economy of millions of people. After these tumultuous events the focus of activities shifted to the northern part of the lowlands, though the south was never completely depopulated and in fact was a last bastion against the Spanish conquerors.

From roughly 1000 to 1250 the site of Chichén Itzá was the most visible political center. Although elite-level ties between the eastern lowlands and western Mesoamerica show up archaeologically from Late Preclassic times on, Early Postclassic Chichén Itzá exhibits especially strong long-distance connections, to El Tajín in Vera Cruz and perhaps to Tula in central Mexico.

As a community Chichén Itzá was vastly different from the earlier Classic sites, north or south. The main focus of the city was a plaza the size of nineteen American football fields (about twelve hectares). In its center was a temple atop a high pyramid. The plaza was flanked by a huge ball court and by a few long, narrow buildings with roofs supported by columns decorated with bas-relief carvings of warriors in full dress. Adjoining this plaza to the east was a secondary plaza bounded by more colonnade structures. A skull rack or platform for sacrifices was built out in the

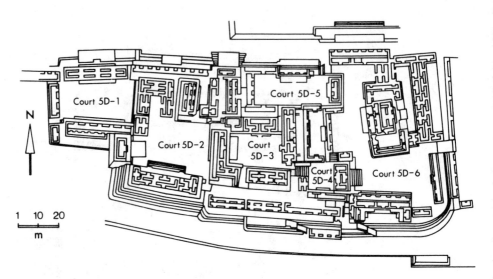

Figure 5.13. The Central Acropolis at Tikal. High-level decision makers, whose quarters were in the upper stories of the palace, were physically screened off from ordinary activities. The complex provided both residential and office space. Redrawn from Harrison (1970: fig. 1).

main plaza, and both plazas had numerous small, perhaps temporary, constructions whose ancient functions are unknown. A *sacbe* ran from the plaza 260 meters straight north to a cenote used for sacrifice. Away from the central plaza, and often connected to the "downtown" area by *sacbeob*, were at least fifteen other plaza groups with plazas that were between fifty and two hundred meters on a side. Usually these groups consisted of relatively few buildings – sometimes only a temple or range structure. Smaller plazas and house mounds occurred between these plaza groups. Nine ball courts are known from the Chichén Itzá vicinity. The large plazas and the ball courts might indicate, if nothing else, at least wider participation in civic-ceremonial activities in the Early Postclassic Period than in the Classic Period.

Cobá was an important Postclassic center in the northeastern Yucatan peninsula, which was an area of substantial population at this time. But about the relationship of the major capital to the northeast, which has somewhat different artifactual styles in the Postclassic, and indeed about Chichén Itzá's role in integrating the rest of the northern lowlands, little is known. Like Mayapán, its successor, Chichén Itzá may have exercised little control over the lives of people in the provinces, functioning mainly as a macroregional, elite-level central place.

The Late Postclassic Period

The first Europeans to see the people of the eastern lowlands were the sailors of Columbus's fourth voyage, who in 1502 encountered a heavily laden trading canoe in the Bay Islands off Honduras. In 1517 the Spanish landed an expedition, which was defeated in battle and forced to flee. Not until 1546 was Yucatan effectively brought under Spanish control. What is known today about the social system of this late period comes from the sixteenth-century written sources as well as from archaeology.

Postclassic Yucatecan houses were most often built like the houses in Figures 5.14 and 5.15, though more elaborate houses were constructed by wealthy families (Fig. 5.16). Most were built on low platforms, some of which today are preserved only as practically formless rock piles. The yard or house lot was usually surrounded by a 0.5–1.5-meter-high rock wall, enclosing an area of between thirty and forty meters in diameter. Postclassic houses in Petén, compared to their typical Classic counterparts, were made with cheaper materials and techniques (less lime plaster and cut stone), and they tend to occur singly more often than in courtyard groups.

Most households were engaged in farming, but they very likely were also active in remunerative, specialized production, such as growing cotton, tree crops, or vegetables, hunting, fishing, fowling, beekeeping, salt collecting, or making pots, sandals, baskets, idols, paper, leather, textiles, stone tools, or charcoal. Almost all households had to obtain at least salt, copal, textiles, fish, pottery, flint, and wooden objects – all items in frequent use – in the market. One of a woman's duties was to buy and sell goods in the market. The basic staple was maize, and manos and metates for corn grinding are commonly found archaeologically in household contexts. Most stone cutting tools were made of flint (usually provided by specialists), although obsidian blades became more available to common households in the Postclassic than they had been in the Classic. Everyone wore cloth mantles, even commoners, but the fancier varieties were reserved for the nobility.

Religious observances were held at the community level, and local communities had patron deities, but the most frequent and important rituals were carried out on

Plate 11. Part of a quadrangle formed by long, multidoorway "range" structures at Uxmal, a major Puuc center. Note the corbeled vaults and the rubble core-stone veneer masonry.

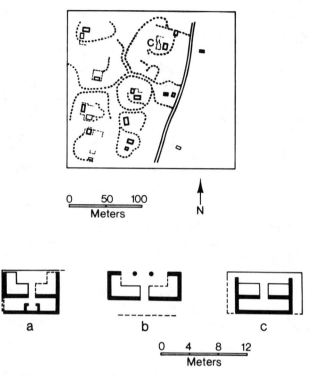

Figure 5.14. A representation of some houses in Mayapán. House c, in the lower part of the figure, is shown with its rock wall and neighboring house lots on the eastern edge of the city. It probably looked like the modern house in Fig. 5.15. Redrawn from A. L. Smith (1962: figs. 1, 8).

a family basis. Small shrines were commonly built next to people's houses, and each family apparently kept idols, which were wooden, clay, or stone representations of one or another of the major beings who inhabited the world of this animistic set of beliefs.

Three social classes – slaves, commoners, and nobles – were legally recognized, but the distinctions among classes were not firm and fast. Slaves were usually war captives, and were owned by lords. Commoners varied considerably in economic status, so that some wealthy and influential people, though commoners, were richer than some families of the nobility. On the whole the nobility was an endogamous caste that controlled political affairs, generally had the most favorable position in economic production and exchange, and had ritual duties that contributed to their power and standing. The overall impression is that status mobility – both up and down – helped make the social system what it was.

Within communities, households were occasionally grouped in clusters of two to four dwelling units on a house lot, in which case one of the residences was a bit larger and more elaborate, and there was a common, outdoor shrine. Men pooled their labor on a small scale in farming tasks, as did women in spinning and weaving. Unlike central Mexico, however, the people of Yucatan had no large, corporate clans like the *calpulli*. Patrilineage groups were recognized, but these were rather loose descent groups, which could include nobles as well as commoners, and as a body they had no common occupation, residential location, or productive assets except for a patron deity. If it were advantageous, ancestry could also be traced through the maternal line. Private property – that is, things not held in common, including houses, personal effects, orchards, cacao plantations, beehives, and slaves – was inherited from father to son.

Almost the entire island of Cozumel, just off the east coast of Yucatan, was divided up into house lots and fields demarcated with Late Postclassic stone boundary walls, all oriented to the same north–south, east–west grid. It is hard to imagine such a system growing by bits and pieces; on the contrary, the 300-square-kilometer land area may have been parceled out among several noble estates worked by families in tribute, tenant, or slave relationships to the landowner.

Mayapán is the best-known Late Postclassic city, but it was by no means a typical community of the times. Between A.D. 1250 and 1450 Mayapán was the leading political center of Yucatan. The settlement covered 4.2 square kilometers, and was contained within an encircling, dry-laid stone wall, which had seven major and five minor gates. Over 4,000 masonry structures were built within the city, of which 2,100 were dwellings, which suggests a population of about 12,000 people. At over 2,800 people per square kilometer, the city had a higher density than any known Classic Period urban center. An area of nineteen hectares – smaller than the "downtown" area of Chichén Itzá – at the center of the site contained all the large buildings. The main plaza was a fairly secluded area of about seventy-five by fifty meters, dominated by a seventeen-meter high temple-pyramid, which was the biggest building at Mayapán. At a volume of only about 10,000 cubic meters, this construction would have been dwarfed by even a second-echelon Classic Period temple. The majority of the structures in this main group were small temples and shrines. Fifteen

Figure 5.15. A modern Yucatecan house similar to the ancient structure c in Fig. 5.14. Redrawn from A. L. Smith (1962: fig. 17e).

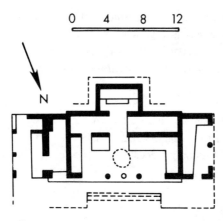

Figure 5.16. An elaborate house in Mayapán. Redrawn from A. L. Smith (1962: fig. 8).

long (thirty to thirty-five meters), open, colonnaded halls, each with an interior shrine, suggest civic-ceremonial activities involving wider participation. Residences in this central area were few, elaborate, and located on the fringes of the precinct. The public, ceremonial buildings at Mayapán were small and decidedly unpretentious monuments compared to those of the Classic Period, and no really large Late Postclassic constructions are known elsewhere in the eastern lowlands. Likewise, Tulum, another late town on the east coast, had a smallish civic-ceremonial precinct with very little residential and no administrative "office" space. Society's energies were clearly being directed toward other pursuits.

Until about 1450 the northern and central parts of the lowlands were loosely integrated into a single state or empire headquartered at Mayapán. After several of the ruling houses revolted, sovereignty reverted to the formerly constituent provinces, and that was the situation when the Spanish arrived. The eastern lowlands were divided into eighteen independent, territorial provinces (see Fig. 5.17). The administrative hierarchy consisted of the *halach uinic*, the greatest lord; *batab*s, who ruled in the town for the *halach uinic*; the *holpop*, "head of the mat," a municipal official; and the *ah cuch cab*s, members of the town council in charge of subdivisions. Tribute was paid to the *halach uinic* through the office of the *batab*, who was also supported by the people. In the days of the Mayapán "joint government" or empire, all of the *halach uinic*s were invited hostages of the ruler at Mayapán. Citizens of the town of Mayapán itself were exempt from tribute, but each of the *halach uinic*s had to be supported by tribute brought from his province by his second-in-command.

Gaspar Antonio Chi, a leading *cacique* and informant for Bishop Diego de Landa's *Relación de las Cosas de Yucatan*, wrote in 1582 that during the Mayapán era the

> lords of Mayapán held in subjection to the entire [country, and] the natives of it were tributary [to them during the period when they ruled]. The tribute [consisted of] small sheets of cotton, native hens, honey, [cacao and] a resin

which served as incense in the temples and sacrifices, [and in all] it was very little, in recognition of vassalage. (Tozzer, ed. and trans. 1941:230)

Granted that Chi (Xiu, one of the leading dynasties), first as a lord, second as a tribute payer to the Spanish, who were trying to drain the wealth of Yucatan through high tribute levies, and third as a person writing a hundred years too late to have had personal knowledge, probably is not an ideal source. Nevertheless, when he wrote that the tribute "was very little, in recognition of vassalage," we are inclined to believe him. Throughout Landa's *Relación* there are references to presents made to lords and priests, but nowhere is there indication that a large number of people were supported by tribute or that tribute was a very efficient engine for generating

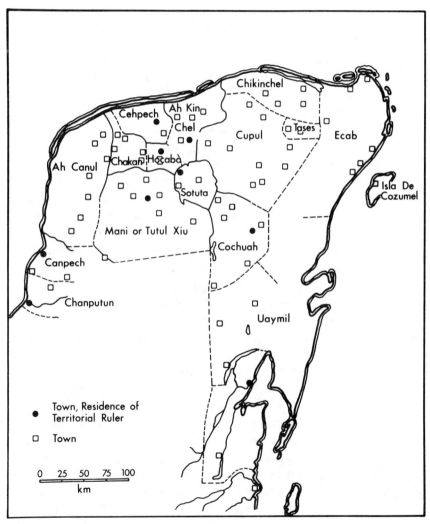

Figure 5.17. The *cuchcabal* or political jurisdictions of Yucatan at the time of the Spanish conquest. Redrawn from Roys (1957: map 1).

revenue. Instead, as we shall see, the lords had their own private means of generating wealth, means that were probably more reliable and efficient.

Closely associated with the nobles who ran affairs of state, and indeed members of the same families, were high-ranking priests. Rulers themselves often served in the temples and at ceremonies. The most important priest was the *ah kin mai*. Respected for his learning, he was responsible for counseling the ruler, educating the sons of the ruling family, and training lesser priests for the towns. Sacrifices, offerings, divination, dances, prophecies, and prayers were engaged in by nobles and commoners, on the community and the individual levels. No single deity, pantheon, or creed unified everyone, for the diversity of idols and oracles was too great. Though some religious practitioners were more important than others, no corporate church hierarchy existed.

What made Yucatan a highly integrated system was not the state or religion, but trade. People made presents to rulers, but they bought and sold with each other. The economic system was horizontally differentiated by individual, local, and regional specializations, and it was vertically differentiated, with several kinds of producer organizations and several kinds of markets. Profound and highly artificial interdependencies were created.

Markets probably operated in most towns, perhaps in the "ceremonial" precincts. Other towns, such as Ecab on the northeast coast, were singled out in the historical sources as commercial centers. Also mentioned as commercial towns in northeastern Yucatan were Chauaca, where lords and merchants were in the majority and where the market was housed in stone buildings, and Cachi, which had a large market plaza and an adjacent court building to settle disputes. Transactions on credit were arranged, and cacao, copper bells, beads, and Pacific-coast red *Spondylus* shells functioned as money. It was said that anything could be bought for cacao.

Lords – the political nobility – had the most advantageous position in Yucatecan trade. The same people who waged war, collected tribute, made laws, settled disputes, and were the spiritually purest, were, not coincidentally, important traders – though the nobles were not the only wealthy merchants. The lords purchased land for development: for orchards, cacao, or copal plantations. Slaves captured in war were used for labor on the lord's estates or in their fisheries. This provided impetus for the slave trade and an economic reason for warfare. Too, captives had exchange value in that they were often held for ransom. However, warfare could interfere with trade, it was said, so it had to be limited. The sign of a state of war, interestingly, was a jaguar skin displayed in the marketplace.

Trade in bulk goods that were in everyday use occurred over long distances. The high-quality salt from the northern coast was probably shipped all over Mesoamerica. Finished cotton cloth in bright colors was carried by sea to Campeche and Tabasco and to Honduras in exchange for cacao. Slaves were another important commodity in long-distance commerce. The Yucatecan demand for cacao was apparently great enough to cause farmers in Tabasco to give up growing maize and concentrate on cacao production for sale. They in turn obtained staples from people farther inland. Coastal–inland trade in maize was probably common in northern Yucatan.

Social ties with people in distant communities were facilitated by the lineage or patronymic system. Travelers could seek out persons of the same surname and be treated as one of the family. As there were about 250 surnames in Yucatan, an individual had potentially a very wide network. Travelers made pilgrimages to famous shrines and oracles, which seem to have been located in commercially important places, as on Cozumel. Indeed the relationship between religious practices and buying and selling was probably quite close. Yucatecos were said to have "earned a great deal by making idols out of clay and wood" – after all, the idols were high-turnover, household items. Each month of the ritual calendar had public feasts and ceremonies, and often the months were dedicated to celebrating the occupations. Thus, special festivals were held for hunters, fishermen, beekeepers, warriors, makers of idols of cedar, makers of pottery idols and braziers, and the professions in general, and also to commemorate cornfields and cacao plantations. These ritual observances were occasions for exchange; in addition, they could not but have stimulated production and consumption (of strong drink, among other things, as all feasts ended only after all present had made wineskins of themselves, according to Landa).

Although the complex commerce that bound households and communities together is apparent in the historical accounts, it is not immediately obvious in the archaeological record of the period. Markets, money, and everyday exchange are by their natures hard to detect archaeologically. One must be aware that the archaeological record may be biased in favor of politics and against commerce, just as it sometimes preserves the animal bone and destroys plant remains, and just as traditional history gave us the king lists and forgot economics.

Evolutionary trends in the eastern lowlands
Several persistent characteristics and determinative relationships can be extracted from the prehistory of the eastern lowlands. These factors made life what it was for the ancient people.

First, the eastern lowlands were never effectively dominated by one primate center (Fig. 5.18). No one city was ever vastly larger than its nearest rivals. No political or economic capital able to dwarf and stifle development over a large realm, as Teotihuacan did, ever evolved in the eastern lowlands. In Classic and Postclassic times there were probably no primate regional systems, even on a scale a tenth the size of the whole area. Early Postclassic Chichén Itzá *might* have politically and militarily controlled a large area, but it very likely did not provide the tight integration that affected all aspects of people's lives.

Instead, leading cities in the eastern lowlands had rivals close in population size and political importance, and close in proximity. Smaller centers, towns, and hamlets were near several larger centers, not just one, as is true in primate systems. Administratively, of course, people would have been "citizens" of only one Preclassic chiefdom or Classic or Postclassic state, but that would not necessarily preclude their interaction with the centers and the people of other, nearby polities. The range of choice in social and economic affairs must have been greater for the people of the eastern lowlands than for ancient Oaxacans, Mexicans, or Chiapas-Guatemalan highlanders. The between-city, horizontal interaction, too, was very different from

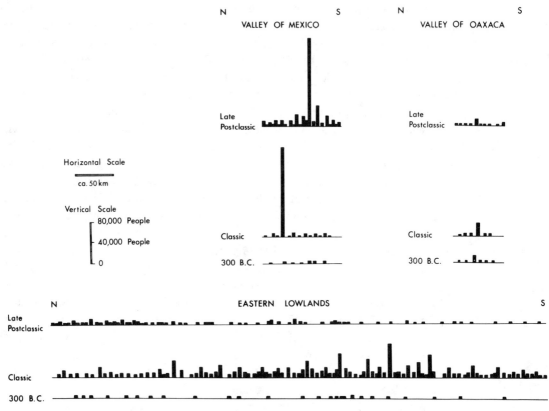

Figure 5.18. A visual representation of settlement patterns over time in the Valley of Mexico, the Valley of Oaxaca, and the eastern lowlands. These are idealized profiles of the sizes and distributions of centers for three successive time periods. The length of the horizontal line represents the length of each study area – the eastern lowlands area is by far the longest. The vertical lines stand for centers, and their heights indicate population size. North is to the left, giving an impression of the general locations of development. For the valleys of Oaxaca and Mexico, the number of secondary centers and their locations are idealized from the data discussed in Chapters 3 and 4. The eastern lowlands profiles are quite impressionistic.

the closed-off, vertical flows that characterized highland primate systems. Not until the Postclassic were there systems in western Mesoamerica that approached the eastern lowlands in horizontal complexity.

The broad, open quality of this area's regional systems needs to be stressed. For many kinds of social behavior (excepting sovereign authority, which will be addressed separately in a later paragraph), the whole network was the entire eastern lowlands. It would be difficult indeed to say where one social or economic system began and another ended. That people belonged to only one or two speech communities and shared the same kinds of household pots from one end of the peninsula to the other attests to regular, unconstrained interaction. Although this kind of everyday activity often escapes archaeologists and historians who are not attuned to it, such repetitive, everyday activity can be crucial in the shaping of social systems.

On the elite level of interaction, there were in the Classic Period regional styles of writing, architecture, and other endeavors associated with the state. Nevertheless these variations were minor compared to what was shared and held in common over the entire area. An area the size of the eastern lowlands in the highlands of Mexico had far greater regional variability in common items such as ceramics, in languages, in burial ritual, and in luxury trappings.

We have made the point that social closure and primacy are tightly associated, as are their opposites, open systems and more equally sized centers. In other words, vertical complexity occurs with a well-defined boundary, whereas, theoretically, horizontal complexity may be boundless. Presumably this relationship obtains at scales of a variety of sizes, and in many types of societies. For the eastern lowlands the point is of interest in several respects, not the least of which is understanding that political interaction had a form of organization related to but quite different from other fields of behavior, such as economics, which may be less vertically complex and less bounded.

In general, chiefdoms and states in the eastern lowlands tended to be unstable and often weak. Chiefdoms and traditional states almost everywhere are notoriously unstable, especially as regards succession to office. In the eastern lowlands, polities had those problems too, but there are also indications of substantial discontinuity in territory, administrative structure, and administrative capitals. Abandonments, cessations of monumental construction and stela erection, and dynastic realignments took place frequently. Polities emerged, gained in strength, and disappeared within one or two archaeological phases. Compare this instability with the Monte Albán polity: sovereign, recognizable, and authoritative for at least 1,200 years. Few political entities in the eastern lowlands are recognizable over that length of time.

In contrast, although the territorial political scene was typically turbulent, somehow the area maintained its basic integration. We suggest that this was accomplished by strong, relatively persistent social and economic institutions unregulated by political administration. These institutions were horizontally differentiated and horizontally integrated, and lacked a great deal of vertical control. They were open systems that were broad in scale, and inclusive rather than exclusive in membership. Market systems would be one such institution; the pan-Yucatecan system of patronymics was another. Thus the eastern lowlands, because of their weak and unstable states and their persistent socioeconomic integrations, contrast strikingly with the highlands.

The strategy for socioeconomic integration adopted by the people of the eastern lowlands had characteristics that mirrored the tropical lowland environment. This does not mean that the environment determined the shape and direction of the human system. But strategies that mimicked the patterns of environmental diversity produced acceptable results for individuals in the short run; manipulating tropical diversity was a way of building exchangeable surplus and amassing wealth. Other strategies – for instance, one borrowed lock, stock, and barrel from the highlands – quite conceivably might have failed from the start or have produced satisfactory returns for only a brief period of time.

Although this subject cannot be exhaustively treated here, we may note, for example, that households were dispersed widely over space. They relied on a variety of agricultural and craft production strategies. Considerable household-level specialization was practiced. Though maize was probably always the most important staple crop, there were many ways to grow it, and there were other crops as well. Large fields that grew a single species were probably rare. In addition to the diversity (horizontal differentiation), large amounts of goods and energy flowed from place to place and from household to household (integration). Some coordination of these exchanges undoubtedly took place, but it did not have to involve a strong vertical control. The low value of any single transaction, where there are many and diverse kinds of transactions, could make regulation unattractive for state administration; states might have developed in those situations in which large economic organizations had previously arisen and were already somewhat vertically coordinated. Little is known about middle-level organization and integration.

The dynamic aspects of conflicts between larger-scale, regional and pan-lowlands integration (including even connections to the rest of Mesoamerica), versus the diverse, middle- and lower-level integrations persistent in this areas's evolution, have a great bearing on understanding change in ecosystems. This line of reasoning leads to specific, testable hypotheses for future research. But instead of offering yet another scenario for the Classic Period collapse, or another speculative analogy for what "the Maya" were really like, we prefer to end this chapter on a note of cautiously optimistic restraint.

Much more can be and needs to be known about regional, local, and middle-scale social/ecological systems in the eastern lowlands. Unfortunately the archaeology of the eastern lowlands has been held back by much of the culture historical approach, the hype of *tumbología* (tombology, an archaeology of spectacular discoveries), and an undisciplined following of fickle intellectual fashions. But we are optimistic that improvements can be made because the means for doing so are simple and widely known: improvements in theoretical guidance, better research design, better methods, maintenance of databases, and cooperative, long-term, large-scale projects. Systematic data have been obtained in spite of the difficult field conditions of the tropical lowlands. A specialist in paleobotany in Yucatan, for example, wrote recently that "[m]uch has been said about the impossibility of recovering organic remains in environments like those that predominate in the Maya lowlands. Nevertheless the problem resides more in the type of excavation that has predominated in this region and in the scant interest in recovering information from activity areas" (Beltrán Frías 1987:227, our translation). And what's true for floral remains applies more broadly here – basic scientific, anthropological questions about the eastern lowlands "may be answered with improved field methods and research designs," as another worker in this field wrote recently. Certainly this would be a big step toward demystifying Mayanist archaeology.

6

Comparisons and conclusions

In this chapter we draw broad conclusions concerning selected aspects of cultural change, focusing on population dynamics, the state, and market systems. We conclude that the regional surveys have been gratifyingly productive in advancing our level of understanding in these areas of human action. However, we also conclude that in order to resolve some of our most important problems a perspective restricted to the analysis of regions is insufficient, and that we need more information on what Mesoamerica was like as a macroregional unit. This level of analysis presents a host of conceptual and methodological problems that anthropology is not now equipped to deal with, but we offer several suggestions for possible directions for future research.

Population dynamics

Some recent studies have proposed that population pressure was the causal variable in key long-term transitions such as those involved in the origins of agriculture and the development of complex societies, as well as in important historical events such as the collapse of the Classic system of the Mesoamerican eastern lowlands. Even Aztec human sacrifice and cannibalism have been explained in these terms. In general, these studies have begun by equating population pressure with rapid population growth. They then demonstrate archaeologically the existence of demographic growth (but not population pressure against an available food supply) and associate it through time with the specific process or event to be explained. Population growth, though rarely uniform either across space or through time, is then asserted to be the independent causal variable.

But population pressure is not a necessary outcome of population growth. The population of the Valley of Oaxaca more than tripled during the Early and Middle Formative periods, yet it was still markedly below the level of population that could have been supported in the region. During the Late Aztec phase in the Basin of Mexico, the population increased from roughly 175,000 people to approximately one million people in some 250 years, yet it was still below the estimated regional carrying capacity. In addition, an association or correlation between variables, especially as measured in archaeological time, does not necessarily imply a linear causal relationship. Even when two factors are seen to change simultaneously, it may not be the case that one of the factors initiated the shift in the other. For example, when population increase and agricultural intensification are observed coincidentally, it does not necessarily mean that a change in one caused a change in the other. The changes may both be the consequences of shifts in a third factor, such as increasing political complexity or changes in marketing or exchange patterns, which could result in intensified household production. Several studies have shown that larger households may be economically more successful and better able to respond to increased demands for labor. In sum, the demonstration of causality, rather than simply its assertion, is an unsolved problem in archaeological studies that put forth population pressure as an explanation.

Is it realistic to think about factors such as demand for labor and its influence on fertility, as we are suggesting, when all one has are archaeological data? Yes, very definitely. Serious methodological problems may be encountered, but if that is the way the world works, it is one's challenge as an archaeologist to come forward with ways to address the problems. Even with the limited information now at our disposal, we are in a position to show the complexity of population processes and their intimate relationships to human organizational factors. The archaeological record of the Valley of Oaxaca shows great variability in the demographic shifts among different topographic zones (piedmont versus alluvium) and among settlements that served diverse functions (administrative versus nonadministrative sites). During Monte Albán I, for example, the population of the piedmont zone increased much more rapidly than did the population of the alluvial zone. Although this difference was in part related to the different agricultural strategies used in these zones, we suggest that the more rapid piedmont population increases were closely tied to the special role the piedmont inhabitants carried out for the valley's administrative elite at Monte Albán. To feed the population of the growing capital, more people had to be encouraged in one way or another to farm the piedmont. Population increase, through increased fertility or immigration, was thus likely to have been a consequence of urban administrative demands.

In Mesoamerica, even at the regional scale, demographic fluctuations were quite complex and neither constant nor regular. In addition, within each region a growth phase in one place was often a period of depopulation in another. This is very clear if one compares the demographic cycles for the survey areas within the Valley of Oaxaca and the Valley of Mexico. Certain zones in all three of our study areas underwent unusually extreme population fluctuations. These shifts cannot be accounted for by those who argue that population growth is a constant phenomenon that occurs generation to generation everywhere, or by "natural population cycles." Obviously in such cases physical environmental features have no explanatory power either. Rather, shifts of this sort are most clearly understood when they are related to major organizational changes, and the effects these had on labor demands, migration, and the strategies that households adopted to cope with shifts in social and economic opportunities.

Finally, in the Valley of Mexico, the Valley of Oaxaca, and the eastern lowlands, major developmental changes in political complexity occurred at times when the populations of these regions were small and substantially below the levels that could have been sustained. In each of these areas, population did not even begin to approach its local "carrying capacity" until after state development, if then. Thus, it would seem suspect to use population pressure as the principal causal variable in the development of complex political institutions in any of these areas. It would appear to be more prudent to examine a wider range of causal factors.

In addressing some problems pertinent to demographic transitions, changes are best viewed on a very large spatial scale. For example, in examining the relatively slow rate of population growth in the Valley of Oaxaca during the Late Postclassic Period (Monte Albán V), one should consider that this rate may have been related to the rapid demographic growth occurring simultaneously during the Late Aztec phase in the Basin of Mexico. If, as is the case today, rapid growth phases in the Valley of Oaxaca were partially due to immigration from the surrounding mountains and highland valleys, one might speculate that the relatively slow rate of growth during Monte Albán V was in part due to a migration rate into the Valley of Oaxaca that was lower than the rates in prior growth phases (for instance, Monte Albán I). We propose that this lower rate may have been related to the very rapid migration at that time into the central highlands, especially the Valley of Mexico. Mountain populations that had previously "donated" migrants to the Valley of Oaxaca may instead have been sending migrants in the direction of the central highlands, because of the more rapidly growing economy of the latter area. Testing this hypothesis will not be easy. We will need some way to identify migrants, and we will need "national-level" data. Thus it is likely that satisfactory explanations of population trends require the researcher to work at different spatial scales: households, localities within regions, whole regions, and, as in the example just presented, large macroregions among which there can be significant flows of migrants.

The state in Mesoamerica
Not all societies have had states; many have fared quite well without them. The state may be defined as a special social institution, the dominant political authority in the region where it exists. The state governs a territory, with territorial subdivisions. States are found in societies with at least two social strata, the rulers and the ruled. In essence the state is an administrative apparatus with usually at least three hierarchical levels of functionaries, who make and carry out political decisions.

The origins and nature of this institution of society have always been an important concern for philosophers, historians, and social scientists, primarily because all of us today, for better or worse, live under the authority of nation-states. So we would like to know how and why our dominant institutions arose. Anthropology has long had the origins of civilization as one of its concerns, but to speak of the origins of the state is often wiser because this concept is easier to define and less value-laden.

The state is a regional phenomenon, and we treat it as such and in fair detail when we discuss its rise in Mesoamerica. Of course the state is not the only kind of regional organization the ancient Mesoamericans had. They also participated in kin groups, cults, and markets, among other organizations. To get a full picture, and even to understand the nature of particular states, one should examine other contemporary social institutions operating at the macroregional and regional scales, and at smaller scales.

By the time of the Spanish conquest, states were established everywhere in Meso-america. In fact, state-level organization was at that time and for a thousand years before a distinguishing characteristic of Mesoamerica, as opposed to the simpler societies beyond the frontier. In the more precocious regions, states were established in the last part of the Middle Preclassic or in the Late Preclassic. In areas like the eastern lowlands the state may not have developed until as late as the Early Classic. In the Valley of Mexico it was in place by A.D. 1. Because of the lack of evidence for a specialized administrative apparatus, we consider the La Venta–San Lorenzo area of the Olmec Horizon (about 1000 B.C.) to have been organized into competing chiefdoms, but not states.

Information about the state in Mesoamerica comes from archaeology and ethno-history. The latter kind of data can be quite detailed about such things as tribute, warfare, and offices and their duties, and it is especially useful for understanding the participants' view. The broad outlines of long-term change in states and the dynamics between states and their societies are accessible through archaeology, though details of diplomacy, functionaries, and so forth are missing.

First we review common features of the Mesoamerican states. The archaeological evidence (and in the case of the Maya, the epigraphic evidence as well) shows rather well that Mesoamerica's early states had territorial subdivisions, and probably at least a three-level administrative hierarchy. The state was maintained by tribute in goods and services paid by small-holders who made up the bulk of the common people. These were societies whose basic dividing line was between the rulers and the common people; other ranked categories may have existed as well. The aristocracy was internally ranked, as manifested in differences in place of burial and mortuary furnishings, and in the relative elaborateness of houses and palaces. Mesoamerica's early states commonly had fixed (as opposed to roving or rotating) capitals. Indeed it would seem that political administration was a primary high-order function of most Mesoamerican cities, although there was variation in time and place in urban functions. The proportion of economic exchange not controlled by the state varied in Mesoamerica. Generally market systems were present. At times they may have been less capacious than tribute systems, at other times more so. The amount of craft and agricultural specialization in Mesoamerica's state societies varied too, but specialized production was certainly present to an archaeologically perceptible degree everywhere.

Additional insights into the workings of Postclassic Mesoamerican states are supplied by the sixteenth-century written source. The following description pertains to Aztec states, but to varying degrees it applies to other Postclassic Mesoamerican states. The difference between the Aztec cases and other Postclassic states are in large part due to scale factors. Because the Tenochtitlan-based state of A.D. 1500 was larger than most, it had a disproportionately high administrative work load. Thus its decision-making and executive structure was larger and more specialized, and the number of managers that oversaw the work of other administrators was greater than in most Postclassic states. Nevertheless there are broad similarities in basic conception, purpose, and form.

The Postclassic state relied for much of its authority and legitimacy on a mythical and legendary historical charter in the oral and written manuscript traditions. This charter justified the existence of sovereignty, established the sacred duties of the ruler, and set down a reciprocal, contractual arrangement whereby the ruler would be materially supported by the commoners while he provided peace, well-being, and security for the whole. The moral order, past and present, was interpreted by priests, but the sovereign himself, his family, and other members of the nobility had sacred ritual burdens, especially self-sacrifice, purity, and penance, which they were obligated to carry for the rest of society. In fact at the highest levels the ranks of the priestly hierarchy were filled with the same people who occupied the highest administrative positions.

State revenues were generated by regular and special-occasion tribute in goods and services. In one way or another all classes, in both home and conquered provinces, contributed to the maintenance of state institutions. The state invested in agricultural production, craft industries, and infrastructure, and had access to a portion of the surplus from these enterprises through special tribute arrangements. Revenue was generated by the manipulation of long-distance trade and large-scale marketing, and by taxes on marketing activities. Warfare was a major way of generating revenue, at least in the short run, though the costs and benefits of military adventures did not always add up advantageously. (We discuss this point further later.)

Diplomacy and warfare were highly formalized. Confederacies of small states and alliances of temporary convenience were common. Terrorism as a relatively cheap method of displaying power, control, and legitimacy was a frequent policy. The state ran schools for the training of rulers and cadres, and it granted and withheld rewards. Several levels of adjudicative functions culminated with the ruler himself. Rulers were assisted by advisers who held formal offices (such as military leader and chief priest), and by a council of the highest nobles, which also was the body charged with selecting a new ruler. A large palace that functioned as the residence of the ruler and as the state's main administrative office building was typical. How much of this description might apply to older Mesoamerican states is not yet resolved, but at least in some areas archaeological methods are probably capable of describing long-term change in state structure and function.

In most respects, then, Mesoamerican states were reminiscent of traditional states elsewhere in the world – for example, China prior to the Ch'in unification, Scythia, Kachari, Angkor, and Peru since the Early Intermediate; Ankole, Axum, Egypt, Jimma, Kuba, Volta, Yoruba, and Zande in Africa; and Mesopotamia from the Uruk Period until the Persian empire. This list does not pretend to be complete, but it shows that in many places and at different times, a similar kind of social institution – the state – evolved.

These traditional states were not the kinds of powerful, far-reaching nation-states of today. They tended to rely on expressions of legitimacy and authority more than on force, and they often did not have very large bureaucracies. Political instability was the rule. The societies of these traditional states did not have the capacity to harness the large amounts of energy that might have overcome the size limits imposed, for example, by relatively poor transportation and communication. *Why* the technology for energy capture was not extended is an interesting question, and one that would perhaps yield a variety of answers for the cases mentioned. In Mesoamerica we suggest that the prerequisite commercial development did not come until quite late; and when it did, the Aztecs indeed tried to consolidate political and economic control over one of Mesoamerica's prime transportation and food-producing resources: the Basin of Mexico lake system. In general, in systems in which increased production depends mostly on massed labor, the limits to state power are set by the state's capacity to bring together and control large numbers of people in a territory small enough so that the costs of administration are not overwhelming. Productive gains cannot all be consumed by administrative needs and the prestige system if the technology of energy capture is to be improved and channeled into basic production and infrastructure.

Thus the basic problems of the traditional Mesoamerican state, and perhaps of traditional states in general, are both organizational and technoenvironmental, and the two domains are so intimately related that it makes little sense to attach general causal priority to either. Traditional states do not grow in size indefinitely, because they are organizationally limited. They are organizationally limited in two senses: (1) Legitimacy as a motivating device requires personal knowledge and intervention to keep functionaries and lesser nobility in line, but presumably this can operate only up to a certain scale before revolt is likely (though the development of writing may help); and (2) growth in the size of the state requires growth in administration, which tends to be funded by essentially predatory means such as costly sumptuary systems, tribute, and warfare, which inhibit basic economic growth. The traditional state is therefore limited too by its physical and socioeconomic environment, because (1) given its structure and strategy, commercial and industrial enterprises have never been promoted or protected sufficiently, and because (2) in some cases, but not in all areas, topographic conditions and the lack of draft animals make the task of improving transportation and communication that much more difficult. The evolution of the nation-state in Europe, nevertheless, demonstrates that these problems can be surmounted.

The problem of state origins

We have been reviewing here some recurrent features of the Mesoamerican state, and have pointed out that elsewhere in the world state institutions very similar in form were developed. Apparently this same general form of institution evolved under many different conditions. The processes that produced states may be quite varied cross-culturally, and may have been different even within Mesoamerica. In some instances elsewhere, states were formed within the historical ken. In these cases (for example, many of the African kingdoms), with the short time scale afforded by written records, particular events, troubles, conquests, migrations, and personalities loom large. Warfare plays a large role, as do the daring and organizational genius of great men. In cases where a broader (and sometimes more objective) time perspective is available, these kinds of particular events are often not known, but the long-term processes look more important after all: problems of ensuring a supply of basic goods in the face of internal or external economic or environmental disturbances, the option of larger-scale integration to increase the volume of commodity flows, long-range problems in maintaining "balance of trade" in elite goods or basic production to support the elite, or difficulties in securing controlled boundaries.

Long-range systemic problems of this sort seem to have been important factors behind the creation of state institutions, even though we often do not know what the particular catalytic events were. Almost certainly the problem of defining and maintaining territory of sufficient size to allow satisfactory production had as one solution greater vertical differentiation and wider regional administrative integration. The securing of stable political integration among horizontally differentiated segments with fissional tendencies was perhaps a crucial factor in several regions, including the eastern lowlands. Functionally specialized segments might require coordination and hence vertical specialization, but this in itself does not necessarily imply a *political* institution. Economic integration might under some conditions proceed without the state. On the other hand, horizontally differentiated units that are not particularly specialized, but are simply territorial, require vertical integration for efficient communication and handling of problems on a larger scale – given that there is a reason for integration in the first place. If the common purpose for a pooling of interests is political in nature – boundary maintenance, offense-defense, or diplomacy, for example – the creation of a state apparatus may be the best and only option. Note that the set of horizontal, conjoined segments is one hierarchical level, and the new institution is primarily seen above this, at the top. If administration is vertically specialized with each segment, then we have a three-tiered administrative hierarchy, though just how integrated the whole is – whether local affairs or many spheres of activity are tightly coordinated – may vary considerably.

Our approach to the rise of the state thus places relatively little emphasis on the particular realms of activity – such as warfare, trade, irrigation, and population growth – that have been used by other scholars either as prime movers or in combination as "systems." No single prime mover is likely to explain very many cases, as states arose under a variety of conditions and in many different physical as well as social environments. At the same time the mere conjoining of these kinds of variables in systems models may sometimes be too speculative, too abstract, and too far removed from real life to be a satisfactory, cross-culturally valid theory. Instead, we believe that the concepts of complexity, integration, scale, and boundedness may provide the formal yet operational dimensions necessary for a general theory; and the notion of more or less inclusive levels of integration provides a way of making the desired links between regional and household-level strategies.

Our intention is to define and to understand the variability in integration, complexity, scale, and boundedness among human social systems and to develop a coherent theory or set of integrated general statements that will permit us to predict how these four variables will change in response to shifts in the coping strategies adopted by the different institutions and decision makers within a society. These changes in institutional strategies and goals often occur as adaptations or adjustments to problems that could be considered examples of the traditionally defined prime movers. To this extent we are interested in changes in factors such as population, exchange, and warfare. But it is our contention that these factors, as they have been conventionally used, are too broad and too simple, and that they may have very different effects on societies of varying scale, complexity, integration, and boundedness. In addition, even within a single society, a factor like demographic change is likely to be viewed very differently by each systemic component, and it may provoke very different responses from them.

It may seem that by this discussion we have unnecessarily complicated the issue of state origins. But on examination our statements concerning the concepts of vertical and horizontal differentiation, integration, and scale are much less abstract and much more operational than the key concepts of many of the current hypotheses of state origins. A look at the data requirements is helpful here. Even with archaeological data alone, one can get a fair idea of numbers of people, administrative territories and their centers, probable directions, kinds and amounts of interaction, boundaries, and the outlines of agricultural and craft specialization. All of these kinds of data can and need to be gathered from entire, behaviorally defined regions in such a manner that household-level activities can be connected with ever larger spheres of integration. State formation is a regional process, not one that can be understood at a single site, but like other regional processes, to be understood it must be related in concrete ways to the strategies of the families or households that make up the broad masses.

State dynamics

Mesoamerican states were not all alike. Even among the three areas we have treated – the valleys of Mexico and Oaxaca and the eastern lowlands – differences are easily detected. Teotihuacan's state was a larger, more complex, and more powerful machine, for example, than the late Postclassic, petty kingdoms of Oaxaca. The available information from other regions in Mesoamerica suggests that other variations existed too. Examination of the variations over time and among our three areas gives us a few tentative ideas about processes.

The Classic Period states of the highlands had the power to control economic activities directly, including food and craft production as well as distribution. They collected massive amounts of tribute, which were allocated to the support of the capital. On the other hand, through most of the Postclassic the highland states were weaker than they were in the Classic. The states of the eastern Mesoamerican lowlands, even in the Classic, were also relatively weak. These states never succeeded in gathering their societies' forces together in a single place, and they did not (except perhaps at the end, fatally) have the means to direct the destiny of whole regional economies, as did the highland Classic states.

In the smaller, less vertically integrated states (that is, the Classic eastern lowlands and the Postclassic cases), "politics" tended to be an activity of the families of the elite caste, who used the advantages of state power and connections as one of a series of ways of acquiring wealth and advancing in the Mesoamerican prestige system. Never could they establish and maintain a monolithic integration of a large population and of all sectors of a regional system, and probably it was not in their interest to do so.

Perhaps the single most important factor behind this somewhat simplified contrast between strong and weak states was the degree of vitality of independent economic formations, especially productive institutions and market systems. We shall return to this idea again in the section on the evolution of market systems.

Some of the differences among Mesoamerican states are matters of scale. The tiny (around 100 square kilometers) political integrations of the Postclassic Valley of Oaxaca had no need for the larger administrative apparatus of the earlier Monte Albán state. Variation in the degree of horizontal specialization at different levels of administrative institutions is also apparent. Perhaps this kind of variation was due to difference in the nature of the tasks being carried out and where in space the activities were undertaken.

An instructive comparison may be made between Teotihuacan and Monte Albán. We suspect that Teotihuacan's state administration may have had greater horizontal specialization, as the tasks overseen were many, varied, and located in different places in space. Teotihuacan's state had to deal with agriculture and tribute close to home, in the rest of the Valley of Mexico, and at farther reaches, in places like Puebla and Morelos; city administration; a large and vertically complex system of craft production and marketing; possibly ideological functions of pan-Mesoamerican importance; and the conduct of diplomacy, warfare, and imperial administration. Each of these activities considered separately is significant, and their coordination would have required yet more complexity. Many of these tasks had to be carried out and supervised in different, widely dispersed places. But in the solution adopted by the Teotihuacan state, most of the coordination and administration of these activities took place not in low-level secondary centers located throughout the territory, but at the highest level, in the major palaces in the "downtown" section of the city.

The form that the Monte Albán state took was rather distinct, due to differences in the tasks and purposes of the institution, which required different numbers and kinds of functionaries, and owing also to the difference in scale between the two systems. Monte Albán, after all, administered a territory considerably smaller and less populous than did Teotihuacan. Thus, even for the same tasks, Monte Albán would have needed fewer overseers and managers. But the nature of the tasks differed too. Monte Albán did not have the pan-Mesoamerican mercantile, imperial, diplomatic, or ideological functions of Teotihuacan. Instead, its principal concerns were boundary maintenance and related activities, and the securing of revenues to pay for what that entailed. Monte Albán's solution was to rely on secondary and tertiary administrative centers within its territory. Even city affairs may have been handled by the site subdivisions and not by the state itself.

Monte Albán created secondary and tertiary centers as part of its strategy of expanding surplus by farming the piedmont. Complexity thus was enhanced at the lower levels of the state administration when the system expanded internally. When it expanded externally, internal integration on the secondary level was relaxed.

Perhaps this process is a less extreme version of Teotihuacan's strategy of concern for external matters, primacy, and attenuation of rural integration.

Problems of state dynamics (including the causes and consequences of changes in complexity, integration, scale, and boundedness) are as theoretically relevant to anthropology as is the question of state origins. Many of the long-term processes involving states can be profitably studied using archaeological data. Variation in the spatial extent of state control can be shown to be related to the size and complexity of administrative institutions. Change in spatial extent may affect the amount of internal interdependence, the total administrative work load, or both. Another way of conceiving of scale here is to treat the size of the organization in terms of the number of participants: more participants means a greater administrative work load, as long as the amount of integration is held constant. If the participants are spread over some distance in a territory, then additional administrative costs are incurred as a function of the distances involved.

Changes in the nature of the tasks a state undertakes and supervises constitute another demonstrable cause of change in state organization. In this regard, asking why and in what ways a region is integrated by its state institution may be quite productive. Certain tasks or purposes may require a great deal of investment in one administrative level. For example, external military concerns are usually the domain of the highest level. They may require certain kinds of horizontal and vertical differentiation and integration, whereas other activities, such as investment in agriculture, require distinct administrative structures.

More research on these kinds of questions is clearly needed. At present we may conclude that changes in state structure result from any of a variety of factors that change the scale of the integrated unit or the nature of its tasks and its degree of integration. Additional factors impinging on state dynamics have to do with the relationship between states and other regional institutions, such as market systems. This we develop further in the next section.

On the dynamic relationship between states and market systems

In the preceding sections we contrasted Mesoamerica's relatively strong states and its relatively weak states. The strength of regional market systems and other kinds of commercial institutions may have a great deal to do with the difference between these states. It is apparently difficult for strong states to emerge in areas serviced by already complex and horizontally integrated commercial institutions, just as autonomous commercial institutions often develop only slowly in situations where integration is provided by powerful early states. For example, craft guilds were either used for governmental ends or simply outlawed in the Roman republic and empire. It wasn't until long after the collapse of Roman power that guilds finally emerged in Europe as autonomous institutions, integral parts of the expanding economy of the Middle Ages.

On the level of the household, a well-developed market system is capable of supplying a relatively broad range of goods and services in large volumes and at a variety of prices and locations. The consumer has choices. The householder living under a strong early state, however, is faced with a narrower range of competing goods and services, often in lower volumes, at administratively fixed prices, and at single, fixed locations. Furthermore, the fact that there are multiple, independently operating suppliers in market-dominated economies means that consumers may still cover their needs if one source of supply is cut off, whereas in central supply systems a perturbation of supply may affect everyone.

On the level of the controlling elite families, too, where one lives – in a market-dominated economy or in a strong early state – will make a difference. Market systems provide another arena for entrepreneurial activity, another potential source of income, and another way to make connections, pick up followers, and increase one's macroregional prestige. Thus in the ethnohistorically known Postclassic Maya societies, the political leaders were also among the most prominent long-distance traders.

Market territories are overlapping areas, defined only loosely by the process of shifting consumer and supplier habits. Thus both suppliers and consumers maximize their freedom to choose optimal marketing destinations. State territories and administrative districts, by contrast, are nonoverlapping and exclusive. If one lives in New Jersey, for example, one cannot go to New York City to obtain a driver's license, even if they are less expensive and better-made there. You may visit Forty-Second Street, however, to buy a cheap stereo. Market systems require more unbounded space for efficient operation, and macroregions with market integration will be resistant to the "tariff walls" or other restrictions on movement that might be erected by administrative institutions. Thus, as in the Mesoamerican eastern lowlands, or the highlands in the Postclassic, states were small in territorial size, and smaller than the economic systems, and they had relatively permeable boundaries. These states were thus not at all coterminous with society, as people's interdependent connections often crossed political boundaries. Note, incidentally, that this is a key difference between the early chiefdoms and the petty states of the Postclassic.

In technologically more sophisticated contexts, especially where rapid transportation over long distances makes foreign competition a real threat, economic organization may need the protection of a relatively large and strong state. Entrepreneurs in England in the latter half of the sixteenth century thus apparently required access to the state administration to protect their nascent capitalist industries. On the other hand, and consistent with a view of certain basic incompatibilities between state and commerce, modern kinds of economic enterprises hardly thrived at all in those sixteenth-century European countries that were dominated by old-fashioned, absolutist monarchies. In Mesoamerica too, such cases of economic institutions needing a certain degree of state intervention can be found. In Aztec times, large-scale coordination and management of the piedmont and lake hydraulic resources in the Valley of Mexico would have been beyond the capabilities of any single city-state. Development of extensive *chinampas* required control of lake levels, which meant coordination of the amount of overflow permitted to reach the lake from piedmont tributaries. Alliances among city-states thus allowed for greater economic integration. But the *chinampas*, their products and their labor force were not under direct control of the Aztec king. Instead, in many instances tracts of *chinampa* lands were granted to other lords as fiefs, the king forfeiting direct control in exchange for tribute, and, he hoped, loyalty. We would interpret this as an illustration not of hand-in-glove harmony, but of a temporary balance between dynamic and mutually antagonistic social forces.

None of this is exclusive to Mesoamerica. These are general processes, seen elsewhere and at different times. African states of historical times also tended to be fairly weak politically, probably because of Africa's strong market systems. These kinds of problems are presently understood only vaguely. Further study is necessary, for example, on the problem of how the size of the state is determined by the demands for economic integration. So far we must conclude that we know very little about this, but in the next section we propose an explanation for why regions or macroregions may become progressively more commercialized as the power of the state declines.

Secular trends in state–market relations

One of Mesoamerica's most prominent secular trends in prehispanic times, one that we have seen in all three of our study areas, was the increased level of commercialization and the decline of governmental power after the Classic Period. To explain this trend, it may again be useful to consider how people may have altered their strategies in order to cope with novel situations. Markets are institutions that always require some sort of regulation to function smoothly. Disputes among market participants must be adjudicated, "con artists" and thieves apprehended and punished, hoarding controlled to keep prices at acceptable levels, and so on. We may also assume, assuredly, that many or perhaps all of these regulatory functions during the Classic were the domain of state institutions. Control, perhaps, may be a more appropriate term than regulation, at least in the highland systems.

Given strong state regulation of market systems, the collapse of these states would have presented serious problems to market participants, who no doubt wanted to maintain at least a minimally acceptable level of market functioning. We suggest that it was under the extreme conditions of collapse of state power that market participants innovated in such a way as to keep commerce going. Exactly what would have been involved is not clear, but perhaps our understanding can be heightened by examining some historically known parallels. Following the collapse of what had been strong Romanized states in western Europe after the seventh century A.D., there began a long period of commercialization and growth in the numbers of markets, accompanied by grow in the number and importance of nongovernmental commercial institutions, such as craft guilds and self-governing cities of merchants. This happened in a climate of declining state controls, involving, for example, the cessation of the Roman impost (the basic market tax that had existed for centuries), a virtual disappearance of financial branches in state bureaucracies, the founding of many new markets without royal authorization, and even the independent minting of coins by various cities no longer under royal control.

China's parallel "medieval revolution" was accompanied by reduced levels of government meddling in market systems. The consequences included a growth of many new towns with economic functions, and a growth in the number, wealth, and power of merchants.

The final word has yet to be written on the nature of local and interregional commercial systems in Late Postclassic Mesoamerica. Considering what little we know, however, it is clear that much economic activity was carried out through various kinds of nongovernmental institutions of the sort that developed in Europe and China. Autonomous commercial cities and "ports of trade," governed by merchants, dotted the eastern Mesoamerican landscape by the time the Spaniards arrived. Included were communities in the regions called Xicalango and Acalan, in the Bay of Chetumal and the Gulf of Honduras, and at the slave-trading center at Tuxtepec in Oaxaca (Fig. 1.2).

Guildlike associations of craftsmen are often mentioned in ethnohistoric sources and in Spanish descriptions of the central highlands urban centers. These organizations were obviously not just extensions of an official structure. The preeminent commercial institutions, which had virtually Mesoamerica-wide significance, were the various *Pochteca* associations. These were found in a number of central highlands cities, but they all seem to have participated in a wider league of *Pochteca*. *Pochteca* judges adjudicated in the market places of the Valley of Mexico. They were responsible for the bulk of long-distance trade in and out of the central highlands, traveling to the ports of trade in Xicalango and the other locations that we mentioned previously. Although the evidence is equivocal, there are indications they alone conquered the province of Soconusco (Fig. 1.2).

Although the precise nature of *Pochteca* organization is not known, we do know that the members resided together in their own *barrios* in each city where they were found, had their own deities and ceremonials and internal hierarchical structures, and, through a moral code and their own courts for judging themselves, maintained a high ethical standard. They were not, strictly speaking, members of the Aztec nobility, but were often very wealthy and highly esteemed, even by the ruler. The *Pochteca* were also not state functionaries, although they did at times cooperate with the ruler in various commercial, espionage, and military activities.

We propose that the developing commercialization of the Postclassic paralleled the changes we described for medieval Europe and China, and that it was based on the increasing separation of governmental and commercial institutions. We would expect these Postclassic commercial institutions to have developed out of Classic Period predecessors such as the solar market system and the walled craftsmen's compounds of Teotihuacan, but we suggest that they became more autonomous and self-regulating after the collapse of the powerful governments. Weaker Postclassic states and commercialization were consequences. Once developed as highly autonomous and firmly established entities, the various market systems, *Pochteca* associations, and so on, could not be easily reincorporated into official structures. As a consequence, compared to earlier, Classic times, levels of state control and state income were precipitously reduced. This allowed the kinds of market arrangements that result in greater economic participation among the general population, and more evenly distributed wealth, to thrive. This is not to argue that strong state control could never again have been instituted, or that states did not attempt to impose controls. But the costs of doing so were certainly higher, and the likelihood of long-term success lower, than when powerful states first developed during the latter part of the Formative.

We have thus far set down our conclusions about states and markets – first seen separately, and then together, in dynamic relationship. It is now time to address the largest-scale problem: not only political and economic arrangements, but the entire social system, and not only of a single region, but of the entire macroregion. This problem is immensely more difficult, as we shall see; nonetheless we ought to begin to resolve the problem by giving our impression of the basic nature of the main linkages among Mesoamerica's regions, the linkages that shaped the macroregional system. Our discussion is only the beginning; much work still must be carried out.

First, we identify several variables we think might be worth taking into consideration in explaining the differences in size that can be observed among the Mesoamerican states. In what follows, we assume that the larger states suffer diseconomies of scale. That is, their administrative costs per capita are higher. But this doesn't imply that all states will remain small and efficient, as under certain conditions large size is advantageous (from the perspective of those who are governing) in spite of the administrative inefficiencies entailed. Visualize a region populated by several competing autonomous polities, among which there is relatively free movement of migrating families. The taxation rate in each polity must remain low, as taxpayers are likely to emigrate when their tax burden is higher than it would be in adjacent areas. The only strategies open to a ruler wishing to raise taxes are to patrol the society's borders to reduce emigration, or conquer adjacent territories to which people might emigrate, leaving them without any desirable residential alternatives. Viewed in this way, larger territorial entities produce more tax revenues; if distance is a variable that is taken into consideration by a potential emigrant (which it surely is), then emigration is inhibited in larger territories because the average distance a family must travel to reach a border is greater than in a smaller territory. (This is assuming that the state has a roughly circular form; this dictum would not apply if the state happened to be long and narrow.) Even the guarding of borders to inhibit emigration is less costly for larger territories, as the ratio of border length to societal area declines with increasing size.

Countering these potential increases in revenue in the larger systems are the costs of military expansion and of the administration of the larger territory. A stable, large political entity can be developed and maintained only so long as the increased tax revenues more than offset the costs of militarism and the diseconomies associated with the governance of the larger area. Here also must be considered the extent to which the state is able to raise taxes even after territorial aggrandizement. Even if emigration becomes a less viable strategy for families oppressed by high taxes, over-taxation could damage economic growth or result in rebellions and strikes.

Similar considerations are relevant to understanding the extent to which states are able to tax trade routes. If a macroregion has multiple trade routes for some valuable commodity, with each route passing through a separate political entity, then taxes on the movement of goods along each route must remain low. Any unit raising taxes will lose traffic along its route. Again, only a territorially large state that controls all possible trade routes is able to raise taxes on the trade goods. Again, though, the large state will be unstable if the costs of expansion and administration of the larger unit are greater than the new revenues.

Applying this set of propositions to the Mesoamerican states (or states anywhere) is not easy because a large number of variables must be considered simultaneously. The likelihood of emigration as a household strategy, for example, is conditioned by a number of factors. Distance to a border is one variable we have already mentioned. Several other factors are relevant. If adjacent territories are environmentally inferior, emigration is less likely as it would entail a decline in standard of living. The same could happen if movement involves loss of access to a well-developed market system. Or, if adjacent territories are overpopulated, emigrants might not be welcomed. Too, emigration is more likely to be adopted as a strategy if adjacent areas are culturally and linguistically like the home territory. A further complication in trying to arrive at values for the variables in the cost–benefit equation for any given region is that the values may change through time.

Overlooking for a moment the extreme difficulties of this kind of analysis, several suggestions can be made with an eye toward explaining some of the differences we have observed among the states in our three study areas. We start by suggesting that territorially large states could not have been particularly viable in the southern highlands macroregion. A polity controlling only the Valley of Oaxaca could, no doubt, have raised taxes on the valley's residents to relatively high levels before suffering mass emigration. In spite of high demands placed on them by the state, valley families would probably have chosen to stay put. Emigrants from the valley would have faced poorer agricultural land virtually everywhere they might have gone in the southern highlands. Too, it is likely they would have suffered even more of a decline in their standard of living by moving away from the valley's relatively well-developed market system (although note that this system worked better at some times than at others). No exceptionally valuable commodity had its source in Oaxaca, so it is not likely that the monopolistic control of trade routes would have been particularly productive of revenues. All in all, the costs of conquering and administering a southern highlands empire could not be offset by significant gains in state revenues. We noted only two periods in which there was any sign of military expansion beyond the limits of the valley: phases II and (to a small extent) V. Neither of these episodes resulted in the creation of a large, enduring Monte Albán "domain" over the southern highlands.

A contrast can be drawn in these regards between the southern highlands and the central highlands. Emigration from the Valley of Mexico was probably always a highly feasible alternative for families oppressed by too-eager tax collectors. Those areas adjacent to the Valley of Mexico, including southern Hidalgo, Tlaxcala, the Puebla Valley, Morelos, and even the Valley of Toluca to the west, are highly similar to the Valley of Mexico from the point of view of potential agricultural production (and probably also in terms of access to market system, although we lack sufficient information on this point). We doubt that a city as large, complex, and wealthy as Teotihuacan could have been supported in the absence of hegemony over a domain extending over thousands of square kilometers into these adjacent valleys, and thus making possible some degree of control over the free interregional movement of families wishing to flee an oppressive tax burden and the inequities of a solar market system.

Recall too that the obsidian mines in and near the northern Valley of Mexico were some of Mesoamerica's most important. We have already noted that the monopoly control of the obsidian trade seems to have been one of Teotihuacan's major economic supports. Similar reasoning can be applied with respect to certain other trade items. A territorially large state, such as Teotihuacan or Tula, interposed between northern Mexico and the rest of Mesoamerica to the south, would have been in a position to monopolistically control the movement of certain precious materials that were mined in the north, and then traded to the south, where they were used in Mesoamerica as symbols of elite status. This would have included "blue-green mineral stones," cinnabar and hematite from the Chalchihuites region of Zacatecas, and turquoise from New Mexico.

Thus we would argue that the cost–benefit calculus favored political integration over very large territories in the central highlands. Can we apply these lines of reasoning to the eastern lowlands? No analogue exists there of the Valley of Mexico obsidian mines, or of the northern-Mexico-to-Mesoamerica trade in precious materials, that would favor the growth of large unified polities based on monopoly control of trade routes. But surely the potential for the free movement of families away from oppressive states would have been very high throughout the eastern lowlands. Not only is agricultural productivity broadly similar over the whole area, but linguistic uniformity (and institutions like the system of patronymics) would have greatly facilitated movement across local political boundaries. Small states would have been forced to keep their demands on families to a minimum. Only those states controlling very large areas – ideally, for those in power, the entire eastern lowlands – could apply pressure on people to produce more and not suffer significant losses of labor power as a consequence. Why, then, didn't such large political entities ever develop and persist in the eastern lowlands? Attempts were made to aggrandize large territories, for example at Mayapán, and probably at Chichén Itzá. But, generally speaking, eastern lowlands polities were territorially rather small. Although we have no final resolution to offer for this enigma, we think it will be important to keep in mind something we suggested earlier: The way people adapted to the eastern lowlands precluded the growth of costly primate centers governing very large territories. The key means of adaptation to the eastern lowlands, involving the "management of diversity," entailed costly, complex exchange mechanisms such as market systems. As is true for all such exchange systems, heavy taxation probably would have resulted in declined productivity rather than increased state revenues. And if governments themselves absorbed the exchange functions, the administrative costs would have been so high as to eliminate any possible gains in tax revenues. Thus the costs of larger system size could never be offset by gains in revenues. Only in the highlands, where monocrop cultivation can produce substantial state revenues with a minimum of administrative costs, could the larger, more cumbersome, and costly political institutions and their primate centers be supported.

Studying macroregional evolution

Certain changes in scale, integration, complexity, and boundedness in our three study areas could be understood largely, but not completely, by analysis at the regional scale. Thus the question of why the capitals of Monte Albán and Tenochtitlan had the forms and functions that they had could not be answered by examining only the sites themselves, however detailed the study. Nor would it be sensible to answer the same question at the very large scale of Mesoamerica, for too much detail of the kind implied by the question would be lost. Instead, satisfactory answers were provided primarily by controlling the relevant variables at an intermediate scale – in these cases, the regions pertaining to Monte Albán and Tenochtitlan. Likewise, the question of how the inhabitants of these capitals were provided with food and basic necessities can be most effectively attacked at the regional scale, once one knows about such factors as the spatial distribution of producers, consumers, and agricultural resources. Then one can ascertain how far afield urban demand must have been felt, and, with knowledge of the urban and outlying administrative apparatus, how the urban demand was dealt with politically.

Other evolutionary changes in regional-scale organization cannot be fully understood without a much more thorough consideration of trends and events operating at a scale much larger than that of the region. In the present state of anthropological abilities, it is possible, given favorable data-gathering conditions, to understand a great deal about regional processes in a systematic way. But social scientists have not yet developed many ways of formulating significant evolutionary questions, or ways of theoretically comprehending the issues, on spatial scales larger than the regional. Furthermore, as social scientists we do not yet have good methods for the systematic collection of data relevant to very broad, macroregional evolution. A national-scale, field-by-field archaeological settlement pattern study exists only as a nightmare among the anxiety-ridden dreams of a survey archaeologist. What are the large-scale problems, exactly? How do trends and events that we understand on a regional scale fit into and help constitute trends perceptible over a whole culture area such as Mesoamerica? Why are some important changes, such as the breakup of large regional primate systems at the end of the Classic Period, repeated (with variations, region to region) more or less simultaneously, not only in the eastern lowlands, with its open systems, but in the Valley of Oaxaca, Veracruz, and even marginal centers in the mountains of the Mixteca?

Currently, with the knowledge gained from our moderately detailed regional studies, we think that we can determine relatively accurately which changes in the history of a region were caused by internal factors and which seem unexplainable on the basis of events taking place within the bounds of the study area. We often suspect that such seemingly unaccountable changes may have been caused by the way the region was linked with other regions into a larger system. In some cases we can

gather further information and make suggestions about the nature of these articulations, as in the case of the founding of Monte Albán, where the stone monuments
seemed to indicate a great concern with systems lying outside the valley. Similarly,
we suspect that weak political boundary conditions were an important factor in the
early and persistent development of strong low-level economic institutions in Mesoamerica's eastern lowlands. And we discussed the conditions favoring the establishment of political domains through conquest of adjacent territories, when states
desire to minimize emigration or control trade routes. But our point is that the perspective is still region-centered. The quality of the thinking and the quality of the
information for questions transcending the region do not match what can be done
now at the regional scale.

The present inability to comprehend macroregional systems is analogous to the
development and denouement of community studies in the social sciences. In the
past, single communities were subjected to in-depth ethnographic examination, and
scientists and the public learned a great deal as a result. Two general methods were
used to specify just what was learned and to relate the community studies to other
researchers and to a larger world. The first was to claim, usually without much
demonstration, that a community was "typical" of a class: For example, the village
of Oraibi told us most of what we wanted to know about the Hopi; Middletown,
USA, spoke for the American town. The sampling difficulties in this approach
should be obvious.

Too, if communities were "typical," then how did they relate to one another,
with their functionally different roles, as parts of a whole system? This problem was
addressed with the second method of giving meaning to community-scale studies,
the "inward–out" approach. Communities were recognized to have had ties with
the outside world, and these were traced by listing the various connections: George
bought bread at the trading post, or several village families became Protestants.
Although this places the community in a somewhat wider perspective, it is not a
regional perspective. To understand the community's role in the region or nation,
one must understand what the region or nation is and how it works. That is a difficult but absolutely necessary requirement if one has gathered community-level
instead of regional-level data.

This is precisely the current theoretical and methodological difficulty with social
evolutionary studies. Just as one community should not be assumed to be typical of
all others in a region, one region is not an archetype of some (usually not well-
defined) class. The Valley of Oaxaca was not just a smaller Valley of Mexico, and
we would never say that our three study areas nicely represent the range of different
kinds of regions in Mesoamerica. Similarly, we believe a region-centered, inward–out
approach is just as inadequate for the study of interregional articulations as a com-
munity-centered approach is for understanding regional processes. The familiar
form for a paper title, "The Macroregion as Seen from X Site," conveys a simple
but intellectually debilitating and ineffectual way of organizing one's thinking. Our
inescapable conclusion is that a different analytical framework is needed for each
different spatial (and temporal) scale of human interaction. As yet a completely sat-

isfactory framework for thinking about phenomena at the macroregional scale has not been developed, although in the following section we put forth several tentative propositions that we think indicate fruitful directions to take. We approach these problems by asking the question, What is Mesoamerica?

What is Mesoamerica?

"Mesoamerica" is not a physiographic unit; *minimally*, it is a culture area, and even then its attributes and its boundaries as a culture area are described differently by various investigators. Objectively, however, more fundamental processes lie behind the existence of this culture area. Mesoamerica came into being as a real, historical entity, self-defined by the patterned behavior of its people. Mesoamerica was a social system. It was, to borrow from Immanuel Wallerstein, a world-system, meaning that its destiny was largely self-defined, and to its participants it represented all the world they wished to care about.

In size Mesoamerica was comparable to the pre-sixteenth-century European world. Each could be traversed with the existing transportation in forty to sixty days. Western Europe's population in 1600 was about 70 million (considerably less in the fifteenth century); pre-Columbian Mesoamerica had perhaps half that number. Western Europe's area was about two million square kilometers; Mesoamerica's, one million. The Chinese world was much larger in territory, and it was a system that produced more people – 60 million in A.D. 180, 200 million in A.D. 1585.

Wallerstein distinguishes between two kinds of world-systems: the world-empire and the world-economy. China is an example of the first. As a society it was unified by its monolithic imperial structure. In a world-economy, however, the nature of the whole is not shaped by the state, because this kind of world-system contains not just one but many, competing, sovereign states. The state is not the structure by which the world social system can be understood. Instead, economic linkages among regions shape the system, as in the developing capitalist world of Europe in the sixteenth century. Both states and the crossing economic linkages have to be understood to comprehend the whole system.

Mesoamerica was neither a world-empire nor a world-economy. The relationships holding it together were neither those of a single empire nor those of separate economic institutions. Nothing like the international markets for basic commodities and capital that characterized Europe were developed in Mesoamerica until perhaps its last two pre-Columbian centuries. What made Mesoamerica an encompassing social system was its structure of elite prestige.

From the chiefdoms of the Preclassic to the states and empires of later times, regional societies in Mesoamerica were composed of two strata: the rulers and the ruled. Distinctive "middle classes" were essentially nonexistent. The elite (the stratum from which rulers could come) of each regional society – our three case examples or others such as the Huasteca, central Veracruz, the Soconusco, the Grijalva depression, the Mixteca Baja, and so forth – had much in common with their counterparts in neighboring and even far-flung regions. Each had to maintain its authority within its own domain, and each was faced with the same kinds of administrative and political problems. On the other hand they were competitors, personally and as representatives of their regional polities. They married each other and visited, feasted, and warred with each other. An elite had more in common with other elites, indeed, than it did with its own commoners. These elite activities were the interregional contacts that made the Mesoamerican world what it was to its participants and what it is to us as twentieth-century archaeologists. Elite-level communication was the principal social mechanism behind the common Mesoamerican culture beliefs and symbols and the widespread distributions of material culture items from 1000 B.C. on.

That this kind of system relied primarily on elite-rank contacts means that it rather easily spread over space. The only requirement was that the participating societies have at least a chiefdom level of sociocultural integration. In this way the boundaries of "Mesoamerica" could change markedly, at times extending down into Central America or, especially in Toltec times, into the southwestern part of the United States.

Other macroregions have witnessed considerable exchange among elites. Heads of state even today give each other gifts, but no one would say that these exchanges are the most important ones in the modern world-system. The Mesoamerican system probably involved mutual gift giving, or a kind of exchange among rulers reminiscent of the prestations made by Southeast Asian princes to the Chinese emperor, or of the "rich trade" in precious items between Europe and Asia in the age of Marco Polo. The historically known exchange of esoteric knowledge among the chiefs of ancient Panama and Colombia, along with the transchiefdom movement of the highly valued symbols of this power and knowledge, was perhaps understood by the Mesoamerican elite even in detail, as they were involved in the same kind of behavior, and sometimes used the same symbols, such as smoke, the sun, and precious metals. The Mesoamerican elite prestige system was quantitatively of greater volume, more regular, and far more sophisticated than the Hopewellian "interaction sphere" that very loosely integrated the ranked societies of the Ohio Valley in the first centuries A.D. Mesoamerica's participants after 500 B.C. played with greater resources and at far higher stakes than did participants in the system's Early Formative Period, or in Peru's Chavín sphere.

We need to specify more precisely why Mesoamerica's elite found it desirable to interact, and what their exchange included. Human carriers moved raw materials and finished items of jade, crystal, metal, feathers, jaguar skins, cotton, and cacao, and the costliest pottery types (Usulatan ware from eastern Mesoamerica, Plumbate from the Pacific side of Chiapas-Guatemala, Nicoya polychrome from Costa Rica, the best Fine Orange from Tabasco, Mixteca-Puebla polychrome, Chalco-Cholula polychrome, and Colima dog pots). Knowledge of writing and the calendar was limited to the elite, yet was pan-Mesoamerican in distribution, as were the ball game and its paraphernalia. Certain pieces of rank-status apparel – headdresses, ear spools, nose plugs, shields – were made to regional sumptuary specifications, but they were likely to be crafted from imported materials. Furthermore, they were universally recognized as symbolic statements about the human versus the animal realm, and about the purity and degree of power of their wearers. In fact many sacred concepts and their physical representations, rituals, and cult figures – such as the feathered serpents, lords of the underworld, rain-lightning deities (Chac, Tlaloc, Dzahui, Cocijo), Ehecatl, and Totec – were transregional. The significances of self-sacrifice, ancestor veneration, and funeral rituals were explicitly understood among the elite all across Mesoamerica.

The elite prestige system did not comprise all of the interregional exchange in Mesoamerica. In addition to the rich trade, some consumer goods flowed among regions. Obsidian, for example, was mined in only two main mining areas (the northern basin of Mexico and highland Guatemala), turned into cores and tools, and carried to all parts of Mesoamerica. Regional economies then saw to its distribution, which was usually differential – in some contexts restricted to the elite, in some places not. Cotton, cacao, and certain other food items may have had interregional distributions, but evidence for this prior to the fifteenth century is scarce.

Apparently the elite exchange provided the stimulus, opportunity, procedures, and established structure for a more irregular traffic in bulk commodities or items in mass demand. There is little evidence for the formation of regular interregional dependencies for goods in common use. Mesoamerica's relatively high cost of transport undoubtedly made a macroregional-scale food economy less feasible than it was in Europe or China. To illustrate, we may consider the problem of supplying maize, a common food, to the Valley of Mexico from Tuxtepec, an important trade center on the Papaloapan River. It had to be moved by *tameme*, human carriers, who typically carried a load of thirty kilos and who traveled twenty-four kilometers a day, according to sixteenth-century evidence. Over the most convenient trails, the journey to Mexico would take eighteen days. A person will consume, however, the equivalent of at least two-thirds of a kilo of corn per day. If we look at the food energy alone, we see that our *tameme* will consume 80 percent of the load over the round trip. This is not to say that bulk items never moved among regions, for other considerations besides the total energy cost may have at times been involved – for example, the providers, not the consumers, may have sometimes paid the cost of transport, as in the Aztec tribute system. These "noneconomic" conditions, however, place the question back in the realm of exchange determined by elite relationships. That is why the Mesoamerican rich trade is not simply an archaeologically preserved proxy for trade in basic commodities. It had a purpose of its own. There is nonetheless a more subtle connection between elite exchange and basic production.

Specific, rational goals and strategies lie behind the exchange of goods, people, and information among Mesoamerica's regional elites. Many of the material items, such as jade or feathers, were important in the scheme of rewards. Control over these prestige items was a key aspect of a ruler's power, because the ability to mass and direct large numbers of people was the measure of greatness. In Mesoamerica, people were the major factor in the production of wealth. More followers meant that more food could be produced, more craft items could be manufactured, and more warriors could be dispatched to the fields of battle. In the absence of coercion, followers had to be enlisted and their captains rewarded with the universally recognized badges of prestige.

In typical Mesoamerican transactions, wealth could not be turned into capital and multiplied in the marketplace, as it is in modern businesses. (Such behavior cannot be ruled out on a local or regional scale, as in the marketing activities suggested for the eastern lowlands.) But power and wealth might be concentrated and enhanced through the clever manipulation of rewards.

Small, lightweight items made of rare materials best suit the needs of this system. Because they are rare, rulers can easily inflate or deflate their value. If the objects come from afar their abundance can be regulated through the ruler's control of foreign trade. Using rare materials means that unauthorized manufacture or use is nearly impossible. Small size and light weight minimize the costs of transport. These qualities also permit a user to display his or her signaling device at all times and to all persons within eyesight. The same qualities allow the object to be easily transferred, taken back, or exchanged. Immovable property (a house, or land) is not so manipulable.

The Mesoamerican prestige system helped a ruler establish his legitimate authority over his subjects. The term "subjects" here refers to commoners, and, even more importantly, to people of rank who were members of the ruler's potential or actual cadres. These persons were the most important targets of Mesoamerican ideology.

Interregional elite interaction also served to regulate basic economic matters, but in roundabout, indirect ways. This network provided the regional elite with information about neighboring polities. Trading ventures, visits, weddings, funerals, cult missions, pilgrimages, ball games, and wars were means of picking up intelligence about the state of competing systems. The quality and abundance of trade items, gifts, and tribute were also measures of the competition. Like the epideictic or display behavior that adjusts the territory sizes and populations of animals, these elite activities signaled relative strengths and weaknesses to competitors. The continual adjustment of borders and the course of diplomacy, alliances, struggles for succession to office, and warfare all affected the concentration of people and economic power.

In this way the elite prestige system was more than a superficial cultural diversion made possible by the surplus and leisure time provided by agriculture. On the contrary, the prestige system, as a regulator of more basic transactions, played a key role in the functioning and dynamics of ancient Mesoamerica.

The Mesoamerican world as a social system was thus formed by its elite prestige system. This world came into existence around 1000 B.C., and it developed within the same basic structure for more than two millennia. There are clues that, in the final centuries before the fateful capture and subjugation of Mesoamerica by the nascent capitalist world-system, Mesoamerica was becoming a system of a different order.

In the Late Postclassic Period, as we have noted earlier, seemingly innovative economic linkages were beginning to threaten the politically based dominance of traditionally reckoned prestige. Ports of trade, at politically neutral places like Acalan, in Tabasco, and perhaps Cozumel, off the Yucatecan coast, served as interregional nodes for the movement of common as well as luxury goods. Coixtlahuaca in the Mixteca Alta was a major center of pan-Mesoamerican exchange for a wide variety of goods, and more specialized markets probably were set up at Matatlan and Chila, in the cotton-producing area of the Puebla-Veracruz border. It seems likely that whole regional economies specialized in the production of particular basic commodities in response to extraregional demands and opportunities. Overall, the Late Postclassic interactions were still dominated by the traditional channels, but new kinds of linkages were emerging. Again, it is interesting to note that the establishment of a new world order was preceded in all areas by the scaling down of the Classic states and the creation of weaker and smaller states with, in many cases, more permeable boundaries.

We hypothesize that the scaling down of states and increased boundary permeabilities came about through a change in the manner in which the elite prestige system was manipulated. This suggestion is based on our identification of two contrastive political-economic strategies employed by the Mesoamerican elite. The first (we call it the "core strategy") is comparatively well known, based on extensive research carried out in key regions like the valleys of Mexico and Oaxaca, which we have described in this book. The other, what we refer to as the "periphery strategy" or "boundary strategy," is less studied because it was played out primarily in the comparatively environmentally marginal, often mountainous or swampy periphery and boundary regions located between cores. We would include here areas like Veracruz and the Mixteca of the western part of the state of Oaxaca.

During periods of preeminence of the core strategy, peripheries and boundaries declined in vitality and political importance. Powerful core states like Teotihuacan suppressed autonomous entrepreneurial activity in peripheries and boundaries by increasing the degree of regional boundedness and by managing interregional flows. This resulted in a situation of "core-periphery hierarchy" (to borrow a phrase from world-systems terminology). When periphery strategists came to the fore, core-periphery hierarchy was blurred and regional boundaries became more permeable, as boundary-zone rulers emerged as important independent players in the context of long-distance interactions.

These two strategies embody important differences in the behavior of elites and in the ways their political systems were built and legitimated. The main political-economic outcomes of the core strategy were:

1   Strongly state-managed economies emerged, including regional-scale agricultural intensification and market-system intervention aimed at supporting large urban populations and costly state apparatuses.
2   Boundary and periphery zones were extensively managed through the establishment of military outposts and extractive and trade enclaves.
3   Powerful core states and their cults were legitimated through connections to religious beliefs and ritual related to rain, earth, sun, and moon, and thus fertility and renewal (including an important female goddess at Teotihuacan).
4   Artistic conventions made use of abstract concepts, standardization of style, and systematization of religious iconography, thus emphasizing collective belonging at the expense of ethnic distinction or individual achievement. Teoti-

huacan art, for example, is described as expressing values that are "impersonal, corporate, and communal."

The institutional arrangements developed by the boundary strategists were clearly unlike those of the core strategists, although too little information is available now to properly characterize them. The main features, as we see it, are:

1 Political power was based to a considerable degree on successful entrepreneurial participation in long-distance networks, including trading, war, and alliances. In these contexts, individual achievement – particularly masculine achievement – was a major source of political legitimation.
2 Individual rulers glorified themselves in written texts describing royal marriages, descent, and success in war. Ethnic distinctions were commonly emphasized in political rhetoric.
3 Religious ritual involving ruler cults, martial cults, and human sacrifice/god nourishment cults legitimated the social position of warrior sodalities.

From the Formative to the Spanish conquest, there was evidently a cyclic alternation in emphasis on one or the other political economy, or in the degree to which one was able to dominate the other, although there was probably always some degree of strained coexistence of the two. The Classic–Postclassic transition in the highlands can be interpreted as a transformation from core to boundary dominance, but was followed by a partial and not entirely successful reemergence of core strategists in the guises of the Toltec, Tarascan, and Aztec empires. The rest of the prehispanic sequence is as yet poorly understood in these terms. We would argue, though, that a theoretical framework capable of understanding the social transformations of the Mesoamerican world over thirty centuries has to have the conceptual ability – and the data – to comprehend both of these main strategies, their interactions, and their contradictions. Both strategies contributed to the culture and institutional arrangements of the Mesoamerican world.

Conclusion

The inadequacies in the current comprehension of macroregional evolution should have been made outstandingly apparent in the preceding section, which attempted to describe what Mesoamerica as a whole was like and how it changed. We can offer little information on flows that would quantify interaction and interdependence. We have few good cases of articulation between well-developed regions and less-developed regions, or of how these linkages changed over time. Few data exist on boundary pulsations or interregional demography. In short, although the regional-level settlement pattern studies have produced much new and stimulating data in recent years, at this time we still have very little systematic data on the changes in scale, complexity, integration, and boundedness within the Mesoamerican system as a whole. Satisfactory answers to some of our most important questions will not be forthcoming until these gaps in our data and theory are filled. The methodological problems will be difficult to solve. But, similarly, methodology must have seemed problematic to those anthropologists who, thirty or more years ago, began to wonder about such matters as the evolution of agricultural strategies, population dynamics, and rural–urban relationships. Once the theoretical questions were posed, the appropriate methods – such as the regional, systematic settlement pattern survey – were soon developed. There is no reason to doubt that new methods will soon be developed to permit the resolution of problems pertaining to the study of change at the Mesoamerican scale.

BIBLIOGRAPHICAL ESSAY

Chapter 1. The growth of Mesoamerican archaeology and ethnohistory
Archaeological method and theory have had bad as well as good moments in Mesoamerica, as discussed in Flannery, ed. (1976), and as characterized succinctly by Flannery on p. 372. On the history of Mesoamerican archaeology, see Willey and Sabloff (1980) and Bernal (1952, 1977). We refer to Morley (1937–8) and Gamio (1922). For "culture area" as a general concept, see Gamio (1922) and Kroeber (1939). A version of the Toltec legend is the "Anales de Cuauhtitlan" (Velázquez, ed. and trans., 1945), and the Tula connection is shown by Jiménez Moreno (1941). Forstemann, by 1894, became the first to relearn the Maya calendar (Tozzer 1907, Marcus 1976c). Vaillant (1930, 1931) did the early work in the Basin of Mexico, and Melgar (1871) discussed the discovery of the first colossal head. For reviews of the "Olmec" problem, see Covarrubias (1957), Bernal (1969), and the volumes edited by Benson (1968) and Sharer and Grove (1989). Publications of the Tehuacán Archaeological and Botanical Project include Byers, ed. (1967), MacNeish, Peterson, and Flannery (1970), Johnson, ed. (1972), and MacNeish et al. (1972). Parsons (1972) reviews archaeological settlement pattern studies, and Willey et al. (1965), Puleston (1973), and Ashmore, ed. (1981) discuss their application in the Maya area. For the Valley of Mexico, see, for example, Armillas (1948, 1971), Wolf and Palerm (1955), Palerm (1973), Acosta (1964a), Piña Chan (1958), Bernal, ed. (1963), and Tolstoy (1958). Several summary works are found in Vogt and Leventhal, eds. (1983). Methodological aspects of regional archaeology are discussed in Fish and Kowalewski, eds. (1990). A follow-up to the 1960 Valley of Mexico conference resulted in a collection of papers (Wolf, ed. 1976). Data from the urban and rural surveys are available in Millon (1973), Millon, Drewitt, and Cowgill (1973), and Sanders, Parsons, and Santley (1979). A few of the important ethnohistorical studies of the Valley of Mexico are Acosta Saignes (1945) on the *Pochteca* (trading specialists), Barlow (1949) and Berdan et al. (in press) on the Aztec empire, Calnek (1976) on Tenochtitlan, Carrasco (1971) on social organization, and Gibson (1964) on the sixteenth century. Among many general works are Brundage (1972), Davies (1973, 1977, 1980), and Soustelle (1961). For early publications on Oaxaca, see Batres (1902) and Bandelier (1884). Caso's bibliography is lengthy, but among the more important works are Caso (1928a, b, c, 1969) and Caso, Bernal, and Acosta (1967). See Bernal (1965), Bernal and Gamio (1974), Paddock, ed. (1966), and Flannery and Marcus, eds. (1983). Results and further references for the Human Ecology project are in Flannery, ed. (1976) and Flannery and Marcus, eds. (1983); for the settlement pattern work see Blanton (1978), Blanton et al. (1982), and Kowalewski et al. (1989). In fact, every archaeologist who has worked more than a little in the Valley of Oaxaca since the 1920s is a member of the scholarly lineage started by Caso. Mayapán's map is published in Pollock et al. (1962), Tikal's in Carr and Hazard (1961), and Dzibilchaltún's in Kurjack (1974). For early settlement pattern studies, see Bullard (1960) and Ricketson and Ricketson (1937). Compare these with Puleston (1960). See Wauchope (1972) for the career of Andrews IV; Spores (1967) is an example of his fine work in the Mixteca Alta. The Lambityeco sherd estimate was done by David Peterson (1976). Acosta reported his budgets for the eleventh through the thirteenth seasons in his 1960, 1961, and 1964b studies.

Thinking about Mesoamerican civilization

Bernal (1977:23) mentions the seventeenth-century diffusionists. See Meggers (1975) for the Shang Chinese–Olmec argument, but contrast it with Grove (1976). A classic in the culture historical literature is Willey's two-volume text on the archaeology of the Americas (1966, 1971). Binford (1965) and Flannery (1967a) critique this approach. Paddock remarked on words like "influence" (1974). The major sources for contemporary sociocultural evolutionary theories are Harris (1979), Service (1975), Steward (1955), White (1959), and Wolf (1982). Of those who rely too heavily on speculative argument from static examples, Harris (1977) is the best known from this century. Spengler (1926) is one of the many birth-development-decline theorists. Single-cause explanations are numerous, but Boserup (1965) and Sanders (Sanders, Parsons, and Santley 1979 being a recent statement) are two examples of what we have in mind. Blanton (1990) critiques Sanders. See Franke (1974) for one discussion of the failure of the green revolution. The volumes on the rise and collapse of Maya civilization were edited by Adams (1977) and Culbert (1973) respectively.

An approach to cultural evolution

Scale, integration, complexity, and boundedness are discussed in Blanton et al. (1982), Kowalewski et al. (1983), Kowalewski et al. (1989), and Kowalewski (1990a). Anthropologists – for example Udy (1959), Johnson (1973, 1978), and Wright (1969) – have considered the implications of the limitations of the human mind in information processing. Much of this is based on sources such as Miller (1965) and Meier (1962). The Colson passage (1978: 161) is found in Barth, ed. (1978), a summary of scale factors in social organization. Goody (1978) considers the argument about population density and social complexity. Concerning scale factors in organizational size, see Boulding (1956), Blau (1968, 1970), Johnson (1982, 1983), Kasarda (1974), and Kosse (1990). The Simon (1969: 98) quote is from his classic article titled "The architecture of complexity." On other aspects of integration and complexity, compare Blau (1968, 1970), Fesler (1968), Johnson (1978, 1980, 1981), Kowalewski, (1990a), McGuire (1983), Simon (1976), and Tainter (1978). Flannery (1972) emphasizes political centralization rather than integration, complexity, scale, and boundedness in his discussion of the cultural evolution of civilizations. Wright (1969), Johnson (1973, 1987), and Wright and Johnson (1975) discuss levels of decision-making hierarchy in states and chiefdoms.

On the interrelationships of governing and economic institutions, see Blanton (1976a) and Blanton et al. (1982), especially the chapter by Feinman (1982). In this area, we have been stimulated primarily by Skinner (1964, 1965a, ed. 1977). In a survey of prestate sedentary societies in the Americas, Feinman and Neitzel (1984) found that economic redistribution was not a major function of leaders.

Societal taxonomies

The major taxonomies are those developed by Service (1971, 1975) and Fried (1967); see also Flannery (1972). Sanders and Price (1968) applied Service's scheme to prehispanic Mesoamerica. Feinman and Neitzel (1984), Sahlins (1958), Earle (1977, 1978), Taylor (1975), and Steponaitis (1978) have discussed chieftainship in relation to redistribution. An argument similar to ours is made by Granovetter (1979: 511, 512).

Explaining culture change

On the transition to coal in England, see Nef (1977). Holland (1975) discusses problem solving in adaptation. Richard N. Adams (1978) was stimulated by Prigogine's (e.g., 1976) concept of "dissipative structures" that exhibit flux due to varying energy inputs. Regarding change as an outcome of adjustment to fluctuating circumstances, we have been stimulated by Schalk, Jorde, and Athens in Binford, ed. (1977), and Earle (1977, 1978), Gall and Saxe (1977), and Holling and Goldberg (1971). See also Rappaport (1978: 67 – 8).

Household consumer behavior, as it relates to houses, is discussed in Blanton (in press c). Goody (1990) summarizes many aspects of household strategies in the preindustrial societies of Eurasia. The literature on fertility decisions in household economics is vast. Pertinent discussions are found in Blanton (1975), Coontz (1957), Cowgill (1975), Easterlin (1978), Jones and Woolf (1969), Lee (1977), and B. White (1973).

The phase I example from Oaxaca is drawn from Blanton et al. (1982) and Kowalewski et al. (1989). Waddell (1972) makes some interesting observations on household time budgets under differing agricultural regimes. T. Smith (1959: e.g., 85, 86) mentions the fact that purchasing certain items from the market can be a time-conserving strategy for households, allowing more time for agricultural intensification. The move to more canal irrigation in phase I is indicated by our surveys (in Blanton et al. 1982 and Kowalewski et al. 1989); see also Flannery et al. (1967) and Neely (1967). Government mediation of conflicts inherent in these irrigation systems is discussed by Hunt and Hunt (1974) and Downing (1974); see also Lees (1973).

The survey methodology used in the valleys of Oaxaca and Mexico is described in Blanton (1978), Blanton et al. (1982), Millon (1973), and Sanders, Parsons, and Santley (1979). This method has its sources in Willey (1953) and in Willey, ed. (1956). See the review in Parsons (1972). Feinman (1982, 1986) and Feinman, Kowalewski, and Blanton (1984) describe the methods used in the analyses of the Valley of Oaxaca ceramic collections. The consequences of varying levels of competition among potters are discussed in Balfet (1965), van der Leeuw (1976), Fontana et al. (1962), Foster (1965), and Birmingham (1975).

On the relationship between functional size and population size, see the summary by Johnson (1977). Primacy is discussed in the works by Beckman (1958), Berry (1961, 1967), Blanton (1976a), Haggett, Cliff, and Frey (1977), Johnson (1977, 1980), Kowalewski (1982a, 1990a), Skinner (1977a), C. A. Smith (1974, 1976a, 1982), and Vapnarsky (1969). Blanton (1989) relates variation in civic architecture to degree of political centralization. Steponaitis (1978) developed the idea about how the locations of secondary centers will reflect the degree of control exercised by the regional capital.

Special topic I. The origins of a market system in the Valley of Oaxaca
On market system development, compare Appleby (1976), Berry (1967), Blanton (1983, 1985, in press a), Feinman, Blanton, and Kowalewski (1984), Hodder and Ukwu (1969), Schwimmer (1976), Skinner (1964), and C. A. Smith (1974). Descriptions of Mesoamerican market systems at the time of the conquest are dealt with in more detail in the following chapters. On the spatial organization of market systems, demand threshold, and so forth, see Christaller (1966) and summaries and comments by Berry (1967), Haggett, Cliff, and Frey (1977), Johnson (1977), and C. A. Smith (1974, 1976a).

Special topic 2. Was there a profit motive in prehispanic Mesoamerica?
The statement about profit motives is found in Sanders, Parsons, and Santley (1979: 296 – 7, 404 – 5). For an introduction to the debate between the substantivists and their critics, refer to Polanyi, Arensberg, and Pearson, eds. (1957), LeClair and Schneider, eds. (1968), Sahlins (1972), and P. Cohen (1967). Sahlins (1965) presented a scheme of different categories of exchange transactions in noncapitalist societies depending on kin and territorial distance. Sahagún (1946: Book 10) describes the various kinds of fraudulent behavior in the market places. Bargaining in the market places is described in Torquemada (1943: 580).

Chapter 2. Preceramic Mesoamerica
Several recent articles evaluate claims of and data purporting to substantiate a pre-Paleo-Indian human presence in the New World in general, including Mesoamerica (Dincauze 1984, Lynch 1990, Meltzer 1989). Bryan (1986), Lorenzo (1978), MacNeish (1983, 1986), and MacNeish and Nelken-Turner (1983) all are proponents of a "pre-projectile" horizon in

Mesoamerica. The recent reanalysis of North American human skeletal material, previously dated to pre-Paleo-Indian times using experimental dating techniques, indicates that none of these specimens is older than 11,000 radiocarbon years (Taylor et al. 1985). The Tlapacoya site report is Lorenzo and Mirambell (eds. 1986), and a brief summary is available in Mirambell (1978). Some of the interpretive problems are discussed by Limbrey (1976). Much of the data from excavations at sites in the region of the Valsequillo reservoir remain unpublished, although several brief discussions are available (Irwin-Williams 1967, 1978). Irwin-Williams (1981), Malde and Steen-McIntyre (1981) and Steen-McIntyre et al. (1973, 1981) debate the very controversial and problematic dating of the artifact-bearing Valsequillo deposits.

Aveleyra Arroyo de Avida (1964) is an early description of Paleo-Indian sites in Mesoamerica that is still among the best and most comprehensive. More recent general summaries are found in Stark (1981, 1986). The evidence for late Pleistocene occupations in the Tehuacán Valley is discussed in the first (MacNeish 1967) and fourth (Johnson and MacNeish 1972) of the five volumes reporting data and results of the Tehuacán Archaeological-Botanical Project. The very sparse evidence for a Paleo-Indian or late Pleistocene human presence in Oaxaca is discussed in Finsten et al. (1989), Flannery (1983a), Flannery and Spores (1983), and Flannery et al. (1981). Gruhn and Bryan (1976) conducted a survey in a region of highland Guatemala to locate preceramic sites, and excavated one dating to the Paleo-Indian period (1977). Brown (1980) analyzes and interprets the distributional and other characteristics of nonceramic sites located in a survey of the Quiche Basin in highland Guatemala, but none of these has been securely dated to either the Paleo-Indian or the Archaic period.

Major programs of research conducted in the Sierra de Tamaulipas of northeastern Mesoamerica (MacNeish 1958) and in the highland valleys of Tehuacán (Byers ed. 1967, MacNeish et al. 1967, Johnson ed. 1972, MacNeish 1973) and Oaxaca (Flannery ed. 1986) have contributed enormously to our understanding of the Mesoamerican Archaic period. MacNeish (1964) summarizes the sequence of change in the Tehuacán Valley. Brief discussions of the Oaxacan Archaic sequence or settlements are found in Finsten and Kowalewski (1991), Finsten et al. (1989), Flannery (1983b), Flannery and Spores (1983), and Flannery et al. (1981). Flannery (ed. 1986) reports the results of the excavation and analysis at Guilá Naquitz.

Very tentative interpretations of nonceramic sites of uncertain age in the Quiche Basin of highland Guatemala (Brown 1980) are suggestive and in some ways consistent with what little is known of the Archaic in highland southwest Mesoamerican from more securely dated contexts (MacNeish 1962).

Niederberger (1979) summarizes evidence for a very rich environment in the Middle Archaic period in the Valley of Mexico and for permanent human occupation. She suggests that an increase in the abundance and size of teosinte pollen grains may be consistent with the widely accepted theoretical position that agriculture had its beginnings in optimal environments, as was the case in the Old World. But the very early evidence for plant domestication in semiarid valleys in Mexico suggests a quite different process.

Blake et al. (1992), Michaels and Voorhies (in press), and Voorhies et al. (1991) report the results of recent research on the Pacific coast of Chiapas. Voorhies et al. carefully describe the reasoning by which they came to the conclusion that the shell sites they report on represent the remains of ancient shrimp collecting and processing stations. Other Pacific coastal Archaic sites in the modern states of Guerrero (Brush 1965) and Nyarit (Mountjoy 1974) have been too incompletely excavated and reported to add to our knowledge of this area. The dating of Archaic levels at the Santa Luisa site on the Río Tecolutla in the modern state of Veracruz, only a few kilometers from the Gulf of Mexico coast, is reported in Wilkerson (1973). Wilkerson (1975) interprets the Archaic remains as those of a permanent, nonagricultural village. However, the only evidence that agriculture or intensive plant collecting was lacking is the absence of grinding stones such as are found at contemporary Tehuacán Valley sites. Year-round occupation is inferred from the size of the site, which is reported on the basis of surface evidence to have extended for a kilometer or more along the river's bank. There are no indicators of seasonality, no hearths or other features, and the size of the excavated area is not reported.

The results of the Belize Archaeological Reconnaissance are mentioned very briefly by MacNeish (1986) and MacNeish and Nelken-Turner (1983). Zeitlin (1984) discusses the general methods of reconnaissance employed, as well as some results and limitations of survey and excavations carried out during the first three of four field seasons. The chronology for preceramic Belize is based predominantly on cross-dating surface artifacts. In the first three seasons, radiocarbon dates had been obtained only for a very small number of late Archaic sites. Stratigraphic excavations were limited to very few localities because of very shallow deposits due to poor soil development. The results of faunal, palynological, and other botanical analyses have not yet been published, so economic interpretations are very tentative and based largely on environmental setting.

Flannery (1967b, 1968a, 1973) discusses economic patterns during the Archaic period in marginal highland environments. Farnsworth et al. (1985) reevaluate dietary reconstructions, based on proportional representation in the archaeological record and tooth wear (MacNeish 1967). The results of chemical analysis of trace elements in human bone, however, are far from conclusive because of the very small sample upon which they are based. The debate about the origin of maize is summarized by Flannery (ed. 1986), who notes that teosinte and maize pollen may not be distinguishable. Benz and Iltis (1990) report the results of their recent reexamination of the earliest known corncobs from the Tehuacán Valley, which supports the argument that these are fully domesticated specimens, rather than the only known examples of "wild maize" as had been reported previously (Mangelsdorf et al. 1967).

Many aspects of social organization in the semiarid highlands during the Archaic period can only be inferred indirectly. Drennan (1983a) discusses ritual and ceremony, based on evidence from Gheo-Shih in the Valley of Oaxaca (Flannery et al. 1981), and using ethnographic analogy. The presence of microbands and macrobands in the preceramic Tehuacán Valley (MacNeish 1972) and in the Valley of Oaxaca (Flannery et al. 1981; Flannery 1983c, ed. 1986) is supported by archaeological evidence, although see Brumfiel (1977) for a critique of settlement pattern analysis and reconstruction in the Tehuacán Valley. Larger organizational units leave little, if any, material trace in the archaeological record. MacNeish (1986) posits localized complexes on the basis of projectile point and other lithic artifact styles and/or frequencies, but these are based on scanty data. However, Wobst (1974) conducted a computer simulation that determined that a minimum group size of 175 – 475 is necessary if, over the long term, all individuals are to be able to find mates who are not close biological relatives. Estimated populations for both the Valley of Oaxaca and the Tehuacán Valley (summarized in Flannery 1983c), where data are most extensive, are well below even this minimum figure, suggesting that larger organizational units in the Archaic linked populations over considerable distances. Marcus (1983a) discusses Proto-Otomanguean and later Otomanguean languages.

Evidence of highland–lowland exchange and/or travel is found in obsidian at late Archaic coastal sites (Nelson and Voorhies 1980, Wilkerson 1975). Flannery (1983c) suggests that the exchange of gifts, in the form of projectile points, may have accompanied the exchange of mates between macrobands.

The role of risk in promoting plant domestication in a semiarid environment is discussed by MacNeish (1972), but Flannery (ed. 1986) emphasizes the importance of interrelationships between annual scarcity, year-to-year unpredictability, the development of food storage methods, and changes in economic practices. See Stark (1981, 1986) for summaries of many of these ideas.

Chapter 3. The Valley of Oaxaca
Readers who require a fuller bibliography should consult the following overviews of Valley of Oaxaca prehistory: Bernal (1965), Paddock (1966), Whitecotton (1977), Blanton et al. (1979),

Blanton and Kowalewski (1981), Flannnery, Marcus, and Kowalewski (1981), Blanton et al. (1982), Flannery and Marcus, eds. (1983), Feinman et al. (1985), Kowalewski et al. (1989), Winter (1989), and Marcus, ed. (1990). Three long-term projects have laid the basis for what is known archaeologically about the valley. First, Alfonso Caso, Ignacio Bernal, and Jorge R. Acosta carried out a series of large-scale excavations at Monte Albán and other valley sites. Bernal also initiated a preliminary surface survey. The major publications resulting from the excavations are Caso, Bernal, and Acosta (1967), Caso (1969), Caso and Bernal (1952), and Bernal and Gamio (1974). Some of the data from Bernal's survey were incorporated into his 1965 article. Second, researchers involved with Kent Flannery's multidisciplinary Oaxaca Human Ecology Project have concentrated on preceramic and Early and Middle Formative adaptations. The project has focused much of its energies on the excavation of living floors of early sites, especially in the Etla arm. The major excavations include San José Mogote (Flannery et al. 1970; Flannery and Marcus 1976; Flannery, Marcus, and Kowalewski 1981; Flannery and Marcus, eds. 1983; Marcus 1989a; Flannery and Marcus 1990), Tierras Largas (Winter 1972), Fábrica San José (Drennan 1976a), and Tomaltepec (Whalen 1981, 1988). Summaries and interpretations of the results of the Human Ecology Project can be found in Flannery et al. (1967), Flannery (1968b), Flannery and Schoenwetter (1970), Flannery (1973), Flannery, ed. (1976), Flannery and Marcus (1976), Flannery, Marcus, and Kowalewski (1981), Flannery and Marcus, eds. (1983), Flannery, ed. (1986), and Marcus, ed. (1990).

The third major archaeological effort is the Valley of Oaxaca Settlement Pattern Project, which has carried out a systematic surface survey of the entire valley (including Monte Albán), and which has produced detailed analyses of the settlement patterns for all prehispanic ceramic periods. For the results of this fieldwork see Kowalewski (1976), Blanton (1978), Blanton et al. (1979), Blanton and Kowalewski (1981), Blanton et al. (1982), Kowalewski et al. (1983), Feinman et al. (1985), Kowalewski et al. (1989), Kowalewski (1990b), and Kowalewski et al. (1990). Feinman and Nicholas (Feinman 1985; Feinman and Nicholas 1988, 1990b) have extended comparable survey coverage into the contiguous Ejutla Valley.

For information about the valley's environment, natural resources, and agriculture, the major source is Kirkby (1973). But see Smith (1978), Kowalewski (1982b), and Flannery, ed. (1986). Motolinía (1950), Cortés (1963), and Durán (1967) contain comments by Aztec and Spanish observers on the fertility of valley lands. Palerm and Wolf (1957) were first to point out the relationship between the valley's environmental potential and its important role as a "nuclear area" in Mesoamerican prehistory. Information on nonagricultural resources comes from scattered sources. Cortés (1963) describes the prehispanic gold mines near the valley, and Caso (1965) comments on the late prehispanic use of gold. W. Taylor (1972), who lists the valley's salt sources, proposed that they were probably insufficient to meet local needs in phase W. Parry (1987) discusses some of the valley sources for chipped-stone tools. Pires-Ferreira (1975, 1976a, 1976b) and Winter and Pires-Ferreira (1976) discuss long-distance exchange, especially the importation and distribution of obsidian. Two sixteenth-century surveys of political and economic conditions in New Spain, the Suma de Visitas (Paso y Troncoso 1905: vol. 1) and the Relaciones Geográficas (Paso y Troncoso 1905: vols. 4, 5; Caso 1928a, 1928b; Barlow 1945) contain further details on valley resources.

For the pre-Monte Albán phases, the major sources are those already mentioned from the Oaxaca Human Ecology Project, along with Feinman (1991), Feinman and Nicholas (1987, 1990a), Fisch (1978, 1982), and Nicholas et al. (1986). *The early Mesoamerican village* (Flannery, ed. 1976) and *The cloud people* (Flannery and Marcus, eds. 1983) examine Formative Period settlements in the valley on a number of analytical scales. Several papers discuss Formative houses (for example, Flannery 1976a) and their related features (Winter 1976a). Flannery and Winter (1976) also examine the range of activities undertaken in the early villages. Flannery (1976b) discusses village catchments, and Kirkby (1973) and Flannery (1973) discuss the potential productivity of early corn farming. Comparative discussions of the productivity of early cultigens and the natural valley-floor vegetation can be found in Flannery (1973), Flannery, ed. (1986), and Robson, Flannery, and Konlande (1976). For information on nonresidential architecture dating to these early phases, see Flannery and Marcus, eds. (1983), Flannery and Marcus (1976, 1990), Flannery, Marcus, and Kowalewski (1981), Marcus (1989a), and Flannery et al. (1970). These works can also be referred to for descriptions of Gheo-Shih, the open-air Archaic site (also see Flannery and Spores 1983; Flannery, ed. 1986; and Finsten, Flannery, and Macnider 1989).

The physical layout of several Formative communities in Oaxaca has been described in Flannery (1976c), Whalen (1976, 1981, 1988), and Winter (1972). Other studies, including Marcus (1976a), Fisch (1982), and Kowalewski et al. (1989) provide information on the sizes of the early villages, and Winter (1976b) has compared growth patterns for a number of these communities. Examining the distribution of certain design elements, Plog (1976) has measured the extent of interaction among five of these settlements and has compared these measurements with actual distances. Pyne (1976) has noted the interesting distribution of the were-jaguar and fire-serpent motifs across several Formative Period communities (see also Marcus 1989a).

Formative burial populations and their associated grave goods have been examined by Winter (1972) and Whalen (1981). These analyses point to increasing social differentiation throughout the Formative Period, an observation supported by the architectural (Flannery and Marcus 1976; Flannery and Marcus, eds. 1983) and settlement pattern data (Blanton et al. 1982; Kowalewski et al. 1989; Feinman 1991). Hodges (1989) has studied skeletal populations to examine the relationship between diet and health. The interrelationship of regional population and potential agricultural productivity in the Valley of Oaxaca Formative Period has been addressed in several studies (Kirkby 1973; Curran 1978; Kowalewski 1980; Fisch 1982; Nicholas et al. 1986; Feinman and Nicholas 1987, 1990a; Nicholas 1989; Feinman 1991). These studies demonstrate that prior to the foundation of Monte Albán the valley's population was only a small fraction of the region's agrarian potential. Although see Sanders and Nichols 1988 (with associated comments) and Blanton (1980, 1983a, 1990) for theoretical background.

Ethnographically, the nature and implications of leader–follower relationships in societies characterized by relatively simple decision-making structures have been discussed most thoroughly for Melanesia (e.g., Paynter and Cole 1980; Meggitt 1973; Sahlins 1963, 1972; Waddell 1972). These studies stress the role that certain influential individuals may play, even in societies without complex administrative organizations, in promoting agricultural intensification, increased labor outputs, and larger household sizes (see also Lightfoot and Feinman 1982). The relationship between increased labor demands and population growth has been reviewed in several studies (Blanton 1975; Cowgill 1975; B. White 1973). In Melanesia, these key leaders or "big-men" also play important roles in maintaining interregional exchange ties and alliances among groups (Paynter and Cole 1980; Strathern 1969, 1978). Callen (1976) also has noted that the big-men with the most prestige and the largest number of followers often reside in the settlements that are centrally located in relation to the regional exchange networks (see also Irwin 1978).

Although the stylistic similarities between the Gulf coast and the Valley of Oaxaca were initially attributed to either Olmec conquest or colonization, most current analyses follow Flannery (1968b), who regards the wide distribution of these highly stylized goods to be the product of an exchange system that connected a large area in Mesoamerica (see Sharer and Grove, eds. 1989). Many of the goods exchanged bore iconographic motifs that were probably associated with individuals of high status (Pires-Ferreira 1975; Drennan 1976b; Flannery and Marcus, eds. 1983; Marcus 1989a). A similar elite exchange system is described in Helms's *Ancient Panama* (1979). These exchange systems also enabled populations to "bank" surpluses as a hedge against years of deficit production (Flannery and Schoenwetter 1970; see also Drennan 1984). The equivalency of long-distance trading and raiding has been discussed by R. Ford (1972).

In his simulation studies, Wobst (1974, 1976) found that human populations must consist of several hundred individuals to assure long-term persistence in isolation. The probability of demographic fluctuation is inversely proportional to population size (Wobst 1975, 1976; cf. Ammerman 1975). This research has provided the logical basis for our model of inter-regional mate exchanges, which also relies heavily on the work of Friedman and Rowlands (1978). The relatively wide range of agricultural strategies available to agriculturalists in the Valley of Oaxaca as compared with the rest of the southern highlands is noted by Palerm and Wolf (1957), who also recognize some of the implications of these differences for long-term development (see also Flannery 1983d).

The organization of the Valley of Oaxaca during the latter part of the Middle Formative Period has been discussed in Flannery, Marcus, and Kowalewski (1981), Blanton et al. (1982), Flannery and Marcus, eds. (1983), and Kowalewski et al. (1989). Marcus (1976b, 1976c, 1980) and Flannery and Marcus (1990) have described the Rosario phase *Danzante* at San José Mogote. Blanton (1976c, 1978) has argued that one of the principal roles of the administrative elite at Monte Albán in phase I was related to offense-defense.

We have made minor modifications in the basic ceramic sequence established by Caso, Bernal, and Acosta (1967). They were able to distinguish a "middle" phase I and a "transition" phase between II and IIIA, primarily on the basis of varying proportions of different pottery types found in their excavations. Because it is necessary to rely on stylistic differences to date surface remains, our chronology simplifies phase I into Early and Late phases, and does not recognize the "transition" phase (see Blanton 1978). Also, John Paddock's unpublished work regarding the phase IV site of Lambityeco enabled us to divide Caso, Bernal, and Acosta's single IIIB–IV into two distinct phases (Blanton et al. 1982; Kowalewski et al., 1989). Our absolute chronology is based on Drennan's (1983b) summary of radiocarbon dates from Valley of Oaxaca excavations.

Blanton (1978) is the primary source for our discussions of Monte Albán's foundation, organization, and population. See also Blanton (1976c). Tuck (1971) is a useful overview of the nature of the League of the Iroquois. For introductions to interaction studies, and the relationship between population, interaction patterns, and organizational change, see Olsson (1965) and Johnson (1977, 1982). Our descriptions of the developments in the Main Plaza were based in large part on Acosta (1965). The quote about Main Plaza construction activities in phase II is from that article. Winter (1974) noted changes in residential architecture and the increasingly formalized use of residential space at Monte Albán. We have relied heavily on the epigraphic and iconographic studies of Joyce Marcus (1976b, 1976c, 1980, 1983b), which expand work begun by Caso (cf. 1928c). She is responsible for identifying place glyphs, for convincingly arguing for a militaristic interpretation of the *Danzantes*, and for noting the valley-wide stylistic shift in IIIA monuments. John Scott (1978) discusses the *Danzantes* and provides a catalog.

The major sources on regional demography, settlement patterns, and changes in political and economic organization in the valley during and after phase I are Blanton et al. (1982), Feinman et al. (1985) and Kowalewski et al. (1989). Feinman (1980, 1982; Feinman, Upham, and Lighfoot 1981) formulated the ceramic production-step index, and analyzed patterns in production and exchange of ceramics (see also Feinman 1986; Feinman, Kowalewski, and Blanton 1984). Preliminary results from a technological analysis of Oaxaca pottery are presented in Feinman et al. 1989. Hunt and Hunt (1974), Downing (1974), and Lees (1973) provide discussions of the social and environmental costs of modern irrigation systems in Oaxaca that we found useful in evaluating the implications of piedmont agricultural development.

Winter (1977, 1984) first pointed out that *comales* were used initially during phase I. Allan (1965:453) discusses how British colonial administrators in Africa hoped to increase village permanency by encouraging a switch in residential architecture away from perishable structures to the more durable mud-brick buildings. The information on architecture at San José Mogote during phase II comes from Flannery and Marcus (1976), Flannery, Marcus, and Kowalewski (1981), and Flannery and Marcus, eds. (1983). Discussions concerning the layout and orientation of nonresidential architecture are drawn mostly from a diachronic, regional analysis completed by Blanton (1989). Elam (1989) summarizes the regional survey findings on hilltop and terrace sites in Oaxaca.

The Classic–Postclassic transition in Oaxaca has been discussed in Finsten (1983), Flannery and Marcus, eds. (1983), Marcus (1989b), and Kowalewski et al. (1989). Information on important phase IV sites can be found in Bernal (1965), Paddock (1966), and Peterson (1976). Excavations that added to our description of phase V regional organization were done by Gallegos (1962, 1963) at Zaachila, Bernal and Gamio (1974) at Yagul, and Caso and de la Borbolla (1936) at Mitla. Spores's studies (1967, 1974, 1984) of the Late Post-classic Mixtec kingdoms built the foundation for our understanding of the phase V polities. Rathje's (1975) suggestions about the Lowland Maya shaped our awareness of the importance of commercial factors in defining the evolutionary significance of the Late Postclassic. Taylor (1971, cited in Cook and Diskin, ed. 1976) pointed out the continuity between early colonial and phase V market systems. Our ethnohistoric interpretations of V are based in part on Appel (1982) and Flannery and Marcus, eds. (1983). See also Spores (1965), W. Taylor (1972), Whitecotton (1977, 1983, 1990), Paddock (1983), and Appel (1986).

A variety of sources was used in developing our arguments about interactions between the Valley of Oaxaca and other areas of Mesoamerica. Caso, Bernal, and Acosta (1967) first pointed out the stylistic isolation of the valley during IIIA and IIIB. Other sources that have been useful in understanding macroregional differences and similarities in ceramic assemblages include MacNeish, Peterson, and Flannery (1970) for Tehuacán, Spencer (1982) and Redmond (1983) for the Cuicatlán area, Spores (1972) in the Nochixtlán Valley to the north, Brockington (1973) and Markman (1981) in the Miahuatlán area, and De Cicco and Brockington (1956), J. Zeitlin (1978), R. Zeitlin (1978), Brockington (1983), and Joyce and Winter (1989) for the Oaxaca coast. Also, Chadwick (1971a) discusses the pan-Mesoamerican distribution of the polychrome pottery found in the valley in phase V.

Our comments on the phase II tributary domain of Monte Albán are based largely on Marcus (1976b, 1980), Spencer (1982), and Redmond (1983). Millon (1973) describes and notes the significance of the Oaxaca *barrio* in Teotihuacan, and Marcus (1980) describes and interprets the Monte Albán stone monuments that depict apparent foreign relations between individuals from the Valley of Oaxaca and individuals from Teotihuacan. Bernal (1965) first discussed the relative weakness of Teotihuacan influence on Valley of Oaxaca artifacts and architecture. Durán (1967), Paso y Troncoso (1905: vol. 4), Barlow (1949), and Burgoa (1934) contain information on the valley's relationship with the Aztec empire and the Mixteca Alta in phase V; see also Appel (1982) and Blanton (1983b). Drennan (1989) noted the filling in of the piedmont surrounding the valley during phase V in his survey north of the Etla arm.

Chapter 4. The Valley of Mexico
The major sources we used in this chapter are the various works that grew out of Eric Wolf's 1960 Valley of Mexico conference. Parsons (1971) lists the proposals made by the conference members. The major publications include those resulting from the Teotihuacan survey, especially R. Millon (1970, 1973, 1976a, 1981, 1988), Millon, Drewitt, and Cowgill (1973), Cowgill (1974, 1983, 1984), and Spence (1967, 1974, 1979a and b, 1981, 1984, 1986). Outside Teotihuacan, surveys were done by Armillas (1971), Blanton (1972a and b), Parsons (1971), Parsons et al. (1982), Sanders (1965), Sanders, ed. (1986), Sanders et al. (1970), Sanders et al. (1975), and Sanders, Parsons, and Santley (1979). Additional summaries and discussions of this work can be found in Parsons (1974), Sanders and Price (1968), Sanders (1981), and Wolf, ed. (1976).

Environment
Refer to Armillas (1971), Blanton (1972a), Lorenzo, ed. (1968), Palerm (1973), Palerm and Wolf (1957), Parsons et al. (1982), Sanders (1965), Sanders et al. (1970), Sanders, Parsons,

and Santley (1979), and West and Armillas (1950). Colinvaux (1973) comments on the significance of patch size in ecological analyses; see also our Chapter 5. Obsidian as a valley resource is described in Santley (1984), Spence (1967), Spence and Parsons (1972), and Charlton (1978, 1984).

Chronology
Tolstoy (1978) summarizes the periods up to A.D. 900; see also Sanders, Parsons, and Santley (1979: ch. 5). The neutral chronological framework for the valley is described by Price (1976) and commented upon by Millon (1976b). Flannery (1977) questions the utility of adding yet another terminological layer. Descriptions of the valley's ceramic sequence can be found in Blanton and Parsons (1971), Parsons (1966), Parsons et al. (1982), Rattray (1966, 1973), Sanders, ed. (1986), Santley (1979), Tolstoy and Paradis (1970), and Tolstoy (1989).

Settlement pattern history of the Valley of Mexico, Teotihuacan
The most useful overview is Sanders, Parsons, and Santley (1979), although we disagree with its population and environmental determinist theory. We have already mentioned sources that resulted from work proposed during Eric Wolf's Valley of Mexico conference. These sources can be supplemented by Cummings (1933), Earle (1976), Piña Chan (1958), Tolstoy (1989), Tolstoy and Fish (1975), Tolstoy et al. (1977), and Vaillant (1930, 1931, 1935). Useful reports on excavations in Teotihuacan include Acosta (1964a), Bernal, ed. (1963), Blucher (1971), Cabrera C. et al., eds. (1982), Cabrera C. et al. (1991), Linné (1934), Matos M. (1980), C. Millon (1972, 1973), R. Millon, Drewitt, and Bennyhoff (1965), and Séjourné (1959, 1966). The spatial organization of Teotihuacan walled compounds is discussed in Hopkins (1987). The poor health of the occupants of one compound is documented by Storey (1985).

Evidence for Teotihuacan control of a central highlands domain is discussed in Dumond (1972), Hirth (1974, 1978, 1980), Hirth and Angulo (1980), Mastache and Crespo (1974), and is summarized in R. Millon (1981, 1988). For Kaminaljuyú, see Kidder, Jennings, and Shook (1946), Sanders and Michels (1969), Sanders and Michels, eds. (1977), Michels and Sanders (1973), Sanders (1978), and the discussion in Sanders (1989). The nature of the Teotihuacan presence outside the central highlands is summarized by R. Millon (1988). A key to understanding Teotihuacan's foreign relations is its role in commodity exchanges, particularly the production and movement of obsidian and its control of obsidian sources in the central highlands and elsewhere. The obsidian industry at Teotihuacan is described in Spence (1981, 1984, 1986); cf. Clark (1986). Santley (1983, 1984, 1989) and Santley et al. (1986) discuss Teotihuacan's involvement in obsidian exchange in Mesoamerica and Teotihuacan's presence at Matacapan (southern Veracruz). Santley and his coauthors propose a commercially based model for Teotihuacan interregional exchange, while Clark (1986) and Drennan et al. (1990) lean toward interpreting Teotihuacan's objectives in more political terms. At this point, our discipline seems to lack the appropriate ethnographic analogues, theoretical models, and data analysis that will be required to fully understand Teotihuacan's role in interregional economics and politics, but we are inching toward a more competent understanding. On the Oaxaca *barrio* at Teotihuacan, refer to R. Millon (1973: 41 – 2, 1981), and Abascal, Harbottle, and Sayre (1974). Tomb 105 of Monte Albán is described in Marquina (1964: láminas 97, 98). Marcus (1980) discusses Monte Albán's stone monuments that depict Teotihuacan emissaries.

The collapse of Teotihuacan; the Coyotlatelco phase; the Mazapan phase
Again, our basic source was R. Millon (1973, 1981, 1988). The quote from Millon on ritual destruction is 1981, pp. 70 – 2. The transition to the Coyotlatelco phase in the valley and in adjacent areas of the central highlands is difficult to interpret (e.g., Dumond and Muller 1972), but recent research in the Tula area (Mastache and Cobean, 1989), and at Xochicalco (Hirth 1989), among other locations, is contributing new insights (a recent summary is Diehl and Berlo, eds., 1989). Diehl (1989) summarizes changes in Teotihuacan after the collapse.

Nigel Davies's (1977, 1980, 1987) summaries of Toltec ethnohistory and archaeology are monumental. See also Chadwick (1971b). Jiménez Moreno (1941) first identified Tula, Hidalgo, as the Tula of the Toltecs. Recent work in and around the center (in addition to the Mastache and Cobean reference already made) has been done by Acosta (e.g., 1956 – 7), Matos M., ed. (1974, 1976), Diehl, ed. (1974), Diehl and Benfer (1975), and Healan (Healan, ed. 1989). Useful summaries of the Tula research are found in Diehl (1981, 1983) and in Healan, Cobean, and Diehl (1989). Alden (1979) analyzes Coyotlatelco and Mazapan settlement patterns in the Valley of Mexico using an interaction model. A number of sources are pertinent to the Tula–Chichén Itzá connection: for example, Kubler (1961), Ruz Lhuiller (1962), Andrews (1965), and the summary in Davies (1977: ch. 5). On Toltec "influence" et El Tajín and the surrounding area, refer to García Payón (1971).

The Early and Late Aztec phases
Comprehensive histories of the Aztec phases have been written by Davies (1973, 1987) and Brundage (1972). The list of primary sources that can be consulted pertaining to the Aztec phases and the earliest period of Spanish contact is a long one, but a mention of prominent sources would include the Codex Xolotl (Dibble 1951), the Codex Mendoza (Berdan and Anawalt 1992), Durán (1967), Ixtlilxochitl (1952), and especially Sahagún (1946, 1950 – 63). Gibson (1964) summarizes the political and economic organization. The political structure of Aztec city-states is discussed in Hodge (1984, 1991, in press). Brumfiel discusses Aztec state-building (1983) and economic change (1976b, 1980, 1986, 1987, 1991), as does Blanton (in press a) and Hassig (1985). Types of markets in and around the Aztec empire are described in Berdan (1985). Evidence for increased economic integration in the Late Aztec phase valley is evident from the ceramic analyses of Hodge and Minc (1990). The basic source for Aztec settlement patterns is Sanders, Parsons, and Santley (1979), supplemented by Gonzalez Aparicio (1973) and by Calnek's work on Tenochtitlan-Tlatelolco (especially 1972 and 1976). Calnek's comment on Tenochtitlan's palaces is from his 1976 article (p. 295).

Sources for Aztec agricultural development include Armillas (1971), Blanton (1972a), Palerm (1973), Parsons (1971), Parsons et al. (1982), Sanders, Parsons, and Santley (1979), and West and Armillas (1950). The energetics of agriculture and transport is analyzed in relation to urban growth in Sanders and Santley (1983), Parsons (1976), and Hassig (1985). Barlow (1949) traced out the extent of the Aztec empire. An expansion and revision of Barlow's empire research is in Berdan et al. (in press). Descriptions of the valley, its cities, markets, and way of life at the time of the conquest were made by the Anonymous Conqueror (1917), Díaz del Castillo (1908 – 16), and Cortés (1963). This kind of information is synthesized in Berdan (1982). The population estimate for Tenochtitlan-Tlatelolco is from Calnek (1976). Summaries of recent work in Tenochtitlan's Templo Mayor are in Broda, Carrasco, and Matos M. (1987), Matos (1988), and Boone, ed. (1987). We measured areas of civic-ceremonial complexes from R. Millon, Drewitt, and Cowgill (1973), Broda et al. (1987), and Marquina (1964: lámina 45). Wittfogel (1957: 86 – 7) briefly contrasts introvert and extrovert architecture. Blanton (1976b) discusses Late Aztec city size relationships. M. Smith found that the distribution of Late Aztec centers conforms to some expectations of marketing location theory (but see Evans 1980 and M. Smith 1980). Blanton (in press a) expanded Smith's central-place analysis and arrived at conclusions similar to his; this led Blanton to conclude that state control of the Late Aztec economic system was not as complete as it is portrayed in sources like Hassig (1985), Hicks (1987), and Carrasco (1971, 1978); this issue is discussed by Offner (1981a; see the exchange between Offner 1981b and Carrasco 1981). Ideational aspects of the Aztec polity are analyzed by Gillespie (1989) and van Zantwijk (1985).

Summary of population trends in the Valley of Mexico; solar markets; city-states
The population values and carrying capacity estimates are from Sanders, Parsons, and Santley (1979). We disagree with their conclusion that population pressure caused sociocultural

change in the valley. Brumfiel, based on analysis of data from the eastern valley (1976a), agrees with our conclusion. She found that during the Ticoman and Patlachique phases only the largest sites could not have been agriculturally self-supporting; this makes sense given that these emergent central places would have had a large component of non-food producers whose activities were supported by surpluses brought in from dependent hamlets and villages. Solar market systems are discussed in C. A. Smith (1974, 1976a). Descriptions of Aztec *calpultin* can be found in Katz (1966), Monzon (1949), and Sanders and Price (1968: 156). Gibson (1964) identifies the fifty Aztec city-states. Bray (1972) summarized their organizational features and discusses league formation among them; see also Hodge (1984, in press).

Chapter 5. The eastern lowlands

The best general text covering the eastern lowlands is Morely, Brainerd, and Sharer (1983). Our treatment of language distributions is necessarily simplified; see McQuown (1956), Swadesh (1961), Thompson (1966:18, 27 – 9), Coe (1987:24 – 7), and Suárez (1983) for fuller discussion. The rainfall statistics are from Roys (1972:10); see also Puleston (1973:240 – 9). Simmons, Tarano, and Pinto (1959) published a soil survey that includes the Department of Petén. Lundell (1937) conducted a vegetation survey; and Puleston (1973:268 – 83) and several authors in *Maya subsistence: studies in memory of Dennis E. Puleston* (Flannery, ed. 1982) have useful discussions of plants and their human uses. Agricultural technology available to the ancient populations is reviewed in Harrison and Turner II, eds. (1978); see also Turner II and Harrison, eds. (1983) and Pohl, ed. (1985). Hellmuth (1977) cites Spanish sources attesting to the productivity and diversity of sixteenth- and seventeenth-century milpas, and see Harrison (1977) and Turner II (1979). Modern applications of ancient intensive agricultural techniques have been undertaken by Mexico's Instituto Nacional sobre Recursos Bióticos and are described by Gómez-Pompa (1979; Gómez-Pompa and Golley 1979; Gómez-Pompa and Kaus 1990). Our estimates of net primary productivity for different vegetation types are extrapolated from Krebs (1972: table 29). Compare, as examples of plant species lists, Lundell (1937) with C. E. Smith (1978) – neither pretends to be complete but the greater diversity of the lowlands is dramatic. Our view of the finely grained, mosaic character of the eastern lowlands is influenced by Puleston's surveys (1973) and by theoretical studies such as Connell's (1978) and the work summarized in Farnworth and Golley, eds. (1973). Compare Connell's study with Sanders (1977). Voorhies (1982) and Graham (1987) also emphasize the rich, fine-grained diversity of the eastern lowlands. An early (1100 B.C.) date for raised-field agriculture in Belize is reported in Puleston (1977:463 – 5) and corroborated in Bloom, Pohl, and Stein (1985) (but see Pohl, ed. 1990). The phrases "organization of diversity" and "replication of uniformity" were coined by Anthony F. C. Wallace (1970:22 – 4). The shapes of interacting territories are treated theoretically by Haggett, Cliff, and Frey (1977:47 – 63). R. E. W. Adams reviews travel times in the eastern lowlands (1978:27). Willey (1981:402, 407) notes that larger centers tend to be spaced at intervals of roughly twenty to thirty kilometers.

Ball (1977a) has a good synthesis of the early prehistory of the northern lowlands; see also Ball (1977b). U. Cowgill et al. (1966) originally reported the Lake Petenxil coring; Wiseman, cited in Hammond (1977a:59 – 60), described the Eckixil results, and Rue (1989) shows *Cheno-Am* disturbance in western Honduras at 4,770 ± 385 B.P. The lake sediment evidence was reviewed by Deevey et al. (1979). For early developments along the Pasión we followed Willey (1973a, 1977), and for northern Belize, Hammond (1977a, b; Andrews V and Hammond 1990). The Olmec phenomena in Mesoamerica were explored by Covarrubias (1957), Bernal (1969), Benson, ed. (1968), Coe and Diehl (1980), and most recently by Sharer and Grove, eds. (1989). The idea that stylistic artifacts, depending on their visibility, communicate different-scale group identities was proposed by Wobst (1977), but Hodder (1982) provides ethnographic examples complicating this. The ideas of Flannery (1968b), Ball (1977a), Hudson (1976), Helms (1979), and Drennan (1976b) were crucial ingredients in the formulation of our view of the nature of Early Formative Mesoamerican societies.

Partial ethnographic parallels to the early societies of the eastern lowlands, and stimulating thoughts on dynamics, were found by reading Pospisil (1963), Bohannan and Bohannan (1953), and Evans-Pritchard (1940) though these are not the only relevant sources. For Early Formative head towns, note the larger settlements in Marcus's array of village sizes (1976a).

Models for the "spread" of farmers in Mesoamerica's eastern lowlands are proposed in R. E. W. Adams, ed. (1977), Puleston and Puleston (1971), and Voorhies (1982). Willey et al. (1965) cover the Belize River area. Their report is one of Mesoamerica's best data monographs. See Culbert (1977a) for the early history of Tikal. Milisauskas (1978:41 – 122) and Barker (1985) review evidence on the early tribal farming societies of Europe.

The data sources cited above for the Early and Middle Preclassic continue to be helpful for the Late Terminal Preclassic. For Cerros, see Freidel (1978, 1979), Robertson and Freidel, eds. (1986), and Garber (1989). Mississippian head towns are discussed in B. Smith, ed. (1978), Welch (1991), and Emerson and Lewis, eds. (1991); see also pp. 57 – 95 of Lanning's (1967) book on Peru. Sahlins (1958), D. Taylor (1975), Helms (1979), Feinman and Neitzel (1984), Drennan and Uribe, eds. (1987), Earle (1989), and Earle, ed. (1991) should be consulted on chiefdoms. Webster (1973) described the Becan entrenchment. Andrews IV (1968), Andrews IV and V (1980), and Kurjack (1974) report on Dzibilchaltún. Population estimates for the Yaxhá-Sacnab area have been made by D. S. and P. M. Rice (Deevey et al. 1979). *The origins of Maya civilization* (R.E.W. Adams, ed. 1977) contains useful general characterizations of Mamom and Chicanel ceramics. On the matter of Floral Park, our opinion is close to that expressed by Rathje (1977), though see Pring (1977) for a culture-historical treatment.

A recent collection of articles deals with the Early Classic (Willey and Mathews, eds. 1985). Research on household variability has been carried out at Copán (Webster and Gonlin 1988) and Cobá (Manzanilla, ed. 1987). Wauchope's (1938) study of modern native houses is useful for comparative purposes. On *chultuns*, see Puleston (1971). The issue of short- versus long-term occupation of house mounds and houses is addressed by Puleston (1973:160 – 4) and Pyburn (1989a). Settlements on the central Petén savannas were examined by P. Rice and D. Rice (1979). The low frequency of *comales* in the eastern lowlands and the differences in cooking styles from the rest of Mesoamerica were noticed fifty years ago (Tozzer, ed. and trans., 1941:90; on cooking see Pyburn 1989b). That different economies have contrasting patterns of "social time" and corresponding differences in household activities has been shown by a variety of studies (e.g., Bates and Lees 1977, Miles 1979, Rotenburg 1979). On variation in houses, see for example Benavides Castillo (1987). On why Mesoamerican societies should be analyzed in a more variation-conscious way than simply the "elite" and "commoner" categories, and for other critical remarks on the current state of archaeology in the Mesoamerican eastern lowlands, see Kowalewski, Feinman, and Finsten (1992). Eastern lowlands obsidian distributions were first examined by Sidrys (1976) and updated by Dreiss and Brown (1989). Welsh (1988) analyzes burial treatment and emphasizes ancestor veneration, going beyond the earlier work by Rathje, Gregory, and Wiseman (1978); see references in Levinson and Malone (1980:144 – 5) on cross-cultural implications. Miksicek (1983) and Beltrán Frías (1987) describe the floral remains from Pulltrouser and Cobá. Ashmore, ed. (1981) is an anthology on settlement patterns and Culbert and Rice edited a volume on population (1990). As Deevey et al. point out, the "logarithmic" population growth on the shores of Lakes Yaxhá and Sacnab had a slow overall rate, 0.17 percent per year, which "must have looked like equilibrium to the oldest inhabitants" (1979:301). Bullard's (1960) mule-trail survey provided a basic framework for settlement pattern studies, along with Morley's (1946:316 – 20) rough classification of centers. Other city typologies (Hammond 1975, Willey and Leventhal 1979) have more types defined by special criteria, but the theoretical purposes of these typologies are unclear. The Copán information is taken from Willey and Leventhal (1979). We follow Puleston's population estimate for Tikal (1973:207) rather than Haviland's (1972), which is lower and based on assumed rather than mapped densities. Puleston and Callender, Jr., describe Tikal's earthworks (1967). Drennan's comparison of within-community densities in Mesoamerica (1988) is the basis for the statement linking dispersed settlement to specific labor patterns. Puleston discussed the orchard and kitchen garden possibilities (1973:199, 292 – 304). The Cobá tree study was done by Folan, Fletcher, and Kintz (1979); maps are available in Folan, Kintz, and Fletcher (1983). The early report on Cobá is Thompson, Pollock, and Charlot (1932). Another recent city project took place at Nohmul (Hammond 1985). Fry's research (1979) on economic organization, which used many pottery collections from a well-sampled area to compare actual distributions against theoretical models, is valuable as one of the few attempts to treat the problem quantitatively; also see Ashmore (1988). The last ten years have seen more studies of chipped stone than ever before: Aldenderfer, Kimball, and Sievert (1989), Lewenstein (1987), McAnany (1989b), and Shafer (1983) are representative of the better work. McAnany (1989a) reviews models of prehistoric eastern Mesoamerican economy (but reaches different conclusions than we do here). Intersite habitation densities are reported for a strip between Tikal and Uaxactún (Puleston 1973) and for a sampled transect between Tikal and Yaxhá (Ford 1979, 1986); see in general Culbert and Rice, eds. (1990).

In the field of Maya hieroglyphics, Proskouriakoff's research made possible new breakthroughs (e.g., Proskouriakoff 1961). Berlin's (1958) discovery of the emblem glyphs was a seminal contribution. The reconstruction of state hierarchies and territories, and of their connection with marriage alliances, was accomplished by Joyce Marcus (1976d). See Houston (1988) on the history of decipherment; Culbert (1988a) has the broadest and easily the most accessible summary of what is known about political history from the glyphs. Compare the Mesoamerican written texts with those of Ur (Wright 1969:99 – 116). See Morley (1946:fig. 1) and Culbert (1988) for an idea of the frequency of monument carving through time. Early Classic dated monuments are shown by Marcus (1976d:31 – 3), who also discusses the relations between Tikal and Uaxactún. A discussion on Palenque rulers continues in Mathews and Schele (1974); the *Palenque Roundtable* volumes; and Schele and Miller (1986). See Ruppert, Thompson, and Proskouriakoff (1955) on Bonampak. Harrison wrote a dissertation (1970) on the Tikal central acropolis; Kowalski wrote a book (1987) on the "House of the Governor" at Uxmal. *Sacbe* construction as boundary maintenance is discussed by Kurjack and Andrews IV (1976). The idea of four regional capitals comes from Joyce Marcus (1976d); see also Culbert (1977b, 1988) and Adams and Jones (1981) on political integration larger than the city-state. Rathje, Gregory, and Wiseman (1978) suggested the commercial functions of the calendar. See the same article for characteristics of Fine Orange pottery that were important from an economic standpoint. Simmons and Brem (1979) discuss the distribution of volcanic ash-tempered pottery. An earlier estimate for the Classic Period in the area is the Ricketsons' 13 to 53 million (Ricketson and Ricketson 1937:23).

The collapse data are from the papers in Culbert, ed. (1973); see also Culbert (1974, 1977b, 1988b). Potter discusses aspects of the Late Classic and Early Postclassic periods in the central lowlands, and Sabloff and Andrews V edited a volume emphasizing the north (1986). Pendergast (1986) argues for continuity at Lamanai. Sabloff and Tourtellot (1991) report on their city-project at Sayil. Chichén Itzá's site map and architectural drawings were published by Ruppert (1952); see also Morris's study of the Temple of the Warriors (Morris, Charlot, and Morris 1931). See Kampen (1972) and Krotser and Krotser (1973) on El Tajín.

The history of early Spanish contact in Yucatan is reviewed by Tozzer, ed. and trans. (1941). A. L. Smith (1962) has drawings of Postclassic houses and house lots, and see D. Rice (1986) on Classic versus Postclassic houses in Petén. Landa described specializations (Tozzer, ed. and trans. 1941:64, 94, 190), as did Roys (1972:30, 46). Landa noted women's market participation (Tozzer, ed. and trans. 1941:127). The primacy of maize is amply documented by Landa, and see Proskouriakoff (1962) for archaeological examples of manos, metates, and obsidian and flint artifacts from Mayapán. Roys (1972:23) discusses dress. Landa describes community and family patterns of ritual and A. L. Smith (1962) documents the archaeological occurrence of household shrines at Mayapán. See also Marcus (1978) for the religion and cosmos of the people of the eastern lowlands. Landa's treatise contains many references to the class system, and Roys (1972:33 – 5) has a brief overview. A. L. Smith noted groupings of houses at Mayapán. Landa mentioned small-scale labor cooperation (Tozzer, ed. and trans. 1941:96, 127); see the same source, p. 99, on lineages and inheritance. The Mayapán monograph (Pollock et al. 1962) is among Mesoamerica's best site reports. Consult Lothrop (1924) and Sanders (1960) for information on Tulum and its surroundings. Landa describes political organization in the Mayapán empire and during later times, and see Roys (1957, 1972). Fox (1978) has a provocative argument that lowland and highland states in Postclassic eastern Mesoamerica were segmentary. See Landa, with Tozzer's well-indexed commentaries (1941) on the organization of religion in Yucatan and on markets, money, and trade; we have also used Roys (1972) and Scholes and Roys (1948). Landa mentions the patronymic system (Tozzer, ed. and trans. 1941:99), which is discussed further by Roys (1957). The quote about making money from idols is Landa's (Tozzer, ed. and trans. 1941:94) and he also describes the monthly festivals (pp. 149 – 66). Landa's wineskin comment is on p. 166. The two scholars urging better research designs are Beltrán Frías (1987:227, our trans.) and Pyburn (1989a:146 – 7); see also Pyburn 1991.

Chapter 6. Comparisons and conclusions

Population dynamics

Population pressure has been viewed as the primary causal factor in sociocultural change by several recent studies that have investigated the issue (e.g., Carneiro 1970; Sanders and Nichols 1988; Sanders, Parsons, and Santley 1979; Smith and Young 1972; Spooner, ed. 1972). Many of these works were inspired by Boserup (1965), whose thesis we find seriously flawed. The approach of Boserup and this group of anthropologists has been challenged on both theoretical (Blanton 1975, Cowgill 1975) and empirical grounds (Blanton et al. 1979; Earle 1978; Feinman et al. 1985; Feinman and Nicholas 1987, 1990a; Johnson 1973; Nicholas 1989). An advocate of population pressure as a causal factor in social and technological change is Cohen (1975, 1977, 1989). Sanders (1973) has argued that population pressure was a major factor in the decline of the Classic Maya, and Harner (1977) has proposed a relationship between population pressure and both human sacrifice and cannibalism among the Aztecs. His argument is seriously faulted and cannot be accepted (Berdan 1982:116 – 18; Ortiz de Montellano 1978; Sahlins 1978).

The relationship between expanded labor demands and increases in fertility and population has been noted in a series of works (cf. Coontz 1957; Easterlin 1978; Nag, White, and Peet 1978; Nerlove 1974; Polgar 1972; White 1973). These studies view fertility decisions in the context of household economic strategies, and regional population shifts as the aggregated result of household choices.

Great variability in intraregional population change has been observed in the Valley of Mexico (Sanders, Parsons, and Santley 1979: 191, 194, 196, 199, 205, 206, 211, 215) and the Valley of Oaxaca, as we have reviewed in Chapter 3. In the Valley of Oaxaca, several studies have pointed out that the complexity that can be observed in such population transitions could not have been due to a constant growth rate or to environmental factors in any simple sense (Blanton 1978, 1980; Blanton et al. 1981; Feinman et al. 1985; Feinman and Nicholas 1987, 1990a; Kowalewski 1980; Nicholas 1989; but see Sanders and Nichols 1988 and Santley 1980). Blanton (1976b) as well as R. Millon (1976a) have made similar interpretations of the Valley of Mexico data (but see Sanders et al. 1976, and Sanders, Parsons, and Santley 1979 for an alternative viewpoint).

Several authors have pointed out that the rapid population growth of the Valley of Mexico in Aztec times was likely due, at least in part, to immigration (Brundage 1972; Davies 1973). Selby and Murphy (1979) have noted that immigrants from outside the Valley of Oaxaca have been a key factor in the rapid growth of Oaxaca City during the last few decades.

The state in Mesoamerica

Recent anthropological considerations of the state include Claessen and van de Velde, eds. (1987), Cohen and Service, eds. (1978), Flannery (1972), Friedman and Rowlands, eds. (1978), Haas (1982), Johnson (1973, 1987), Jones and Kautz, eds. (1981), Service (1975), and Wright (1977, 1986). The comparative framework and some of the descriptive terminology and examples we use follow closely the cross-cultural study *The early state* (Claessen and Skalník, eds. 1978). Some archaeologists would differ with our view that La Venta and San Lorenzo were chiefdoms, not states. Examples of ethnohistoric accounts or works based on ethnohistoric accounts that give details of state organization include Durán (1967), the *Codex Ramirez* (Orozco y Berra, ed. 1979), Hodge (1984, 1991, in press), Offner (1983), Tozzer, ed. and trans. (1941). On the matter of confederacies and alliances, see, for example, Davies (1968). The examples of states are largely from Claessen and Skalník's study of what they call "early states" (that is, traditional, evolutionarily "early," not necessarily pristine or chronologically early). We made several additions to and deletions from their list. The argument on the limits to growth of the traditional state owes much to Wallerstein's writing (1974) and to Claessen and Skalník. Political administration was often an important function of Mesoamerican cities, but we disagree with Sanders and Webster (1988) that Mesoamerican cities were "regal-ritual" (see M. Smith 1989). Marcus (1983c) describes some of the variability in Mesoamerican cities. Blanton (1982) discusses early urbanism in a broader framework. Writing and some of its social consequences are discussed by Marcus (1976c). Cowgill's (1983) discussion of the Ciudadela at Teotihuacan is an example of how archaeological data can be used to infer state structure and function. Bringing members of the nobility into the palace as retainers, wives, or even hostages (as at Mayapán), was a common way for a ruler to try to solve the problem of maintaining vertical integration between himself and a too-numerous second echelon. A general review of African kingdoms from an anthropological perspective is Mair (1977). See Flannery's (1972) criticism of prime-mover arguments and Athens (1977) for a critique of systems models (but note that Athens himself then reverts to a prime-mover argument). See Spores (1972) on the Mixteca Alta, Sanders and his colleagues (Sanders and Michels, eds. 1977) on the Valley of Guatemala, and Fox (1978) on the Quiche for other Mesoamerican cases of state development.

On the dynamic relationship between states and market systems

Lopez (1976) discusses guilds under Rome (p. 9) and in medieval times (p. 127). C. A. Smith (1976b: 354) outlines the essential features of fully developed ("fully commercialized") market systems. Christaller (1966) first contrasted the territorial properties of market versus administrative institutions (see also Blanton 1976a). Blanton (1983c, 1985) discusses the origin and evolution of market systems in a comparative framework. Wallerstein (1974) discusses the role of the state in nascent capitalist development. Palerm (1973) points to the hydraulic potentials of the Valley of Mexico. On African market systems, see Hopkins (1973). An introduction to medieval European commercialization and the decline in state controls can be found in Lopez (1976) and Pirenne (1952, 1957). Skinner (1977b) comments on China's parallel "medieval revolution." We comment on these matters in more detail in Blanton et al. (1982: ch. 8; cf. Blanton 1983d).

Acosta Saignes (1945), Chapman (1957), and Bittman and Sullivan (1978) are useful introductory sources on the *Pochteca* and the Mesoamerican ports of trade. Bittman and Sullivan (1978), Blanton (in press a), Brumfiel (1976b), and Hicks (1987) consider the nature of Aztec state attempts to reimpose controls on commercial institutions during the Late Postclassic. The ideas about the sizes of states in relation to control of emigration and trade routes are largely from Friedman (1977). See also Blanton (in press b) on how this figured into strategies of the Aztec empire.

What is Mesoamerica?

The term "Mesoamerica" became established after the publication of Kirchoff's article (1943). See also Saucr (1941), Helms (1975), Andrews (1977), and Mathien and McGuire, eds. (1986) for views on Mesoamerica and its frontiers. Wallerstein's (1974) world-system concept was devised for the Old World and applied to Mesoamerica as empire and to its relationship to the U.S. Southwest (Pailes and Whitecotton 1979; Whitecotton and Pailes 1979), but the tendency to empire, we think, does not effectively characterize Mesoamerican macroregional interaction. Mesoamerica as a world-system is discussed in Blanton and Feinman (1984). The literature discussing macroregional interactions and the applicability of world-systems concepts to early civilizations is a "growth industry." See, for example, Champion, ed. (1989), Chase-Dunn and Hall, eds. (1991), Ekholm and Friedman (1982), Kohl (1989), Price (1977), Renfrew and Cherry, eds. (1986), Rowlands, Larsen, and Kristiansen, eds. (1987), Schneider (1977), Schortman and Urban (1987), Whitecotton and Pailes (1986), and Wolf (1982). Population estimates for Mesoamerica are discussed in Cook and Simpson (1948), Cook and Borah (1960), Borah and Cook (1960, 1963), and Sanders (1972). The figure for Mesoamerica's areal extent comes from R. E. W. Adams (1977: 11). Mesoamerican – Southwestern connections are discussed in Mathien and McGuire, eds. (1986). Europe's population figures are those given by Spooner (1968: 33). China's are from Skinner (1977b: 19). The shared interests of Mesoamerican nobility are discussed in M. Smith (1986). The embassies and tribute of Southeast Asia in the pre-Portuguese period are described by Wheatley (1961). Lattimore (1962) writes about the Old World silk trade. R. M. Adams (1974) reviews research on ancient trade, including luxury goods; see also Helms (1988), Peregrine (1991), and Schneider (1977). The transchiefdom sharing of esoteric knowledge used for political legitimacy is elegantly presented by Helms (1979). For Hopewell see Caldwell (1964), Struever and Houart (1972), and Seeman (1977). For Chavín see Lanning (1967). The estimates of human carrier efficiencies are based on figures provided to us from a study by H. Ball (ms.); see also Drennan (1984). Estimates of food consumption were complied by Kowalewski (1982). Martin Wobst (1977) points out that symbols have different material requirements that depend on their use for signaling at various levels within social groups. Wynne-Edwards (1962) discusses epideictic displays in animal populations. For ports of trade, see Chapman (1957) and Sabloff et al. (1974). Interregional marketing is described in Durán (1967: vol. 2: 185, 357) and suggested by later *relaciones* (García Payón, ed. 1965); see Berdan (1985). We discuss core and boundary strategies in Blanton, Kowalewski, and Feinman (1992). The quote about Teotihuacan art is from Pasztory (1988: 50). The chapters in Diehl and Berlo (eds. 1989) stimulated our thinking about boundary strategists.

Abascal, Rafael M., Gordon Harbottle, and E. V. Sayre. 1974. Correlation between terra cotta figurines and pottery from the Valley of Mexico and source clays by activation analysis. In *Archaeological Chemistry*, ed. Curt W. Beck, pp. 81 – 99. Washington: American Chemical Society.

Acosta, Jorge R. 1956 – 7. Interpretación de algunos de los datos obtenidos en Tula relativos a la epoca Tolteca. *Revista Mexicana de Estudios Antropológicos 14:75 – 110*.

1960. Las exploraciones arqueológicas en Tula, Hidalgo, durante la XI temporada, 1955. *Anales del Instituto Nacional de Antropología e Historia* 11:39 – 72.

1961. La doceava temporada de exploraciones en Tula, Hidalgo. *Anales del Instituto Nacional de Antropología e Historia* 13:29 – 58.

1964a. *El Palacio del Quetzalpapalotl*. Mexico: Memorías del Instituto Nacional de Antropología e Historia 10.

1964b. La decimotercera temporada de exploraciones en Tula, Hidalgo. *Anales del Instituto Nacional de Antropología e Historia* 16:45 – 76.

1965. Preclassic and classic architecture of Oaxaca. In *Handbook of Middle American Indians*, vol. 3, part 3, ed. G. Willey, pp. 814 – 36. Austin: University of Texas Press.

Acosta Saignes, Miguel. 1945. Los Pochteca: ubicación de los mercados en la estructura social Tenochca. *Acta Antropológica*, epoca 1, 1(1).

Adams, Richard E. W. 1973. Maya collapse: transformations and termination in the ceramic sequence at Altar de Sacrificios. In *The Classic Maya collapse*. ed. T. Patrick Culbert, pp. 133 – 63. Albuquerque: University of New Mexico Press.

1977. *Prehistoric Mesoamerica*. Boston: Little, Brown.

1978. Routes of communication in Mesoamerica: the Northern Guatemalan Highlands and the Petén. In *Mesoamerican communication routes and cultural contacts*, ed. Thomas A. Lee, Jr., and Carlos Navarete, pp. 27 – 35. *New World Archaeological Foundation, Papers* 40.

Adams, Richard E. W., ed. 1977. *The origins of Maya civilization*. Albuquerque: University of New Mexico Press.

Adams, Richard E. W., and Richard C. Jones. 1981. Spatial patterns and regional growth among Classic Maya Cities. *American Antiquity* 46:301 – 22.

Adams, Richard N. 1978. Man, energy and anthropology: I can feel the heat, but where's the light? *American Anthropologist* 80:297 – 309.

Adams, Robert McC. 1974. Anthropological perspectives on ancient trade. *Current Anthropology* 15:239 – 58.

Alden, John. 1979. A reconstruction of Toltec Period political units in the Valley of Mexico. In *Transformations: mathematical approaches to culture change*, ed. C. Renfrew and K. Cooke, pp. 169 – 200. New York: Academic Press.

Aldenderfer, Mark S., Larry R. Kimball, and April Sievert. 1989. Microwear analysis in the Maya lowlands: the use of functional data in a complex society setting. *Journal of Field Archaeology* 16:47 – 60.

Allan, William. 1965. *The African husbandman*. New York: Barnes & Noble Books.

243

Ammerman, Albert J. 1975. Late Pleistocene population dynamics: an alternative view. *Human Ecology* 3, no. 4:219 – 34.

Andrews, E. Wyllys, IV. 1965. Archaeology and prehistory of the Northern Maya lowlands: an introduction. In *Handbook of Middle American Indians*, vol. 2, ed. R. Wauchope, pp. 288 – 330. Austin: University of Texas Press.

1968. Dzibilchaltún, a Northern Mayan metropolis. *Archaeology* 21:36 – 47.

1973. The development of Mayan civilization after abandonment of the southern cities. In *The Classic Maya collapse*, ed. T. Patrick Culbert, pp. 243 – 65. Albuquerque: University of New Mexico Press.

1977. The southeastern periphery of Mesoamerica: a view from Eastern El Salvador. In *Social processes in Maya prehistory: studies in honour of Sir Eric Thompson*, ed. Norman Hammond, pp. 113 – 34. London: Academic Press.

Andrews, E. Wyllys, IV, and E. Wyllys Andrews V. 1980. *Excavations at Dzibilchaltún, Yucatan, Mexico* Middle American Research Institute, Publication 48.

Andrews, E. Wyllys, V, and Norman Hammond. 1990. Redefinition of the Swasey phase at Cuello, Belize. *American Antiquity* 55:570 – 84.

Anonymous Conqueror, 1917. *Narrative of some things of New Spain and of the great city of Temestitan, Mexico*. trans. Marshall H. Saville. New York: The Cortés Society.

Appel, Jill. 1982. The postclassic: a summary of the ethnohistoric information relevant to the interpretation of late postclassic settlement pattern data, the central and Valle Grande survey zones. In R. E. Blanton et al., *Monte Albán's hinterland*, part I: *Prehispanic settlement patterns of the central and southern parts of the Valley of Oaxaca, Mexico*, Museum of Anthropology, University of Michigan, Memoirs 15:139 – 48.

1986. A central-place analysis of Classic and Late Postclassic settlement patterns in the Valley of Oaxaca. In *Economic aspects of prehispanic highland Mexico*, ed. B. L. Isaac, pp. 375 – 418. Research in Economic Anthropology, Supplement 2. Greenwich: JAI Press.

Appleby, Gordon. 1976. The role of urban food needs in regional development, Puno, Peru. In *Regional analysis*, vol. 1: *Economic systems*, ed. Carol Smith, pp. 147 – 77. New York: Academic Press.

Armillas, Pedro. 1948. A sequence of cultural development in Meso-America. In *A reappraisal of Peruvian archaeology*, ed. Wendell C. Bennett, pp. 105 – 11. *Society for American Archaeology Memoirs* 13(4).

1971. Gardens in swamps. *Science* 174:653 – 61.

Ashmore, Wendy. 1988. Household and community at Classic Quirigua. In *Household and community in the Mesoamerican past*, ed. Richard R. Wilk and Wendy Ashmore, pp. 153 – 70. Albuquerque: University of New Mexico Press.

Ashmore, Wendy, ed. 1981. *Lowland Maya settlement patterns*. Albuquerque: University of New Mexico Press.

Athens, J. Stephen. 1977. Theory building and the study of evolutionary process in complex societies. In *For theory building in archaeology*, ed. Lewis R. Binford, pp. 353 – 84. New York: Academic Press.

Aveleyra Arroyo de Avida, Luis. 1964. The primitive hunters. In *Handbook of Middle American Indians*, vol. 1: *Natural environment and early cultures*, ed. Robert C. West, pp. 384 – 412. Austin: University of Texas Press.

Balfet, Hélène. 1965. Ethnographic observations in North Africa and archaeological interpretation: the pottery of Maghreb. In *Ceramics and man*, ed. Fred R. Matson, pp. 161 – 77. Chicago: Aldine.

Ball, Hugh G. The Aztec tribute: an investigation of manpower requirements. Unpublished ms. in the files of the authors.

Ball, Joseph W. 1977a. The rise of the Northern Maya chiefdoms: a socioprocessual analysis. In *The origins of Maya civilization*, ed. R. E. W. Adams, pp. 101 – 32. Albuquerque: University of New Mexico Press.

1977b. An hypothetical outline of Coastal Maya prehistory: 300 B.C. – A.D. 1200. In *Social process in Maya prehistory: studies in honour of Sir Eric Thompson*, ed. Norman Hammond, pp. 167 – 96. London: Academic Press.

Bandelier, A. F. 1884. *Report of an archaeological tour in Mexico, in 1881.* The Archaeological Institute of America, American Series 2, 2nd ed.

Barker, Graeme. 1985. *Prehistoric farming in Europe.* Cambridge: Cambridge University Press.

Barlow, Robert H. 1945. Dos relaciones antiguas del pueblo de Cuilapa, Estado de Oaxaca. *Tlalocan* 2:18 – 28.

1949. The extent of the empire of the Culhua Mexica. *Ibero-Americana* 28.

Barth, Fredrik, ed. 1978. *Scale and social organization.* Oslo: Universitetsforlaget.

Bates, Daniel, and Susan H. Lees. 1977. The role of exchange in productive specialization. *American Anthropologies* 79(4):824 – 41.

Batres, Leopoldo. 1902. *Exploraciones de Monte Albán.* Mexico, D.F.: Casa Editorial Gante.

Becker, Marshall Joseph. 1973. Archaeological evidence for occupational specialization among the Classic Period Maya at Tikal, Guatemala. *American Antiquity* 38:396 – 406.

Beckmann, Martin. 1958. City hierarchies and the distribution of city size. *Economic Development and Culture Change* 6:243 – 8.

Beltrán Frías, Luis. 1987. Subsistencia y aprovechamiento del mundo. In *Cobá, Quintana Roo: análisis de dos unidades habitacionales Mayas*, ed. Linda Manzanilla, pp. 213 – 40. Instituto de Investigaciones Antropológicas, Universidad Nacional Autónoma de México. Serie Antropológica 82.

Benavides Castillo, Antonio. 1987. Arquitectura doméstica en Cobá. In *Cobá, Quintana Roo: análisis de dos unidades habitacionales Mayas*, ed. Linda Manzanilla, pp. 25 – 67. Instituto de Investigaciones Antropológicas, Universidad Nacional Autónoma de México. Serie Antropológica 82.

Benson, Elizabeth P., ed. 1968. *Dumbarton Oaks Conference on the Olmec.* Washington, D.C.: Dumbarton Oaks.

Benz, Bruce F., and Hugh H. Iltis. 1990. Studies in archaeological maize I: The "wild" maize from San Marcos Cave reexamined. *American Antiquity* 55(3):500 – 11.

Berdan, Frances F. 1982. *The Aztecs of central Mexico: an imperial society.* New York: Holt, Rinehart, and Winston.

1985. Markets in the economy of ancient Mexico. In *Markets and marketing*, ed. Stuart Plattner, pp. 339 – 67. Lanham, Md.: University Press of America.

Berdan, Frances F., and Patricia R. Anawalt. 1992. *The Codex Mendoza*, 4 vols. Berkeley: University of California Press.

Berdan, Frances F., Richard E. Blanton, Elizabeth H. Boone, Mary G. Hodge, Michael E. Smith, and Emily Umberger. In press. *Aztec imperial strategies.* Washington, D.C.: Dumbarton Oaks.

Berlin, Heinrich. 1953. *Archaeological reconnaissance in Tabasco.* Carnegie Institution of Washington. Current Reports 1(7).

1958. El glifo "emblema" en las inscripciones Mayas. *Journal de la Société des Américanistes* 47:111 – 19.

Bernal, Ignacio. 1952. La Arqueología Mexicana de 1880 a la fecha. *Cuadernos Americanos* 65:121 – 45.

1965. Archaeological synthesis of Oaxaca. In *Handbook of Middle American Indians*, vol. 3, ed. G. R. Willey, pp. 788 – 813. Austin: University of Texas Press.

1969. *The Olmec world*, trans. Doris Heyden and Fernando Horcasitas. Berkeley: University of California Press.

1977. Maya antiquaries. In *Social process in Maya prehistory: studies in honour of Sir Eric Thompson*, ed. Norman Hammond, pp. 19 – 43. London: Academic Press.

Bernal, Ignacio, ed. 1963. *Teotihuacan: descubrimientos, reconstrucciones.* Mexico, D.F.: Instituto Nacional de Antropología e Historia.

Bernal, Ignacio, and Lorenzo Gamio. 1974. *Yagul: el Palacio de los Seis Patios.* Mexico, D.F.: Instituto de Investigaciones Antropológicas, Universidad Nacional Autónoma de Mexico.

Berry, Brian J. L. 1961. City-size distributions and economic development. *Economic Development and Culture Change* 9:573 – 87.

1967. *Geography of market centers and retail distribution.* Englewood Cliffs, N.J.: Prentice-Hall.

Binford, Lewis R. 1965. Archaeological systematics and the study of culture process. *American Antiquity* 31:203 – 10.

Binford, Lewis R., ed. 1977. *For theory building in archaeology.* New York: Academic Press.

Birmingham, Judy. 1975. Traditional potters of the Kathmandu Valley: an ethnoarchaeological study. *Man* 10:370 – 86.

Bittman, Bente, and Thelma Sullivan. 1978. The pochteca. In *Mesoamerican communication routes and cultural contacts,* ed. Thomas A. Lee, Jr., and Carlos Navarete, pp. 211 – 18. New World Archaeological Foundation, Papers 40.

Blake, Michael, Brian S. Chisholm, John E. Clark, Barbara Voorhies, and Michael W. Love. 1992. Prehistoric subsistence in the Soconusco region. *Current Anthropology* 33(1):83 – 94.

Blanton, Richard E. 1972a. *Prehispanic settlement patterns of the Ixtapalapa Peninsula region, Mexico.* Department of Anthropology. Pennsylvania State University, Occasional Papers 6.

1972b. Prehispanic adaptation in the Ixtapalapa region, Mexico. *Science* 175:1317 – 26.

1975. The cybernetic analysis of human population growth. *Memoirs of the Society for American Archaeology* 30:116 – 26.

1976a. Anthropological studies of cities. *Annual Review of Anthropology* 5:249 – 64.

1976b. The role of symbiosis in adaptation and sociocultural change in the Valley of Mexico. In *The Valley of Mexico,* ed. Eric R. Wolf, pp. 181 – 202. Albuquerque: University of New Mexico Press.

1976c. The origins of Monte Albán. In *Cultural change and continuity,* ed. C. Cleland, pp. 223 – 32. New York: Academic Press.

1978. *Monte Albán: settlement patterns at the ancient Zapotec capital.* New York: Academic Press.

1980. Cultural ecology reconsidered. *American Antiquity* 45:145 – 51.

1982. Urban beginnings: a view from anthropological archaeology. *Journal of Urban History* 8:427 – 46.

1983a. The ecological approach in highland Mesoamerican archaeology. In *Archaeological hammers and theories,* ed. J. A. Moore and A. S. Keene, pp. 221 – 33. New York: Academic Press.

1983b. The Aztec garrison of "Acatepec." In *The cloud people: divergent evolution of the Zapotec and Mixtec civilizations,* ed. K. V. Flannery and J. Marcus, pp. 318 – 22. New York: Academic Press.

1983c. Factors underlying the origin and evolution of market systems. In *Economic anthropology: topics and theories,* ed. Sutti Ortiz, pp. 51 – 66. Lanham, Md.: University Press of America.

1983d. Advances in the study of cultural evolution in prehispanic highland Mesoamerica. In *Advances in world archaeology,* vol. 2, ed. F. Wendorf and A. Close, pp. 245 – 88. New York: Academic Press.

1985. A comparison of early market systems. In *Markets and marketing,* ed. Stuart Plattner, pp. 399 – 416. Lanham, Md.: University Press of America.

1989. Continuity and change in public architecture: periods I through V of the Valley of Oaxaca, Mexico. In S. A. Kowalewski et al., *Monte Albán's hinterland,* part II: *Prehispanic settlement patterns in Tlacolula, Etla, and Ocotlán, the Valley of Oaxaca, Mexico.* Museum of Anthropology, University of Michigan, Memoirs 23:409 – 47.

1990. Theory and practice in Mesoamerican archaeology: a comparison of two modes of scientific inquiry. In *Debating Oaxaca archaeology,* ed. J. Marcus. Museum of Anthropology, University of Michigan, Anthropological Papers 84:1 – 16.

In press a. The Basin of Mexico market system and the growth of empire. In *Aztec imperial strategies*, ed. Frances Berdan, Richard Blanton, Elizabeth Boone, Mary Hodge, Michael Smith, and Emily Umberger. Washington, D.C.: Dumbarton Oaks.

In press b. A consideration of causality in the growth of empire: a comparative perspective. In *Aztec imperial strategies*, ed. Frances Berdan et al. Washington, D.C.: Dumbarton Oaks.

In press c. *Households and the built environment: a cross-cultural study of dwellings in social and cultural contexts*. New York: Plenum Press.

Blanton, Richard E., Jill Appel, Laura Finsten, Stephen A. Kowalewski, Gary M. Feinman, and Eva Fisch. 1979. Regional evolution in the Valley of Oaxaca, Mexico. *Journal of Field Archaeology* 6:369 – 90.

Blanton, Richard E., and Gary M. Feinman. 1984. The Mesoamerican world-system. *American Anthropologist* 86:673 – 92.

Blanton, Richard E., and Stephen A. Kowalewski. 1981. Monte Albán and after in the Valley of Oaxaca. In *Supplement to the handbook of Middle American Indians*, vol. 1, ed. Jeremy Sabloff, pp. 94 – 115. Austin: University of Texas Press.

Blanton, Richard E., Stephen A. Kowalewski, and Gary M. Feinman. 1992. The Mesoamerican world-system. *Review* XV: 419–26.

Blanton, Richard E., Stephen A. Kowalewski, Gary M. Feinman, and Jill Appel. 1982. *Monte Albán's hinterland*, part I: *Prehispanic settlement patterns of the central and southern parts of the Valley of Oaxaca, Mexico*. Museum of Anthropology, University of Michigan, Memoirs 15.

Blanton, Richard E., and Jeffrey R. Parsons. 1971. Ceramic markers used for period designations. In J. R. Parsons, *Prehistoric settlement patterns in the Texcoco region, Mexico*, pp. 255 – 314. Museum of Anthropology, University of Michigan, Memoirs 3.

Blau, Peter M. 1968. The hierarchy of authority in organizations. *The American Journal of Sociology* 73:453 – 67.

1970. A formal theory of differentiation in organizations. *American Sociological Review* 35:2:201 – 18.

Bloom, Paul R., Mary Pohl, and Julie Stein. 1985. Analysis of sedimentation and agriculture along the Río Hondo, northern Belize. In *Prehistoric lowland Maya environment and subsistence economy*, ed. Mary Pohl, pp. 21 – 33. Papers of the Peabody Museum of Archaeology and Ethnology. Harvard University, vol. 77. Cambridge.

Blucher, Darlena. 1971. Late preclassic cultures in the Valley of Mexico: pre-urban Teotihuacan. Ph.D. dissertation, Brandeis University.

Bohannan, Laura, and Paul Bohannan. 1953. *The Tiv of Central Nigeria*. London: International Institute.

Boone, Elizabeth H., ed. 1987. *The Aztec Templo Mayor*. Washington, D.C.: Dumbarton Oaks.

Borah, Woodrow, and Sherburne F. Cook. 1960. The population of central Mexico in 1548. *Ibero-Americana* 48.

1963. The aboriginal population of Central Mexico on the eve of the Spanish conquest. *Ibero-Americana* 54.

Boserup, Esther. 1965. *The conditions of agricultural growth: the economics of agrarian change under population pressure*. Chicago: Aldine.

Boulding, Kenneth. 1956. Toward a general theory of growth. *General Systems* 1:66 – 75.

Brainerd, George W. 1958. *The archaeological ceramics of the Yucatan*. University of California, Anthropological Records 19.

Bray, Warwick. 1972. The city state in Central Mexico at the time of the Spanish conquest. *Journal of Latin American Studies* 4:161 – 85.

Brockington, Donald L. 1973. *Archaeological investigations at Miahuatlán, Oaxaca*. Nashville: Vanderbilt University Publications in Archaeology, 1.

1983. The view from the Coast: relationships between the Coast and the Valley of Oaxaca. *Notas Mesoamericanas* 9:25 – 31.

Broda, Johanna, Davíd Carrasco, and Eduardo Matos Moctezuma. 1987. *The Great Temple of Tenochtitlan: center and periphery in the ancient world.* Berkeley: University of California Press.

Brown, Kenneth L. 1980. A brief report on PaleoIndian-Archaic occupation in the Quiche Basin, Guatemala. *American Antiquity* 45(2):313 – 24.

Brumfiel, Elizabeth M. 1976a. Regional growth in the eastern Valley of Mexico: a test of the "population pressure" hypothesis. In *The early Mesoamerican village*, ed. Kent V. Flannery, pp. 234 – 50. New York: Academic Press.

1976b. Specialization and exchange at the Late Postclassic (Aztec) community of Huexotla, Mexico. Ph.D. dissertation, University of Michigan.

1977. Archaeological research 2: Tehuacán. *Latin American Research Review* 12(1):203 – 11.

1980. Specialization, market exchange, and the Aztec state: a view from Huexotla. *Current Anthropology* 21:459 – 78.

1983. Aztec state making: ecology, structure, and the origin of the state. *American Anthropologist* 85:261 – 84.

1986. The division of labor at Xico: The chipped stone industry. In *Research in economic anthropology*, supplement 2, ed. Barry Isaac, pp. 245 – 79. Greenwich, Conn.: JAI Press.

1987. Elite and utilitarian crafts in the Aztec state. In *Specialization, exchange, and complex societies*, eds. Elizabeth Brumfiel and Timothy Earle, pp. 102 – 18. Cambridge: Cambridge University Press.

1991. Agricultural development and class stratification in the southern valley of Mexico. In *Land and politics in the Valley of Mexico: a two-thousand year perspective*, ed. H. R. Harvey, pp. 43 – 62. Albuquerque: University of New Mexico Press.

Brundage, Burr Cartwright. 1972. *A rain of darts: the Mexica Aztecs.* Austin: University of Texas Press.

Brush, Charles F. 1965. Pox pottery: earliest identified Mexican ceramic. *Science* 149:194 – 5.

Bryan, Alan L., ed. 1986. *New evidence for the Pleistocene peopling of the Americas.* Orono: Center for the Study of Early Man.

Bullard, William R., Jr. 1960. Maya settlement pattern in northeastern Petén, Guatemala. *American Antiquity* 25:355 – 72.

Burgoa, Fray Francisco de. 1934. *Geográfica descripción*, 2 vols. Mexico: Archivo General de la Nación.

Byers, Douglas S., ed. 1967. *The prehistory of the Tehuacán Valley*, vol. 1: *Environment and subsistence.* Austin: University of Texas Press.

Cabrera Castro, Rubén, Ignacio Rodríguez Garcia, and Noel Morelos Garcia, eds., 1982. *Teotihuacan 80 – 82: primeros resultados.* Mexico City: Instituto Nacional de Antropología e Historia.

Cabrera Castro, Rubén, Saburo Sugiyama, and George L. Cowgill. 1991. The Temple de Quetzalcoatl project at Teotihuacan. *Ancient Mesoamerica* 2:77 – 92.

Caldwell, Joseph R. 1964. Interaction spheres in prehistory. In *Hopewellian studies*, ed. Joseph R. Caldwell and Robert L. Hall, pp. 133 – 43. *Illinois State Museum, Scientific Papers* 12(6).

Callen, Jay S. 1976. *Settlement patterns in pre-war Siwai: an application of central-place theory to a horticultural society.* Solomon Island Studies in Human Biogeography 5.

Calnek, Edward. 1972. Settlement pattern and *chinampa* agriculture at Tenochtitlan. *American Antiquity* 37:104 – 15.

1976. The internal structure of Tenochtitlan. In *The Valley of Mexico*, ed. Eric R. Wolf, pp. 287 – 302. Albuquerque: University of New Mexico Press.

Carneiro, Robert. 1970. A theory of the origin of the state. *Science* 169:733 – 8.

Carr, Robert F., and James E. Hazard. 1961. *Map of the ruins of Tikal, El Petén, Guatemala.* The University Museum, University of Pennsylvania, Museum Monographs, Tikal Report 11.

Carrasco, Pedro. 1971. Social organization of ancient Mexico. In *Handbook of Middle America Indians*, vol. 10, ed. G. F. Eckholm and Ignacio Bernal, pp. 349 – 75. Austin: University of Texas Press.

1978. La economía del México prehispánico. In *Economía política e ideología en el México prehispánico*, eds. Pedro Carrasco and Johanna Broda, pp. 15 – 76. Mexico: Editorial Nueva Imagen.

1981. Comment on Offner. *American Antiquity* 46:62 – 8.

Caso, Alfonso. 1928a. Relación de la vicaria y partido de Sta. Cruz que en Mexicano se dice Iztepec y en Zapoteco Quialoo. *Revista Mexicana de Estudios Historicos*, 2, suplemento, 180 – 4.

1928b. Descripción de Tehuantepec. *Revista Mexicana de Estudios Historicos*, 2, suplemento, 164 – 75.

1928c. *Las estelas Zapotecas*. Mexico, D.F.: Secretaría de Educación Pública.

1965. Lapidary work, goldwork, and copperwork from Oaxaca. In *Handbook of Middle American Indians*, vol. 3, part 2, ed. R. Wauchope, pp. 896 – 930. Austin: University of Texas Press.

1969. *El tesoro de Monte Albán*. Mexico: Memorías del Instituto Nacional de Antropología e Historia 3.

Caso, Alfonso, and Ignacio Bernal. 1952. *Urnas de Oaxaca*. Mexico: Memorías del Instituto Nacional de Antropología e Historia 2.

Caso, Alfonso, Ignacio Bernal, and Jorge R. Acosta. 1967. *La cerámica de Monte Albán*. Mexico: Memorías del Instituto Nacional de Antropología e Historia 13.

Caso, Alfonso, and D. F. Rubin de la Borbolla. 1936. *Exploraciones en Mitla, 1934 – 35*. Mexico: Instituto Panamericano de Geografía e Historia, pub. 21.

Chadwick, Robert. 1971a. Postclassic pottery of the central valleys. In *Handbook of Middle American Indians*, vol. 10, part 1, ed. Gordon Ekholm and Ignacio Bernal, pp. 228 – 57. Austin: University of Texas Press.

1971b. Native pre-Aztec history of Central Mexico. In *Handbook of Middle American Indians*, vol. 11, ed. R.Wauchope, G. F. Eckholm, and I. Bernal, pp. 474 – 505. Austin: University of Texas Press.

Champion, T. C., ed. 1989. *Centre and periphery: comparative studies in archaeology*. London: Unwin Hyman.

Chapman, Anne C. 1957. Port of trade enclaves in Aztec and Maya civilization. In *Trade and market in the early empires*, ed. Karl Polanyi, Conrad M. Arensberg, and Harry W. Pearson, pp. 114 – 53. Glencoe, Ill.: Free Press.

Charlton, Thomas H. 1978. Teotihuacan, Tepeapulco and obsidian exploitation. *Science* 200:1227 – 36.

1984. Production and exchange: variables in the evolution of a civilization. In *Trade and exchange in early Mesoamerica*, ed. Kenneth Hirth, pp. 17 – 42. Albuquerque: University of New Mexico Press.

Chase-Dunn, Christopher, and Thomas D. Hall, eds. 1991. *Core/periphery relations in precapitalist worlds*. Boulder, Colo.: Westview Press.

Christaller, Walter. 1966. *Central places in southern Germany*, trans. C. W. Baskin. Englewood Cliffs, N.J.: Prentice-Hall (orig. pub. 1933).

Claessen, Henri J. M., and Peter Skalník, eds. 1978. *The early state*. The Hague: Mouton.

Claessen, Henri J. M., and Pieter van de Velde, eds. 1987. *Early state dynamics*. Leiden: E. J. Brill.

Clark, John E. 1986. From mountains to molehills: A critical review of Teotihuacan's obsidian industry. In *Research in economic anthropology* supplement 2, ed. Barry Isaac, pp. 23 – 74. Greenwich, Conn.: JAI Press.

Coe, Michael D. 1961. *La Victoria, an early site on the Pacific Coast of Guatemala*. Peabody Museum of Archaeology and Ethnology, Papers 53. Cambridge: Harvard University.

1962. *Mexico.* New York: Praeger.

1966. *The Maya.* New York: Praeger.

1968. *America's first civilization: discovering the Olmec.* New York: American Heritage.

1987. *The Maya.* 4th ed. New York: Thames and Hudson.

Coe, Michael D., and Richard A. Diehl. 1980. *In the land of the Olmec,* 2 vols. Austin: University of Texas Press.

Cohen, Mark N. 1975. Population pressure and the origins of agriculture. In *Population ecology and social evolution,* ed. Steven Polgar, pp. 79 – 121. The Hague: Mouton.

1977. *The food crisis in prehistory.* New Haven: Yale University Press.

1989. *Health and the rise of civilization.* New Haven: Yale University Press.

Cohen, Percy. 1967. Economic analysis and economic man: some comments on a controversy. In *Themes in economic anthropology,* ed. R. Firth, pp. 91 – 118. London: Tavistock Publications.

Cohen, Ronald, and Elman R. Service, eds. 1978. *The origins of the state: the anthropology of political evolution.* Philadelphia: ISHI.

Colinvaux, Paul. 1973. *Introduction to ecology.* New York: Wiley.

Colson, E. 1978. A redundancy of actors. In *Scale and social organization,* ed. Fredrik Barth, pp. 150 – 62. Oslo: Universitetsforlaget.

Connell, Joseph H. 1978. Diversity in tropical rain forests and coral reefs. *Science* 199:1302 – 10.

Cook, Scott, and Martin Diskin. 1976. The peasant market economy of the Valley of Oaxaca in analysis and history. In *Markets in Oaxaca,* ed. Scott Cook and Martin Diskin, pp. 5 – 26. Austin: University of Texas Press.

Cook, Sherburne F., and Woodrow Borah. 1960. The Indian population of Central Mexico, 1531 – 1610. *Ibero-Americana* 44.

Cook, Sherburne F., and Leslie Byrd Simpson. 1948. The population of central Mexico in the 16th century. *Ibero-Americana* 31.

Coontz, Sydney H. 1957. *Population theories and the economic interpretation.* London: Routledge.

Cortés, Hernando. 1963. *Cartas y documentos.* Mexico: Editorial Porrua, S.A.

Covarrubias, Miguel. 1957. *Indian art of Mexico and Central America.* New York: Knopf.

Cowgill, George L. 1974. Quantitative studies of urbanization at Teotihuacan. In *Mesoamerican archaeology: new approaches,* ed. Norman Hammond, pp. 363 – 96. Austin: University of Texas Press.

1975. On causes and consequences of ancient and modern population changes. *American Anthropologist* 77:505 – 25.

1983. Rulership and the Ciudadela: political inferences from Teotihuacan architecture. In *Civilization in the ancient Americas,* ed. R. Leventhal and A. Kolata, pp. 313 – 43. Albuquerque: University of New Mexico Press.

1984. Spatial analysis of Teotihuacan: a Mesoamerican metropolis. In *Intrasite spatial analysis in archaeology,* ed. H. Hietala, pp. 154 – 95. Cambridge: Cambridge University Press.

Cowgill, Ursula M., G. Goulen, E. Hutchinson, R. Patrick, A. Pacec, and M. Tsukuda. 1966. *The history of Laguna de Petenxil.* Memoirs of the Connecticut Academy of Arts and Sciences 17.

Culbert, T. Patrick. 1973. The Maya downfall at Tikal. In *The Classic Maya collapse,* ed. T. Patrick Culbert, pp. 63 – 92. Albuquerque: University of New Mexico Press.

1974. *The lost civilization: the story of the Classic Maya.* New York: Harper & Row.

1977a. Early Maya development at Tikal, Guatemala. In *The origins of Maya civilization,* ed. R. E. W. Adams, pp. 27 – 43. Albuquerque: University of New Mexico Press.

1977b. Maya development and collapse: an economic perspective. In *Social process in Maya prehistory: studies in honour of Sir Eric Thompson,* ed. Norman Hammond, pp. 509 – 30. London: Academic Press.

1988a. Political history and the decipherment of Maya glyphs. *Antiquity* 62:135 – 52.

1988b. The collapse of Classic Maya civilization. In *The collapse of ancient states and civilizations,* ed. Norman Yoffee and George Cowgill, pp. 69 – 101. Tucson: University of Arizona Press.

Culbert T. Patrick, ed. 1973. *The Classic Maya collapse.* Albuquerque: University of New Mexico Press.

Culbert, T. Patrick, and Don S. Rice, eds. 1990. *Precolumbian population history in the Maya lowlands.* Albuquerque: University of New Mexico Press.

Cummings, Byron. 1933. *Cuicuilco and the Archaic culture of Mexico.* University of Arizona, Science Bulletin 4(8).

Curran, Margaret. 1978. An examination of the relationship between population density and agricultural productivity in the prehispanic Valley of Oaxaca, Mexico. Paper presented at the 43rd annual meeting of the Society for American Archaeology, Tucson, Ariz.

Dahlgren, Barbro. 1954. *La Mixteca, su cultura e historia prehispánicas.* Mexico, D.F.: Imprenta Universitaria.

Davies, Nigel B. 1968. *Los Señorios independientes del imperio Azteca.* Mexico: Instituto Nacional de Antropología e Historia.

1973. *The Aztecs.* London: Macmillan.

1977. *The Toltecs: until the fall of Tula.* Norman: University of Oklahoma Press.

1980. *The Toltec heritage.* Norman: University of Oklahoma Press.

1987. *The Aztec empire: the Toltec resurgence.* Norman: University of Oklahoma Press.

De Cicco, Gabriel, and Donald Brockington. 1956. *Reconocimiento arqueológico en el suroeste de Oaxaca.* Instituto Nacional de Antropología e Historia, Dirección de Monumentos Prehispánicos, Informe 6.

Deevey, E. S., Don S. Rice, Prudence M. Rice, H. H. Vaughn, Mark Brenner, and M. S. Flannery. 1979. Mayan urbanism: impact on a tropical karst environment. *Science* 206:298 – 306.

Diaz del Castillo, Bernal. 1908 – 16. *The true history of the conquest of New Spain,* 5 vols., trans. A. P. Maudslay. New York: Hakluyt Society.

Dibble, Charles. 1951. *Códice Xolotl.* Publicaciones del Instituto de la Historia, primera serie, 22, Mexico.

Diehl, Richard A. 1981. Tula. In *Supplement to the handbook of Middle American Indians,* ed. Jeremy A. Sabloff, pp. 277 – 95. Austin: University of Texas Press.

1983. *Tula, the Toltec capital of ancient Mexico.* London: Thames and Hudson.

1989. A shadow of its former self: Teotihuacan during the Coyotlatelco Period. In *Mesoamerica after the decline of Teotihuacan: A.D. 700 – 900,* eds R. Diehl and J. C. Berlo, pp. 9 – 18. Washington, D.C.: Dumbarton Oaks.

Diehl, Richard A., ed. 1974. Studies of ancient Tollan. Department of Anthropology, University of Missouri. *Monographs in Anthropology* 1.

Diehl, Richard A., and Robert Benfer. 1975. Tollan the Toltec capital. *Archaeology* 28:112 – 24.

Diehl, Richard A., and Janet C. Berlo, eds. 1989. *Mesoamerica after the decline of Teotihuacan: A.D. 700 – 900.* Washington, D.C.: Dumbarton Oaks.

Dincauze, Dena F. 1984. An archaeological evaluation of the case for pre-Clovis occupations. In *Advances in world archaeology,* vol. 3, ed. F. Wendorf and A. Close, pp. 275 – 323. New York: Academic Press.

Downing, Theodore. 1974. Irrigation and moisture-sensitive periods: a Zapotec case. In *Irrigation's impact on society,* ed. T. Downing and M. Gibson. *University of Arizona Anthropological Papers* 25:113 – 22.

Dreiss, Meredith L., and David O. Brown. 1989. Obsidian exchange patterns in Belize. In *Research in economic anthropology,* supplement 4: *Prehistoric Maya economies of Belize,* ed. Patricia A. McAnany and Barry Isaac, pp. 57 – 90. Greenwich, Conn.: JAI Press.

Drennan, Robert D. 1976a. *Fábrica San José and Middle Formative society in the Valley of Oaxaca.* Museum of Anthropology, University of Michigan, Memoirs 8.

1976b. Religion and social evolution in Formative Mesoamerica. In *The early Meso-american village,* ed. Kent V. Flannery, pp. 345 – 68. New York: Academic Press.

1983a. Ritual and ceremonial development at the hunter-gatherer level. In *The cloud people: divergent evolution of the Zapotec and Mixtec civilizations,* ed. Kent V. Flannery and Joyce Marcus, pp. 30 – 2. New York: Academic Press.

1983b. Appendix: radiocarbon dates for the Oaxaca region. In *The cloud people: divergent evolution of the Zapotec and Mixtec civilizations,* ed. K. V. Flannery and J. Marcus, pp. 363 – 70. New York: Academic Press.

1984. Long-distance transport costs in pre-hispanic Mesoamerica. *American Anthropologist* 86:105 – 12.

1988. Household location and compact versus dispersed settlement in prehispanic Meso-america. In *Household and community in the Mesoamerican past: case studies in the Maya area and Oaxaca,* ed. Richard Wilk and Wendy Ashmore, pp. 273 – 93. Albuquerque: University of New Mexico Press.

1989. The mountains north of the valley. In S. A. Kowalewski et al., *Monte Albán's hinter-land,* part II: *Prehispanic settlement patterns in Tlacolula, Etla, and Ocotlán, the Valley of Oaxaca, Mexico.* Museum of Anthropology, University of Michigan, Memoirs 23:367 – 84.

Drennan, Robert D., Philip T. Fitzgibbons, and Heinz Dehn. 1990. Imports and exports in Classic Mesoamerican political economy: the Tehuacán Valley and the Teotihuacan obsidian industry. In *Research in economic anthropology,* vol. 12, ed. Barry Isaac, pp. 177 – 99. Greenwich, Conn.: JAI Press.

Drennan, Robert D., and Carlos A. Uribe, eds. 1987. *Chiefdoms in the Americas.* Lanham, Md.: University Press of America.

Drucker, Phillip. 1943a. *Ceramic sequences at Tres Zapotes, Veracruz, Mexico.* Bureau of American Ethnology Bulletin 140. Washington, D.C.: Smithsonian Institution.

1943b. *Ceramic stratigraphy at Cerro De Las Mesas, Veracruz, Mexico.* Bureau of American Ethnology Bulletin 141. Washington, D.C.: Smithsonian Institution.

Dumond, Don. 1972. Demographic aspects of the Classic Period in Puebla-Tlaxcala. *Southwestern Journal of Anthropology* 28:101 – 30.

Dumond, Don, and Florencia Muller. 1972. Classic to Postclassic in highland Central Mexico. *Science* 175:1208 – 15.

Durán, Fray Diego. 1967. *Historia de las Indias de Nueva España e Islas de la Tierra Firme,* 2 vols., ed. Angel Garibay K. Mexico: Editorial Porrua.

Durant, Will. 1944. *Caesar and Christ.* New York: Simon & Schuster.

Earle, Timothy. 1976. A nearest-neighbor analysis of two Formative settlement systems. In *The early Mesoamerican village,* ed. K. Flannery, pp. 196 – 222. New York: Academic Press.

1977. A reappraisal of redistribution: complex Hawaiian chiefdoms. In *Exchange systems in prehistory,* ed. T. Earle and J. Ericson, pp. 213 – 29. New York: Academic Press.

1978. *Economic and social organization of a complex chiefdom: the Halelea District, Kaua'i, Hawaii.* Museum of Anthropology, University of Michigan, Anthropological Papers 63.

1989. The evolution of chiefdoms. *Current Anthropology* 30(1):84 – 8.

Earle, Timothy, ed. 1991. *Chiefdoms, power, and economy.* Cambridge: Cambridge University Press.

Easterlin, Richard A. 1978. The economies and sociology of fertility: a synthesis. In *Historical studies of changing fertility,* ed. Charles Tilly, pp. 57 – 134. Princeton: Princeton University Press.

Eaton, Jack. 1975. Ancient agricultural farmsteads in the Río Bec region of Yucatan. *Contributions of the University of California Archaeological Research Facility* 27:56 – 82.

Ekholm, Gordon F. 1944. *Excavations at Tampico and Panuco in the Huasteca.* American Museum of Natural History, Anthropological Papers 38 (part 5).

Ekholm, Kasja, and Jonathan Friedman. 1982. 'Capital' imperialism and exploitation in the ancient world-systems. *Review* 6:87 – 110.

Elam, J. Michael. 1989. Defensible and fortified sites. In S. A. Kowalewski et al., *Monte Albán's hinterland*, part II: *Prehispanic settlement patterns in Tlacolula, Etla, and Ocotlán, the Valley of Oaxaca, Mexico*. Museum of Anthropology, University of Michigan, Memoirs 23:385 – 407.

Emerson, Thomas E., and R. Barry Lewis, eds. 1991. *Cahokia and the hinterlands: middle Mississippian cultures of the Midwest*. Urbana: University of Illinois Press.

Evans, Susan. 1980. Spatial analysis of Basin of Mexico settlement: problems with the use of the central place model. *American Antiquity* 45:866 – 75.

—— 1991. Architecture and authority in an Aztec village: Farm and function of the Tecpan. In *Land and politics in the Valley of Mexico: a two-thousand year perspective*, ed. H. R. Harvey, pp. 63 – 92. Albuquerque: University of New Mexico Press.

Evans-Pritchard, E. E. 1940. *The Nuer: a description of the modes of livelihood and political institutions of a Nilotic people*. New York: Oxford University Press.

Farnsworth, Paul, James E. Brady, Michael J. DeNiro, Richard S. MacNeish. 1985. A reevaluation of the isotopic and archaeological reconstructions of diet in Tehuacan Valley. *American Antiquity* 50(1):102 – 16.

Farnworth, Edward G., and Frank B. Golley, eds. 1973. *Fragile ecosystems: evaluation of research and application in the neotropics*. New York: Springer-Verlag.

Feinman, Gary M. 1980. The relationship between administrative organization and ceramic production in the Valley of Oaxaca, Mexico. Ph.D. dissertation, City University of New York.

—— 1982. Patterns in ceramic production and distribution, periods Early I through V. In Blanton et al., *Monte Albán's hinterland, part 1: Prehispanic settlement patterns of the central and southern parts of the Valley of Oaxaca, Mexico*. Museum of Anthropology, University of Michigan, Memoirs 15:181 – 206.

—— 1985. Investigations in a near-periphery: regional settlement pattern survey in the Ejutla Valley. *Mexicon* 7:60 – 8.

—— 1986. The emergence of specialized ceramic production in formative Oaxaca. In *Economic aspects of prehispanic highland Mexico*, ed. B. L. Isaac, pp. 347 – 73. Research in Economic Anthropology, Supplement 2. Greenwich, Conn.: JAI Press.

—— 1991. Demography, surplus, and inequality: early political formations in highland Mesoamerica. In *Chiefdoms and their evolutionary significance*, ed. T. K. Earle, pp. 229 – 62. Cambridge: Cambridge University Press.

Feinman, Gary M., Sherman Banker, Reid F. Cooper, Glen B. Cook, and Linda M. Nicholas. 1989. A technological perspective on changes in the ancient Oaxacan grayware ceramic tradition: preliminary results. *Journal of Field Archaeology* 16:331 – 44.

Feinman, Gary M., Richard E. Blanton, and Stephen A. Kowalewski. 1984. Market system development in the prehispanic Valley of Oaxaca, Mexico. In *Trade and exchange in early Mesoamerica*, ed. Kenneth Hirth, pp. 157 – 78. Albuquerque: University of New Mexico Press.

Feinman, Gary M., Stephen A. Kowalewski, and Richard E. Blanton. 1984. Modelling ceramic production and organizational change in the prehispanic Valley of Oaxaca, Mexico. In *The many dimensions of pottery: ceramics in archaeology and anthropology*, ed. S. E. van der Leeuw and A. C. Pritchard, pp. 297 – 337. Amsterdam: University of Amsterdam.

Feinman, Gary M., Stephen A. Kowalewski, Laura Finsten, Richard E. Blanton, and Linda Nicholas. 1985. Long-term demographic change: a perspective from the Valley of Oaxaca. *Journal of Field Archaeology* 12:333 – 62.

Feinman, Gary M., and Jill Neitzel. 1984. Too many types: an overview of sedentary prestate societies in the Americas. In *Advances in archaeological method and theory*, vol. 7, ed. Michael B. Schiffer, pp. 39 – 102. Orlando: Academic Press.

Feinman, Gary M., and Linda M. Nicholas. 1987. Labor, surplus, and production: a regional analysis of formative Oaxacan socio-economic change. In *Coasts, plains and deserts: essays in honor of Reynold J. Ruppé,* ed. S. Gaines. Arizona State University, Anthropological Research Papers 38:27 – 50.

1988. The prehispanic settlement history of the Ejutla Valley, Mexico: a preliminary perspective. *Mexicon* 10:5 – 13.

1990a. Settlement and land use in ancient Oaxaca. In *Debating Oaxaca archaeology,* ed. J. Marcus. Museum of Anthropology, University of Michigan, Anthropological Papers 84:71 – 113.

1990b. At the margins of the Monte Albán state: settlement patterns in the Ejutla Valley, Oaxaca, Mexico. *Latin American Antiquity* 1:216 – 46.

Feinman, Gary M., Steadman Upham, and Kent G. Lightfoot. 1981. The production step measure: an ordinal index of labor input in ceramic manufacture. *American Antiquity* 46:871 – 84.

Fesler, James W. 1968. Centralization and decentralization. *International Encyclopedia of the Social Sciences* 2:370 – 9.

Finsten, Laura. 1983. The classic–postclassic transition in the Valley of Oaxaca, Mexico: a regional analysis of the process of political decentralization in a prehistoric complex society. Ph.D. dissertation, Purdue University.

Finsten, Laura, Kent V. Flannery, and Barbara Macnider. 1989. Preceramic sites and cave occupations. In S. A. Kowalewski et al., *Monte Albán's hinterland,* part II: *Prehispanic settlement patterns in Tlacolula, Etla, and Ocotlán, the Valley of Oaxaca, Mexico.* Museum of Anthropology, University of Michigan, Memoirs 23:39 – 53.

Finsten, Laura, and Stephen A. Kowalewski. 1991. The Peñoles Project: results. Paper presented at the 90th annual meeting of the American Anthropological Association. Chicago, Nov. 24, 1991.

Fisch, Eva. 1978. The Early Formative in the Valley of Oaxaca, Mexico: a regional analysis. Paper presented at the 43rd annual meeting of the Society for American Archaeology, Tucson, Ariz.

1982. The early and middle formative periods. In R. E. Blanton et al., *Monte Albán's hinterland,* part I: *Prehispanic settlement patterns of the central and southern parts of the Valley of Oaxaca, Mexico.* Museum of Anthropology, University of Michigan, Memoirs 15:27 – 36.

Fish, Suzanne K., and Stephen A. Kowalewski. 1990. *The archaeology of regions: a case for full coverage survey.* Washington, D.C.: Smithsonian Institution Press.

Flannery, Kent V. 1967a. Culture history vs. cultural process: a debate in American archaeology. *Scientific American* 217:119 – 22.

1967b. The vertebrate fauna and hunting patterns. In *The prehistory of the Tehuacán Valley,* vol. 1: *Environment and subsistence,* ed. Douglas S.Byers, pp. 132 – 77. Austin: University of Texas Press.

1968a. Archaeological systems theory and early Mesoamerica. In *Anthropological archaeology in the Americas,* ed. Betty J. Meggars, pp. 67 – 87. Washington: Anthropological Society of Washington.

1968b. The Olmec and the Valley of Oaxaca: a model for inter-regional interaction in formative times. In *Dumbarton Oaks Conference on the Olmec,* ed. Elizabeth P. Benson, pp. 79 – 110. Washington, D.C.: Dumbarton Oaks.

1972. The cultural evolution of civilizations. *Annual Review of Ecology and Systematics* 3:399 – 426.

1973. The origins of agriculture. *Annual Review of Anthropology* 2:271 – 310.

1976a. The early Mesoamerican house. In *The early Mesoamerican village,* ed. Kent Flannery, pp. 16 – 24. New York: Academic Press.

1976b. Empirical determination of site catchments in Oaxaca and Tehuacán. In *The early Mesoamerican village,* ed. Kent V. Flannery, pp. 103 – 17. New York: Academic Press.

1976c. Two possible village subdivisions: the courtyard group and the residential ward. In *The early Mesoamerican village,* ed. Kent V. Flannery, pp. 72 – 5. New York: Academic Press.

1977. Review of *The Valley of Mexico*, ed. Eric R. Wolf. *Science* 196:759 – 61.

1983a. Pleistocene fauna of Early Ajuereado type from Cueva Blanca, Oaxaca. In *The cloud people: divergent evolution of the Zapotec and Mixtec civilizations*, ed. Kent V. Flannery and Joyce Marcus, pp. 18 – 20. New York: Academic Press.

1983b. Tentative chronological phases for the Oaxaca Preceramic. In *The cloud people: divergent evolution of the Zapotec and Mixtec civilizations*, ed. Kent V. Flannery and Joyce Marcus, pp. 26 – 29. New York: Academic Press.

1983c. Settlement, subsistence, and social organization of the proto-Otomangueans. In *The cloud people: divergent evolution of the Zapotec and Mixtec civilizations*, eds. Kent V. Flannery and Joyce Marcus, pp. 32 – 6. New York: Academic Press.

1983d. Precolumbian farming in the Valleys of Oaxaca, Nochixtlán, Tehuacán, and Cuicatlán: a comparative study. In *The cloud people: divergent evolution of the Zapotec and Mixtec civilizations*, ed. K. V. Flannery and J. Marcus, pp. 323 – 39. New York: Academic Press.

Flannery, Kent V., ed. 1976. *The early Mesoamerican village*. New York: Academic Press.

1982. *Maya subsistence: studies in memory of Dennis E. Puleston*. New York: Academic Press.

1986. *Guilá Naquitz: archaic foraging and early agriculture in Oaxaca, Mexico*. New York: Academic Press.

Flannery, Kent V., Michael J. Kirkby, Anne V. T. Kirkby, and Aubrey W. Williams, Jr. 1967. Farming systems and political growth in ancient Oaxaca. *Science* 158:445 – 54.

Flannery, Kent V., and Joyce Marcus. 1976. Evolution of the public building in Formative Oaxaca. In *Cultural change and continuity: essays in honor of James B. Griffin*, ed. Charles Cleland, pp. 205 – 21. New York: Academic Press.

1990. Borrón y cuenta nueva: setting Oaxaca's archaeological record straight. In *Debating Oaxaca archaeology*, ed. J. Marcus. Museum of Anthropology, University of Michigan, Anthropological Papers 84:17 – 69.

Flannery, Kent V., and Joyce Marcus, eds. 1983. *The cloud people: divergent evolution of the Zapotec and Mixtec civilizations*. New York: Academic Press.

Flannery, Kent V., Joyce Marcus, and Stephen Kowalewski. 1981. The Pre-ceramic and Formative of the Valley of Oaxaca. In *Supplement to the handbook of Middle American Indians*, ed. Jeremy A. Sabloff, pp. 48 – 93. Austin: University of Texas Press.

Flannery, Kent V., and James Schoenwetter. 1970. Climate and man in Formative Oaxaca. *Archaeology* 23:144 – 52.

Flannery, Kent V., and Ronald Spores. 1983. Excavated sites of the Oaxaca preceramic. In *The cloud people: divergent evolution of the Zapotec and Mixtec civilizations*, ed. K. V. Flannery and J. Marcus, p. 20 – 6. New York: Academic Press.

Flannery, Kent V., and Marcus C. Winter. 1976. Analyzing household activities. In *The early Mesoamerican village*, ed. Kent V. Flannery, pp. 34 – 47. New York: Academic Press.

Flannery, Kent V., Marcus C. Winter, Susan Lees, James A. Neely, James Schoenwetter, Suzanne Kitchen, and Jane C. Wheeler. 1970. Preliminary archaeological investigations in the Valley of Oaxaca, Mexico, 1966 – 1969. Mimeographed report submitted to the Instituto Nacional de Antropología e Historia and the National Science Foundation.

Folan, William J., Laraine A. Fletcher, and Ellen R. Kintz. 1979. Fruit, fiber, bark and resin: social organization of a Maya urban center. *Science* 204:697 – 701.

Folan, William J., Ellen R. Kintz, and Laraine A. Fletcher. 1983. *Cobá: a classic Maya metropolis*. New York: Academic Press.

Fontana, Bernard, William Robinson, Charles Cormack, and Ernest Leavitt, Jr. 1962. *Papago Indian pottery*. Seattle: University of Washington Press.

Ford, Anabel. 1979. A reevaluation of Late Classic Maya settlement in light of new data from the Tikal-Yaxhá intersite area. Paper presented at the 44th annual meeting of the Society for American Archaeology, Vancouver, B. C.

1986. *Population growth and social complexity: an examination of settlement and environment in the central Maya lowlands*. Arizona State University Anthropological Research Papers 35.

Ford, Richard I. 1972. Barter, gift or violence: an analysis of Tewa intertribal exchange. In *Social exchange and interaction,* ed. Edwin N. Wilmsen, pp. 21 – 45. Museum of Anthropology, University of Michigan, Anthropological Papers 46.

Foster, George M. 1965. The sociology of pottery: questions, hypotheses, arising from contemporary Mexican work. In *Ceramics and man,* ed. F. R. Matson, pp. 43 – 61. Chicago: Aldine.

Fox, John W. 1978. *Quiche conquest: centralism and regionalism in highland Guatemalan state development.* Albuquerque: University of New Mexico Press.

1987. *Maya Postclassic state formation: segmentary lineage migration in advancing frontiers.* Cambridge: Cambridge University Press.

Franke, Richard W. 1974. Miracle seeds and shattered dreams in Java. *Natural History* 83: 11 – 18, 84 – 8.

Freidel, David A. 1978. Maritime adaptation and the rise of Maya civilizations: the view from Cerros, Belize. In *Prehistoric coastal adaptations: the economy and ecology of maritime Middle America,* ed. Barbara L. Stark and Barbara Voorhies, pp. 239 – 65. New York: Academic Press.

1979. Culture areas and interaction spheres: contrasting approaches to lowland Maya evolution in light of evidence from Cerros, northern Belize. *American Antiquity* 44: 36 – 54.

Fried, Morton. 1967. *The evolution of political society.* New York: Random House.

Friedman, David. 1977. A theory of the size and shape of nations. *Journal of Political Economy* 85:59 – 77.

Friedman, J., and M. J. Rowlands, 1978. Notes toward an epigenetic model of the evolution of "civilization." In *The evolution of social systems,* ed. J. Friedman and M. J. Rowlands, pp. 201 – 78. Pittsburgh: University of Pittsburgh Press.

Fry, Robert E. 1979. The economics of pottery at Tikal, Guatemala: models of exchange for serving vessels. *American Antiquity* 44:494 – 512.

Gall, Patricia L., and Arthur Saxe. 1977. The ecological evolution of culture: the state as a predator in succession theory. In *Exchange systems in prehistory,* ed. T. Earle and J. Ericson, pp. 255 – 68. New York: Academic Press.

Gallegos, Roberto. 1962. Exploraciones en Zaachila, Oaxaca. *Bolitín del Instituto de Antropología e Historia* 8:6 – 8.

1963. Zaachila: the first season's work. *Archaeology* 16:226 – 33.

Gamio, Manuel. 1922. *La población del Valle de Teotihuacan,* 2 vols. Mexico: Secretaría de Educación Pública.

Garber, James F. 1989. *Archaeology at Cerros, Belize, Central America,* vol. II: *The Artifacts.* Dallas: Southern Methodist University Press.

García Cook, Angel. 1976. *El desarrollo cultural en el norte de Valle Poblano: inferéncias.* Departmento de Monumentos Prehispánicos, Serie Arqueología 1. Mexico, D. F.: Instituto Nacional de Antropología e Historia.

García Payón, José. 1950. Restos de una cultura prehispánica encontrados en la Región de Zempoala, Veracruz. *Uni-Ver* 2 (15). Jalapa: Universidad Veracruzana.

1971. Archaeology of Central Veracruz. In *Handbook of Middle American Indians.* vol. 2, ed. R. Wauchope, G. F. Ekholm, and I. Bernal, pp. 505 – 43. Austin: University of Texas Press.

García Payón, José, ed. 1965. *Descripción del Pueblo de Gueytlapan (Zacatlán. Jujupango, Matatlán y Chila Papantla) por el Alcalde Mayor Juan de Carrion, 30 de Mayo de 1581.* Jalapa: Universidad Veracruzana.

Gibson, Charles. 1964. *The Aztecs under Spanish rule: a history of the Indians of the Valley of Mexico, 1519 – 1810.* Stanford: Stanford University Press.

Gillespie, Susan D. 1989. *The Aztec kings: the construction of rulership in Mexica history.* Tucson: University of Arizona Press.

Gómez-Pompa, Arturo. 1979. *Agricultura intensiva precolombina*. Instituto Nacional de Investigaciones sobre Recursos Bióticos, Documento AE-79-003. Jalapa: Universidad Veracruzana.

Gómez-Pompa, Arturo, and Frank Golley. 1979. *Estudio de las estrategias del uso del suelo y sus recursos por las culturas Mesoamericanas y su applicación para satisfacer las demandas actuales.* Instituto Nacional de Investigaciones sobre Recursos Bióticos, Documento AE-79-004. Jalapa: Universidad Veracruzana.

Gómez-Pompa, Arturo, and Andrea Kaus. 1990. Traditional management of tropical forests in Mexico. In *Alternatives to deforestation: steps toward alternative use of the Amazon rainforest,* ed. Anthony Anderson, pp. 45 – 64. New York: Columbia University Press.

Gonzalez Aparicio, Luis. 1973. *Plano reconstructivo de la Región de Tenochtitlan*. Mexico: Instituto Nacional de Antropología e Historia.

Goody, Jack. 1978. Population and polity in the Voltaic region. In *The evolution of social systems,* ed. J. Friedman and M. J. Rowlands, pp. 535 – 46. Pittsburgh: University of Pittsburgh Press.

1990. *The oriental, the ancient, and the primitive: systems of marriage and the family in the preindustrial societies of Eurasia.* Cambridge: Cambridge University Press.

Graham, Elizabeth. 1987. Resource diversity in Belize and its implications for models of lowland trade. *American Antiquity* 52:753 – 67.

Graham, John A. 1972. *The hieroglyphic inscriptions and monumental art of Altar de Sacrificios.* Peabody Museum of Archaeology and Ethnology, Papers 64(2). Cambridge: Harvard University.

Granovetter, Mark. 1979. The idea of "advancement" in theories of social evolution and development. *American Journal of Sociology* 85(3):489 – 515.

Grove, David. 1976. Olmec origins and transpacific diffusion: reply to Meggers. *American Anthropologist* 78:634 – 7.

Gruhn, Ruth, and Alan L. Bryan. 1976. An archaeological survey of the Chichicastenango area of highland Guatemala. *Cerámica de la Cultura Maya* 9:75 – 119.

1977. Los Tapiales: a Paleo-Indian campsite in the Guatemalan highlands. *Proceedings of the American Philosophical Society* 121:235 – 73.

Haas, Jonathan. 1982. *The evolution of the prehistoric state*. New York: Columbia University Press.

Haggett, Peter, Andrew D. Cliff, and Allan Frey. 1977. *Locational models,* vol. 1, 2nd ed. New York: Halsted Press.

Hammond, Norman. 1974. The distribution of Late Classic Maya major ceremonial centers in the central area. In *Mesoamerican archaeology: new approaches,* ed. Norman Hammond, pp. 313 – 34. Austin: University of Texas Press.

1975. Maya settlement hierarchy in northern Belize. In *Studies in ancient Mesoamerica,* vol. 2, ed. John A. Graham, pp. 40 – 55. University of California, Archaeological Research Facility, Contributions 27.

1977a. Ex Oriente Lux: a view from Belize. In *The origins of Maya civilization,* ed. R. E. W. Adams, pp. 45 – 76. Albuquerque: University of New Mexico Press.

1977b. The Early Formative in the Maya lowlands. In *Social process in Maya prehistory: studies in honour of Sir Eric Thompson,* ed. Norman Hammond, pp. 77 – 101. London: Academic Press.

1985. *Nohmul: a prehistoric Maya community in Belize, excavations 1973 – 1983.* BAR International Series 250 (i, ii). Oxford.

Harner, Michael. 1977. The ecological basis for Aztec sacrifice. *American Ethnologist* 4:117 – 35.

Harris, Marvin. 1977. *Cannibals and kings: the origins of cultures*. New York: Random House.

1979. *Cultural materialism: the struggle for a science of culture.* New York: Random House.

Harrison, Peter. 1970. The central acropolis, Tikal, Guatemala: a preliminary study of the functions of its structural components during the Late Classic period. Ph.D. dissertation, University of Pennsylvania.

1977. The rise of the *bajos* and the fall of the Maya. In *Social process in Maya prehistory: studies in honour of Sir Eric Thompson,* ed. Norman Hammond, pp. 469 – 508. London: Academic Press.

Harrison, Peter, and B. L. Turner, II, eds. 1978. *Prehispanic Maya agriculture.* Albuquerque: University of New Mexico Press.

Hassig, Ross. 1985. *Trade, tribute, and transportation: the sixteenth-century political economy of the Valley of Mexico.* Norman: University of Oklahoma Press.

Haviland, William A. 1972. Family size, prehistoric population estimates, and the ancient Maya. *American Antiquity* 37:135 – 9.

Healan, Dan M. 1989. *Tula of the Toltecs: excavations and survey.* Iowa City: University of Iowa Press.

Healan, Dan M., Robert H. Cobean, and Richard A. Diehl. 1989. Synthesis and conclusions. In *Tula of the Toltecs,* ed. Dan Healan, pp. 239 – 52. Iowa City: University of Iowa Press.

Heizer, Robert H. 1968. New observations on La Venta. In *Dumbarton Oaks Conference on the Olmec,* ed. Elizabeth P. Benson, pp. 9 – 36. Washington, D.C.: Dumbarton Oaks.

Hellmuth, Nicholas. 1977. Cholti-Lacandon (Chiapas) and Petén-Ytzá agriculture, settlement pattern and population. In *Social process in Maya prehistory: studies in honour of Sir Eric Thompson,* ed. Norman Hammond, pp. 421 – 48. London: Academic Press.

Helms, Mary W. 1975. *Middle America: a culture history of heartland and frontiers.* Englewood Cliffs, N.J.: Prentice-Hall.

1979. *Ancient Panama: chiefs in search of power.* Austin: University of Texas Press.

1988. *Ulysses' sail.* Cambridge: Cambridge University Press.

Hicks, Frederic. 1987. First steps toward a market-integrated economy in Aztec Mexico. In *Early state dynamics,* ed. Henri Claessen and Pieter van de Velde, pp. 91 – 107. Leiden: E. J. Brill.

Hirth, Kenneth G. 1974. Pre-Columbian population development along the Río Amatzinac: the Formative through Classic periods in Eastern Morelos, Mexico. Ph.D. dissertation, University of Wisconsin.

1978. Teotihuacan regional population administration in Eastern Morelos. *World Archeology* 9:320 – 33.

1980. *The Teotihuacan Classic: a regional perspective from eastern Morelos.* Vanderbilt University, Publications in Anthropology 25.

1989. Militarism and social organization at Xochicalco, Morelos. In *Mesoamerica after the decline of Teotihuacan: A.D. 700 – 900,* ed. R. Diehl and J. Berlo, pp. 69 – 82. Washington, D.C.: Dumbarton Oaks.

Hirth, Kenneth G., and Jorge Angulo Villaseñor. 1981. Early state expansion in central Mexico: Teotihuacan in Morelos. *Journal of Field Archaeology* 8:135 – 50.

Hodder, B. W., and U. Ukwu. 1969. *Markets in West Africa.* Ibadan: Ibadan University.

Hodder, Ian. 1982. *Symbols in action: ethnoarchaeological studies of material culture.* Cambridge: Cambridge University Press.

Hodge, Mary G. 1984. *Aztec city-states.* University of Michigan, Museum of Anthropology, Memoirs 18.

1991. Land and lordship in the Valley of Mexico: the politics of Aztec provincial administration. In *Land and politics in the Valley of Mexico: a two-thousand year perspective,* ed. H. R. Harvey, pp. 113 – 39. Albuquerque: University of New Mexico Press.

In press. Political organization of the central provinces. In *Aztec imperial strategies,* ed. Frances F. Berdan, Richard E. Blanton, Elizabeth H. Boone, Mary G. Hodge, Michael E. Smith, and Emily Umberger. Washington, D.C.: Dumbarton Oaks.

Hodge, Mary G., and Leah D. Minc. 1990. The spatial patterning of Aztec ceramics: implications for prehispanic exchange systems in the Valley of Mexico. *Journal of Field Archaeology* 17:419 – 37.

Hodges, Denise. 1989. *Agricultural intensification and prehistoric health in the Valley of Oaxaca, Mexico.* Museum of Anthropology, University of Michigan, Memoirs 22.

Holland, John H. 1975. *Adaptation in natural and artificial systems.* Ann Arbor: University of Michigan Press.

Holling, C. S., and M. A. Goldberg. 1971. Ecology and planning. *Journal of the American Institute of Planners* 37:221 – 30.

Holms, William H. 1895 – 7. *Archaeological studies among the ancient cities of Mexico.* Field Museum, Anthropological Series 1(1). Chicago.

Hopkins, A. G. 1973. *An economic history of West Africa.* New York: Columbia University Press.

Hopkins, M. R. 1987. Network analysis of the plans of some Teotihuacan apartment compounds. *Environment and planning B: planning and design* 14:387 – 406.

Houston, Stephen D. 1988. The phonetic decipherment of Maya glyphs. *Antiquity* 62: 126 – 35.

Hudson, Charles. 1976. *The Southeastern Indians.* Knoxville: University of Tennessee Press.

Hunt, Eva, and R. Hunt. 1974. Irrigation, conflict and politics: a Mexican case. In *Irrigation's impact on society,* ed. T. Downing and M. Gibson. University of Arizona, Anthropological Papers 25:129 – 57.

Irwin, Geoffrey. 1978. Pots and entrepôts: a study of settlement, trade and the development of economic specialization in Papuan prehistory. *World Archaeology* 9:299 – 319.

Irwin-Williams, Cynthia. 1967. Associations of early man with horse, camel, and mastodon at Hueyatlaco, Valsequillo (Puebla, Mexico). In *Pleistocene extinctions: the search for a cause,* ed. Paul S. Martin and Henry E. Wright, Jr., pp. 337 – 47. New Haven: Yale University Press.

1978. Summary of archaeological evidence from the Valsequillo region, Puebla, Mexico. In *Cultural continuity in Mesoamerica,* ed. David L. Browman, pp. 7 – 22. The Hague: Mouton.

1981. Letter to the Editor: commentary on geologic evidence for age of deposits at Hueyatlaco archaeological site, Valsequillo, Mexico. *Quaternary Research* 16:258.

Ixtlilxochitl, Fernando de Alva. 1952. *Obras históricas,* 2 vols., ed. Alfredo Chavero. Mexico: Editorial Nacional.

Jiménez Moreno, Wigberto. 1941. Tula y los Toltecas segun las Fuentes históricas. *Revista Mexicana de Estudios Antropológicas* 5:79 – 85.

Johnson, Frederick, ed. 1972. *The prehistory of the Tehuacán Valley,* vol. 4: *Chronology and irrigation.* Austin: University of Texas Press.

Johnson, Frederick, and Richard S. MacNeish. 1972. Chronometric dating. In *The prehistory of the Tehuacán Valley,* vol. 4: *Chronology and irrigation,* ed. Frederick Johnson, pp. 3 – 58. Austin: University of Texas Press.

Johnson, Gregory A. 1973. *Local exchange and early state development in southwestern Iran.* Museum of Anthropology, University of Michigan, Anthropological Papers 51.

1977. Aspects of regional analysis in archaeology. *Annual Review of Anthropology* 6: 479 – 508.

1978. Information sources and the development of decision-making organizations. In *Social archaeology: beyond subsistence and dating,* ed. Charles Redman et al., pp. 87 – 112. New York: Academic Press.

1980. Rank-size convexity and system integration: a view from archaeology. *Economic Geography* 56:234 – 47.

1981. Monitoring complex system integration and boundary phenomena with settlement size data. In *Archaeological approaches to the study of complexity,* ed. S. E. van der Leeuw, pp. 143 – 88. Amsterdam: Albert Egges van Giffen Instituut voor Prae- en Protohistorie, University van Amsterdam.

1982. Organizational structure and scalar stress. In *Theory and explanation in archaeology: the Southampton conference,* ed. C. Renfrew, M. J. Rowlands, and B. A. Seagraves, pp. 389 – 421. New York: Academic Press.

1983. Decision-making organization and pastoral nomad camp size. *Human Ecology* 11:175 – 99.

1987. The changing organization of Uruk administration on the Susiana plain. In *The archaeology of Western Iran: settlement and society from prehistory to the Islamic conquest*, ed. Frank Hole, pp. 107 – 40. Washington, D.C.: Smithsonian Institution Press.

Jones, E. L., and S. J. Woolf. 1969. Introduction: the historical role of agrarian change in economic development. In *Agrarian change and economic development*, ed. E. L. Jones and S. J. Woolf, pp. 1 – 21. London: Methuen.

Jones, Grant D., and Robert R. Kautz, eds. 1981. *The transition to statehood in the new world*. Cambridge: Cambridge University Press.

Jorde, L. B. 1977. Precipitation cycles and cultural buffering in the prehistorical Southwest. In *For theory building in archaeology*, ed. Lewis Binford, pp. 385 – 95. New York: Academic Press.

Joyce, Arthur, and Marcus Winter. 1989. Investigaciones arqueológicas en la cuenca del Río Verde Inferior, 1988. *Notas Mesoamericanas* 11:249 – 62.

Kampen, Michael E. 1972. *The sculptures of El Tajín, Veracruz, Mexico*. Gainesville: University of Florida Press.

Kasarda, J. D. 1974. The structural implications of social system size: a three-level analysis. *American Sociological Review* 39(1):19 – 28.

Katz, Friedrich. 1966. *Situación social y económica de los Aztecas durante los Siglos XV y XVI*. Mexico: Instituto de Investigaciones Históricas, Universidad Nacional Autónoma de Mexico.

Kidder, Alfred V., Jesse D. Jennings, and Edwin M. Shook. 1946. *Excavations at Kaminaljuyú, Guatemala*. Carnegie Institution of Washington, Publication 561.

Kirchhoff, Paul. 1943. Mesoamérica, sus límites geográficos, composición étnica y carácteres culturales. *Acta Americana* 1:92 – 107.

Kirkby, Anne V. T. 1973. *The use of land and water resources in the past and present Valley of Oaxaca*. Museum of Anthropology, University of Michigan, Memoirs 5.

Kohl, Philip L. 1989. The use and abuse of world systems theory: the case of the "pristine" West Asian state. In *Archaeological thought in America*, ed. C. C. Lamberg-Karlovsky, pp. 218 – 40. Cambridge: Cambridge University Press.

Kosse, Krisztina. 1990. Group size and societal complexity: thresholds in the long-term memory. *Journal of Anthropological Archaeology* 9:275 – 303.

Kowalewski, Stephen A. 1976. Prehispanic settlement patterns of the central part of the Valley of Oaxaca, Mexico. Ph.D. dissertation, University of Arizona.

1980. Population-resource balances in Period I of Oaxaca, Mexico. *American Antiquity* 45:151 – 65.

1982a. The evolution of primate regional systems. *Comparative Urban Research* IX:60 – 78.

1982b. Population and agricultural potential: Early I – V. In R. E. Blanton et al., *Monte Albán's hinterland*, part I: *Prehispanic settlement patterns of the central and southern parts of the Valley of Oaxaca, Mexico*. Museum of Anthropology, University of Michigan, Memoirs 15:389 – 96.

1990a. The evolution of complexity in the Valley of Oaxaca. *Annual Review of Anthropology* 19:39 – 58.

1990b. Merits of full-coverage survey: examples from the Valley of Oaxaca, Mexico. In *The archaeology of regions*, ed. S. K. Fish and S. A. Kowalewski, pp. 33 – 85. Washington, D.C.: Smithsonian Institution Press.

Kowalewski, Stephen A., Richard E. Blanton, Gary M. Feinman, and Laura Finsten. 1983. Boundaries, scale, and internal organization. *Journal of Anthropological Archaeology* 2: 32 – 56.

Kowalewski, Stephen A., Gary M. Feinman, and Laura Finsten. 1992. "The elite" and assessment of social stratification in Mesoamerican archaeology. In *Mesoamerican elites: an archaeological assessment*, ed. D. Z. Chase and A. F. Chase, pp. 259 – 77. Norman: University of Oklahoma Press.

Kowalewski, Stephen A., Gary M. Feinman, Laura Finsten, and Richard E. Blanton. 1990. Panorama arqueológica del Valle de Oaxaca. In *Lecturas históricas del estado de Oaxaca,* volumen 1, ed. M. C. Winter, pp. 223 – 86. Mexico: Instituto Nacional de Antropología e Historia.

Kowalewski, Stephen A., Gary M. Feinman, Laura Finsten, Richard E. Blanton, and Linda M. Nicholas. 1989. *Monte Albán's hinterland,* part II: *Prehispanic settlement patterns in Tlacolula, Etla, and Ocotlán, the Valley of Oaxaca, Mexico.* Museum of Anthropology, University of Michigan, Memoirs 23.

Kowalski, Jeff Karl. 1987. *The House of the Governor: a Maya palace at Uxmal, Yucatan, Mexico.* Norman: University of Oklahoma Press.

Krebs, Charles J. 1972. *Ecology: the experimental analysis of distribution and abundance.* New York: Harper & Row.

Kroeber, A. L. 1939. *Cultural and natural areas of native North America.* University of California, Publications in American Archaeology and Ethnology 38.

Krotser, Paula H., and G. R. Krotser. 1973. The lifestyle of El Tajín. *American Antiquity* 38:199 – 205.

Kubler, George. 1961. Chichén Itzá y Tula. *Estudios de Cultura Maya.* 1:47 – 80.

Kurjack, Edward B. 1974. *Prehistorical lowland Maya community and social organization: a case study at Dzibilchaltún, Yucatan, Mexico.* Middle American Research Institute, Publication 38.

Kurjack, Edward B., and E. Wyllys Andrews, IV. 1976. Early boundary maintenance in northwest Yucatan, Mexico. *American Antiquity* 41:318 – 25.

Landa, Diego de. 1941. *Landa's Relación de las cosas de Yucatan,* ed. and trans. Alfred M. Tozzer. Peabody Museum of Archaeology and Ethnology, Papers 18. Cambridge: Harvard University.

Lanning, Edward P. 1967. *Peru before the Incas.* Englewood Cliffs, N.J.: Prentice-Hall.

Lattimore, Owen. 1962. *Studies in frontier history: collected papers, 1928 – 1958.* New York: Oxford University Press.

LeClair, Edward E., and H. Schneider, eds. 1968. *Economic anthropology.* New York: Holt, Rinehart and Winston.

Lee, Ronald D. 1977. Introduction. In *Population patterns in the past,* ed. R. Lee, pp. 1 – 16. New York: Academic Press.

Lees, Susan H. 1973. *Sociopolitical aspects of canal irrigation in the Valley of Oaxaca.* Museum of Anthropology, University of Michigan, Memoirs 6.

Levinson, David, and Martin J. Malone. 1980. *Toward explaining human culture: a critical review of the findings of worldwide cross-cultural research.* New Haven: HRAF Press.

Lewenstein, Suzanne M. 1987. *Stone tool use at Cerros: the ethnoarchaeological and use-wear evidence.* Austin: University of Texas Press.

Lightfoot, Kent, and Gary Feinman. 1982. Social differentiation and leadership development in early pithouse villages on the Mogollon region of the American Southwest. *American Antiquity* 47:64 – 86.

Limbrey, S. 1976. Tlapacoya: problems of interpretation of lake margin sediments at an early occupation site in the Basin of Mexico. In *Geoarchaeology: earth science and the past,* ed. D. A. Davidson and M. L. Shackley, pp. 213 – 26. Boulder, Colo.: Westview Press.

Linné, Sigvald. 1934. *Archaeological researches at Teotihuacan, Mexico.* Ethnographic Museum of Sweden, Publication 1.

Lopez, Robert. 1976. *The commercial revolution of the Middle Ages, 950 – 1350.* Cambridge: Cambridge University Press.

Lorenzo, José Luis, ed. 1968. *Materiales para la arqueología de Teotihuacan.* Instituto Nacional de Antropología e Historia, Serie Investigaciones 17.

 1978. Early man research in the American hemisphere: appraisal and perspectives. In *Early Man in America from a circum-Pacific perspective,* ed. Alan L. Bryan, pp. 1 – 9. Department of Anthropology, University of Alberta, Occasional Papers 1.

Lorenzo, José Luis, and Lorena Mirambell, eds. 1986. *Tlapacoya: 35,000 Años de Historia del Lago de Chalco.* Serie Prehistoria. Mexico: Instituto Nacional de Antropología e Historia.

Lothrop, Samuel K. 1924. *Tulum: an archaeological study of the East Coast of Yucatan.* Carnegie Institution of Washington. Publication 335.

Lowe, Gareth W. 1959. *The Chiapas project, 1955 – 58.* New World Archaeological Foundation Papers 1.

Lundell, Cyrus Longworth. 1937. *The vegetation of Petén.* Carnegie Institution of Washington. Publication 478.

Lynch, Thomas F. 1990. Glacial-age man in South America? a critical review. *American Antiquity* 55(1):12 – 36.

McAnany, Patricia A. 1989a. Economic foundations of prehistoric Maya society: paradigms and concepts. In *Research in economic anthropology,* supplement 4: *Prehistoric Maya economies of Belize,* ed. Patricia A. McAnany and Barry Isaac, pp. 347 – 72. Greenwich, Conn.: JAI Press.

1989b. Stone tool production and exchange in the eastern Maya lowlands: the consumer perspective from Pulltrouser Swamp, Belize. *American Antiquity* 54:332 – 46.

McGuire, Randall. 1983. Breaking down cultural complexity. Inequality and heterogeneity. In *Advances in archaeological method and theory* 6, ed. Michael Schiffer, pp. 91 – 142. New York: Academic Press.

MacNeish, Richard S. 1958. Preliminary archaeological investigations in the Sierra de Tamaulipas, Mexico. *Transaction of the American Philosophical Society* n.s. 48, part 6.

1962. *The Santa Marta rockshelter, Ocozocuautla, Chiapas, Mexico.* Papers of the New World Archaeological Foundation, Number 14.

1964. Ancient Mesoamerican civilization. *Science* 143:531 – 37.

1967. A summary of the subsistence. In *The prehistory of the Tehuacán Valley,* vol. 1: *Environment and subsistence,* ed. Douglas S. Byers, pp. 290 – 310. Austin: University of Texas Press.

1972. Summary of the cultural sequence and its implications in the Tehuacán Valley. In *The prehistory of the Tehuacán Valley.* Vol. 5: *Excavations and reconnaissance.* ed. Richard S. MacNeish, pp. 496 – 504. Austin: University of Texas Press.

1983. Mesoamerica. In *Early man in the New World,* ed. Richard Shutler, Jr., pp. 125 – 35. Beverly Hills: Sage Publications.

1986. The Preceramic of Middle America. In *Advances in world archaeology,* vol. 5, ed. Fred Wendorf and Angela E. Close, pp. 93 – 129. New York: Academic Press.

MacNeish, Richard S., Melvin L. Fowler, Angel García Cook, Frederick A. Peterson, Antoinette Nelken-Terner, and James A. Neely. 1972. *The prehistory of the Tehuacán Valley,* vol. 5: *Excavations and reconnaissance.* Austin: University of Texas Press.

MacNeish, Richard S., and Antoinette Nelken-Turner. 1983. The Preceramic of Meso-america. *Journal of Field Archaeology* 10:71 – 84.

MacNeish, Richard S., Antoinette Nelken-Turner, and Irmgard W. Johnson. 1967. *The prehistory of the Tehuacán Valley,* vol. 2.: *Nonceramic artifacts.* Austin: University of Texas Press.

MacNeish, Richard S., Frederick A. Peterson, and Kent V. Flannery. 1970. *The prehistory of the Tehuacán Valley,* vol. 3: *Ceramics.* Austin: University of Texas Press.

McQuown, Norman A. 1956. The classification of the Maya languages. *International Journal of American Linguistics* 22:191 – 5.

Mair, Lucy. 1977. *African kingdoms.* New York: Oxford University Press.

Malde, H. E. and V. Steen-McIntyre. 1981. Letter to the editor: reply to comments by C. Irwin-Williams: archaeological sites, Valesquillo, Mexico. *Quarternary Research* 16: 418 – 21.

Mangelsdorf, Paul C., Richard S. MacNeish, and Walton C. Galinat. 1967. Prehistoric wild and cultivated maize. In *The prehistory of the Tehuacán Valley,* vol. 1: *Environment and subsistence,* ed. Douglas S. Byers, pp. 178 – 200. Austin: University of Texas Press.

Manzanilla, Linda, ed. 1987. *Cobá, Quintana Roo: análisis de dos unidades habitacionales Mayas*. Instituto de Investigaciones Antropológicas, Universidad Nacional Autónoma de Mexico, Serie Antropológica 82.

Marcus, Joyce. 1973. Territorial organization of the lowland Classic Maya. *Science* 180: 911 – 16.

1976a. The size of the early Mesoamerican village. In *The early Mesoamerican village*, ed. Kent V. Flannery, pp. 79 – 90. New York: Academic Press.

1976b. The iconography of militarism at Monte Albán and neighboring sites in the Valley of Oaxaca. In *Origins of religious art and iconography in Pre-Classic Mesoamerica*, ed. H. B. Nicholson, pp. 123 – 39. Los Angeles: Latin American Center, UCLA.

1976c. The origins of Mesoamerican writing. *Annual Review of Anthropology* 5:35 – 67.

1976d. *Emblem and state in the Classic Maya lowlands: an epigraphic approach to territorial organization*. Washington, D.C.: Dumbarton Oaks.

1978. Archaeology and religion: a comparison of the Zapotec and Maya. *World Archaeology* 10:172 – 91.

1980. Zapotec writing. *Scientific American* 242:50 – 64.

1983a. The genetic model and the linguistic divergence of the Otomangueans. In *The cloud people: divergent evolution of the Zapotec and Mixtec civilizations*, ed. Kent V. Flannery and Joyce Marcus, pp. 4 – 9. New York: Academic Press.

1983b. The conquest slabs of Building J. Monte Albán. In *The cloud people: divergent evolution of the Zapotec and Mixtec civilizations*, ed. Kent V. Flannery and Joyce Marcus, pp. 106 – 8. New York: Academic Press.

1983c. On the nature of the Mesoamerican city. In *Prehistoric settlement patterns*, eds. Evon Vogt and Richard Leventhal, pp. 195 – 242. Albuquerque: University of New Mexico Press.

1989a. Zapotec chiefdoms and the nature of formative religions. In *Regional perspectives on the Olmec*, ed. R. J. Sharer and D. C. Grove, pp. 148 – 97. Cambridge: Cambridge University Press.

1989b. From centralized systems to city-states: possible models for the Epiclassic. In *Mesoamerica after the decline of Teotihuacan: A.D. 700 – 900*, ed. R. A. Diehl and J. C. Berlo, pp. 201 – 8. Washington, D.C.: Dumbarton Oaks.

Marcus, Joyce, ed. 1990. *Debating Oaxaca archaeology*. Museum of Anthropology, University of Michigan, Anthropological Papers 84.

Marcus, Joyce, Kent V. Flannery, and Ronald Spores. 1983. The cultural legacy of the Oaxacan Preceramic. In *The cloud people: divergent evolution of the Zapotec and Mixtec civilizations*, ed. Kent V. Flannery and Joyce Marcus, pp. 36 – 9. New York: Academic Press.

Markman, Charles W. 1981. *Prehistoric settlement dynamics in Central Oaxaca, Mexico: a view from the Miahuatlán Valley*. Vanderbilt University, Publications in Anthropology 26.

Marquina, Ignacio. 1964. *Arquitectura prehispánica*, 2nd ed. Mexico: Instituto Nacional de Antropología e Historia, Memorias 1.

Mastache, Alba Guadalupe, and Robert H. Cobean. 1989. The Coyotlatelco culture and the origins of the Toltec state. In *Mesoamerica after the decline of Teotihuacan: A.D. 700 – 900*, ed. R. Diehl and J. Berlo, pp. 49 – 68. Washington, D.C.: Dumbarton Oaks.

Mastache, Alba Guadalupe, and Ana Crespo. 1974. La ocupación prehispánica en el area de Tula, Hgo. In *Proyecto Tula*, part 1, ed. E. Matos Moctezuma, Colección Cientifica (Arqueología) 15, pp. 71 – 103. Mexico: Instituto Nacional de Antropología e Historia, Departmento de Monumentos Prehispánicos.

Mathews, Peter, and Linda Schele. 1974. Lords of Palenque: the glyphic evidence. In *Primera Mesa Redonda de Palenque*, part 1, ed. Merle Greene Robertson, pp. 63 – 76. Pebble Beach, Calif.: Robert Louis Stevenson School.

Mathien, Frances J., and Randall H. McGuire, eds. 1986. *Ripples in the Chichimec Sea: new considerations of Southwestern-Mesoamerican interactions*. Carbondale: Southern Illinois University Press.

Mato Moctezuma, Eduardo. 1976. *Proyecto Tula,* part 2. Instituto Nacional de Antropología e Historia, Colección Cientifica 33.

    1980. Teotihuacan: Excavaciones en la calle de los muertos (1964). *Anales de Antropología* 17:69 – 90.

    1988. *The great temple of the Aztecs.* New York: Thames and Hudson.

Matos Moctezuma, Eduardo, ed. 1974. *Proyecto Tula,* part 1. Instituto Nacional de Antropología e Historia, Colección Cientifica 15.

Maudslay, Alfred P. 1889 – 1902. *Archaeology, biologia Centrali Americana,* 4 vols. London: R. H., Porter and Dulau and Co.

Medellin-Zenil, A. 1960. *Cerámicas del Totonacapan.* Jalapa: Universidad Veracruzana.

Meggers, Betty J. 1975. The transpacific origin of Mesoamerican civilization: a preliminary view of the evidence and its theoretical implications. *American Anthropologist* 77:1 – 27.

Meggitt, M. J. 1973. The pattern of leadership among the Mae-Enga of New Guinea. In *Politics in New Guinea,* ed. R. M. Brandt and P. Lawrence, pp. 191 – 206. Seattle: University of Washington Press.

Meier, R. 1962. *A communications theory of urban growth.* Cambridge: MIT Press.

Melgar, José. 1871. Estudio sobre la antiqüedad y el origen de la cabeza colosal de tipo Etiópico. *Boletín de la Sociedad Mexicana de Geografía y Estadistica,* 2a época, 3:104 – 18.

Meltzer, David J. 1989. Why don't we know when the first people came to North America? *American Antiquity* 54(3):471 – 90.

Michaels, George H., and Barbara Voorhies. In Press. Late Archaic Period coastal collectors in Southern Mesoamerica: the Chantuto people revisited, Part 3: Developments of hunting-fishing-gathering maritime societies on the Pacific. In *Proceedings of the Circum-Pacific Prehistory Conference.* Seattle, August 2 – 6, 1989.

Michels, Joseph, and William T. Sanders. 1973. *The Pennsylvania State University Kaminaljuyú Project–1969/1970 season,* part 1: *Mound excavations.* Department of Anthropology, Pennsylvania State University, Occasional Papers in Anthropology 9.

Miksicek, Charles H. 1983. Macrofloral remains of the Pulltrouser area: settlements and fields. In *Pulltrouser Swamp: ancient Maya habitat, agriculture, and settlement in northern Belize,* ed. B. L. Turner, II, and Peter D. Harrison, pp. 94 – 104. Austin: University of Texas Press.

Miles, Douglas. 1979. The finger knife and Ockham's razor: a problem in Asian culture history and economic anthropology. *American Ethnologist* 6:223 – 43.

Milisauskas, Sarunas. 1978. *European prehistory.* New York: Academic Press.

Miller, J. G. 1965. Living systems: basic concepts. *Behavioral Science* 10:193 – 257.

Millon, Clara. 1972. The history of mural art at Teotihuacan. In *Mesa Redonda: Teotihuacan XI,* 2:1 – 16. Mexico: Sociedad Mexicana de Antropología.

    1973. Painting, writing, and polity in Teotihuacan, Mexico. *American Antiquity* 38(3): 294 – 314.

Millon, René. 1970. Teotihuacan: completion of map of giant ancient city in the Valley of Mexico. *Science* 170:1077 – 82.

    1973. *Urbanization at Teotihuacan, Mexico,* vol. 1: *The Teotihuacan map,* part 1: *Text.* Austin: University of Texas Press.

    1976a. Social relations in ancient Teotihuacan. In *The Valley of Mexico,* ed. Eric R. Wolf, pp. 205 – 48. Albuquerque: University of New Mexico Press.

    1976b. Chronological and developmental terminology: why they must be divorced. In *The Valley of Mexico,* ed. Eric R. Wolf, pp. 23 – 8. Albuquerque: University of New Mexico Press.

    1981. Teotihuacan: city, state, and civilization. In *Supplement to the handbook of Middle American Indians,* ed. Jeremy Sabloff, pp. 198 – 243. Austin: University of Texas Press.

    1988. The last years of Teotihuacan dominance. In *The collapse of ancient states and civilizations,* ed. N. Yoffee and G. Cowgill, pp. 102 – 64. Tucson: The University of Arizona Press.

Millon, René, Bruce Drewitt, and James Bennyhoff. 1965. The Pyramid of the Sun at Teotihuacan: 1959 investigations. *Transactions of the American Philosophical Society* 55(6):3 – 93.

Millon, René, Bruce Drewitt, and George Cowgill. 1973. *Urbanization at Teotihuacan. Mexico*, vol. 1: *The Teotihuacan map*, part 2: *Maps*. Austin: University of Texas Press.

Mirambell, Lorena. 1978. Tlapacoya. In *Early man in America from a circum-Pacific perspective*, ed. Alan L. Bryan, pp. 221 – 30. Department of Anthropology, University of Alberta, Occasional Papers 1.

Monzon, Arturo. 1949. *El Calpulli en la organización social de los Tenochca*. Mexico: Instituto de Historia, Universidad Nacional Autónoma de México.

Morley, Sylvanus Griswold. 1937 – 8. *The inscriptions of Petén*. 5 vols. Carnegie Institution of Washington, Publication 437.

1946. *The ancient Maya*. Stanford: Stanford University Press.

Morley, Sylvanus G., George W. Brainerd, and Robert J. Sharer. 1983. *The ancient Maya*, 4th ed. Stanford: Stanford University Press.

Morris, Earl H., Jean Charlot, and Ann Axtell Morris. 1931. *The Temple of the Warriors at Chichén Itzá, Yucatan*, 2 vols. Carnegie Institution of Washington, Publication 406.

Motolinía, Toribio de Benavente. 1950. *History of the Indians of New Spain*, ed. and trans. Elizabeth Foster. In *Documents and narratives concerning the discovery and conquest of Latin America*, vol. 4. Berkeley: The Cortés Society.

Mountjoy, J. B. 1974. San Blas complex ecology. In *The archaeology of West Mexico*, ed. B. Bell, pp. 106 – 119. Ajijic: Sociedad de Estudios Avanzados del Occidente de México.

Nag, Moni, Benjamin N. F. White, and R. Creighton Peet. 1978. An anthropological approach to the study of the economic value of children in Java and Nepal. *Current Anthropology* 19:293 – 301.

Neely, James. 1967. Organización hidráulica y systemas de irrigación prehistóricas en el Valle de Oaxaca. *Instituto Nacional de Antropología e Historia, Boletín* 27:15 – 17.

Nef, John U. 1977. An early energy crisis and its consequences. *Scientific American* 237: 140 – 51.

Nelson, Fred W., and Barbara Voorhies. 1980. Trace element analysis of obsidian artifacts from three shell midden sites in the littoral zone, Chiapas, Mexico. *American Antiquity* 45:540 – 50.

Nerlove, Marc. 1974. Household and economy: toward a new theory of population and economic growth. *Journal of Political Economy* 82(2):200 – 18.

Nicholas, Linda M. 1989. Land use in prehispanic Oaxaca. In S. A. Kowalewski et al., *Monte Albán's hinterland*, part II: *Prehispanic settlement patterns in Tlacolula, Etla, and Ocotlán, the Valley of Oaxaca, Mexico*. Museum of Anthropology, University of Michigan, Memoirs 23:449 – 505.

Nicholas, Linda M., Gary M. Feinman, Stephen A. Kowalewski, Richard E. Blanton, and Laura Finsten. 1986. Prehispanic colonization of the Valley of Oaxaca, Mexico. *Human Ecology* 14:131 – 62.

Niederberger, Christine. 1979. Early sedentary economy in the basin of Mexico. *Science* 203:131 – 42.

Noguera, Eduardo. 1945. Excavaciones en el Estado de Puebla. *Anales* 1. Mexico, D.F.: Instituto Nacional de Antropología e Historia.

Offner, Jerome A. 1981a. On the inapplicability of "oriental despotism" and the "asiatic mode of production" to the Aztecs of Texcoco. *American Antiquity* 46: 43 – 61.

1981b. On Carrasco's use of theoretical "first principles." *American Antiquity* 46:69 – 74.

1983. *Law and politics in Aztec Texcoco*. Cambridge: Cambridge University Press.

Olsson, Gunnar. 1965. *Distance and human interaction: a review and bibliography*. Bibliography Series 2. Philadelphia: Regional Science Research Institute.

Orozco y Berra, Manuel, ed. 1979. *Códice Ramírez: relación del origen de los Indios que habitan esta Nueva España según sus historias*. Mexico: Editorial Innovación.

Ortiz de Montellano, Bernard. 1978. Aztec Cannibalism: an ecological necessity? *Science* 200:611 – 17.

Paddock, John. 1966. Oaxaca in ancient Mesoamerica. In *Ancient Oaxaca,* ed. John Paddock, pp. 83 – 242. Stanford: Stanford University Press.

1974. Comment on "The prehistory of the southeastern Maya periphery," by Robert J. Sharer. *Current Anthropology* 15:181.

1983. *Lord 5 Flower's family: rulers of Zaachila and Cuilapan.* Vanderbilt University, Publications in Anthropology 29.

Pailes, Richard A., and Joseph W. Whitecotton. 1979. The greater Southwest and the Meso-american "world" system: an exploratory model of frontier relationships. In *The frontier: comparative studies,* vol. 2, ed. William W. Savage, Jr., and Stephen Thompson, pp. 105 – 21. Norman: University of Oklahoma Press.

Palerm, Angel. 1973. *Obras hidráulicas prehispánicas en el sistema lacustre del Valle de México.* Mexico, D.F.: Instituto Nacional de Antropología e Historia.

Palerm, Angel, and Eric R. Wolf. 1957. Ecological potential and cultural development in Mesoamerica. *Pan American Union Social Science Monograph* 3:1 – 37.

Parry, William J. 1987. *Chipped stone tools in formative Oaxaca, Mexico: their procurement, production and use.* Museum of Anthropology, University of Michigan, Memoirs 20.

Parsons, Jeffrey R. 1966. The Aztec ceramic sequence in the Teotihuacan Valley, Mexico. Ph.D. dissertation, University of Michigan.

1971. *Prehistoric settlement patterns of the Texcoco region, Mexico.* Museum of Anthropology, University of Michigan, Memoirs 3.

1972. Archaeological settlement patterns. *Annual Review of Anthropology* 1:127 – 50.

1974. The development of prehistoric complex society: a regional perspective from the Valley of Mexico. *Journal of Field Archaeology* 1:81 – 108.

1976. The role of chinampa agriculture in the food supply of Aztec Tenochtitlan. In *Cultural change and continuity: essays in honor of James Bennett Griffin,* ed. Charles Cleland, pp. 233 – 57. New York: Academic Press.

Parsons, Jeffrey R., Elizabeth Brumfiel, Mary H. Parsons, and David J. Wilson. 1982. *Prehispanic settlement patterns in the southern Valley of Mexico: the Chalco-Xochimilco Region.* Museum of Anthropology, University of Michigan, Memoirs 14.

Parsons, Lee A. 1969. *Bilbao, Guatemala: an archaeological study of the Pacific Coast, Cotzu-malhuapa region.* Milwaukee Public Museum, Publications in Anthropology 12, vol. 2.

Paso y Troncoso, Francisco del, ed. 1905. *Papeles de Nueva España.* Segunda serie, vols. 1 and 4. Madrid: Sucesores de Rivadeneyra.

Pasztory, Esther. 1988. A reinterpretation of Teotihuacan and its mural painting tradition. In *Feathered serpents and flowering trees: reconstructing the murals of Teotihuacan,* ed. Kathleen Berrin, pp.45 – 77. Seattle: University of Washington Press.

Paynter, Robert, and John W. Cole. 1980. Ethnographic overproduction, tribal political economy and the Kapauku of Irian Jaya. In *Beyond the myths of culture,* ed. E. B. Ross, pp. 61 – 99. New York: Academic Press.

Pendergast, David M. 1986. Stability through change: Lamanai, Belize, from the ninth to the seventeenth century. In *Late lowland Maya civilization: Classic to Postclassic,* ed. Jeremy A. Sabloff and E. Wyllys Andrews, V., pp. 223 – 50. Albuquerque: University of New Mexico Press.

Peregrine, Peter. 1991. Some political aspects of craft specialization. *World Archaeology* 23: 1 – 11.

Peterson, David A. 1976. Ancient commerce. Ph.D. dissertation, State University of New York at Binghamton.

Piña Chan, Román. 1958. *Tlatilco.* Instituto Nacional de Antropología e Historia, Serie Investigaciones 1.

Pirenne, Henri. 1952. *Medieval cities,* trans. Frank D. Halsey. Princeton: Princeton University Press.

1957. *Mohammed and Charlemagne*. Cleveland: World Publishing Co.

Pires-Ferreira, Jane W. 1975. *Exchange networks in Formative Mesoamerica, with special reference to the Valley of Oaxaca*. Museum of Anthropology, University of Michigan, Memoirs 7.

1976a. Obsidian exchange in Formative Mesoamerica. In *The early Mesoamerican village*, ed. Kent Flannery, pp. 292 – 305. New York: Academic Press.

1976b. Shell and iron-ore mirror exchange in Formative Mesoamerica, with comments on other commodities. In *The early Mesoamerican village*, ed. Kent V. Flannery, pp. 311 – 25. New York: Academic Press.

Plog, Stephen. 1976. Measurement of prehistoric interaction between communities. In *The early Mesoamerican village*, ed. Kent V. Flannery, pp. 255 – 72. New York: Academic Press.

Pohl, Mary, ed. 1985. *Prehistoric lowland Maya environment and subsistence economy*. Papers of the Peabody Museum of Archaeology and Ethnology, Harvard University, vol. 77, Cambridge.

1990. *Ancient Maya wetland agriculture: excavations on Albion Island, northern Belize*. Boulder: Westview Press.

Polanyi, Karl, Conrad Arensberg, and Harry Pearson, eds. 1957. *Trade and market in the early empires*. Glencoe, Ill.: Free Press.

Polgar, Steven. 1972. Population history and population policies from an anthropological perspective. *Current Anthropology* 13:203 – 11.

Pollock, H. E. D., Ralph L. Roys, T. Proskouriakoff, and A. Ledyard Smith. 1962. *Mayapán, Yucatan, Mexico*. Carnegie Institution of Washington, Publication 619.

Pospisil, Leopold. 1963. *Kapauku Papuan economy*. Yale University, Publications in Anthropology 67.

Potter, David F. 1976. Prehispanic architecture and sculpture in central Yucatan. *American Antiquity* 41:430 – 48.

Price, Barbara. 1976. A chronological framework for cultural development in Mesoamerica. In *The Valley of Mexico*, ed. Eric R. Wolf, pp. 13 – 22. Albuquerque: University of New Mexico Press.

1977. Shifts in production and organization: a cluster-interaction model. *Current Anthropology* 18:209 – 33.

Prigogine, Ilya. 1976. Order through fluctuation: self organization and social system. In *Evolution and consciousness*, ed. E. Jantsch and C. Waddington, pp. 93 – 133. Reading, Mass.: Addison-Wesley.

Pring, D. C. 1977. Influence or intrusion? the "Protoclassic" in the Maya lowlands. In *Social process in Maya prehistory: studies in honour of Sir Eric Thompson*, ed. Norman Hammond, pp. 135 – 65. London: Academic Press.

Proskouriakoff, Tatiana. 1961. The lords of the Maya realm. *Expedition* 4:14 – 21.

1962. *The artifacts of Mayapán. Mayapán, Yucatan, Mexico*. Carnegie Institution of Washington, Publication 619, part 4.

Puleston, Dennis E. 1971. An experimental approach to the function of Classic Maya chultuns. *American Antiquity* 36:322 – 35.

1973. Ancient Maya settlement patterns and environment at Tikal, Guatemala: implications for subsistence models. Ph.D. dissertation, University of Pennsylvania.

1977. The art and archaeology of agriculture in the Maya lowlands. In *Social process in Maya prehistory: studies in honour of Sir Eric Thompson*, ed. Norman Hammond, pp. 449 – 67. London: Academic Press.

Puleston, Dennis E., and Donald W. Callender, Jr. 1967. Defensive earthworks at Tikal. *Expedition*. 9:40 – 8.

Puleston, Dennis E., and Olga S. Puleston. 1971. An ecological approach to the origins of Maya civilization. *Archaeology* 24:330 – 7.

Pyburn, K. Anne. 1989a. *Prehistoric Maya community and settlement at Nohmul, Belize*. BAR International Series 509. Oxford.

1989b. Maya cuisine: hearths and the lowland economy. In *Research in economic anthropology*, supplement 4: *Prehistoric Maya economies of Belize*, ed. Patricia A. McAnany and Barry Isaac, pp. 325 – 44. Greenwich, Conn.: JAI Press.

1991. *Prehispanic Maya states: the evidence for absence*. Paper presented at the 11th annual meeting of the Society for Economic Anthropology, Bloomington, Ind.

Pyne, Nanette M. 1976. The fire-serpent and were-jaguar in Formative Oaxaca: a contingency table analysis. In *The early Mesoamerican village*, ed. Kent V. Flannery, pp. 272 – 82. New York: Academic Press.

Rands, Robert L. 1973. The Classic Maya collapse: Usumacinta zone and the northwestern periphery. In *The Classic Maya collapse*, ed. T. Patrick Culbert, pp. 165 – 205. Albuquerque: University of New Mexico Press.

Rappaport, Roy. 1978. Maladaptation in social systems. In *The evolution of social systems*, ed. J. Friedman and M. J. Rowlands, pp. 49 – 72. Pittsburgh: University of Pittsburgh Press.

Rathje, William L. 1975. Last tango in Mayapán: a tentative trajectory of production-distribution systems. In *Ancient civilization and trade*, ed. J. Sabloff and C. C. Lamberg-Karlovsky, pp. 409 – 48. Albuquerque: University of New Mexico Press.

1977. The Tikal connection. In *The origins of Maya civilization*, ed. R. E. W. Adams, pp. 373 – 82. Albuquerque: University of New Mexico Press.

Rathje, William L., David A. Gregory, and Frederick M. Wiseman. 1978. Trade models and archaeological problems: classic Maya examples. In *Mesoamerican communication routes and cultural contacts*, ed. Thomas A. Lee and Carlos Navarete, pp. 147 – 76. New World Archaeological Foundation, papers 40.

Rattray, Evelyn. 1966. An archaeological and stylistic study of Coyotlatelco pottery. *Mesoamerican Notes* 7 – 8:87 – 193.

1973. The Teotihuacan ceramic chronology: early Tzacualli to early Tlamimilolpa phases. Ph.D. dissertation, University of Missouri.

Redmond, Elsa M. 1983. *A fuego y sangre: early Zapotec imperialism in the Cuicatlán Cañada*. Museum of Anthropology, University of Michigan, Memoirs 16.

Renfrew, Colin R., and John F. Cherry, eds. 1986. *Peer polity interaction and socio-political change*. Cambridge: Cambridge University Press.

Rice, Don S. 1986. The Petén Postclassic: a settlement perspective. In *Late lowland Maya civilization: Classic to Postclassic*, ed. Jeremy A. Sabloff and E. Wyllys Andrews, V. pp. 301 – 44. Albuquerque: University of New Mexico Press.

Rice, Prudence M., and Don S. Rice. 1979. Home on the range: aboriginal Maya settlement in the central Petén savannas. *Archaeology* 32:16 – 25.

Ricketson, Oliver G., and Edith Bayles Ricketson. 1937. *Uaxactún, Guatemala: Group E – 1926 – 1931*. Carnegie Institution of Washington, Publication 477.

Robertson, Robin A., and David A. Freidel, eds. 1986. *Archaeology at Cerros, Belize, Central America*, vol. 1: *An interim report*. Dallas: Southern Methodist University Press.

Robson, J., R. Ford, K. Flannery, and J. Konlande. 1976. The nutritional significance of maize and teosinte. *Ecology of Food and Nutrition* 4:243 – 9.

Rotenberg, Robert. 1979. Intra-regional differences in public schedules: a social time approach to regional process. Paper presented at the 14th annual meeting of the Southern Anthropological Society, Memphis, Tenn.

Rowlands, Michael, Mogens Larsen, and Kristian Kristiansen, eds. 1987. *Centre and periphery in the ancient World*. Cambridge: Cambridge University Press.

Roys, Ralph L. 1957. *The political geography of the Yucatan Maya*. Carnegie Institution of Washington, Publication 613.

1972. *The Indian background of colonial Yucatan*. Norman: University of Oklahoma Press (orig. pub. 1943).

Rue, David J. 1989. Archaic Middle American agriculture and settlement: recent pollen data from Honduras. *Journal of Field Archaeology* 16:177 – 84.

Ruppert, Karl. 1952. *Chichén Itzá: architectural notes and plans.* Carnegie Institution of Washington, Publication 595.

Ruppert, Karl, and John H. Denison, Jr. 1943. *Archaeological reconnaissance in Campeche, Quintana Roo and Petén.* Carnegie Institution of Washington, Publication 543.

Ruppert, Karl, Eric S. Thompson, and Tatiana Proskouriakoff. 1955. *Bonampak, Chiapas, Mexico.* Carnegie Institution of Washington, Publication 602.

Ruz Lhuiller, Alberto. 1962. Chichén Itzá y Tula: comentarios a un ensayo. *Estudios de Cultura Maya* 2:205 – 23.

Sabloff, Jeremy A. 1973. Continuity and disruption during Terminal Late Classic times at Seibal: ceramic and other evidence. In *The Classic Maya collapse,* ed. T. Patrick Culbert, pp. 107 – 31. Albuquerque: University of New Mexico Press.

Sabloff, Jeremy A., William L. Rathje, David A. Freidel, Judith G. Connor, and Paula L. W. Sabloff. 1974. Trade and power in Postclassic Yucatan. In *Mesoamerican archaeology: new approaches,* ed. Norman Hammond, pp. 397 – 416. Austin: University of Texas Press.

Sabloff, Jeremy A., and E. Wyllys Andrews, V, eds. 1986. *Late lowland Maya civilization: Classic to Postclassic.* Albuquerque: University of New Mexico Press.

Sabloff, Jeremy A., and Gair Tourtellot. 1991. *The ancient Maya city of Sayil: the mapping of a Puuc region center.* Middle American Research Institute, Publication 60. New Orleans: Tulane University.

Sahagún, Fray Bernardino de. 1946. *Historia general de las cosas de Nueva España,* ed. Miguel Acosta Saignes. Mexico: Editorial Nueva España.

1950 – 63. *General history of the things of New Spain,* 12 vols., trans. A. Anderson and C. Dibble. Salt Lake City: University of Utah Press.

Sahlins, Marshall D. 1958. *Social stratification in Polynesia.* Seattle: University of Washington Press.

1963. Poor man, rich man, big man, chief: political types in Melanesia and Polynesia. *Comparative Studies in Society and History* 5:285 – 303.

1965. On the sociology of primitive exchange. In *The relevance of models for social anthropology,* ed. M. Banton, pp. 139 – 236. London: Tavistock Publications.

1972. *Stone age economics.* Chicago: Aldine.

1978. Culture as protein and profit. *New York Review of Books* 25:18:45 – 53.

Sanders, William T. 1960. *Prehistoric ceramics and settlement patterns in Quintana Roo, Mexico.* Carnegie Institution of Washington, Publication 606, contribution 60, pp. 155 – 264.

1965. The cultural ecology of the Teotihuacan Valley. Ms. on file, Pennsylvania State University, Dept. of Anthropology.

1972. Population, agricultural history, and societal evolution in Mesoamerica. In *Population growth: anthropological implications,* ed. Brian Spooner, pp. 101 – 53. Cambridge: MIT Press.

1973. The cultural ecology of the lowland Maya: a reevaluation. In *The Classic Maya collapse,* ed. T. Patrick Culbert, pp. 325 – 65. Albuquerque: University of New Mexico Press.

1977. Environmental heterogeneity and the evolution of lowland Maya civilization. In *The origins of Maya civilization,* ed. R. E. W. Adams, pp. 287 – 97. Albuquerque: University of New Mexico Press.

1978. Ethnographic analogy and the Teotihuacan horizon style. In *Middle Classic Mesoamerica,* ed. E. Pasztory, pp. 35 – 44. New York: Columbia University Press.

1981. Ecological adaptation in the Basin of Mexico: 23,000 B.C. to the present. In *Supplement to the handbook of Middle American Indians,* vol. 1, ed. Jeremy Sabloff, pp. 147 – 97. Austin: University of Texas Press.

1986. *The Teotihuacan Valley project final report: the Toltec Period occupation of the valley.* Department of Anthropology, Pennsylvania State University, Occasional Papers in Anthropology 13.

1989. The Epiclassic as a stage in Mesoamerican prehistory: an evaluation. In *Mesoamerica after the decline of Teotihuacan: A.D. 700 – 900,* eds. Richard Diehl and Janet Berlo, pp. 211 – 18. Washington, D.C.: Dumbarton Oaks.

Sanders, William T., Anton Kovar, Thomas Charlton, and Richard Diehl. 1970. *The Teotihuacan Valley project final report,* vol. 1: *The natural environment, contemporary occupation and 16th-century population of the valley.* Department of Anthropology, Pennsylvania State University, Occasional Papers in Anthropology 3.

Sanders, William T., and Joseph W. Michels. 1969. *The Pennsylvania State University Kaminaljuyú project–1968 season,* part 1: *The excavations.* Department of Anthropology, Pennsylvania State University, Occasional Papers in Anthropology 2.

Sanders, William T., and Joseph W. Michels, eds. 1977. *Teotihuacan and Kaminaljuyú: a study in prehistoric culture contact.* University Park: Pennsylvania State University.

Sanders, William T., and Deborah L. Nichols. 1988. Ecological theory and cultural evolution in the Valley of Oaxaca. *Current Anthropology* 29:33 – 80.

Sanders, William T., Jeffrey R. Parsons, and Michael Logan. 1976. Summary and conclusions. In *The Valley of Mexico,* ed. Eric Wolf, pp. 161 – 78. Albuquerque: University of New Mexico Press.

Sanders, William T., Jeffrey R. Parsons, and Robert S. Santley. 1979. *The Basin of Mexico: ecological processes in the evolution of a civilization.* New York: Academic Press.

Sanders, William T., and Barbara Price. 1968. *Mesoamerica.* New York: Random House.

Sanders, William T., and Robert S. Santley. 1983. A tale of three cities: Energetics and urbanization in Pre-Hispanic central Mexico. In *Prehistoric settlement patterns,* ed. Evon Vogt and Richard Leventhal, pp. 243 – 91. Albuquerque: University of New Mexico Press.

Sanders, William T., and David L. Webster. 1988. The Mesoamerican urban tradition. *American Anthropologist* 90:521 – 46.

Sanders, William T., Michael West, Charles Fletcher, and Joseph Marino. 1975. *The Formative Period occupation of the valley.* The Teotihuacan Valley project final report, vol. 2. Department of Anthropology, Pennsylvania State University, Occasional Papers in Anthropology 10.

Santley, Robert S. 1979. The ceramic sequence of the Basin of Mexico. In William T. Sanders, Jeffrey R. Parsons, and Robert S. Santley, *The Basin of Mexico,* pp. 435 – 74. New York: Academic Press.

1980. Disembedded capitals reconsidered. *American Antiquity* 45:132 – 45.

1983. Obsidian trade and Teotihuacan influence in Mesoamerica. In *Highland-Lowland interaction in Mesoamerica: interdisciplinary approaches,* ed. A. Miller, pp. 69 – 124. Washington, D.C.: Dumbarton Oaks.

1984. Obsidian exchange, economic stratification, and the evolution of complex society in the Basin of Mexico. In *Trade and exchange in early Mesoamerica,* ed. Kenneth Hirth, pp. 43 – 87. Albuquerque: University of New Mexico Press.

1989. Obsidian working, long-distance exchange, and the Teotihuacan presence on the south Gulf coast. In *Mesoamerica after the decline of Teotihuacan: A.D. 700 – 900,* ed. R. Diehl and J. Berlo, pp. 131 – 51. Washington, D.C.: Dumbarton Oaks.

Santley, Robert S., Janet M. Kerley, and Ronald Kneebone. 1986. Obsidian working, long-distance exchange, and the politico-economic organization of early states in Central Mexico. In *Research in Economic Anthropology,* supplement 2, ed. Barry Isaac, pp. 101 – 132. Greenwich, Conn.: JAI Press.

Sauer, Carl O. 1941. The personality of Mexico. *Geographical Review* 31:353 – 64.

Schalk, Randall E. 1977. The structure of an anadromous fish resource. In *For theory building in archaeology,* ed. Lewis R. Binford, pp. 207 – 44. New York: Academic Press.

Schele, Linda, and Mary Ellen Miller. 1986. *Blood of kings: dynasty and ritual in Maya art.* New York: George Braziller.

Schneider, Jane. 1977. Was there a precapitalist world-system? *Peasant Studies* 6:20 – 9.

Scholes, Francis V., and Ralph L. Roys. 1948. *The Maya Chontal Indians of Acalan-Tixchel.* Carnegie Institution of Washington, Publication 560.

Schortman, Edward M. and Patricia A. Urban. 1987. Modelling interregional interaction in prehistory. In *Advances in archaeological method and theory,* ed. Michael Schiffer, pp. 37 – 95. New York: Academic Press.

Schwimmer, Brian. 1976. Periodic markets and urban development in southern Ghana. In *Regional analysis,* vol. 1: *Economic systems,* ed. Carol Smith, pp. 123 – 46. New York: Academic Press.

Scott, John F. 1978. *The Danzantes of Monte Albán,* parts 1 and 2. Washington, D.C.: Dumbarton Oaks.

Seeman, Mark F. 1977. Stylistic variation in Middle Woodland pipe styles: the chronological implications. *Midcontinental Journal of Archaeology* 2:47 – 66.

Séjourné, Laurette. 1959. *Un palacio en la Ciudad de los Dioses: exploraciones en Teotihuacan, 1955 – 58.* Mexico, D.F.: Instituto Nacional de Antropología e Historia.

1966. *Arquitectura y pintura en Teotihuacan.* Siglo 21. Mexico: Editores S. A.

Selby, Henry, and Arthur Murphy. 1979. *The City of Oaxaca: final technical report.* Office of Urban Development, Technical Assistance Bureau, Agency for International Development.

Service, Elman. 1971. *Primitive social organization,* 2nd ed. New York: Random House.

1975. *The origins of the state and civilization: the process of culture evolution.* New York: Norton.

Shafer, Harry J. 1983. The lithic artifacts of the Pulltrouser area: settlements and fields. In *Pulltrouser Swamp: ancient Maya habitat, agriculture, and settlement in northern Belize,* ed. B. L. Turner, II, and Peter D. Harrison, pp. 212 – 45. Austin: University of Texas Press.

Sharer, Robert J., and David C. Grove, eds. 1989. *Regional perspectives on the Olmec.* Cambridge: Cambridge University Press.

Sidrys, Raymond V. 1976. Classic Maya obsidian trade. *American Antiquity* 41:449 – 64.

Simmons, Charles S., José Manuel Tarano T., and José Humberto Pinto S. 1959. *Clasificación de reconocimiento de los suelos de la República de Guatemala.* Guatemala: Ministerio de Educación Pública.

Simmons, Michael, and Gerald Brem. 1979. The analysis and distribution of volcanic ash-tempered pottery in the lowland Maya area. *American Antiquity* 44:79 – 91.

Simon, Herbert A. 1969. The architecture of complexity. In H. Simon, *The sciences of the artificial,* pp. 84 – 118. Cambridge: MIT Press.

1976. *Administrative behavior,* 3rd ed. New York: Free Press.

Skinner, G. William. 1964. Marketing and social structure in rural China, part 1. *Journal of Asian Studies* 24:3 – 43.

1965a. Marketing and social structure in rural China, part 2. *Journal of Asian Studies* 24:195 – 228.

1965b. Marketing and social structure in rural China, part 3. *Journal of Asian Studies* 24:363 – 99.

1977a. Regional urbanization in nineteenth-century China. In *The city in Late Imperial China,* ed. G. William Skinner, pp. 211 – 49. Stanford: Stanford University Press.

1977b. Introduction: urban development in Imperial China. In *The city in Late Imperial China,* ed. G. William Skinner, pp. 3 – 31. Stanford: Stanford University Press.

Skinner, G. William, ed. 1977. *The city in Late Imperial China.* Stanford: Stanford University Press.

Smith, A. Ledyard. 1950. *Uaxactún, Guatemala: excavations of 1931 – 1937.* Carnegie Institution of Washington, Publication 588.

1955. *Archaeological reconnaissance in central Guatemala.* Carnegie Institution of Washington, Publication 608.

1962. *Residential and associated structures at Mayapán. Mayapán, Yucatan, Mexico.* Carnegie Institution of Washington, Publication 619, part 3.

Smith, Bruce D., ed. 1978. *Mississippian settlement patterns.* New York: Academic Press.

Smith, C. Earle, Jr. 1978. *The vegetational history of the Oaxaca Valley.* Museum of Anthropology, University of Michigan, Memoirs 10, part 1.

Smith, Carol A.1974. Economics of marketing systems: models from economic geography. *Annual Review of Anthropology* 3:167 – 201.

1976a. Regional economic systems: linking geographical models and socioeconomic problems. In *Regional analysis,* vol. 1: *Economic systems,* ed. C. A. Smith, pp. 3 – 63. New York: Academic Press.

1976b. Exchange systems and the spatial distribution of elites: the organization of stratification in agrarian societies. In *Regional analysis,* vol. 2: *Social systems,* ed. C. A. Smith, pp. 309 – 74. New York: Academic Press.

1982. Modern and premodern urban primacy. *Comparative Urban Research* 9:79 – 96.

Smith, Michael E. 1979. The Aztec marketing system and settlement pattern in the Valley of Mexico: a central place analysis. *American Antiquity* 44:110 – 24.

1980. The role of the marketing system in Aztec society and economy: reply to Evans. *American Antiquity* 45:876 – 83.

1986. The role of social stratification in the Aztec empire: a view from the provinces. *American Anthropologist* 88:70 – 91.

1989. Cities, towns, and urbanism: response to Sanders and Webster. *American Anthropologist* 91:454 – 60.

Smith, Phillip E., and T. Cuyler Young. 1972. The evolution of early agriculture and culture in greater Mesopotamia: a trial model. In *Population growth: anthropological implications,* ed. Brian Spooner, pp. 5 – 19. Cambridge: MIT Press.

Smith, Thomas. 1959. *The agrarian origins of modern Japan.* Stanford: Stanford University Press.

Soustelle, Jacques. 1961. *Daily life of the Aztecs on the eve of the Spanish conquest,* trans. Patrick O'Brian. Stanford: Stanford University Press.

Spence, Michael W. 1967. The obsidian industry of Teotihuacan. *American Antiquity* 32:507 – 14.

1974. Residential practices and the distribution of skeletal traits in Teotihuacan, Mexico. *Man* 9:262 – 73.

1979a. The development of the Teotihuacan obsidian production system. Ms. on file. University of Western Ontario, Dept. of Anthropology.

1979b. Obsidian production and the state in Teotihuacan, Mexico. Ms. on file, University of Western Ontario, Dept. of Anthropology.

1981. Obsidian production and the state in Teotihuacan, Mexico. *American Antiquity* 46:769 – 88.

1984. Craft production and polity in early Teotihuacan. In *Trade and exchange in early Mesoamerica,* ed. Kenneth Hirth, pp. 87 – 114. Albuquerque: University of New Mexico Press.

1986. Locational analysis of craft specialization areas in Teotihuacan. In *Research in Economic Anthropology,* supplement 2, ed. Barry Isaac, pp. 75 – 100. Greenwich, Conn.: JAI Press.

Spence, Michael W., and Jeffrey R. Parsons. 1972. Prehispanic obsidian exploitation in central Mexico: a preliminary synthesis. In *Miscellaneous studies in Mexican prehistory,* pp. 1 – 44. Museum of Anthropology, University of Michigan, Anthropological Papers 45.

Spencer, Charles S. 1982. *The Cuicatlán Cañada and Monte Albán: a study of primary state formation.* New York: Academic Press.

Spengler, Oswald. 1926. *The decline of the West: form and actuality,* trans. Charles Francis Atkinson. New York: Knopf.

Spooner, Brian, ed. 1972. *Population growth: anthropological implications.* Cambridge, Mass.: MIT Press.

Spooner, Frank C. 1968. The economy of Europe, 1559 – 1609. In *The new Cambridge modern history*, vol. 3: *The counterreformation and price revolution, 1559 – 1610*, ed. R. B. Wernham, pp. 14 – 43. Cambridge: Cambridge University Press.

Spores, Ronald. 1965. The Zapotecs and Mixtecs at Spanish Conquest. In *Handbook of Middle American Indians*, vol. 3, ed. R. Wauchope and G. Willey, pp. 962 – 87. Austin: University of Texas Press.

1967. *The Mixtec kings and their people*. Norman: University of Oklahoma Press.

1972. *An archaeological settlement survey of the Nochixtlan Valley, Oaxaca*. Vanderbilt University Publications in Anthropology 1.

1974. Marital alliances in the political integration of Mixtec kingdoms. *American Anthropologist* 76: 297 – 311.

1984. *The Mixtecs in ancient and colonial times*. Norman: University of Oklahoma Press.

Stark, Barbara L. 1981. The rise of sedentary life. In *Handbook of Middle American Indians*, supplement 1: *Archaeology*, ed. Jeremy A. Sabloff, pp. 345 – 72. Austin: University of Texas Press.

1986. Origins of food production in the New World. In *American archaeology past and future*, ed. David J. Meltzer, Don D. Fowler, and Jeremy A. Sabloff, pp. 277 – 321. Washington, D.C.: Smithsonian Institution Press.

Steen-McIntyre, V., R. Fryxell, and H. E. Malde. 1973. Unexpectedly old age of deposits of Hueyatlaco archaeological site, Valsequillo, Mexico, implied by new stratigraphic and petrographic findings. *Geological Society of American Abstracts* 5:820.

1981. Geologic evidence for age of deposits at Hueyatlaco archaeological site, Valsequillo, Mexico. *Quaternary Research* 16:1 – 17.

Stephens, John L. 1973. *Incidents of travel in Yucatan*. New York: Dover.

Steponaitis, Vincas P. 1978. Location theory and complex chiefdoms: a Mississippian example. In *Mississippian settlement patterns*, ed. Bruce Smith, pp. 417 – 53. New York: Academic Press.

Steward, Julian H. 1955. *Theory of culture change*. Urbana: University of Illinois Press.

Stirling, Matthew W. 1943. *Stone monuments of southern Mexico*. Bureau of American Ethnology, Bulletin 138. Washington, D.C.: Smithsonian Institution.

Stone, Doris S. 1957. *The archaeology of central and southern Honduras*. Peabody Museum of Anthropology and Ethnology, Papers 29(3). Cambridge: Harvard University.

Storey, Rebecca. 1985. An estimate of mortality in a pre-Columbian population. *American Anthropologist* 87:519 – 35.

Strathern, Andrew. 1969. Finance and production: two strategies in New Guinea Highlands exchange systems. *Oceania* 40:42 – 67.

1978. Tambu and Kina: profit, exploitation and reciprocity in two New Guinea exchange systems. *Mankind* 11:253 – 64.

Struever, Stuart, and Gail L. Houart. 1972. An analysis of the Hopewell interaction sphere. In *Social exchange and interaction*, ed. Edwin N. Wilmsen. Museum of Anthropology, University of Michigan, Anthropological Papers 46:47 – 79.

Suárez, Jorge A. 1983. *The Mesoamerican Indian languages*. Cambridge: Cambridge University Press.

Swadesh, Maurice. 1961. Interrelaciones de las lenguas Mayas. *Anales del Instituto Nacional de Antropología e Historia* 13:231 – 67.

Tainter, Joseph. 1978. Modeling change in prehistoric social systems. In *For theory building in archaeology*, ed. Lewis R. Binford, pp. 327 – 51. New York: Academic Press.

Taylor, Donna. 1975. Some locational aspects of middle-range hierarchical societies. Ph.D. dissertation, City University of New York.

Taylor, R. E., L. A. Payen, C. A. Prior, P. J. Slota, Jr., R. Gillespie, J. A. J. Gowlett, R. E. M. Hedges, A. J. T. Jull, T. H. Zabel, D. J. Konahue, and R. Berger. 1985. Major revisions in the Pleistocene age assignments for North American human skeletons by C-14 accelerator mass spectrometry: none older than 11,000 C-14 years B. P. *American Antiquity* 50(1):136 – 40.

Taylor, William. 1971. The colonial background to peasant economy in the Valley of Oaxaca. Paper presented at the joint annual meetings of the Southwestern Anthropological Association and the American Ethnological Society, Tucson, Ariz.

1972. *Landlord and peasant in colonial Oaxaca.* Stanford: Stanford University Press.

Thompson, J. Eric S. 1966. *The rise and fall of Maya civilization.* Norman: University of Oklahoma Press.

Thompson, J. Eric S., Harry E. D. Pollock, and Jean Charlot. 1932. *A preliminary study of the ruins of Cobá, Quintana Roo, Mexico.* Carnegie Institution of Washington, Publication 424.

Tolstoy, Paul. 1958. Surface survey of the northern Valley of Mexico: the Classic and Postclassic periods. *Transactions of the American Philosophical Society* 48(5).

1978. Western Mesoamerica before A.D. 900. In *Chronologies in New World archaeology,* ed. R. E. Taylor and C. W. Meighan, pp. 241 – 84. New York: Academic Press.

1989. Coapexco and Tlatilco: sites with Olmec materials in the Basin of Mexico. In *Regional perspectives on the Olmec,* ed. Robert Sharer and David Grove, pp. 85 – 121. Cambridge: Cambridge University Press.

Tolstoy, Paul, and Suzanne K. Fish. 1975. Surface and subsurface evidence for community size at Coapexco, Mexico. *Journal of Field Archaeology* 2:97 – 104.

Tolstoy, Paul, Suzanne K. Fish, Martin W. Boksenbaum, and Kathryn Blair Vaughn. 1977. Early sedentary communities of the Basin of Mexico. *Journal of Field Archaeology* 4: 91 – 106.

Tolstoy, Paul, and Louise I. Paradis. 1970. Early and Middle Preclassic culture in the Basin of Mexico. *Science* 167:344 – 51.

Torquemada, Fray Juan de. 1943. *Monarquia Indiana,* tomo 2. Mexico: Editorial Chaves Hayhoe.

Tozzer, Alfred M. 1907. Ernst Förstemann. *American Anthropologist* 9:153 – 9.

1957. *Chichén Itzá and its cenote of sacrifice.* Peabody Museum of Archaeology and Ethnology, Memoirs, vols. 11 and 12. Cambridge: Harvard University.

Tozzer, Alfred M., ed. and trans. 1941. *Landa's relación de las cosas de Yucatan.* Peabody Museum of Archaeology and Ethnology, Papers 18.

Tuck, James. 1971. The Iroquois confederacy. *Scientific American* 224:32 – 42.

Turner, B. L., II. 1979. Prehispanic terracing in the central Maya lowlands: problems of agricultural intensification. In *Maya archaeology and ethnohistory,* ed. Norman Hammond and Gordon R. Willey, pp. 103 – 15. Austin: University of Texas Press.

Turner, B. L., II, and Peter Harrison, eds. 1983. *Pulltrouser Swamp: ancient Maya habitat, agriculture, and settlement in northern Belize.* Austin: University of Texas Press.

Udy, Stanley H., Jr. 1959. *Organization of work.* New Haven: HRAF Press.

Vaillant, George C. 1930. *Excavations at Zacatenco.* American Museum of Natural History, Anthropological Papers 32:1.

1931. *Excavations at Ticoman.* American Museum of Natural History, Anthropological Papers 32:2.

1935. *Excavations at El Arbolillo.* American Museum of Natural History, Anthropological Papers 35:2.

van der Leeuw, Sander Ernst. 1976. *Studies in the technology of ancient pottery.* Amsterdam: Organization for the Advancement of Pure Research.

van Zantwijk, R. 1985. *The Aztec arrangement.* Norman: University of Oklahoma Press.

Vapnarsky, C. A. 1969. On rank-size distributions of cities: an ecological approach. *Economic Development and Cultural Change* 17:584 – 95.

Varner, Dudley. 1974. Prehispanic settlement patterns in the Valley of Oaxaca, Mexico: the Etla arm. Ph.D. dissertation, University of Arizona.

Velázquez, Primo Feliciano, ed. and trans. 1945. Anales de Cuauhtitlán. In *Códice Chimalpopoca: Anales de Cuauhtitlán y Leyenda de los Soles*. Mexico: Universidad Nacional de México, Imprenta Universitaria.

Vogt, Evon Z., and Richard M. Leventhal, eds. 1983. *Prehistoric settlement patterns*. Albuquerque: University of New Mexico Press.

Voorhies, Barbara. 1982. An ecological model of the early Maya of the central lowlands. In *Maya subsistence: studies in honor of Dennis E. Puleston,* ed. Kent V. Flannery, pp. 65 – 95. New York: Academic Press.

Voorhies, Barbara, George H. Michaels, and George M. Riser, 1991. Ancient shrimp fishery. *National Geographic Research and Exploration* 7(1):20 – 35.

Waddell, Eric. 1972. *The mound builders*. Seattle: University of Washington Press.

Wallace, Anthony F. C. 1970. *Culture and personality*, 2nd ed. New York: Random House.

Wallerstein, Immanuel. 1974a. *The modern world system: capitalist agriculture and the origins of the European world-economy in the sixteenth century*. New York: Academic Press.

1974b. The rise and future demise of the world capitalist system: concepts for comparative analysis. *Comparative Studies in Society and History* 16:387 – 415.

Warner, Rex. 1954. *Thucydides: the Peloponnesian War*. Harmondsworth, England: Penguin Books.

Wauchope, Robert. 1938. *Modern Maya houses*. Carnegie Institution of Washington, Publication 502.

1972. Edward Wyllys Andrews, IV, 1916 – 1971. *American Antiquity* 37:394 – 401.

Webster, David. 1973. *Becan: an early Maya lowland fortified site*. Department of Anthropology, Pennsylvania State University, Occasional Papers in Anthropology 8.

Webster, David, and Nancy Gonlin. 1988. Household remains of the humblest Maya. *Journal of Field Archaeology* 15:169 – 90.

Weigand, Phil. 1968. The mines and mining techniques of the Chalchihuites culture. *American Antiquity* 33:45 – 61.

1980. The prehistory of the state of Zacatecas: an interpretation, part 1. *Anthropology* 1(2):67 – 87.

Weigand, Phil, Garman Harbottle, and Edward Sayre. 1977. Turquoise sources and source analysis: Mesoamerica and the Southwestern U.S.A. In *Exchange systems in prehistory,* eds. T. Earle and J. Ericson, pp. 15 – 34. New York: Academic Press.

Welch, Paul D. 1991. *Moundville's economy*. Tuscaloosa: University of Alabama Press.

Welsh, W. B. M. 1988. *An analysis of Classic lowland Maya burials*. BAR International Series 409. Oxford.

West, R. C., and P. Armillas. 1950. Las chinampas de México. *Cuadernos Americanos* 50: 165 – 92.

Whalen, Michael E. 1976. Zoning within an Early Formative community in the Valley of Oaxaca. In *The early Mesoamerican village,* ed. Kent V. Flannery, pp. 75 – 9. New York: Academic Press.

1981. *Excavations at Santo Domingo Tomaltepec: evolution of a Formative community in the Valley of Oaxaca, Mexico*. Museum of Anthropology, University of Michigan, Memoirs 11.

1988. Small community organization during the Late Formative Period in Oaxaca, Mexico. *Journal of Field Archaeology* 15:291 – 306.

Wheatley, Paul. 1961. *The golden Khersonese: studies in the historical geography of the Malay Peninsula before A.D. 1500*. Kuala Lampur: University of Malaya Press.

White, Benjamin N. F. 1973. Demand for labor and population growth in colonial Java. *Human Ecology* 1:217 – 36.

White, Leslie. 1959. *The evolution of culture*. New York: McGraw-Hill.

Whitecotton, Joseph W. 1977. *The Zapotecs: princes, priests, and peasants*. Norman: University of Oklahoma Press.

———. 1983. The genealogy of Macuilxochitl: a 16th-century Zapotec pictorial from the Valley of Oaxaca. *Notas Mesoamericanas* 9:59 – 75.

———. 1990. *Zapotec elite ethnohistory: pictorial genealogies from eastern Oaxaca*. Vanderbilt University, Publications in Anthropology 39.

Whitecotton, Joseph W., and Richard A. Pailes. 1979. Mesoamerica as an historical unit: a world-system model. Paper presented at the 43rd International Congress of Americanists, Vancouver, B.C.

———. 1986. New World precolumbian World systems. In *Ripples in the Chichimec Sea*, eds. Frances Mathien and Randall McGuire, pp. 183 – 204. Carbondale: Southern Illinois University Press.

Wilkerson, S. Jeffrey K. 1973. An archaeological sequence from Santa Luisa, Veracruz, Mexico. *Contributions of the University of California Archeological Research Facility* 18:37 – 50.

———. 1975. Pre-agricultural village life: the Late Preceramic Period in Veracruz. *Contributions of the University of California Archaeological Research Facility* 27:111 – 22.

Willey, Gordon R. 1953. *Prehistoric settlement patterns in the Virú Valley, Peru*. Bureau of American Ethnology Bulletin 155.

———. 1966. *An introduction to American archaeology*, vol. 1: *North and Central America*. Englewood Cliffs, N.J.: Prentice-Hall.

———. 1971. *An introduction to American archaeology*, vol. 2: *South America*. Englewood Cliffs, N.J.: Prentice-Hall.

———. 1973a. *The Altar de Sacrificios excavations: general summary and conclusions*. Peabody Museum of Archaeology and Ethnology, Papers 64, no. 3. Cambridge: Harvard University.

———. 1973b. Certain aspects of the Late Classic to Postclassic periods in the Belize Valley. In *The Classic Maya collapse*, ed. T. Patrick Culbert, pp. 93 – 106. Albuquerque: University of New Mexico Press.

———. 1977. The rise of Classic Maya civilization: a Pasión Valley perspective. In *The origins of Maya civilization*, ed. R. E. W. Adams, pp. 133 – 57. Albuquerque: University of New Mexico Press.

———. 1981. Maya lowland settlement patterns: a summary review. In *Lowland Maya settlement patterns*, ed. W. Ashmore, pp. 385 – 415. Albuquerque: University of New Mexico Press.

Willey, Gordon R., ed. 1956. *Prehistoric settlement patterns in the New World*. Viking Fund Publications in Anthropology 23.

Willey, Gordon R., William R. Bullard, Jr., John B. Glass, and James C. Gifford. 1965. *Prehistoric Maya settlements in the Belize Valley*. Papers of the Peabody Museum of Archaeology and Ethnology, Harvard University, vol. 59. Cambridge.

Willey, Gordon R., and Richard M. Leventhal. 1979. Prehistoric settlement at Copán. In *Maya archaeology and ethnohistory*, eds. Norman Hammond and Gordon R. Willey, pp. 75 – 102. Austin: University of Texas Press.

Willey, Gordon R., and Peter Mathews, ed. 1985. *A consideration of the early Classic period in the Maya lowlands*. Institute for Mesoamerican Studies, State University of New York at Albany, Publication 10.

Willey, Gordon R., and Jeremy A. Sabloff. 1974. *A history of American archaeology*. San Francisco: Freeman.

———. 1980. *A history of Mesoamerican archaeology*, 2nd ed. San Francisco: Freeman.

Willey, Gordon R., and Demitri B. Shimkin. 1973. The Maya collapse: a summary view. In *The Classic Maya collapse*, ed. T. Patrick Culbert, pp. 457 – 501. Albuquerque: University of New Mexico Press.

Winter, Marcus C. 1972. Tierras Largas: a formative community in the Valley of Oaxaca, Mexico. Ph.D. dissertation, University of Arizona.

1974. Residential patterns at Monte Albán, Oaxaca, Mexico. *Science* 186:981 – 7.

1976a. The archaeological household cluster in the Valley of Oaxaca. In *The early Mesoamerican village,* ed. Kent V. Flannery, pp. 25 – 31. New York: Academic Press.

1976b. Differential patterns of community growth in Oaxaca. In *The early Mesoamerican village,* ed. Kent V. Flannery, pp. 227 – 34. New York: Academic Press.

1977. Paper presented at Congreso de Evaluación de la antropología in Oaxaca, Mexico.

1984. Exchange in formative highland Oaxaca. In *Trade and exchange in early Mesoamerica,* ed. K. G. Hirth, pp. 179 – 214. Albuquerque: University of New Mexico Press.

1989. *Oaxaca: the archaeological record.* Mexico: Minutiae Mexicana.

Winter, Marcus C., and Jane W. Pires-Ferreira. 1976. Distribution of obsidian among households in two Oaxacan villages. In *The early Mesoamerican village,* ed. Kent V. Flannery, pp. 306 – 11. New York: Academic Press.

Wittfogel, Karl. 1957. *Oriental despotism.* New Haven: Yale University Press.

Wobst, H. Martin. 1974. Boundary conditions for Paleolithic social systems: a simulation approach. *American Antiquity* 39:147 – 79.

1975. The demography of finite populations and the origins of the incest taboo. *Memoirs of Society for American Archaeology* 30:75 – 81.

1976. Locational relationships in Paleolithic society. *Journal of Human Evolution* 5:49 – 58.

1977. Stylistic behavior and information exchange. In *For the director: research essays in honor of James B. Griffin,* ed. Charles E. Cleland, pp. 317 – 42. Museum of Anthropology, University of Michigan, Anthropological Papers 61.

Wolf, Eric R. 1959. *Sons of the shaking earth.* Chicago: University of Chicago Press.

1982. *Europe and the people without history.* Berkeley: University of California Press.

Wolf, Eric R., ed. 1976. *The Valley of Mexico.* Albuquerque: University of New Mexico Press.

Wolf, Eric R., and Angel Palerm. 1955. Irrigation in the old Acolhua domain, Mexico. *Southwestern Journal of Anthropology* 11:265 – 81.

Wright, Henry T. 1969. *The administration of rural production in an early Mesopotamian town.* Museum of Anthropology, University of Michigan, Anthropological Papers 38.

1977. Recent research on the origin of the state. *Annual Review of Anthropology* 6:379 – 97.

1986. The evolution of civilizations. In *American archaeology: past and future,* eds. D. Meltzer, D. Fowler, and J. Sabloff, pp. 323 – 65. Washington, D.C.: Smithsonian Institution Press.

Wright, Henry T., and Gregory Johnson. 1975. Population, exchange, and early state formation in southwestern Iran. *American Anthropologist* 77:267 – 89.

Wynne-Edwards, V. C. 1962. *Animal dispersion in relation to social behavior.* Edinburgh: Oliver and Boyd.

Zeitlin, Judith F. 1978. Changing patterns of resource exploitation, settlement distribution, and demography on the Southern Isthmus of Tehuantepec, Mexico. In *Prehistoric coastal adaptations,* ed. B. L. Stark and B. Voorhies, pp. 151 – 78. New York: Academic Press.

Zeitlin, Robert N. 1978. Long-distance exchange and the growth of a regional center on the Southern Isthmus of Tehuantepec. In *Prehistoric coastal adaptations,* ed. B. L. Stark and B. Voorhies, pp. 183 – 210. New York: Academic Press.

1984. A summary report on three seasons of field investigations into the Archaic period prehistory of lowland Belize. *American Anthropologist* 86:358 – 68.